"From the onset of colonization until well into the present, the discourse and histories of Two-Spirit Indigenous peoples have remained a puzzle for Indigenous and non-Indigenous people alike. *Reclaiming Two-Spirits* will help you solve that puzzle. Using familiar and obscure stories, Smithers skillfully reveals the centrality of Two-Spirit struggles within the matrix of settler-colonial domination and the Indigenous struggle for freedom. He reveals the destructive nature of colonial violence and the possibilities of a Two-Spirit future. An original contribution to Indigenous cultural and intellectual histories, an understanding of the links between language and power and Indigenous futures, this book will not only educate your mind but will also touch your spirit."

—Kyle T. Mays (Black/Saginaw Chippewa), author of
An Afro-Indigenous History of the United States

"Lost teachings are found in this compelling revelation on the complexity of Two-Spirit people. Based on chronicles of Native culture and historical documents, as well as oral histories and interviews, *Reclaiming Two-Spirits* offers an understanding of how Two-Spirit gives balance in a binary world. A reminder to everyone to have more empathy and compassion."

—Lynette Allston, chief of the Nottoway Indian Tribe of Virginia

"Smithers's *Reclaiming Two-Spirits* compels readers to rethink gender and sexuality from the nonbinary point of view of Indigenous cultures, which uses gender-neutral and polyvalent words to express an array of identities. Smithers recovers the Two-Spirits who lie hidden beneath the homophobic language of archival records, obliging not only historians but everyone who cares about Indigenous peoples to be more aware of gender biases and how language is a tool of colonization."

—David Martínez (Akimel O'odham/Hia Ced
O'odham/Mexican), author of *Life of the Indigenous Mind*

"Gregory D. Smithers's *Reclaiming Two-Spirits* sheds welcome light on the deeply misunderstood topic of how Native Americans with diverse sexual and gender identities relate to both their native cultures and the settler societies—they embrace traditional roles that are often disavowed in their native cultures due to the legacy of colonialism, while at the same time resisting conflation with LGBT identities of Eurocentric origin. Smithers's obvious sympathy for his subject, along with his cogent scholarship, engaging storytelling, and lucid prose, makes the complexly contested space that Two-Spirit people occupy accessible and understandable to general audiences of Natives and settlers alike."

—Susan Stryker, author of *Transgender History: The Roots of Today's Revolution*, and founding co-editor of *TSQ: Transgender Studies Quarterly*

"*Reclaiming Two-Spirits* is by far the most compelling study to date of an evolving tradition and way of life that has always operated according to a cultural logic of its own and that we can appreciate fully only by taking that cultural logic seriously. Setting aside Anglo-American assumptions and categories, Smithers has listened closely to Two-Spirit people in the present and to traces of their voices in historical sources. This book is a major contribution to our understanding of Native American cultures and to an authentically diverse history of gender and sexuality."

—Richard Godbeer, author of *Sexual Revolution in Early America*

"*Reclaiming Two-Spirits* is the book that we've been waiting for! Finally, a readable and reliable guide to the history of America's Two-Spirit people."

—Rachel Hope Cleves, author of *Charity and Sylvia: A Same-Sex Marriage in Early America*

RECLAIMING
TWO-SPIRITS

ALSO BY GREGORY D. SMITHERS

*The Cherokee Diaspora: An Indigenous History
of Migration, Resettlement, and Identity*

*Native Southerners: Indigenous History
from Origins to Removal*

*Native Diasporas: Indigenous Identities and Settler
Colonialism in the Americas* (coedited
with Brooke N. Newman)

*Racism in American Popular Media: From Aunt Jemima to
the Frito Bandito* (coauthored with Brian D. Behnken)

*Slave Breeding: Sex, Violence, and Memory
in African American History*

*Science, Sexuality, and Race in the United States
and Australia, 1780s–1940s*

QUEER ACTION/QUEER IDEAS

A unique series addressing pivotal
issues within the LGBTQ movement

RECLAIMING

TWO-SPIRITS

SEXUALITY,
SPIRITUAL RENEWAL
& SOVEREIGNTY
IN NATIVE AMERICA

GREGORY D. SMITHERS

FOREWORD BY **RAVEN E. HEAVY RUNNER**

BEACON PRESS BOSTON

BEACON PRESS
Boston, Massachusetts
www.beacon.org

Beacon Press books
are published under the auspices of
the Unitarian Universalist Association of Congregations.

25 24 23 22   8 7 6 5 4 3 2 1

This book is printed on acid-free paper that meets the uncoated paper
ANSI/NISO specifications for permanence as revised in 1992.

Text design and composition by Kim Arney

Library of Congress Cataloging-in-Publication Data
Name: Smithers, Gregory D., 1974– author.
Title: Reclaiming Two-Spirits : sexuality, spiritual renewal,
and sovereignty in Native America / Gregory D. Smithers.
Description: Boston : Beacon Press, [2022] | Series: Queer action/queer
ideas | Includes bibliographical references and index. | Summary: "A
sweeping history of Indigenous traditions of gender and sexuality that
decolonizes North America's past and reveals how Two-Spirit people are
reclaiming their place in Native nations"—Provided by publisher.
Identifiers: LCCN 2021034778 (print) | LCCN 2021034779 (ebook) |
ISBN 9780807003466 (hardcover) | ISBN 9780807003473 (ebook)
Subjects: LCSH: Two-spirit people—History. | Indians of North America—
Social life and customs. | Gender identity—North America—History.
Classification: LCC E98.S48 (print) | LCC E98.S48 (ebook) |
DDC 306.7608997—dc23
LC record available at https://lccn.loc.gov/2021034778
LC ebook record available at https://lccn.loc.gov/2021034779

CONTENTS

FOREWORD

WHEN I WAS YOUNG, my grandmother often told us that our words have power. "Be mindful of how you talk as you have the power to hurt or heal one another." The medicine one carries is evident by what one says and, today, by what one writes. As a young person, I realized early I was not like my heterosexual counterparts and they in turn let me know this. As adolescence turned into my later teen years, that reality became even more stark. I sought to find who I was, to gather strength in a colonized world that told me I did not belong. Although we as Indigenous people have fought against weapons of war, disease, and famine, it was the education system that has caused most harm to those of us remaining from this onslaught. Not until I came across the books of Walter Williams, Will Roscoe, and others did I find a path toward healing. Along the way, I heard of a gathering of others like me seeking power to overcome the plight brought by Europeans. I found myself in the company of Wesley Thomas, Beverly Little Thunder, Richard LaFortune, Janet Spotted Eagle, Michael Red Earth, Muriel Miguel, and Clyde Hall. I learned much of who I am as a Two-Spirit from those elders. They walked before us, sharing all they had learned, guiding us toward a role that would help our nations.

When I was asked by Dr. Smithers to write this foreword, I wondered what medicine he added to this path. I have in my own journey read many books of Two-Spirit people and spoken with many of my contemporaries about what these words meant to us as Indigenous LGBTQ2S+ people. We discussed how and who should convey this medicine. Although I've been suspicious of non-Native people doing this work, I also realized that a lot of this information would have been lost were it not for the non-Native people who recorded their journeys through Turtle Island, as Indigenous people call North

America. Although their intent may not have been to empower us, the remnants of their words have allowed for a glimpse of who we were in past centuries. Like those of us who have turned the hurtful words of "queer" into words of power, we have looked past their ignoble intent to glean the chaff and make for ourselves sustenance to carry on the work intended by our people and our Creator. In the pages of Dr. Smithers's *Reclaiming Two-Spirits*, I see woven a beautiful basket of words from Marty Fixico, Candi Brings Plenty, Lee Staples, Heather Purser, and Sheldon Raymore. Although our tribal governments have a way to go, I know the work that these warriors do will awaken the power and place of where our Two-Spirits rightfully deserve to be: back into the circle of our nations. I thank you, Dr. Smithers, for being that kind conduit toward that laudable goal.

All Our Relations,

RAVEN E. HEAVY RUNNER, MSW (he, him, his)
Blackfeet, Montana, Two-Spirit Society, Enrolled Board Member
Northwest Two-Spirit Society, Co-Chair
International Council of Two-Spirit Societies, Leadership Circle Member

SERIES NOTE

IN THE DECADES since the Stonewall riots we have seen rapidly unfolding projects of "uncovering queer history." More than ever LGBTQ+ people have become increasingly fascinated by people who have preceded them with whom they can identify in any number of ways. But the very term "queer history" is a misnomer. There is no unified, cohesive, universal queer history but instead a series of sometimes overlapping, sometimes not overlapping, queer histories. There are very few concrete connections to be made between male sexualized mentorship relationships in ancient Greece, the hijra of India, nineteenth-century women in American social reform movements who loved other women, the activists of the gay liberation movement, and people today who identify as gender-queer or nonbinary. Each of these histories, which span the globe and the centuries, is unique. All are important and all deserve to be examined in their singularity and their historical richness.

Gregory D. Smithers's *Reclaiming Two-Spirits: Sexuality, Spiritual Renewal & Sovereignty in Native America* presents us with a complex, layered, and deeply researched portrait of Two-Spirit people, traditions, and cultures. It is a book that expands our understanding of the breadth and depth of Two-Spirit experiences. Smithers's research covers five hundred years of Indigenous people's history in America; it is the most comprehensive study of this material published to date. While the term "Two-Spirit" is a contemporary coinage and usage derived from the Northern Algonquin word *niizh manitoag*, denoting the coexistence of feminine and masculine qualities in a single person, the cultural, religious, and spiritual legacy it embodies is centuries old.

Smithers charts the historical legacies of how European invasions, social prejudices, government policy, and Native resistance have shaped cultural understandings of Two-Spirit cultures. More important, he traces how Native people have kept these traditions and identities alive and have reclaimed them, ensuring that they move into the future. *Reclaiming Two-Spirits* is not simply a history or a reclamation of legacies that have been forgotten but the charting of a celebratory reawakening in a contemporary age of an identity. Drawing on a wide range of traditional historical texts, Indigenous oral histories, tribal accounts, historical memory, and contemporary interviews with Two-Spirit people, the book brings into focus a living history and legacy that is a central and vibrant aspect of Native culture today.

Reclaiming Two-Spirits explores complex issues of cultural sovereignty, not only in how it relates to wider issues of legal and political freedoms but in how it expands our ideas about gender and sexuality. For readers who know aspects of this legacy and for those who are new to it, Smithers's book will be a revelation.

—Michael Bronski

A NOTE
ABOUT LANGUAGE

HOW WE THINK, talk, and write about Indigeneity, gender, and sexuality changes over time. Today's nomenclature applied to the past can alter history's meaning in ways that make little sense to the people who made that history possible. With this in mind, throughout this book I've tried to hew as closely as possible to language that reflects usage during the time periods described. For example, I don't use the term "queer" (or add the "Q" to LGBT) until the late 1980s, when activists began inverting the word's pejorative connotation. Readers may find the presence of other terms strange, awkward, or even offensive. Read through the lens of contemporary culture, they are. But understanding the past is not the same as agreeing with it, politically or at any other level. In the pages that follow, the term "Two-Spirit" does, at face value, the work of an English-language noun: it divides people into groups or arbitrary categories. The goal of this work is explicitly decolonial: to reveal how Indigenous people associate dynamic sets of meanings to words that allow them to actively build on the traditions of their ancestors and create new knowledge for the future. In this sense, I am expanding on the work of the Cherokee scholar Joshua Nelson in that I use "Two-Spirit" in ways that emphasize action, doing, and becoming (and highlight the selective ways in which Two-Spirit people use terms like "gay," "lesbian," or "transgender").[1] I historicize the term "Two-Spirit" to account for chronological, cultural, and tribal dynamism. Events and people from the past are referred to in the past tense. Analyses of the contemporary world are narrated in the present tense. When appropriate, I use tribally specific language but also employ "Indian," "Native American," and "Indigenous." I use these pancultural and panpolitical terms interchangeably, recognizing the inadequacy and contested historical nature of them all. Finally, I follow the conventions established by the National Congress of American Indians in using the term "Indian Country" to refer to Native spaces and places, and to underscore the continued existence of self-governing, sovereign, tribal nations.

ABOUT THE COVER ART

RETURNING REPRESENTS TWO-SPIRITS in one blanket, the blanket representing the fabric of society, showing that it's made up of many pieces, none like the other but all strong and beautiful together. The blue represents seeing clearly or truly and beyond what others see. The figures are stripped of clothing and anything identifiable by gender so that they truly represent just spirits. The red dot in the background is everything that tries to steal your eyes or attention away from what is important. The yellow and white lines represent creator and ancestors, and the red marks represent the four directions. The vertical line on the left represents both water and smoke, the life force and prayer connection. The spirits come together in reclamation of self and love.

—Asa Wright (Klamath/Modoc), *Returning*,
https://mightymodoc.com

PROLOGUE

Two Spirit Natives are sacred
Lesbian Natives are sacred
Gay Natives are sacred
Bisexual Natives are sacred
Trans Natives are sacred
Queer Natives are sacred
Intersex Natives are sacred
Non-Binary Natives are sacred

—NATIVE AMERICANS in Philanthropy[1]

"THERE'S ONLY ONE LEAK IN THE ROOF," the parking attendant joked as a small group of people strolled toward the Festival Pavilion at Fort Mason. Sipping their morning coffee and sidestepping puddles of rainwater, some of the people in that small group smiled at the attendant's joke as they headed toward the cover of the Pavilion. They, like me, were more interested in getting out of the wet and cold of an early February morning in San Francisco.

February 2, 2019, dawned with gray skies and scattered rain showers. As carloads of family members and friends pulled into the Festival Pavilion parking lot, the morning breeze whisked the rain clouds apart, revealing a pale blue sky and sunshine that was more in keeping with the bright mood inside the Pavilion.

The Festival Pavilion sits on San Francisco Bay, not far from the tourist bottlenecks of Fisherman's Wharf and Pier 39. The Pavilion is a cavernous and drafty building, and on this morning, I spotted two leaks, not one. No one really cared, though. On February 2, the Festival Pavilion was warmed by the sound of L. Frank Manriquez's voice over the PA system, people's smiles, a hug for a relative or friend, and the sounds of conversation and laughter. Roger Kuhn, a member of the Poarch Band of Creek Indians, described the atmosphere in the Pavilion as "full of love."[2]

He was right. As I walked through the Pavilion talking and laughing with friends new and old, the morning vibe at the eighth annual Two-Spirit powwow was one of warmth and welcoming. Like other modern powwows, this one is a mixture of commerce and tradition. You can buy a T-shirt with a witty punch line—"Homeland Security: Fighting Terrorism Since 1492"—and you can enter a dance, like the Fancy Bussle. The official powwow brochure encourages these different forms of participation. The brochure also makes the cultural purpose of the powwow and its parent body, the Bay Area American Indian Two-Spirits (BAAITS), clear: "to restore and recover the role of Two-Spirit people within American Indian/First Nations community by creating a forum for the spiritual, cultural and artistic expression of Two-Spirit people."

Starting with the Grand Entry and the opening blessing, the eighth annual Two-Spirit powwow served that purpose and more. People from myriad tribal nations, embodying a spectrum of sexual and gendered identities—gay, lesbian, transgender, bisexual, straight, ace—danced, reminisced, ate, and laughed together. The eighth annual Two-Spirit powwow advanced the BAAITS mission, but it was doing something else, something more: Two-Spirit people were reclaiming connections to communities, celebrating sexual and gender diversity, and renewing social roles that were part of the fabric of sovereign tribal nations before colonizers invaded and tried to destroy them.

. . . .

The BAAITS powwow is one of numerous similar events held across the United States and Canada each year. In recent decades, the number of Two-Spirit powwows has grown dramatically, reflecting the collective pride and self-confidence that Two-Spirit people feel in both urban and reservation settings. Still, as I reveal throughout this book, Two-Spirit people are acutely aware of the challenges they face. They know that colonialism continues to intrude into their lives.

To understand the recent history of Two-Spirit people requires a journey back to the summer of 1990. That summer, a small group of Native Americans met at the third annual spiritual gathering of lesbian, gay, bisexual, and transgender Natives in Winnipeg, Manitoba.

Despite what most history books told them, that small group of Indigenous people knew that their spiritual traditions, stories, and kinship communities weren't relics of a time that most Americans—including substantial numbers of Native Americans—had forgotten. Delegates discussed how they could access their own histories by using a language that celebrated Indigenous diversity throughout North America. They knew that accessing the traces of those histories started by transcending the labels imposed on them by colonial cultures. They wanted to consign offensive terms like "berdache" to the dustbin of history, while also searching for a collective, Pan-Indian identity that was more affirming than labels such as "gay," "lesbian," or "transgender."

In Winnipeg, the delegates swapped stories and found what they'd been searching for. They agreed on their name, an umbrella term that captures the fluidity of their sexual identities and dynamism of gender in Native cultures. That term: *Two-Spirit.*

Winnipeg, located at the intersection of the Red and Assiniboine Rivers, proved an ideal location for this reclaiming. For well over six thousand years, people from nihi'wawin Cree, Dakota, Ojibwe, Oji-Cree, and Diné language groups met in and around what is today Winnipeg to trade and engage in diplomacy. It was here, at this historic crossroads, that a new generation of Indigenous leaders assembled. Together, they discussed how they could use the term "Two-Spirit" to reclaim their histories, spiritual traditions, and stories. What does it mean to be a Two-Spirit person?

"Two-Spirit" is derived from the Northern Algonquin word *niizh manitoag*, which denotes the existence of feminine and masculine qualities in a single person. Since that Winnipeg gathering, the Two-Spirit umbrella has grown. It includes people working to reclaim and renew tribal knowledge, individuals who experience life along a spectrum of gendered identifications, and others who incorporate aspects of LGBTQ identity into their sense of self and place in community. Above all, Two-Spirit people continue to work tirelessly to increase their visibility and acceptance throughout Indian Country and beyond.[3]

Throughout this book I use "Two-Spirit" to highlight the active, creative ways in which Indigenous people continue to reclaim their gendered traditions and renew their sexual sense of self. This is a conscious decision, made in consultation with Two-Spirit people and designed to highlight the blended, overlapping, and dynamic nature of Two-Spirit identities. Understanding Two-Spirit solely as a static noun rearticulates colonial logic; it objectifies and fetishizes people whose identities, social roles, and histories are far more vibrant and actively created than Western binary logics suggest. Additionally, if we try to attach the mainstream LGBTQ movement's pronouns to Two-Spirit people the result is a recolonization of Indigenous cultures, sexualities, and social roles that obscures the spectrum of sexual relationships and gendered roles and identities among Two-Spirit and gender-nonconforming people in Indian Country.[4] Indeed, pronouns create arbitrary divisions, as does that other Western invention, mind-body dualism. Western culture has left Europeans and Euro-Americans ill equipped to grasp Indigenous epistemologies of spirituality and body—a *wholeness* understood to exist along a continuum or living spectrum that unites the metaphysical with the physical.[5]

I discussed this dynamism with Ken Pinkham at the BAAITS Powwow in San Francisco in February 2019.[6] Pinkham, a Two-Spirit elder from the Nimiipuu (Nez Percé tribe), remembers those early gatherings in the 1990s as an exhilarating time. The adoption of the term "Two-Spirit" was, he recalls, a major breakthrough.

We sat by San Francisco Bay and chatted as a midafternoon rain shower swept over us. Pinkham sipped a can of Diet Coke and enjoyed a number of cigarettes as he shared his stories with me. He told me that "Two-Spirits" gained popularity because it helped Native Americans undermine the homophobic stigmas associated with labels like "gay" and "lesbian" in Indian Country during the 1980s and early 1990s, a time when HIV/AIDS struck down a number of Pinkham's friends.

By embracing a new language, Two-Spirit people began reclaiming their historical roles and, as the Hunkpapa Lakota activist Barbara Cameron put it, became "more visible in our communities."[7] In the early 1990s, some anthropologists followed the lead of Cameron and other Two-Spirit people by adopting the terminology in their research and teaching. Historians, a stubbornly empirical lot, slowly caught on, too, and started using the term "Two-Spirit" in interdisciplinary histories.[8]

Why was this new terminology needed? Pinkham shared with me part of the answer. But answering this question fully requires us to dig deeper; it is therefore one of the main focal points of this book. It requires a reexamination of colonialism's ongoing destructiveness and its different forms of violence—disease, physical acts of war and genocide, the cultural destructiveness caused by boarding schools, and the corrosive impact of corporations and capitalism on Indigenous communities.[9] In spite of five centuries of colonialism, it is still possible for Two-Spirit people to reclaim their traditions, identities, roles, and their sacred status. For still other Native people, the term "Two-Spirit" is a starting point for telling new stories.

Language reclamation and renewal is key to understanding Two-Spirit storytelling. From Mesoamerica to sub-Arctic tribal communities, Native languages routinely avoided the use gender pronouns. Lakota speakers, for example, tended to use the linguistically neuter "it" instead of gendered pronouns. Throughout Indian Country, distinctions of animate and inanimate, thing and person, human and more-than-human kinship, carried greater meaning than Western-style gender pronouns.[10] The Hopi, who speak an Uto-Aztecan language, distinguish people and things not according to gender but according to the categories animate, inanimate, and vegetable.[11] Athabaskan speakers didn't historically use gender pronouns and as a consequence had what Europeans perceived as confusing gender distinctions. Among Dakota-speaking people, gender is understood in lots of different ways, but historically the language has never involved the use of gender-specific pronouns. And Iroquoian speakers, like the Cherokees, did not use gender-specific pronouns either.[12]

These examples only scratch the surface of linguistic and cultural understandings of how Native Americans blended gender roles and identities and engaged in sexual activity they considered normal and healthy. Traditionally, Indigenous people tended to avoid using anatomy or physical appearance as crude markers of gender. They developed much more complex social and cultural systems that made room for gender blending and sexual fluidity within kin-based communities.[13]

The idea that an individual might blend multiple gender identities into their conception of self is an alien concept in virtually every Western culture. But when Europeans began invading the Americas during the late fifteenth century, most Native communities did not connect gender to anatomical concepts of "sex" in the way we do today. Instead, Indigenous people blended occupational roles, physical characteristics and clothing, speech patterns and jewelry, and spiritual and ceremonial participation into dynamic and ever-changing identities. The idea of static gender or sexual categories made little sense for people who strove to bring balance and harmony to their communities.

The rigid world of categories that Europeans constructed during the Scientific Revolution and the Enlightenment had limited utility for Native nations as geographically distant as the Cherokees and Diné (Navajo) peoples. In Diné culture, a *nadleeh* is an individual who blends their gendered identities into kinship communities based on the principals of change over time, ambiguity, and reciprocity.[14] According to Diné anthropologist Wesley Thomas, the nadleeh is one of five dynamic genders in Diné culture—*asdzaan* (or woman, and the primary gender), men, nadleeh, masculine female, feminine male. In terms of sexuality, Thomas contends that Two-Spirit people were likely asexual. Thomas dates the sexualization of the nadleeh to the mid-twentieth century. Before that, "most of them were asexual because their roles had so much to do with the ceremonies."[15]

Reconnecting with dynamic cultures, ceremonies, language traditions, and community isn't easy, but that work continues in the twenty-first century. Two-Spirit elders, artists, scholars, writers, and activists are proving instrumental in reconnecting with tribal histories, culture, and language. That's what DeLesslin "Roo" George-Warren is doing for the Catawba Nation. George-Warren's work highlights the dynamism of Native language and culture (it is featured in the final section of this book). George-Warren is one of a younger generation of LGBTQ2S+ people who are undermining sexual stigmas and gendered stereotypes.[16] Their work reveals that Native people don't need academics to validate their history, culture, or efforts to reclaim traditions.[17] Rick Bacigalupi's 2019 documentary, *Two-Spirit Powwow*, reveals that Two-Spirit people are doing just fine getting on with the work of reclaiming their identities, traditions, and connections to sovereign Native nations. This is an important point, underscored by Cherokee author and scholar Daniel Heath Justice, who writes, "The sacred fire doesn't burn only for straight folks. We queer folks dance around the fire too, our voices strong, our hearts full, our spirits shining. We have gifts of healing to bring too."[18]

The language of Two-Spiritedness, and the fluidity of its meaning, empowers Native people to celebrate their blended gender and sexual identities, and to selectively incorporate non-Native terms like "homosexual," "gay," "lesbian," "transgender," "ace," "queer," or "intersex." These terms are part of a Western intellectual and cultural tradition that dates back to the late nineteenth and early twentieth centuries. Some, like "homosexual," are clinical in the way they categorize people. Other terms demean. "Queer," for example, derives from a sixteenth-century Germanic term meaning strange or peculiar. By the nineteenth century "queer" was used as an adjective to describe something that was spoiled or ruined. Not until the 1920s and 1930s did the term "queer" appear in Europe and North America as a derogatory term to designate a sexually suspect person.[19]

Two-Spirit people attempt to transcend gendered and sexual epithets by reopening doors to tribally specific histories, cultures, and sacred traditions that went underground in response to the violent and eliminationist policies of settler-colonial governments. In the United States, it wasn't until the federal government passed the American Indian Religious Freedom Act of 1978 that thousands of Native people felt safe honoring their traditions in public.[20] Psychologically, reimagining and reclaiming connections to the past continues to prove life-affirming for Two-Spirit people. In doing this work, Two-Spirit people enact traditions of resilience and resistance to the destructiveness of settler colonialism. These qualities empower Two-Spirit people as they grapple with feelings of isolation and work to reconnect with community. The bonds of community were, and remain, central to collective identities and the politics of Indigenous sovereignty. They begin with the nurturing love for family and branch out to larger kinship communities. Through oral traditions, the reintegration of Two-Spirit people into the ceremonial and social life of Native American communities, and their telling of new stories and coining new terms—like "Indigiqueer"—Two-Spirit people continue to reweave themselves into the fabric of family and community throughout Indian Country.

Reclaiming Two-Spirits tells these stories. It reveals stories of spirituality, resilience, and community across Indian Country and beyond. It's a history that enriches our understanding of North America's Indigenous past while also informing hot-button contemporary debates about gender and sexuality in the United States. To begin grasping the magnitude of this history it's necessary to go beyond the 1990s and the adoption of the term "Two-Spirit." We need to reach back even further in time and revisit key events in the early colonial history of North America. The genocidal events that punctuated colonialism and bore witness to episodes of physical and psychological terrorism have left deep wounds in the collective psyche of Native Americans.[21] Remembering those events, strewn across Turtle Island over five centuries, reveals how colonialism disconnects people from traditional knowledge, community relationships, language, and futures filled with hope.[22]

These wounds also inspire determination to reclaim Two-Spirit histories. Two-Spirit identities in the twenty-first century are products of Native American and colonial histories. Since 1492, the people who made colonialism possible have attacked and attempted to reshape the gendered and sexual identities, and the social and cultural life, of Native Americans. Addressing these complex histories is critical to understanding the choices Indigenous people make in relation to the fluid identities embodied by Two-Spirit people today.

The stories that I share in this book will shock, disturb, and hopefully inspire readers. They are stories that most readers know virtually nothing about because the scholars and journalists who write about LGBTQ history all too often ignore Two-Spirit people. Omitting Two-Spirit histories impoverishes our collective understanding of Indigenous cultures and detracts from the extraordinarily rich traditions of gender and sexual diversity in North America. This book cuts through those silences. It is an Indigihistory—a history centered on Indigenous sources and stories, Native experiences and emotions, which decolonize colonialism's archives. It is also a history that seeks to reclaim Two-Spirit pasts in both tribal-centric contexts and in the larger history of Native America's ongoing encounters with colonialism in North America.

Reclaiming Two-Spirits focuses on contemporary events, people, and cultures. However, I contextualize these recent histories by taking readers on historical journeys to places and moments that are now foreign to us all. This approach makes it possible to see how physical and psychological violence almost destroyed Two-Spirit people and their tribal communities. It also illustrates how colonialism's destructiveness failed (and continues to fail) to silence Two-Spirit people. By organizing the book around major themes and a chronological trajectory, my goal is to demonstrate how Two-Spirit people draw strength from the wounds of the past and continually strive to renew cultural traditions that guide them in reclaiming their place in the circle of community.

. . . .

It is not easy for Two-Spirit people to reclaim their histories. Over 80 percent of transgender, gay, lesbian, and Two-Spirit Native people experience physical violence in their lifetimes.[23] That violence highlights how colonialism continues to lay siege to Indian Country. For Two-Spirit people, contemporary forms of trauma are contextualized by a painful history of settler-colonial practices and policies that separated Indigenous people from their communities, religious beliefs, and languages. White Americans routinely draw on their racial privilege to forget about darker, genocidal moments in American history. Native communities haven't forgotten; most don't have that luxury.

The lens through which Native people view American history is shaded by their ongoing interactions with settler colonialism. Recent statistics capture part of this story, especially in relation to issues of gender, sexuality, and racial violence. During the opening decade of the twenty-first century, four out of five Native women reported experiencing violence. For those Native women reporting sexual assault, over 80 percent of cases involved a non-Native assailant; a disproportionate number of these cases resulted from the "man camps" that spring up to house oil and gas workers in Indian Country.[24]

Among Indigenous trans and Two-Spirit people in the United States, disproportionately high rates of violence within intimate queer relationships, workplace discrimination, food insecurity, homophobia (both in Native communities and in the broader settler society), homelessness, and violence shape their realities.[25] One study found that 85 percent of Two-Spirit women experience sexual assault during their lifetimes.[26] Additionally, trans and Two-Spirit Native Americans routinely encounter obstacles in accessing appropriate medical and mental health services, all of which culminates in disturbingly high rates of suicidal ideation.

Addressing these issues underscores the importance of sovereignty in Native communities. For Indigenous North Americans, sovereignty is expressed through culture, religious belief, and language. Cultural sovereignty is the foundation of political sovereignty; culture empowers communities to decolonize settler legal structures. It also provides the language needed to decolonize gender and sexuality by embracing sexual sovereignty through the legal recognition of same-sex marriage, passing laws that address sexual violence, and giving recognition to nonbinary gender identities. Throughout the twentieth and into the twenty-first century, the inability of federally recognized tribal nations to police and prosecute non-Indigenous people who commit crimes of a violent and sexual nature against members of tribal communities has undermined Native sovereignty and perpetuated the worst abuses of settler colonialism.[27]

It remains unclear how a 2020 Supreme Court decision affirming the eastern half of Oklahoma as an "Indian reservation" will in practice impact the criminal justice system in relation to sexually violent crimes.[28] There's little doubt, however, that the position from which Two-Spirit people experience contemporary forms of colonialism and understand its history differs from non-Indigenous LGBTQ and gender-fluid people. Not surprisingly, Native positionality shapes the historical consciousness of Two-Spirit people.[29]

Positionality refers to a body of knowledge that became popular on college campuses and among activists during the poststructuralist turn at the end of the twentieth century. Poststructural and feminist theorists, building on the insights of early-twentieth-century philosophers, have produced important insights into how markers of identity—specifically race, gender, and sexuality—shape how people see the world, and are seen in it.[30] Theories of positionality provide invaluable insights into how and why Indigenous people frame narratives about the past in ways that give meaning to their present realities.

I've brought up the question of positionality with people I've spoken with while writing this book. I do this because I've never pretended to be something I'm not. This is in contrast to examples of individuals laying claim to Native identities in academia, politics, and, as Terry Tofoya's fraudulent claim to an Indigenous identity revealed, in recent Two-Spirit history.[31] When I asked Ken Harper (Cherokee Nation) if he thought my being foreign (I was born in Australia), white, and straight was going to be a problem he replied matter-of-factly, "You're going to take some heat."[32]

He's right. Candi Brings Plenty, a Two-Spirit, cis-gender Oglala Lakota Sioux and descendent of Crazy Horse's band, echoed Harper's observation. She wasn't "angry" about my "cis-straight white privileged male identity" but noted that "a lot of folks do get triggered" by non-Natives writing Indigenous histories.[33] This concern is something I take seriously and think about often. For too long, scholars and scientists engaged in unethical research practices, misrepresented Native history and culture, and wrote in a detached, supposedly "objective" tone that concealed their own cultural baggage and biases, incomplete understanding of Indigenous epistemologies, and interpretive shortcomings.

Today, historians have an opportunity to write ethical histories by collaborating with Indigenous people. These types of histories can act as meeting places, locations where the dusty, ink-faded documents that historians traditionally rely upon meet and engage in conversation with Indigenous people and the panoply of sources—from oral histories to art, dance, and more—they use to make sense of the present. As historian Katherine Ellinghaus and Pitjantjatjara scholar Barry Judd insist, we should nurture Indigenous histories through a "scholarship of engagement" with Native people. This work will help us all to better contextualize the present and foster new meeting places, starting points for future conversations about the meaning of the past.[34]

In writing this book, I am indebted to the scores of Indigenous people who met with me, expressed excitement about the project, and indicated it had deep significance to them. Without this engagement, I wouldn't have persisted in writing the book. I should underscore that my goal isn't to speak for, or write about, Native Americans. My goal has been two-fold: to collaborate with Indigenous people to craft historical knowledge and to actively listen to the diversity of stories that exist throughout Indian Country. This ethic is informed by my engagement with the ideas and experiences of some incredible people. For instance, I recall years ago, Daniel Wildcat (Yuchi Nation) instructed a packed auditorium at Virginia Commonwealth University to view anyone who claims to speak for all Native people with deep suspicion. As Wildcat reminded that audience, and later shared with me over dinner, Indian Country is filled with many voices.

To hear those voices, to actually listen and comprehend the meaning of Indigenous storytelling, requires radical empathy. The ethics of radical empathy should inspire us to leave our comfort zones and make connections, to accept time frames established by Indigenous people, and to allow ourselves to be vulnerable so we become open to building new connections and supportive of Native people as they forge new paths of understanding. That openness will help decolonize American history and highlight Indigenous ways of knowing and narrating the past.[35] I encourage readers to empathize with the richness and complexity that lives among the culturally and politically sovereign communities of Indian Country. I invite you to do so critically, to actively engage with Native storytelling and writing, community organizing among Two-Spirit people, and the life experiences that Two-Spirit people have shared with me in oral histories. In some cases, my positionality as an outsider proved an asset because my knowledge of Native culture and language (and my reading of sources written in Cherokee) wasn't assumed or taken for granted by the Indigenous people I interviewed for this book. In recognizing my outsider status, the people I spoke to demonstrated a duty of care to their culture, explaining sensitive topics to me with care and levels of detail that might not have seemed necessary had they been talking to another Two-Spirit person.[36] I opened myself to being led by Two-Spirit elders; I opened myself to learning. Those conversations proved lively and enriching; many were moving and raw. I treasure them all.

. . . .

The questions I ask about colonialism's written archives and how they represent (or, just as revealingly, ignore) Two-Spirit people and their histories are informed by Two-Spirit storytelling, art, politics, and a decolonial reading of sources. Let me give you a sense of what I'm talking about. To do so I want to transport you back in time to a now-foreign world. The tale I'm about to share with you is a true story of European invasion, violence, and deep trauma. It's also a story that helps us understand the importance of reclaiming and renewing Two-Spirit histories in our own time.

The story begins after a long day of work. As they had done on untold occasions, a small group of Cuchendado Indians toiled through the daylight hours, tending to their crops and working together to complete tasks essential to the community's well-being. It had always been this way; no one could recall life being any different. The Cuchendados worked and talked together, ate meals from a "common pot" together, and shared in ceremonial traditions.[37]

Life seemed balanced, orderly. People who performed the gender roles of women used skills refined over generations to raise crops and prepare food to nourish the community. Those who identified with more masculine social identities also had roles to fulfill. They received instructions from women on how to work the fields, in addition to hunting game and accompanying women in harvesting wild fruits, nuts, and seeds. This work helped to maintain a sense of equilibrium in the world that the Cuchendados shared with one another and with their more-than-human kin. In Cuchendado villages, nestled along the southwestern coast of what is today Texas, people lived *with* the land, not *on* it. Individuals formed relationships that stood as testaments to the importance of kinship, collaboration, and community cohesion.

The world of the Cuchendados wasn't a utopia. They had their problems—war, slavery, crop failures, and infidelities. By the early sixteenth century, these challenges seemed to arrive in increasingly intense waves. Climate change, migration, violence. Life was changing, and as a result the Cuchendados began rethinking old social and political systems. As other Native communities began to realize at this time, the Cuchendados understood that they needed to adapt their traditions to the changes occurring around them if they hoped to keep them alive.

And then, a new threat arrived.

In 1527, Álvar Núñez Cabeza de Vaca stepped onto land that Europeans referred to as the New World. De Vaca was part of the Narváez expedition, one of many waves of Spanish invasion that swept through the Caribbean and the Americas during the sixteenth century. The Spaniards began their incursions into Indigenous communities at Santo Domingo, home to the Taino people. From there, de Vaca traveled with the Narváez expedition to Cuba and finally to Florida.

When the Spaniards arrived in mainland North America they clung to the coastline of the Gulf region. They were curious but cautious. The Spaniards wanted to find riches, but they did not want to die. And yet, death loomed large in the sixteenth century, whether one was Indian or European. For Native people along the Gulf Coast, Spanish invasions meant the spread of diseases and outbreaks of violence, factors that further destabilized populations and hastened political changes that sent growing numbers of Indigenous people inland in search of refuge.

De Vaca wasn't looking for refuge, but he couldn't avoid his own mortality. Hunger and fear shadowed de Vaca and every other European invader in the Americas during the sixteenth century. De Vaca's anxiety intensified as his journey continued. While traveling through Florida, a band of Native warriors detained the Spaniard and held him captive. In an age when male captives in this part of North America routinely met prolonged and painful deaths, de Vaca may well have assumed the end of his life was near.

It wasn't. The Spaniard survived, perhaps the beneficiary of a band of Native people eager for information, trade, or both, as much as they wanted to send a warning to these foreigners. On his release, de Vaca beat a hasty path out of the Indian village. He set a westward course and resumed his journey. It was during this part of his incursion through Indigenous communities in North America's Southeast that he claimed he saw something unbelievable, something "devilish."

De Vaca had stumbled into a Cuchendado village, an intrusion the Cuchendados weren't particularly pleased about. Given that extensive networks of communication and trade already existed among Native North Americans, it's likely that word of foreign invaders had reached the Cuchendados before de Vaca arrived. Tribal elders may also have learned that wherever these outsiders went, sickness and death followed.[38] What we know for certain is that de Vaca believed he'd witnessed "a devilish thing" among the Cuchendados. What had he seen?

The nature of what de Vaca thought he saw was colored by his religious beliefs, his orders from the Spanish Crown, and his heterosexuality. If, in contrast, a group of Native American travelers unrelated to the Cuchendados had entered these small village communities they would not have seen anything out of the ordinary. However, what de Vaca believed he saw, and how he described it, caused as much violence to the historical representation of the Cuchendados as assaults with canons and harquebuses could inflict. Like scores of other European invaders, de Vaca expressed shock to discover families that included a number of "impotent, effeminate men."

De Vaca claimed he had seen men married to other men. De Vaca, a devout Catholic, was disturbed. These were unmanly men. He reported that these men "go about dressed as women, and do women's tasks, and shoot with a bow, and carry great burdens, . . . and they are huskier than other men, and taller."[39]

De Vaca passed over this encounter with noticeable abruptness. He offered little in the way of analysis, reflection, and certainly no empathy—something at odds with his historical reputation as a man with a nuanced appreciation of Native American cultures.[40] De Vaca might have felt moral repugnance at the sight of men married to men, but his captivity among the Florida Indians taught him the importance of strategic silences if he wanted to continue living. These men might have been engaged in "a devilish thing," the women's clothing they wore hinting at their "impotent, effeminate" characteristics, but they were also "huskier than other men, and taller."[41] There was no time for nuanced analysis. De Vaca wanted to get away from these "savages," and fast.

There's more to this scene, however, than de Vaca was willing to let on. Like other European invaders, and the Euro-Americans who came after them in subsequent centuries, narrative silences mingled with logical contradictions and moral judgments in an attempt to dismiss, judge, or eliminate gender-fluid Native people from the historical record. The written records of settler-colonial societies in the northern half of the Americas from Panama to Alaska present only fragmentary written evidence of the individuals we know today as Two-Spirit people.

. . . .

For all of its condescension and chauvinism, de Vaca's description of men "dressed as women" constitutes a written fragment that echoes the reports of other colonial documents. I've combed through colonialism's written archives to unearth these historical fragments. They are painful and offensive. They include documents that allude to "sodomites," "semen eaters," men wearing "the garb of women," "hermaphrodites," and the "berdache," the latter being a term with etymological roots in the ancient Arabic terms *bardaj* or *barah* and used to refer to a "kept boy," "male prostitute," or "catamite." By the eighteenth century, English and French documents refer to the "berdache" in Native North American communities, the Italians to "berdasia," and the Spanish to "bardaxa" or "bardaje." According to the Merriam-Webster dictionary, "berdache" was popularly used in the above ways by the early nineteenth century, but the word was in use long before this.[42] Why did Europeans and Euro-Americans use these labels? How did intergenerational violence and offensive language impact Native communities? And, most importantly, how can books like this one contribute to the decolonization of historical writing to shed light on the past and illuminate paths for future Two-Spirit histories?[43]

Reclaiming Two-Spirits addresses these questions by challenging both the offensiveness and the silences embedded in settler-colonial archives. Where other historians see gaps in historical knowledge, I see opportunities to be led by the knowledge of Two-Spirit people. This book therefore weaves the oral narratives, art, and dance of Two-Spirit people into historical understandings of Native cultures nurtured over millennia.

The following chapters are divided into three parts: "Judgments," "Stories," and "Reclaiming." The chapters focus on how Two-Spirit people have navigated five centuries of settler colonialism and responded to changes in Native cultures, kinship systems, and communal identities. What emerges are dynamic histories—Indigihistories—that require us to trace the intellectual and cultural history of Two-Spirits in ways that are sensitive to the multiple meanings the term "Two-Spirits" embraces.[44] The epigraphs from twentieth- and early-twenty-first-century Two-Spirit people at the beginning of each chapter serve as a reminder of how Native people actively interpret their past and explain to those willing to listen how history impacts contemporary Indigenous lives. Those acts of historical interpretation continue to make it possible for Two-Spirit people to come together in a sense of Pan-Indigenous community while also empowering them to reclaim tribally specific identities. These include *hwame, winkte, Na'dle, Agokwa*, and myriad other gendered and sexual identities that people change, blend, adapt, and innovate over time and in different social settings.

If mystery surrounds Two-Spirit histories—and much of Native American history, for that matter—then that mysteriousness is a product of the colonial archive and the inadequacies of empirical historical and anthropological methodologies. It is also a product of racial stereotypes perpetuated in American culture. Over the past century, a steady diet of Hollywood films, novels, and the continued use of "redface" Indians as mascots has presented audiences with distorted images of Native American history and culture. Alternatively, the neoliberalism of modern LGBTQ politics has tended to follow settler colonialism's logical trail of written documents and empirical data. The result is the marginalization of Two-Spirit people. As Candi Brings Plenty told me, "White LGBTQ people are part of the problem."[45]

I've heard a lot of statements like that over the years. The sense that "white LGBTQ people are part of the problem" reveals how Two-Spirit people recognize the ongoing physical and spiritual violence of colonialism, and the abuses perpetrated against them in the name of Christianity, civilization, science, and more. We should stop for a moment and consider the implications of that violent, often predatory, history. Indeed, it wasn't always the violence committed with firearms, canons, nor even the diseases that spread through Native communities and targeted people we know today as Two-Spirit. The violence perpetuated by Europeans and Euro-Americans against Two-Spirit people, Native women, and Indigenous children was repetitive and systematic; it is also ongoing. It remains present in American politics, in religion, and in how Americans think about "authentic Indians." And it exists in the way non-Native LGBTQ people appropriate Native language and tradition to "Com[e] Out as Two Spirit," as the singer Jason Mraz did in 2018.[46]

. . . .

Fortunately, history and the cultures and languages that give it meaning aren't owned by any one group, political party, or corporation. The portals to the past do not unfold in a linear manner; they have a habit of circling back on us and revealing knowledge and insights once thought lost. History's cycles, its openness, means that the story of what we today call Two-Spirit people is as much a tale of Indigenous knowledge, loss, and reclaiming as it is a lesson in European "discovery," violence, and prejudice. It's a "devilish" history that's full of seemingly queer side notes that link Two-Spirit people to the past, connect them to communities in the present, and help them imagine possible futures.

PART 1

. . . .

JUDGMENTS

CHAPTER 1

INVASION

Balboa set his dogs on people he considered "sodomites."
The understanding was that homosexuality being an
abomination, it really did help further their ability to subjugate
people, especially if in these communities you had people who
were Two-Spirit who had prominent roles.

—RAVEN HEAVY RUNNER (Blackfeet Nation)[1]

Gender-nonconforming people were living as an accepted
part of Native culture, and of course, Europeans looked
at that through that lens they were looking through
and described it in that derogatory language.

—MARCA CASSITY (Osage Nation)[2]

THE CUEVA INDIANS LIVED QUIET, dignified lives on the isthmus that connects North and South America. Enjoying a tropical maritime climate, the Cueva cared for a diversity of interconnected biomes, ranging from tropical mountain forests to freshwater wetlands and coral reefs. Their world was filled with examples of human frailty, human strength, and, occasionally, a little magic and wonder. For these Indigenous Americans, spiritual forces and ceremonial traditions that were hundreds—probably thousands—of years in the making held their communities together. Cueva traditions gave life meaning, reinforced kinship ties, and reminded people of their responsibilities to the larger community.

In 1500, Cueva-speaking people lived in one of approximately eighty-seven chiefdoms. These relatively small communities structured social and political life. So, too, did the architecture of Cueva communities. Thatched dwellings arranged in a circle reminded residents of the importance of community and the intimate connection between community members and the local environment. For the Cueva, like the neighboring Coiba-speaking people, time did not move in a linear trajectory but flowed according to the cycles of the seasons.

The Cueva paid attention to these cycles. They tied their spiritual, medicinal, and cultural traditions to the environment. The production of food was also connected to seasonal changes. Growing crops like beans and cocoa and adding protein to the diet from meats acquired through hunting and fishing demanded that the Cueva pay attention to local ecologies and fluctuating seasons.

But the Cueva were more than simply a farming and hunting people who lived from season to season. Like the Cuchendados along the Gulf Coast and scores of Indigenous communities from the Pacific coast to the Atlantic seaboard, the Cueva lived in vibrant, creative communities. For instance, Cueva mariners built canoes that transported as many as fifty to sixty passengers along the Pacific coastline of Central America. They were also skilled craftspeople—potters, stonecutters, and goldsmiths.

It's not clear how large the Cueva-speaking population was when they first encountered Europeans in the early sixteenth century. They might have numbered a few hundred thousand; then again, their population could also have exceeded one million. Like so much about the world the Cueva Indians made, we're unlikely to ever know the exact size of their population. To Cueva-speaking peoples in the Darién region of what is today Panama, demographic precision probably wasn't their most pressing concern at the opening of the sixteenth century. They faced other, more urgent issues. Their history was about to take a cruel turn.

Scores of Native communities throughout the Americas confronted wave after wave of European invasion. Some, like the Cueva, experienced searing levels of violence at the hands of the Spanish. Others, such as the Cofitachequis in what is today the American South, flirted with diplomatic relationships with European intruders. In still other instances Indigenous people tried to hold on to their art, oral narratives, and ceremonial traditions—Native archives that bore testimony to vibrant and creative communities. The Spanish attacked these archives when they assaulted Indigenous villages whose members engaged in

gender roles and sexual activity that didn't conform to their understanding of "civilization."[3] One of the ways conquistadors terrorized
Indigenous communities from the earliest phase of colonial invasion
was to normalize assaults on people who displayed gender-fluid identities.[4] That violence became endemic to colonialism. Like tornados
whirling across the landscapes, the volatile mix of prejudice and greed
meant that the Spanish hovered like storm clouds ever ready to cut a
path of destruction through Indigenous communities.

. . . .

Invasion. It's an ugly word. European jurists shied away from the
word when describing the colonization of the Americas during the
sixteenth and seventeenth centuries. They preferred words like "discovery" and, later, "the right of conquest." To be sure, these were legal
fictions. Ultimately, though, legalese failed to elide the basic fact that
Europeans invaded the sovereign homelands of Indigenous people.[5]
"Invasion," derived from the Latin *invasionem*, connotes intrusion,
infringement, incursion. It also evokes images of violence, plunder,
and theft. Since the late fifteenth century, invasion has structured colonialism's expansion across North America and given shape to its
persistence. In a physical and psychological sense, Spanish invasion
proved uneven; it was also overseen by Spanish officials whose incom-
petence and corruption often undermined their ability to fulfill their
ambition.[6] Still, Spanish invasions had the potential to destroy Indigenous communities and traumatize survivors. And Spanish written
records, like the archives of other European colonizers, perpetuated a
lie by recasting invasion as exploration, settlement, and the sharing of
Christianity. Lofty tales about brave soldiers, explorers, and missionaries contrasted with references to "sodomites," *hombres afeminados*
("effeminate men") who wore *habito mujeril* ("feminine dress"), and
mujeres varoniles ("masculine women") among Indigenous communities. The authors of documents lodged in colonialism's archives misrepresented these people; it distorted the meaning of kinship and stole
from Indigenous people the fullness of their humanity.

   This is what the Cueva faced in 1500: a Spanish invasion that
resulted in a theft of the body and soul so profound that it reverberates in the historical consciousness of Two-Spirit people today. The
Cueva weren't the first, and wouldn't be the last, to navigate European

attacks on their system of gender and sexuality. During Christopher Columbus's second voyage to the Americas, his doctor, Diego Alvarez Chanca, claimed that a link existed between cannibalism and sodomy among the Native people of the Caribbean. The Caribs, he wrote in 1494, castrated boys caught during warfare and kept them until fully grown. Upon reaching manhood, the Caribs purportedly killed their captives and ate them. The following year, Michele di Cuneo, an Italian, asserted that Caribs passed sodomy on to the Arawak people like a "virus." Once "indulged in, it will prove too pleasurable to ever be resisted again, resulting in permanent and polluted emasculation."[7]

By the time the Spanish invaded the Cueva homelands in 1515, Europeans had already accumulated a catalog of half-truths and outright fictions about Indian "savagery." In the Darién region, Christian feelings of revulsion quickly transformed into actions designed to terrorize the locals. Armed Spaniards spread fear through Native communities as they unleashed one unrelenting wave of violence after another. The carnage was often swift and bloody. Not satisfied with taking captives, the Spanish engaged in intense and localized outbreaks of violence that sometimes involved the unleashing of attack dogs into the Native communities.

The Indigenous people of the Darién region bore the brunt of these early Spanish assaults. They endured both physical violence and sustained political and cultural attacks on their sovereignty. The Spanish rationalized their violent invasions by deploying the Spanish Requirement (or "Requerimiento") in 1513. Written for the Council of Castile by the jurist Juan López de Palacios Rubios, the Requerimiento was a "requirement," or "demand," for Native Americans to renounce their religious faith, accept Catholicism, and submit to Spanish rule. Any resistance to the Spanish risked enslavement or death.[8]

The Requerimiento was the opening gambit in Spanish colonial efforts to sever the social ties that bound Native people together in community. Spanish attacks followed a familiar pattern of terror: if Indigenous people refused the Requerimiento, soldiers would rush into the villages, surprise the inhabitants, and release their attack dogs.[9] When this happened, people screamed in fear as they tried to warn their kin. Those failing to escape endured agonizing deaths as the razor-sharp teeth of the Spanish dogs tore people's bodies apart.[10]

The Flemish engraver Theodor de Bry captured the terror and bloodshed of one of these attacks in 1594. In de Bry's engraving we glimpse Spanish exterminatory violence in action. Spanish soldiers mingle casually as they engage in conversation while their dogs devour the bodies of Indigenous people—dead and lifeless "heathens." It's a chilling scene, a reminder of how Europeans brought with them not only trade goods, diseases, and ideas about the territorial conquest but also searing levels of violence.

What triggered this carnage? Vasco Núñez de Balboa knew. In 1515, the Spanish explorer and conquistador invaded the Cueva Indian province of Dabaiba. His invasion force included a man whose name became synonymous with the brutality of Spanish colonialism in the Americas: Hernando de Soto.[11] De Soto learned a valuable lesson from Balboa in 1515. Colonial conquest involved the exercise of extreme cruelty. De Soto learned another lesson from Balboa: what he "discovered" wouldn't always sit well with his Catholic sensibilities.

De Soto, like Balboa before him, wrote about his "discoveries" of Indigenous peoples. Those descriptions also included details about the land and water resources of the Americas. Spanish incursions into the interior portions of North America disclosed Native social relationships that outraged European sensibilities.[12]

. . . .

The Spaniards who invaded the Americas in the sixteenth century arrived with the intention of exploiting the resources of this "New World." They knew they needed allies and local informants if they hoped to succeed in their quest for wealth. This meant they couldn't kill every Indian, at least not immediately. So, some Spaniards looked for similarities in Native social and political life and their own. If the Spanish intended to exploit Indigenous people and local resources, they'd need to understand them, at least on a rudimentary level. And yet, differences seemed insurmountable.[13]

Spanish reports of these early encounters spawned spirited debate among Iberian intellectuals. In the 1520s and 1530s, academics at the University of Salamanca posited that Native Americans weren't "natural slaves." Instead, Indigenous peoples displayed barbarous habits that education could rectify. Bartolomé de las Casas, a graduate of the

University of Salamanca, championed this idea. A Dominican friar and Spanish colonist, las Casas arrived on the island of Hispaniola in 1502. He participated in the enslavement of Native people, and served as a missionary among the Mayan. By midcentury, however, las Casas had come to reject the idea that Indigenous people weren't human because they lacked Christianity. In the Valladolid debate of 1550 with Juan Ginés de Sepúlveda, in which Sepúlveda defended Spanish violence against Indigenous people on the grounds that they were "natural slaves," las Casas countered with arguments grounded in "milieu theory," a belief that American Indians remained at an earlier stage of human development.[14]

In the Americas, Sepúlveda's view held sway: Native Americans were heathens; they were therefore "natural slaves" whose barbarism invited war. When Spanish conquistadors encountered social relationships that they considered repugnant or a challenge to Spanish conquest, they directed waves of violence against Native people. Among the most feared instruments of Spanish cruelty were dogs. Spanish mastiffs and greyhounds, trained to track the scent of humans, proved highly effective killers. When the dogs caught the scent of their human prey they encircled their intended victims, cut off their escape, and attacked.[15]

The Spanish mastiffs that Balboa deployed against the Indians of Panama in 1515 were muscular, well-trained animals. Weighing as much as two hundred pounds, these dogs must surely have terrified Native people, whose only experience with dogs was with small breeds like the Chihuahua, a petite dog that, according to Spanish accounts, Native people either ate or bred as "bed warmers."[16] Nothing prepared the Indigenous peoples of Central and North America for the mastiff breeds that accompanied the Spaniards during the sixteenth century. For the Spanish invaders, these well-trained killers became a technology of colonization and intimidation. These dogs performed their role with brutal efficiency.

The Spanish nurtured an ideology in which Indians were a brutal, heathenish people, inclined to savage acts of violence and uncivilized rituals. These characterizations shaped Spanish colonial politics over the coming centuries, with the authors of written documents shaping historical perceptions of Indians as people who killed Christian missionaries without provocation, engaged in ritualistic acts of human sacrifice, and tormented the recently arrived Spaniards with sadistic acts of torture. Moreover, the Indians allegedly practiced cannibalism, a claim that persisted in Spanish descriptions of Native sexuality and gender roles.[17]

This could not stand. God-fearing Spaniards needed to defend themselves. With great speed the invaders cast themselves as the champions of Christian civilization as they "murdered and massacred" their way through the Darién region and other parts of the Americas.[18] Catholic priests and settlers would ultimately follow the conquistadors and initial waves of invasion, transforming the "savage" spaces of the so-called New World into stable, orderly, and above all, civilized places. This transformation could only happen if the Spanish stamped out sin among the "natural slaves" of the Americas. Few sins, at least in the minds of early modern Europeans, were in more urgent need of eradication than sodomy.[19]

. . . .

The Spanish claimed they saw "sodomites" throughout the Americas. In Native communities, the people Europeans labeled as sodomites sometimes played important social and cultural roles. This included the preservation of sacred knowledge, overseeing important ceremonies, and acting as teachers and healers. In the Darién region, as in other parts of Central and South America, gender-fluid people played important roles in binding kinship communities together. For Native people, kinship constituted the basis for one's identity and a tangible link to collective knowledge and memory. The Spanish recognized the importance of "sodomites" to Cueva kinship. This recognition, combined with feelings of moral repugnance, explains why the Spaniards targeted them with enslavement or even death.[20]

The epithets used by the Spanish to denigrate gender-fluid people in Cueva society were not chosen by accident. That language had a deep history and it justified physical violence. The term "sodomite" was derived from *Sadeh Adom*, contracting to "Sodom." The cities of Sodom, located near the salt mines of the Dead Sea, and nearby Gomorrah appear in the Book of Genesis, the New Testament, the Tankh, and Quran. By the time the Spanish invaded the Caribbean and the American mainland, Sodom and Gomorrah had become shorthand for sin, especially "sin" involving anal and oral sex.

This bothered the Spanish, but it didn't concern them as much as the social relationships that the people they labeled sodomites formed. Back in Europe, the Inquisition focused on what sodomites thought and how their connections to a local community enabled their sexual behavior. The typical Spaniard saw a sodomite's sexual and social relations as expressions of their inner moral and religious failings that manifested in "antisocial" behavior and could infect entire communities.[21]

The logic that informed episodes of genocidal violence against the Cueva and other Native communities therefore originated in the culture and politics of early modern Spain. As noted, medieval Spain wasn't a safe place for sodomites. By the sixteenth and seventeenth centuries, emerging legal and scientific knowledge heightened this danger. As nascent civil states began forming across Europe, Spanish legal and theological authorities sharpened distinctions involving male-male, male-female, male-animal, and female-female acts of sodomy (the latter occurring when the "active" female partner penetrated the "passive" with their "abnormally large clitoris").[22] Significantly, as legal thinkers differentiated types of sexual crimes, the Catholic clergy clung to the idea that all forms of sodomy were sinful.

The Catholic Church's opposition to sodomy stemmed from a reading of the Bible that reached back to the story of Sodom and Gomorrah. Catholic priests used this story to warn parishioners away from this most sinful of sexual activities. Priests issued regular reminders that all sexual activity—starting with masturbation, an act of sexual self-gratification that theologians associated with the biblical story Onan and the "spilling of seed"—was sinful. The biblical story of Onan in Genesis 38 cautioned male readers against the spilling of "his seed on the ground," a passage that can be interpreted as an admonition against masturbation, sodomical acts, or practicing coitus interruptus during heterosexual sex. The Spanish clergy also judged sexual activity along a hierarchy of sin. Sodomy was at the top of the hierarchy. In cases of sodomy both the active and passive participants in a sexual act were deemed guilty of the most egregious breach of God's law.[23] At the bottom of the hierarchy of sexual sin was vaginal intercourse.[24]

By the early sixteenth century, Spanish legal authorities joined the Catholic clergy in taking a dim view of sodomites. Unlike the Catholic Church, though, the Spanish state used the law to bring criminal charges against an active participant in a sodomical act. A man accused of penetrating the anus of another male became a target for prosecution by the state. The penetrated male was considered the passive sexual partner and legally defined as a victim of rape. Interestingly, the Spanish state's use of the law to address sodomy in this way departed from the practice in much of the rest of the Mediterranean world. In sodomy trials throughout the region, *guarrones*, or sexual partners engaged in the "active" performance of anal penetration, might avoid prosecution because they were deemed to be engaging in a masculine act. The penetrated, or "passive," partner (*maricas*) was not viewed in this masculine light and faced the possibility of a harsh sentence.[25]

This wasn't the case in the Spanish legal system. In Spanish popular culture, however, sexual attitudes reflected those throughout Europe, with the passive participant in sodomy cases viewed in an increasingly negative light. Early modern Spaniards viewed male passivity as a sign of weakness and inferiority. Linguistically, Spaniards used the word *puto* as an epithet to insult and mock an allegedly effeminate male who was anally penetrated. In the eyes of Spanish Catholics, weakness, passivity, and effeminacy were also hallmarks of the Moors—the Muslim inhabitants of the Iberian Peninsula. When the Spanish declared war on the Moors and ultimately defeated them at the end of the fifteenth century, Spanish popular culture emphasized the active, strong, and masculine nature of the Spanish in relation to the passive, weak, and racially inferior Moors.[26] Thus, the Spanish had already connected military conquest with gender and sexuality before they reached the Americas.[27]

. . . .

Understanding Spanish attitudes helps to explain their explicit attacks on Native elders and knowledge keepers—people integral to maintaining kinship ties and communal bonds. When Spaniards recast elders, shamans, and healers as "effeminates" or "sodomites," they rationalized their violence against these people. In the minds of Spanish conquistadores, taking action against the Cueva sodomites was just. Recognizing this enables us to see that when the Spanish attacked Native sodomites, they assaulted individuals with fluid gender identities and who were integral to the health and stability of Indigenous communities. Spanish violence, both physical and intellectual, constituted the first step in the conquerors' efforts to unravel Indigenous kinship bonds and ultimately compel the members of sovereign tribal communities to submit to Spanish rule.

The Cueva, like scores of Native cultures throughout the Americas, left us with no written words to help us understand how they resisted Spanish assaults, or how they felt when elders and knowledge keepers were literally thrown to the dogs. That silence is both painful and haunting. Where complex human societies once thrived, there's now a void, historical silences filled only with records of Spanish brutality. We can try to imagine the terror that the Spanish and their dogs visited on the Cueva, but that imagining feels like an injustice to those who lost their lives.

The Cueva-speaking people weren't alone in encountering the violent firestorms of Spanish colonialism. Nahuatl-speaking people, who appear to have had a considerable social and cultural influence on the Mayans, reportedly engaged in forms of sodomy that the Spaniards found repulsive. Nahua noblemen reportedly sated their lust by engaging in sexual activity with "passives." In some cases, the existence of "passives" appeared to help Native rulers solidify social hierarchy. In Mayan society, the existence of sodomy and pederasty, sexual activity involving a man and a catamite (a boy kept for sexual activity; the term's usage increased during the 1500s), helped to reinforce both structural political ranks and social hierarchy.[28]

What concerned the Spanish—and had the potential to stymie colonial invasion and expansion—was the leading roles that "sodomites" and "pederasts" appeared to hold in Native communities. If one of the pillars of Spanish colonialism involved Indigenous submission to Catholicism—elders and knowledge keepers who stood in the way of this needed to be eliminated. Labeling key members of kinship communities sodomites or pederasts therefore served an important purpose: they rationalized genocide.

Still, the fact remains that gender-fluid people played important roles in scores of Indigenous communities and enjoyed healthy sexual lives unburdened by labels like "sodomite" and "catamite." Indigenous oral traditions, art, and archaeology reveal the existence of same-sex relationships in Native communities. Where it occurred, same-sex intimacy was not sinful but a marker of maturity, ceremony, tradition, or pleasure. In some instances, when a young boy fellated an older boy the sex act represented a marker of maturity as much as it might have signified an act of sexual desire and gratification.[29] In Nahua culture, for instance, virtually no written evidence survives to suggest that this behavior was defined in purely "homosexual" terms.[30] To use labels like "homosexual" or "sodomite" is Eurocentric, and in the case of "homosexual," it is ahistorical to use this term for an era prior to its being coined in the late nineteenth century.

In fact, the Indigenous people whose lives were interrupted by Spanish invasions gave meaning to iconography that told their own stories about sexual intercourse. What the Spanish perceived as sinful acts of sodomy, Native people may have understood as a ceremonial marking of maturation. Alternatively, warfare and military victory involved sexual acts in which victorious warriors engaged in intercourse with the vanquished male warriors. This type of sexual activity was designed to reinforce the strength and recently won superiority of the victorious warriors and to transform the defeated men "into a passive."[31] The point here is that there existed no single reason for people engaging in sexual behaviors in Native American societies during the sixteenth century.

Sexual expression constituted an important facet of mental and physical well-being for Indigenous people throughout the Americas. On Peru's north coast, the Moche produced art and architecture that scholars have long compared to that of Mayan civilization. Like the Mayan, Moche roots connected them to the "mother cultures" of the Olmec and Chavin-Cupisnique cultures.[32] And like the Mayans, Moche artists produced pieces with clean lines that emphasized realism. That's evident in Moche erotic pottery.

A highly portable and widely available art form, Moche pottery depicted scenes ranging from the ceremonial to the everyday, everything from sacrifice scenes to people fishing. Within this genre, the Moche produced erotic art that included representations of fellatio.[33] Bahía archaeology also provides glimpses into the world the Spanish tried to destroy. Bahía culture stretched from the Pacific coast to the Andean foothills between 500 BCE to 500 CE. Bahía artists produced sculpture and artworks that reveal heterosexual and same-sex couples. That art suggests that same-sex couples played active roles in maintaining kinship bonds and balancing the needs of the community by raising children or tending to nutritional needs.[34]

The Spanish tended to look past, or willfully ignore, the social and sexual complexity conveyed in Moche and Bahía art. Nowhere was this clearer than when the Spanish unleashed their attack dogs on people they characterized as sodomites. In turning their dogs into an extermination force, the Spanish destroyed generations of knowledge and rich stores of information about the cultural, military, and spiritual traditions associated with gender-fluid identities and the variety of motives for engaging in sexual acts. Gendered traditions in Native communities gave meaning to human maturation and warfare. They also defined cultural traditions in ways that emphasized the interconnected and shape-shifting powers of all living and spiritual beings—a belief system that made European gender binaries and sexually prescribed behaviors seem anachronistic across Native America.[35]

. . . .

Some six thousand miles northeast of the Cueva homelands, Spanish colonial archives provide another imperfect glimpse into the gendered worlds of Native Americans. In the early spring of 1540, in what is today South Carolina, an Indigenous woman whose name is lost to history began diplomatic negotiations with the Spanish conquistador Hernando de Soto. According to the written accounts of de Soto's incursion into the American South between 1539 and 1542, this Indigenous woman appeared to occupy a position of considerable political power. Garcilaso de la Vega, a Spanish soldier, lauded "her discretion" and "great beauty, which she had in extreme perfection."[36]

De la Vega, who wrote under the pseudonym "El Inca," didn't travel to North America with de Soto. He accumulated information from men who accompanied de Soto, a group that began its North American incursion at Ozita in 1539, not far from modern-day Tampa, with 625 men and 250 horses. Whereas other accounts of de Soto's invasion were written by men who accompanied him, de la Vega's writings offer a stark reminder of the ethnographic limitations of Spanish representations of Indigenous history and culture.[37] We should read these documents with extreme caution, and considerable skepticism.

We do know that after the Spaniards set out from Ozita they traveled parallel to the coastline. As they moved over and through landscapes that Indigenous people had nurtured for generations they used chains and iron collars to secure women and slaves, routinely demanded canoes, stole food, and terrorized entire communities.[38] De Soto, a veteran of Pizarro's violent march through Inca homelands that led to the death of the Inca emperor Atahualpa—strangled by an iron collar—in 1533, understood the intimidatory benefits of physical violence. But in the spring of 1540, as de Soto's conquistadors changed course and headed north toward Yupaha, another name that Indigenous people purportedly associated with the residents of the Cofitachequi chiefdom, they paused their violence. The Spanish were entering a society in which a great chieftainess purportedly ruled over a rich land.[39]

The Spanish referred to this leader as the *cacica* of Cofitachequi, *cacica* being the feminine of *cacique*, an Arawak term for a hereditary chief, which the Spanish appropriated.[40] Europeans had known queens to rule over their societies; Queen Isabella's "manly" virtues had attracted praise from the high-ranking men of Castile, but praise of this nature rarely extended to other women.[41] In Europe, queens surrounded themselves with male advisors. At Cofitachequi, the cacica's advisors were not men but other elite women.

The power that the cacica of Cofitachequi wielded and the gendered composition of her closest advisors was not something the Spaniards were accustomed to.[42] Influenced by Aristotelian precepts of humanity, Spanish writers from playwrights to Jesuit priests crafted a vision of the world in which men discovered, shaped, and ruled societies. *Homo agens*, "man the doer," became naturalized in Spanish culture, as men conquered vast lands and ruled over large numbers of people. In the Americas, Spaniards enacted their masculinity—their machismo—through invasion, violence against effeminate men and sodomites, and attempts to establish colonial rule over societies governed by matrilineal traditions.[43]

Cofitachequi was a matrilineal society that did not fit neatly into Spanish ideals of masculinity.[44] The magnitude of the cacica's power, the reputed wealth of her chiefdom, and her fluid gender identity puzzled the Spanish. Reading between the lines of the Spanish chroniclers, we glimpse the cacica's power as she dictated the terms of her first meeting with de Soto along the banks of the Wateree River. Traveling in an elaborately decorated piragua and accompanied by her most trusted female advisors, the cacica began laying the groundwork for a possible alliance. One of de Soto's chroniclers known merely as "A Gentleman of Elvas" wrote that the cacica offered the Spaniards gifts, including "a long string of pearl beads" and "all her canoes." The cacica was opening the white path of friendship. Elvas suggested that de Soto negotiated with the cacica in a bid to get information from her and secure an alliance that would benefit the Spanish.[45] What Elvas failed to grasp was that the Spanish were a small part of the cacica's diplomatic calculations—mere bit players.

The cacica ruled over Cofitachequi, a society anthropologists and archaeologists refer to as a chiefdom. Chiefdoms shaped the political landscape from the Great Lakes to the Gulf Coast. Chiefdoms varied in size and complexity, from simple chiefdoms with as few as one hundred to two hundred people to complex chiefdoms, a hierarchical political structure combining smaller chiefdoms under a single para-mount chief, monumental architecture, and populations that ran into the thousands. Cofitachequi was a complex chiefdom. The people of Cofitachequi probably spoke a Muskogean dialect, but Siouan and Iroquoian speakers likely also called Cofitachequi home.[46]

As a matrilineal society, the women of Cofitachequi played leading roles in politics, medicine, agriculture, and in overseeing kinship ties. Like the Cusabo, Guale, Yamasee, and other matrilineal societies in the Southeast, women, and people who took on skilled roles associ-ated with women, held positions of considerable power and social esteem. The Spanish chroniclers wrote about the influence of these women without ever fully grasping their significance as markers of fluid gender roles and matrilineal kinship communities. Only when we decolonize these written artifacts of Spanish colonialism and sup-plement them with archaeological evidence do we begin to grasp the historical significance of women like the cacica of Cofitachequi.

Matrilineality confounded European concepts of paternal descent and inheritance, but it proved the norm among Indigenous people in the Southeast. The world of the Cofitachequis, and nearby chief-doms such as Guale and Mocama, differed substantially from the patriarchal societies of Europe. In these and other societies across the Native South, women inherited positions of political power and influence. This proved the case in Cofitachequi, just as it did among the neighboring Cusabo people.[47] Additionally, women determined the structure of kinship ties. For instance, when a man married, he moved into the home of his wife. And when that couple had children, the women of the house (and in adolescence, the mother's brothers) assumed the responsibility for educating children.[48]

But in 1540, Cofitachequi was weakened. There was no guarantee that its matrilineal structures would endure in the form de Soto had encountered them. There were several reasons for this. First, an extended war with Ocute had strained Cofitachequi's resources. Second, warfare exacerbated resources shortages caused by a severe "Pestilence," an extended drought that crippled much of the Southeast between 1565 and 1575 that depleted Cofitachequi's stockpiles of food.[49] Third, other regional powers, such as Coosa, were growing in power and ambition, further exposing the frailties of Cofitachequi.[50]

Given this context, it's reasonable to speculate that the cacica was looking for new allies. Perhaps de Soto could form part of a new alliance that could help the cacica shore up Cofitachequi's regional stability. De Soto, however, had other plans. He'd heard of a powerful chiefdom named Chiaha and its male leader, the "lord of Coca." De Soto wanted the cacica to help him meet this wealthy chief. We don't know why, but the cacica did eventually agree to accompany de Soto and his men, the Spanish promising to provide her with an enslaved man named Vascoucellos in exchange for her guidance to Chiaha.[51]

After setting out for Chiaha in May 1540, the Spaniards resumed their violent and sexually exploitative practices, although not always successfully. According to the chronicler Rodrigo Rangel, an Indigenous woman encountered during their journey took offense at the sexual overtures of a Spanish soldier. She reportedly grabbed the Spaniard "by the genitals and held him very fatigued and submissive, and perhaps if other Christians had not passed and aided him, the Indian woman would have killed him." Rangel tried to explain away the seriousness of this incident, writing that it "was not that he wished to have intercourse with her as a lustful man, but rather that she wished to liberate herself and flee."[52]

The cacica likely heard about such incidents, prompting growing suspicions of Spanish motives. Moreover, as the cacica arrived at the borderlands of her chiefdom she would have recognized the danger of being taken captive by warriors from rival chiefdoms. The cacica was an astute leader; it wouldn't have surprised her to learn that "some caciques [of neighboring Ocute and Cofoque]" promised to provision de Soto's men if the Spaniards "would declare war against the Queen of Cofitachequi."[53] Preexisting rivalries among Indigenous chiefdoms thus stymied any hopes the cacica might have had of forming an alliance with the Spanish. The time had come to cut her losses and leave these foreigners. This she did, departing, to the surprise of the Spaniards, with an enslaved woman.[54]

. . . .

From the Darién region to the Gulf Coast and into the interior portions of the Native South, Spanish invasions had unsettling and sometimes deadly effects on Indigenous communities. In Cofitachequi's cacica, de Soto saw an opportunity to exploit a *mujeres varoniles*—"masculine woman." He miscalculated, failing to see that the cacica had a mind of her own and a tradition of matrilineal empowerment to draw strength from as she strategized about how best to manage the domestic and foreign affairs of Cofitachequi.[55] In contrast, the Cueva "sodomites" experienced a very different, bloody fate. In both cases, Spanish violence, real and threatened, loomed over Spanish-Indigenous encounters.[56]

As the early sixteenth century examples outlined in this chapter remind us, decolonizing Spanish colonial archives and critiquing the acts that gave rise to the *leyenda negra*—the black legend, a term used to refer to Spanish cruelty and intolerance for Indigenous cultures in the Americas—also demands that we not lose sight of Indigenous people. Their art, the structure of their communities, the way Native people moved over landscapes and waterscapes in response to European invasion continued to tell us a number of complex stories about the calculations that Indigenous people made in relation to early forms of colonial intrusion. Some, like the Cueva, confronted genocidal violence. Others, like the Moche and Bahía peoples, created material objects that survived and can today reconnect Indigenous people to traditions that colonizers willfully tried to destroy. And in the leadership of the cacica of Cofitachequi we see the outlines of a gendered system of kinship and political power struggling to adapt to a changing world around it and prepare for the challenges of the future.

For colonizers, these initial encounters with Indigenous communities and people whose gendered roles and sexual practices seemed at odds with their own norms ignited feelings of anxiety, contempt, and superiority. Who were these people, and why did many of them appear to move effortlessly between male and female identities? Were they trying to deceive the colonizers? Why didn't Native people conform to the male-female binary that Europeans increasingly saw as a natural part of life?[57] Perhaps answers to these questions lie in closer examinations of Indigenous bodies.

CHAPTER 2

"HERMAPHRODITES"

It wasn't until I got older that I knew who I was,
that I was different from everyone else.

—TIMOTHY "TWIX" WARD (San Carlos Apache Tribe, Arizona)[1]

Happily I recover.
Happily my interior becomes cool.
Happily I go forth.
My interior feeling cool, may I walk.
No longer sore, may I walk.
Happily, with abundant dark clouds, may I walk.
Happily, with abundant showers, may I walk.
Happily, with abundant plants, may I walk.
Happily, on a trail of pollen, may I walk.
Happily, may I walk.

— "PRAYER OF THE NIGHT CHANT" (Diné)[2]

DURING HIS SECOND VOYAGE to North America, the French Hugue-
not explorer René Goulaine de Laudonnière wrote of "deer gambol-
ing across the open spaces" and a "great green valley" that led to "the
most beautiful prairies in all the world." Laudonnière immodestly
called this place shielded by "a tall forest" and irrigated by "little
fresh-water streams" the Vale of Laudonnière.

After pausing briefly to enjoy the landscape he had no right to
name, Laudonnière and his men pushed on. They traveled along "a
little trail" before meeting "an Indian woman of tall bodice, an hermaphrodite, who came to our front with a large vessel." Laudonnière
wrote that he and his men happily drank the cool, clear water from

the hermaphrodite's "large vessel." Laudonnière recalled that "the succor of that *Indian Hermaphrodite*" restored his party's strength.[3]

This incident was one of two encounters that Laudonnière had with "hermaphrodites." Laudonnière made both of these observations during the second of his four voyages to "La Florida" between 1562 and 1567. Notably, his descriptions of "hermaphrodites" among the Timucuan Indians—a community of Indigenous people who lived on lands between modern-day Georgia and Florida—were noticeably brief. Who was this mysterious "hermaphrodite"? Laudonnière provided few details. Typical of sixteenth-century accounts, Laudonnière's description relied on a word with roots in the ancient Greek *hermaphroditos*, a person possessing the attributes of both male and female.[4] Today, the preferred term is "intersex."

Laudonnière's brief account leaves us with mere traces of information about intersex people. That brevity has further contributed to the mischaracterization of Indigenous gender identities and sexual roles in the written archives of colonialism. However, despite their flaws, written documents are starting points for understanding how colonial cultures, medicine, and science imposed categories of difference on Native people.

First, let's return to the historical context in which Laudonnière claimed he encountered Timucuan hermaphrodites. Laudonnière, along with Jean Ribault, was one of the founders of Fort Caroline, a short-lived French colony located somewhere near present-day Jacksonville, Florida, before Spanish forces destroyed it in 1565.[5] Over the next two decades, "La Florida" remained a volatile place. The Spanish presence in the region proved particularly disruptive to Native polities and exacerbated preexisting rivalries among Indigenous chiefdoms.[6]

Laudonnière described the Timucuan hermaphrodites in this fraught context. He insinuated that hermaphrodites, like women, performed the bulk of the work—the drudgery of daily life. As far as Laudonnière could tell, the hermaphrodites' unique blend of masculine strength and feminine caregiving qualities equipped them to tend to the needs of weary travelers and perform labor-intensive work. How Laudonnière knew that these were intersex people wasn't clear; he gave no indication that he performed an anatomical examination of these so-called hermaphrodites—an invasive process that Timucuans would

likely have rejected. Like so many European observations, Laudonnière's recollections amounted to little more than conjecture.[7]

Conjecture, like prejudice, informed centuries of ethnographic
misrepresentation of Indigenous cultures. Laudonnière contributed to
this inglorious canon of colonial writing. In addition to observing the
hospitality and labors of hermaphrodites, he emphasized the savagery
and subhuman qualities of Native people by criticizing their gender
roles. Timucuan men did not adhere to the rules of "just war" but instead indulged in guerrilla-style "surprise attacks" on their enemies.[8]
Laudonnière also expressed some harsh views of Timucuan women.
They, like hermaphrodites, were burden bearers who suffered under
the tyranny of Native men.

Laudonnière expressed mixed emotions about Timucuan gender
roles and sexuality. He was disgusted by Timucuan men who "love
women and maydens" to excess—a clear sign that they lacked moral
scruples. He pitied Timucuan women, his descriptions of their "burdens" revealing his condescension. Laudonnière's portrayal of the
Timucuan hermaphrodites was most damning. Like Indian women,
hermaphrodites carried the burdens of Timucuan society. And in times
of war the hermaphrodites did double duty, carrying the "victuals"
and bodies of the dead, while they also "paint their faces and fluff out
their hair with feathers in order to make themselves as repulsive as
possible."[9]

. . . .

Who were the Timucuan hermaphrodites? To answer this question,
we first need to understand what Laudonnière meant when he used the
term "hermaphrodite." The hermaphrodite was more than a person
with both male and female attributes; by the fifteenth and sixteenth
centuries it was someone who "improperly occupies two offices." Like
the term "ambidexter"—a term medieval lawyers used in charging
"misconduct"—Europeans used the word "hermaphrodite" as an epithet to denote unnaturalness, the devil, or a figure of tragicomedy. Just
as church and civil authorities defined "sodomites" as disruptive to
evolving understandings of the natural and social order, they defined
hermaphrodites with similar levels of approbation.[10]

Today, the defamatory connotations associated with the word
"hermaphrodite" means that it is rightly considered offensive. It's a

pejorative label, used for people who now refer to themselves as intersex.[11] Intersex people don't fit neatly into the tidy world of Western medical and scientific categories—the binary of male and female.

Appreciating intersex identities requires a crash course in human biology. A person with an egg-producing body has two X chromosomes, while a body that produces sperm possesses X and Y chromosomes. When these chromosomes fuse as a result of sexual reproduction, the chromosomes are paired in a process known as karyotyping and which can produce what Western science labels a male (XY chromosomes) or female (XX chromosomes).

Nature sometimes confounds the neat categories that Western scientists and doctors began refining during the sixteenth century. Take, for example, a child born with XXY or XO chromosomes. These combinations produce what medical professionals call anomalies in the development of sexual organs. In these cases, a newborn might enter the world with what looks like both male and female genitals. Another child might be born with XX chromosomes but lack a vagina, womb, or ovaries.

These intersex newborns enter the world with the capacity to live full and dignified lives. However, cultural, religious, and medical prejudices have circumscribed the lives of intersex people in Western culture for millennia. As far back as ancient Greek and Roman mythology, philosophers developed ableist discourses that included the category of "hermaphrodite." In the Hippocratic writings of the ancient Greeks, hermaphrodites existed as "in-between" types. In contrast, the Aristotelian tradition posited that intersex people had an "overabundance of generative material." Ancient Greek writers such as Aristotle and Galen postulated a one-sex model—male—as normative and to which all other human physical types were compared. Ancient thinkers viewed those who diverged from the male standard as incomplete, or inversions. Female bodies diverged from male bodies in being wetter, cooler, and possessed of an anatomical peculiarity: the uterus. Ancient writers identified hermaphrodites as a human anomaly. Like people born with an extra nipple or a sixth toe, these people attracted medicalized labels like "anomalous" or "monstrous."[12] For many in the ancient world, hermaphrodites belonged alongside people born with dwarfism, albinism, one eye, or other physical "abnormalities." In still other instances, the birth of intersex infants was assumed to foretell calamity, and in some cases, these infants were killed.[13]

In Europe between the fifth and fifteenth centuries, theologians, jurists, doctors, and alchemists elaborated on ancient ideas about hermaphrodites. Ovid's tale of the water nymph Salmacis became one of the best-known legends of Europe's ancient mythology. Ovid's tale is the story of Salmacis's unsuccessful attempt to seduce the son of Hermes and Aphrodite, Hermaphroditus. Unhappy with Hermaphroditus's rebuke of her overtures, Salmacis summoned the gods and created a creature that fused male and female body parts.

Ancient mythology appealed to alchemists. Medieval alchemists borrowed liberally from ancient stories, the Bible, and the writings of theologians. Tales about hermaphrodites provided useful metaphors in explaining complex chemical processes. Similarly, medical, religious, and legal authorities drew on a cross-section of literary tropes to associate the hermaphrodite with the monstrous, social disorder, or misconduct.

These cultural traditions guided jurists and priests at a time when male and female identities were not as fixed as they became in the centuries after the Reformation.[14] The imprecise language used to describe differences between men and women during the fifteenth and sixteenth centuries meant that the meanings attached to terms like "hermaphrodite" remained unstable. In some medical and theological texts, eunuchs received the label of hermaphrodite. Others posited that the hermaphrodite's genitalia combined an amalgam of male and female sexual organs.[15]

By the late fifteenth century, a concerted effort to end uncertainty about sex began. In Spain and Portugal, the establishment of the Inquisition saw church authorities redeploy ancient mythology and biblical teachings to establish a knowledge base to police people's thoughts and actions. The Inquisition had broad reach. Jurists and priests monitored Jewish converts to Catholicism, called conversos. They also maintained a keen eye on sexual matters and policed the social behavior of men and women. At the same time, European intellectuals and medical experts began reassessing the one-sex model—the ancient Greek world's idea of male normativity and female divergence. In its place they prescribed a two-sex model of male and female bodies. Anomalies, or human beings who blended male and female genitalia, blurred the categories of man and woman and invited religious, legal, and medical scrutiny. In this context, the Inquisition played an important role in crystallizing a language of exclusion that defined hermaphrodites as "monstrous" because they departed from "normal" understandings of male and female bodies.[16]

The medical invention of the hermaphrodite became fodder for political, cultural, and religious debates in seventeenth-century Europe. Medical writers and theologians continued expressing concern about the "unnatural" physical attributes of hermaphrodites. Growing numbers of doctors linked social status, behavior, and biology to perceived physical abnormalities, while theologians maintained that differences between men and women were part of natural, or God's, law.[17] Among other things, Europeans used the figure of the hermaphrodite to refine a language of difference deemed vital to governing large numbers of people.[18]

How Europeans represented hermaphrodites spoke to a growing preoccupation with prescribing social order. During the Renaissance, theologians and physicians associated hermaphrodites with behaviors they considered sinful, such as cross-dressing. In Germany, writers linked hermaphroditism with *Monstrositäten* (monstrosities). The theologian Albertus Magnus went further, linking the hermaphrodite's body with a predilection for lying. Physicians added to this discussion by proposing categories of hermaphrodites. For instance, the Frenchman Ambroise Paré identified four types of hermaphrodites: the male hermaphrodite, the female hermaphrodite, the male-female hermaphrodite, and a neutral hermaphrodite.[19] However, more research was needed. By the early decades of the seventeenth century, German physicians joined their colleagues throughout Europe in looking to dissection as a way to gain greater empirical understanding of the hermaphrodite's anomalous reproductive organs. Given speculation that the hermaphrodite's male and female genitalia existed one above the other or side by side on their bodies, dissection might dispel myths and provide scientific certainty.[20] By the latter half of the century, medical writers emphasized how the hermaphrodite diverged from those with "normal" male or female genitalia suitable for human reproduction and was physically incomplete.[21]

These harsher European representations of hermaphrodites also coincided with the Reformation in Christianity and the invasion of the

Caribbean and Americas. These events impacted how Europeans saw Native American people. In fact, sixteenth- and seventeenth-century representations of hermaphrodites became so embedded in Western culture that they endured into the eighteenth century and beyond. Theodor de Bry's late-sixteenth-century portrayal of Florida hermaphrodites echoed Laudonnière's descriptions and those of medical and theological texts. During these centuries Europeans wrote matter-of-factly about Native Americans' holding hermaphrodites in "great Contempt, believing them to be something so evil as not to deserve the Comforts of Life."[22]

But did they? Or do these descriptions tell us more about Europeans and their intellectual assumptions, social anxieties, or idiosyncratic readings of ancient mythology and biblical texts? What if Europeans were looking at Native Americans but not really seeing them?

. . . .

Most Indigenous societies across North America did not subject intersex people to the types of prejudices characteristic of European Christianity and medical science. Intersex people weren't common, but at the same time Native communities generally didn't ostracize intersex people by placing them outside the boundaries of kinship. In a number of instances, intersex people played important ceremonial and spiritual roles in mediating relationships between people with clearly identifiable male or female features, while others helped to maintain balance and harmony in society by renewing a community's connection to both place and sacred traditions. Indigenous religious traditions contained strong medicine; it connected people to kinship networks and was powerful because it was responsive to ecological change.[23] In many Native philosophies, gender roles and sexual identities were (and remain) dynamic.[24]

With this in mind, let's return to Laudonnière and the Europeans who accompanied him through the area the Spanish called La Florida: territorial claims that extended from the Atlantic seaboard west along the Gulf Coast to modern-day Louisiana and Texas. At the time that Laudonnière published his account, La Florida was governed by Indigenous polities. But Europeans—particularly the Spanish, Portuguese, French, and English—had their eyes on this vast region and the potential riches it contained. All of these European powers sent exploratory parties into La Florida in search of wealth, to seek out suitable agricultural lands, and to investigate the viability of diplomatic and trade partnerships with Native polities. These objectives dominate colonialism's written archives. Those documents also contain references to hermaphroditism, a phenomenon that so puzzled a number of writers that they, like Laudonnière, felt compelled to record it.

Jacques Le Moyne de Morgues claimed he saw hermaphrodites—or at least men who adopted what he understood as female roles. Le Moyne was part of Laudonnière and Ribault's efforts to establish a French colony in what is today northern Florida. At the same time, the Spanish wanted to establish a permanent colonial presence, which they took steps toward doing with the founding of St. Augustine in 1565.

The year 1565 proved to be pivotal in La Florida, as European rivalries played out on Indian lands. The result was a massacre. The Spanish attacked Fort Caroline and slaughtered French soldiers. After suffering heavy losses, the French abandoned their colonial ambitions in this part of La Florida for the time being.[25]

Le Moyne escaped the violence of La Florida and returned to Paris in 1566, where he remained until 1572. In 1572, he again fled from violence, and the St. Bartholomew's Day massacre of Huguenots by Catholics. He made his way to England and after settling in to his new life published an account of his experiences in the northern portion of La Florida. In 1591, an English translation of his writings appeared. Theodor de Bry provided engravings for Le Moyne's account. The resulting book was entitled *Les Grands Voyages.*

De Bry's engravings depict numerous scenes from the Americas. Like other representations of the New World during this era, de Bry's depictions portray a "virgin land," "fertile" and waiting to be "penetrated" by a "civilized" people. Unlike the works of John White, an English artist whose sixteenth-century watercolors aimed to bring North America alive for European audiences, de Bry's renderings of Indian life tended to flatten a world that in reality was filled with complexity and nuance.[26] This is particularly evident in de Bry's representation of violence and death. In this respect, one of his engravings remains particularly striking.

In *The Employments of the Hermaphrodites*, de Bry depicts a scene of suffering and trauma. In the foreground, two muscular figures with long wavy hair carry a dead warrior. The deceased warrior's left arm hangs limp beside his body, his right arm carefully placed across his chest. The semi-naked warrior looks skyward, his eyes closed. In death the physical pain that marked his final moments are etched on his face, de Bry's engraving freezing these emotions in time.

De Bry never visited the Americas, and in style and form his engravings of Native Americans resembled his representations of the Scottish Picts. His engravings were therefore a product of imagination as much as it tried to illustrate Le Moyne's recollections. *The Employments of the Hermaphrodites* presented a stylized snapshot of carnage. In the background of de Bry's engraving, another dead warrior is stretchered away from the field of battle. Two seriously wounded warriors are carried away from the field of battle as four hermaphrodite figures follow behind, stretchering fallen warriors to safety. All of the bodies in this image possess classically muscular physiques. The hermaphrodites, all muscle and sinew, appear as so many Europeans perceived them: burden bearers.

De Bry's *Employments of the Hermaphrodites* tells a visual story about the aftermath of war and the role the "hermaphrodites" played in clearing the broken bodies from the battlefield. The engraving represented both the foreignness and familiarity of the Americas to European audiences. An alien landscape gestured to the foreignness of this place, yet the ritual of taking the injured and dead from the battlefield reflected the melancholy labors that Europeans also performed at the conclusion of hostilities. Although most of de Bry's engravings homogenize Native Americans, this one is different: it nods to a social hierarchy in Indigenous societies recognizable to Europeans. Through his representation of *Employments*, de Bry provides visual clues about the hermaphrodites' lowly rank and apparently marginal status. Their name, "the hermaphrodites," couldn't be more apt.

Le Moyne's written description of *The Employments of the Hermaphrodites* reinforced de Bry's visual imagery: "Hermaphrodites partaking of the nature of each sex, are quite common in these parts." His remarks echoed Laudonnière's contention about the ubiquity of hermaphrodites in North America. But were they ubiquitous?

Data on intersex people is historically unreliable. Even today, medical estimates place the number of intersex births at between 1 in 1,500 to 1 in every 2,000. These figures mask the diversity within the intersex community because they lump into statistical estimates people born with XXY chromosomes, individuals possessing vaginal agenesis (a rare condition in which the vagina and uterus partly develop, or do not develop at all), hypospadias (the opening of the urethra is on the underside of the penis instead of at the tip), and a number of other birth and developmental possibilities.[27] Given the imperfect nature of demographic understandings about intersex people in the twenty-first century, it's not a stretch to assume that the sixteenth-century assertion about hermaphrodites being "quite common" was hyperbole. At the same time, we have to remain open to the possibility of Native men choosing to follow female roles (and Indigenous women performing the roles of men), thereby contributing to the balance and harmony of their society—and confounding European observers.

What of Timucuan perceptions of hermaphrodites? These, too, prove difficult to get at. Le Moyne contended that hermaphrodites "are considered odious by the Indians themselves." Socially marginalized yet physically strong, they were allegedly employed by the Timucuans as "beasts of burden."

De Bry's engraving reinforced Le Moyne's narrative imagery. Take that post-battle scene. Le Moyne described it as follows:

> When a chief goes out to war, the hermaphrodites carry the provisions. When any Indian is dead of wounds or disease, two hermaphrodites take a couple of stout poles, fasten cross-pieces on them, and attach to these a mat woven of reeds. On this they place the deceased. . . . Then [the hermaphrodites] take thongs of hide, three or four fingers broad, fasten the ends to the ends of the poles, and put the middle over their heads, which are remarkably hard; and in this manner they carry the deceased to the place of burial. Persons having contagious diseases are also carried to places appointed for the purpose, on the shoulders of the hermaphrodites, who supply [those ill] with food, and take care of them, until they get quite well again.[28]

According to Le Moyne, hermaphrodites occupied the bottom rung on the Timucuan social ladder. The Timucua did live in a society of ranked clans. These kinship communities centered on the village as the core of political life. Each village had a chief, and chiefs often gained their status through matrilineal inheritance, a system that existed in neighboring communities and imbued women with significant political, social, and cultural power. Female inheritance proved important to Timucuans because it connected members of kinship groups who might reside in different villages.[29]

Timucuan people represented social and political status in a number of ways. Ritualized behavior, greetings, and the use of covered platforms on which chiefs sat, like those used by the cacica of Cofitachequi, signaled a person's occupation or social status. So, too, did tattoos, clothing, and accessories like shell beads. Other Native communities throughout southeastern North America displayed similar ranked social systems and political structures during this period. Despite these similarities, the Timucuan people and neighboring Apalachees lived in distinct types of political communities. Timucuans lived in less demographically dense communities and did not rely on intensive agricultural production for their economic survival, contrary to the case across much of the Native South.[30]

What the Timucuans had in common with their Indigenous neighbors was a commitment to kinship as a means of establishing the responsibilities of kin members and defining non-kin outsiders, particularly captives and slaves.[31] So where did the hermaphrodites exist in this social system?[32]

The written and visual sources that Laudonnière, Le Moyne, and de Bry left suggest that people "partaking of each sex" occupied a servile status in Timucuan society. The hermaphrodites pictured in de Bry's engraving might therefore have been captives. But if that was the case, why were these kinless people charged with a task of considerable religious and ceremonial importance?

Le Moyne confessed that he didn't know the spiritual significance of the work being performed by the Timucuan hermaphrodites. We now know that the task of tending to the needs of the recently deceased was an important ceremonial occasion among southeastern Indian communities; it wasn't a job for the kinless or enslaved. Administering to the needs of the dead, bridging the transition between the living and the afterlife, was a spiritually significant task that was vital to maintaining balance and harmony in Indigenous societies.

It was European cultural chauvinism, Christianity, and the superficiality of Laudonnière and Le Moyne's observations that imposed a marginalized status on the Timucuan hermaphrodites. That the people Laudonnière and Le Moyne described possessed physical strength, performed labor associated with women, and took on ceremonial roles similar to priests suggests that the hermaphrodites occupied an important position in the Timucuan kinship system. As people who internally and externally embodied the qualities of both men and women, the people Laudonnière and Le Moyne labeled hermaphrodites were likely viewed by their peers as possessing spiritual knowledge of immense power.[33]

If hermaphrodites occupied esteemed social and religious positions, why then did they perform seemingly mundane tasks? The short answer is that Europeans didn't really have an answer; in fact, they didn't even ask the question—they made an assumption. This is an important point that speaks to what we think we know about the past. It is also an invitation to pause and recognize that history isn't a simple list of facts; it's a form of storytelling that requires both evidence and imagination. However, the visual evidence that de Bry and other European artists produced has lulled historians and anthropologists into a false sense of certainty. Sixteenth-century engravings tend to freeze Native Americans in time and depict them engaging in tasks that appear to fall along clearly defined gender lines. Indigenous men and women did perform separate, albeit complementary, tasks, on a daily basis. It is also true that gender was not a fixed category in most Native communities. European sources imply the opposite, suggesting that gendered certainty existed when, in truth, a dynamic spectrum of gendered roles and identities existed, one that included space for intersex people.

European sources close off possibilities for gender roles and identities that transcended the male-female binary which was solidifying in European culture.[34] Across a range of literary genres, European writers conflated hermaphrodites, sodomites, eunuchs, and cross-dressers. They did this to highlight what they saw as abnormalities in Native American societies. Two other labels that received increasing use during the late sixteenth century were "catamite" and "berdache." These terms have a long history dating back to the ancient world. In ancient Greek and Roman society, a catamite was a "kept boy," the intimate companion of an adult male in a pederastic relationship. By the late sixteenth century, Europeans used this term as a slur. Similarly, the ancient Arabic *bardaj* or *barah* evolved into the Spanish terms *bardaxa* and *bardaje*, and the French *berdache*. Collectively these words referred to a "kept boy," slave, or sodomite. Whether uttered by civil or church authorities, all of these terms carried negative connotations in European cultures.[35]

The Laguna Pueblo poet and activist Paula Gunn Allen lamented the use of these labels and their imposition onto Native American cultures. Looking back over the history of European colonialism in North America, Allen identified European notions of patriarchy and Christianity as the root cause of these developments. Europeans combined gender, sexual, and racial ideologies to justify invasion, the territorial dispossession of Indigenous communities, and genocide. For Allen, feminist approaches to Native history and culture offered a path to "ameliorating the effects of patriarchal colonialism, enabling many of the tribes to reclaim their ancient gynarchical, egalitarian, and sacred traditions."[36]

Allen, who identified as a lesbian and lamented the "devaluation of lesbian and gay tribal members as leaders, shamans, healers, or ritual participants," advanced an unapologetically Indigenous perspective on North American history.[37] It's a historical consciousness that helps us appreciate the enduring impact that labels like "hermaphrodite" had (and have) on the collective psyche of Native communities.

Use of such labels was and is the language of European colonizers—a destructive rhetoric that aimed to undermine Native kinship communities. Recognizing this, we can begin to empathize with people like Timothy "Twix" Ward and their quest to arrive at a more enriching sense of their place in their tribal communities. We can also appreciate the healing involved in journeys of personal and communal reclamation, journeys—as Allen's quotation in "Prayer of the Night Chant" at the beginning of this chapter reveals—that begin optimistically: "Happily I recover."

Recovery isn't easy. It is ongoing. How, after all, do you reclaim something that attack dogs destroyed, conquistadors tried to exploit, civil authorities criminalized, and European writers misrepresented? And how do you heal when Christian missionaries told your ancestors they were wrong, sinful, unnatural?[38]

CHAPTER 3

SIN

That influence [Christianity] is very powerful.
I'm not saying it's all bad or anything, I just think . . .
it can be bad and it can hurt.

— BEN LUCERO WOLF (Kiowa)[1]

Transformation or mutation is at the heart of the sacred. The
ceremonial understandings of the Native world revolve around
the concept. It is the process we call "ritual," which means "to
change something or someone from one state to another."

— PAULA GUNN ALLEN (Laguna Pueblo)[2]

THE CUEVA "SODOMITES," the cacica with "manly courage" of Cofitachequi, and the Timucuan "hermaphrodites" left Europeans with
more questions than answers about Native people. As the Spanish,
the French, and waves of other European intruders moved across the
landscape and into Indigenous communities, they recorded examples
not only of *mujeres varoniles* ("manly women," or women with manly
qualities) but also of *hombres afeminados*, "effeminate men." Who
were these "men"? How numerous were they? What role did "effeminate men" play in Indigenous societies? Why the cross-dressing? Was
same-sex marriage an accepted part of Native life? Were these people
unredeemable sinners?

Indigenous people didn't share the punitive understandings of sin
that Europeans brought with them to North America during the sixteenth and seventeenth centuries. Native religions did (and do) change
over time—through daily activity and ceremonial renewal. Indigenous

religions also connected humans and more-than-human relatives to specific places, with women and people with gender-fluid identities being imbued with considerable powers to reproduce life and act as conduits to connect kin. These were multidimensional belief systems. Those in the kinship circle didn't go out of their way to convert or persecute nonbelievers, but the pursuit of balance through wisdom and spiritual fulfillment meant that there was a place for everyone who adhered to the responsibilities of reciprocity.[3]

Europeans brought a different religious worldview with them to North America. Christian belief systems defined the boundaries of civilization, justified war, and shaped the administration of the law and the policing of sin. The word "sin" dates back to the proto-Germanic *Sundiō* and the Old English *synn*. In Genesis 4:7, God warns Cain that sin is "crouching at the door" and he must "rule over it," lest it get the better of him. From its Old Testament moorings, "sin" developed a variety of applications in religious thought, the law, politics, and popular culture. By the time Europeans began invading the Americas, "sin" denoted guilt, mischief, an "offense against God," or "a moral wrong."[4] Early European accounts of North America gave the impression that Indigenous people were addicted to "sin."[5]

This impression is partly a product of authorship. Soldiers and missionaries wrote accounts of Indigenous people that ranged from the superficial to the judgmental. In Spanish and French colonial contexts from the sixteenth and seventeenth centuries, these accounts provide glimpses of Native people with fluid gender roles or partaking in sexual activity that flew in the face of accepted European standards of heteronormativity. But they're only glimpses; the greatest impact that these military diaries and missionary ethnographies have on historical knowledge is to distort the spiritual and physical worlds of Indigenous people.

. . . .

Juan Pardo claimed he saw a cross-dressing Indian. The Spanish conquistador embarked on two incursions into the southeastern corner of North America between December 1566 and March 1568. His mission was twofold: to find reliable Indian trading partners and to scout the landscape for suitable locations for Spanish forts.[6] During his second expedition, Pardo and his men marched into the town of Cauchi.[7] It was October 2, 1567. On this day, as on others, Pardo tried to remain faithful to the instructions of Pedro Menéndez, the first governor of Florida (1565–1574), to "be very friendly" with the Indians and to "persuade them to the obedience of His Majesty."[8] Cauchi, located along the French Broad River in what is today North Carolina, looked like an orderly community of farms and sturdy dwellings. To Spanish eyes, it seemed like a prosperous place—ideal trading partners.

Six Cauchi caciques, male leaders, met the Spanish that fall. According to Spanish records, the most prominent one was Cauchi Orata. An interpreter purportedly asked Cauchi Orata and the five other caciques what they "should do in the service of God and your Majesty's and for the salvation of so many souls, and the aggrandizement of your kingdoms and your royal estates."[9] Cauchi Orata's reply was brief: "Yaa."[10]

The Spanish interpreted this response as an indication of submission. In return for the Indians' "subjection and submission," the Spanish presented gifts of "a small wedge and a large knife and a little green and red taffeta." Everyone seemed pleased, or so the Spanish thought. The Spanish interpreters assured their superiors that the Indians agreed to work in the "service of God and His Majesty." More likely, and as occurred throughout the Americas, the Cauchi elders' apparent "obedience" was more like an overture, an opening gambit, as they sized up these intruders and decided whether they were the type of people to conduct future talks with.

On October 3, the Spanish prepared to leave Cauchi. Pardo believed he'd achieved a bloodless conquest. But as Pardo prepared to lead his men on to the next Indigenous town he spotted "an Indian walking among the Indian women with an apron before him as [the women] wear it and he did what they did." Was this an *hombre afeminado*? His curiosity piqued, Pardo summoned Guillermo Ruffin, an interpreter, to "ask why that Indian went among the Indian women, wearing an apron as they did."[11] Ruffin, who was joined by a small group of interpreters and soldiers, cornered a cacique and asked him about the cross-dressing man. The cacique reportedly responded that the cross-dresser was his brother and "not a man for war nor carrying on the business of a man."[12]

. . . .

Pardo was by no means the first, and wouldn't be the last, to inquire after the meaning of public displays of cross-dressing in Indigenous communities. In 1540, Captain Hernando Alarcon spotted "three or foure men in womens apparell" during an expedition through California. Alarcon claimed that these cross-dressing men were part of a group of women who "goe naked, and weare a great wreath of fethers behind them, and before painted and glued together, and their haire like the men."[13]

Spanish soldiers proved poor ethnographers. Like French traders and the steady stream of Dutch, Swiss, Italian, Scottish, and English traders who traveled into Indian Country, their packhorses overflowing with trade goods, these men were generally not interested in crafting detailed ethnographic analyses. Their priorities lay elsewhere—survival, establishing forts, subduing "savages," making money.[14]

In 1608 Samuel de Champlain set about putting the French presence in North America on a more permanent footing when he oversaw the construction of a small fort that became known as Quebec. In this and subsequent French efforts to establish permanent settlements in North America, the French, knowing that they were in competition with other colonial powers, became acutely aware that they needed allies—Indigenous allies. These were, after all, the sovereign lands of communities that included the Micmac, Abenaki, Passamaquoddy, and Anishinaabeg.[15]

Missionaries added detail, if not ethnographic depth, to military and exploratory accounts of Indigenous life during the seventeenth century. In both Spanish and French colonies, Jesuit and Franciscan missionaries began contributing to a written colonial archive about Native cross-dressing, sodomy, "hermaphroditism," and sin that distorted Indigenous culture and misled historians for centuries.

To understand the archival fragments that missionaries created it's important to reflect on the intellectual context that shaped Catholic missionaries. In medieval Europe, stories about transvestite saints, romances involving gender inversions, and cross-dressing men and women in military service circulated among the literate sections of society.[16] Playwrights sometimes used these stories to evoke humor. The clergy and legal community saw little to laugh about. By the sixteenth century, men dressed in women's clothing invited serious questions about their masculinity—questions reflective of a sharpening male-female gender binary.[17]

After they arrived in North America, missionaries began making a variety of assumptions about the rationale behind cross-dressing and "sodomy" among Indigenous men. In their zeal to save souls, Catholic missionaries offered a blanket assessment of such behavior: sin.

Few missionaries proved as zealous and energetic in identifying and rooting out sin as Francisco Pareja. Pareja, a Spanish-born Franciscan missionary, served at San Juan del Puerto, near present-day Jacksonville. Sometime in late 1607 or early 1608, Pareja joined two other Franciscans in targeting communities such as the Timucuans, whose villages included "hermaphrodites" and medicine people whose healing practices both fascinated and disturbed missionaries. Pareja observed these cultural and medicinal practices, compiling ethnographic and linguistic information that he hoped would aid in converting Timucuans to Christianity.[18]

Pareja's method for extracting information from Timucuans flouted the local Indigenous people's standards of communalism. Pareja's commitment to the Catholic Church's catechism and use of the confessional led him to isolate Timucuan "infidels" in a bid to coerce information out of them and encourage individuals to live what he defined as a moral life.[19] In the *confesionario*, the confessional box, Pareja asked highly personal and intrusive questions. Often these questions reflected an obsession with sexual behavior, particularly among same-sex couples.[20]

Pareja's questions were also voyeuristic. They highlighted the lack of knowledge that the Spanish and other European invaders had about Indigenous social, cultural, and religious life. Acquiring this knowledge, however, was considered vital to the success of European trade and, ultimately, colonial conquest in the Americas. Informational conquest, or gaining knowledge of and over Native cultural and social systems, was a priority for missionaries wanting to save souls and mold Indigenous people in the image of their God.

Pareja's inquiries were part of that imperial quest. He directed his questions at a broad cross-section of Timucuan society. Midwives, herbalists, men and women, married couples, the very young and the old, chiefs and "sorcerers" and "sodomites." Pareja had questions for them all. He was particularly interested in sexual activity and gender roles. For example, Pareja queried married women about their sexual desires. "Mujer con mujer, has tenido acto, como si fuero hombre?" ("Woman with woman, have you acted as if you were a man?") was one intrusive question that Pareja asked.

He also asked men about their sexual encounters with other men: "Have you had intercourse with another man? Or have you gone around trying out or making fun in order to do that?" And when young boys entered the confessional he'd ask, "Has someone been investigating you from behind? Did you consummate the act?"

Pareja wanted confessions; he wanted to know the intimate behaviors and ceremonial secrets of Timucuan society so that he could eventually destroy their culture. Pareja stole ideas, ritual practices, and language—critical elements that defined the souls of Timucuan people and their community. And he displayed no scruples about breaching the trust of the confessional. From Pareja's deception—his theft—he concluded that among Timucuans "both female and male homosexuality occurred, with some special emphasis on boyish pederasty."[21]

Other Indigenous communities in Florida such as the Guales and the Apalachees also navigated the incessant intrusions of missionaries and their questions about marriage, gender roles, and sexual activity. It is not impossible to imagine that Native people in Florida and along the Gulf Coast learned to manipulate the missionaries in much the same way that Indigenous people in Central and South America navigated the *confesionario*. By seeming to answer the missionary's questions about cross-dressing, masturbation, sodomy, pederasty, and reproduction, Florida's Native people could provide these voyeuristic outsiders with titillating anecdotes while at the same time calculating the costs of using the missionaries to access trade and diplomatic networks in the hope of outmaneuvering a rival Native polity.[22]

Pareja was not alone in seeking out "confessions." In 1634, Don Bartolomé de Alva published *Confesionario mayor*, a confessional guide for priests ministering to the Nahuatl. De Alva's concerns ranged from idolatry to autoeroticism. He expressed particular concern about female masturbation. He wanted to know who, or what, women thought about when they stimulated their vagina or anus. Did female penitents imagine themselves having carnal communications with Jesus, Mary, or a group of saints?[23] To de Alva, the answer mattered. Saving Indians' souls meant controlling their thoughts and sexual desires.

Other authors focused on marriage. In 1695, Fray Clemente de Ledesma, a Franciscan, published a confessional guide entitled *Confesionario del despertador de noticias de los Santos Sacramentos.* Among the sacraments emphasized by de Ledesma was reproductive sex within marriage. Married heterosexual couples must service the conjugal debt (*debito conjugal*) but they must do so for purposes of procreation only. De Ledesma's prescriptive guidelines for marital sex emphasized the importance of a couple not letting their passions rule them "like an animal." To do so, de Ledesma cautioned, was "a very grave sin."[24]

These and countless other confessional guides revealed the importance of sex—whom one does it with, how often, when, and why—in controlling (or governing) Indigenous people and prescribing social order. In colonized spaces, policing sex empowered missionaries and colonial officials to incentivize reproductive sex acts by linking promises of land to family size and providing access to natural resources, legal protections, or eternal salvation. Ideally, colonial families, as their numbers grew, would drive demand for more land and ultimately dispossess sovereign Indigenous nations. Missionaries helped create this world, a world in which nonreproductive sex, from masturbation to anal penetration, was criminalized and the heteronormativity of Christianity was used to structure settler-colonial expansion.[25]

Pareja's *Confesionario major* and his willingness to learn the Timucuan language aided his efforts to police and prescribe social and sexual behavior. The intimate details of what penitents told Pareja are unknown. But the traces of evidence that remain reveal an insidious story of missionaries working to undermine the culture and language of the people they claimed to want to protect.[26] Pareja's scruples, his constant worry about the "weight of sin," meant that he remained focused on knowing with whom Timucuans had *a dúo contigo* (literally "duet with you," a Spanish euphemism for sexual intercourse), whether pederasty—*hurgandote por detrás* ("poking from behind")—was indulged in, and whether pregnant women were inclined to induce miscarriages, the "grave sin" of homicide. Why did Pareja want this information? To facilitate Indian conversion and prescribe Catholic mores so the souls of "savages" might be saved.[27] If Pareja extracted a confession of sin, his remedy was straightforward: "From now on do not do these things or consent to them, only with herbs and baths cure yourself, because they have virtue in that God gave and created them to heal us, and all other things that you do and pray for are not of benefit, but instead harm us since they are sins."[28]

. . . .

It's important not to overstate the power and influence of missionaries over Indigenous people. The Jesuits abandoned their first missionary incursion into French colonial America in 1613 (but later resumed their efforts). In 1615, Champlain turned to the Récollets (literally, Recollects), a Franciscan order, to try to make headway with the Natives. The Récollets' vow of poverty appealed to civil authorities. Trade and diplomacy with Indigenous nations was an expensive business, so French authorities were hopeful that missionaries could help colonize Native people on the cheap.[29]

Missionaries worked to enmesh themselves in Native communities. In 1625, the Jesuits renewed their evangelical work. Over the next century, Jesuit missionaries slowly worked their way from the Hudson Bay to French Louisiana. In expanding the cause of French colonialism, Jesuits saw the Americas as an opportunity to extend the pastoral work that they had begun among France's urban lower classes. To Jesuits, Native Americans represented a new opportunity to "improve" the daily life and religious culture of an impoverished people. Undermine poverty, Jesuit missionaries insisted, and you could unshackle Indigenous people from sin and the grip of the devil.[30]

Jesuits took these attitudes with them as they fanned out across North America during the seventeenth century. During their time among the Mohawks between the 1630s and 1650s, Jesuit missionaries grew in their conviction that the relocation of a select few promising Natives to Quebec would set an example for other Indigenous people by ending their "extreme poverty" and enriching their spiritual embrace of Catholicism. Far to the north, Jesuits expressed similar views about the Innu, whom the French called Montaignais. The Montaignais, Jesuits reported, remained mired in poverty and addicted to superstition. Eradicating superstition was the true test of the conversion power of Christianity.[31]

But it was far to the south that Jesuits focused the bulk of their energies from the mid-seventeenth century onward. Throughout the *pays d'en haut* (or the Upper Country), a vast territory of New France west of Montreal that included the Great Lakes, the Anishinaabeg controlled access to land, rivers, and resources coveted by the French and other European colonizers. This was no "middle ground," but a region characterized by intersecting trade and diplomatic networks controlled by Native people.[32] The truth of the *pays d'en haut*—its wealth, its sovereign Native polities, and their deep cultural and ecological connections to the region—drew fur trappers and traders like moths to a flame. They simply couldn't resist the riches they imagined were on offer.

On the southern portions of the Great Lakes, Jesuit missionaries took a keen interest in Native life in Illinois Country. Here, the French found sovereign Indigenous nations prospering on fertile soils and rich riparian ecosystems. Despite the wealth, cultural sophistication, and sovereign independence of the Native people throughout this region, missionaries and their civil allies crafted narratives about a vast landscape of untapped potential filled with peoples who committed the vilest sins. This region, a homeland filled with spiritual powers for the Miami, Sauk, Winnebago, Potawatomi, Kickapoo, and others, was in truth no wilderness. In French hands, an alternative history of this place was written that transformed Indigenous communities into dark places, a chaotic backcountry full of sin and desperately poor people.[33]

Throughout the *pays d'en haut*, Jesuit missionaries made observations about cross-dressing that echoed the impressions of missionaries in other parts of North America. The Jesuits intruded into Indigenous life with both their questions and their self-righteousness. Jacques Marquette was one of these missionaries. Between 1673 and 1677 Marquette set out from the Great Lakes with a small flotilla of canoes. Aided by the French-Canadian explorer Louis Jolliet, Marquette and his Native guides traveled down the Mississippi and Illinois Rivers. During his travels Marquette took a particular interest in the culture and customs of the Illinois and Nadouessi Indians. Marquette recorded his impressions of these people in his journal and also sketched a map of the Upper Mississippi.[34] Although crude and often inaccurate, maps

like these helped shape French colonial knowledge of a region popu-
lated by thriving Indigenous communities.[35]

Marquette, Jolliet, and their Indian guides left Lake Superior and
set a southerly course. They were "taken by the great river called by
the natives Missisipi [*sic*], which must empty somewhere in the region
of the Florida sea." Marquette claimed that "some of the Savages
have assured us that this is so noble a river that, at more than three
hundred leagues' distance from its mouth, it is larger than the one
flowing before Quebec."[36]

Marquette seemed particularly struck by the habits and beliefs of
the Native people he met. He recorded in his journal a curious tale, a
story of Illinois and Nadouessi boys who, "while still young, assume
the garb of women, and retain it throughout their lives." Marquette
was puzzled and made several inquiries, hoping to uncover the cultural meaning of cross-dressing.[37] The Illinois and Nadouessi elders,
however, refused to respond. The perplexed Marquette wrote, "There
is some mystery in this." He observed that these cross-dressing men
"never marry and glory in demeaning themselves to do everything that
the women do."[38]

It's unlikely that the people Marquette described thought that they
were "demeaning themselves."[39] The Illinois tribes, which included
the Peoria, Miami, Koskasia, and other Algonquin-speaking communities, retained cultural connections dating back to the Mississippi
mound-building societies that flourished throughout the eastern half
of North America after 700 CE. The Illinois shared a number of other
cultural characteristics, including polygyny and clans structured along
patrilineal lines.[40]

The people Marquette called the Nadouessi—a French version of
the Dakota word *natowessiwa* ("people of an alien tribe")—were a
Dakota people. The garbled French name led missionaries, fur traders,
and civil authorities to carry the confusion forward: they also referred
to Dakota peoples as Naduesiu, Nadoessi, and Nadoeuessioux, the
last word being a Dakota word for "snake."[41] The Dakota trace kinship descent along matrilineal lines, although chieftainship appeared
to follow patrilineal inheritance patterns at the time Marquette encountered them. Polygynous relationships existed but weren't overly
common. What proved more routine among the Dakota—which included the eastern Dakota, the central Nakota, and the Lakota—were

blended gender roles and identities. Within the different Dakota kinship divisions, which they referred to as *oyate* (people), gender fluidity
had a place in community life.[42]

Marquette's unfamiliarity with Indigenous kinship and his single-
minded devotion to his mission meant that he didn't fully grasp the
nuances within Illinois and Dakota communities. His Christianity
blinded him to the complex system of gender relations that Illinois
and Dakota peoples used to structure their communities. The Illinois
and Dakotas did not live under the tyranny of a European-style gender
binary; no rigid hierarchy of men and women existed, at least not as
Marquette would have understood it. In Illinois and Dakota societies,
the ethos of reciprocity and community drove people to strive for harmony in their social relations and for balance in affairs of a physical
and spiritual nature.

This emphasis on balance and harmony began early in a child's
life. Illinois and Dakota children weren't immediately prescribed a
permanent gender identity after they were born. Gendered identities
remained fluid, multiple, complex. Their identities changed with age,
geography, and skills or after a dream or vision. Marquette lacked the
language and cultural insights to appreciate the fluid social roles and
cultural identities of male-bodied women and female-bodied men. In
the kinship world of the Illinois and Dakotas there existed a place for a
female-bodied person wearing men's clothing. And if that person took
up bow and arrow and headed out to hunt or onto the battlefield, their
kin generally supported them.

While Marquette struggled to understand gender-fluid roles and
identities, he did acknowledge that some people seemed blessed with
special gifts. These people performed roles "at all the juggleries, and
at the solemn dances in honor of the Calumet." Marquette's reference
to jugglers referred to practitioners of magic, or what became known
as shamanism. He went on to suggest that their songs carried special
significance, and they "are summoned to the Councils, and nothing
can be decided without their advice." Marquette concluded that these
people lead "an Extraordinary life," something that became evident to
him when he observed that "they pass for Manitous,—That is to say,
for Spirits;—or persons of Consequence."[43]

Manitou. It intrigued Europeans; it worried missionaries. What
was it? Men like Marquette speculated that Manitou were spirits

that inhabited the supernatural world. But they couldn't be certain. From their interactions with Native people around the Great Lakes and across northeastern North America, missionaries puzzled at this mysterious Manitou. European invaders heard stories about Manitou, of tricksters and powerful grandmothers, of dances performed in masquerade, and tales of spirit beings springing from the forest wilderness.[44]

Marquette feared what he did not know or understand; missionaries feared the power of the Manitou. In a region dominated by the lucrative fur trade, Marquette and fellow missionaries quickly realized the futility of trying to transform Indians into European-style farmers; but they could still conquer souls. He took solace from those moments when he spotted a Christian cross "erected in the middle of the village" with prayers and offerings to the "great Manitou" acting as a conduit to the Christian god.[45]

Manitou was spiritual power. It filled all things but could appear most visibly and powerfully in specific forms, like animals. Anyone could summon Manitou, be it through warfare, ceremony, or in forging reciprocal relationships with non-kin outsiders. This latter point is significant because many Native communities believed that Europeans possessed Manitou. This meant that efforts to establish peaceful relations with outsiders had the potential to take on particular importance.[46]

Summoning Manitou wasn't an individual pursuit, however. When shamans and priests summoned its power, they relied on ceremonies involving dreams, dances, chanting, and tobacco smoking. In some Native communities, gender-fluid people led these communal efforts. People filled with Manitou were sources of great wonder and power. Their kin viewed them as special people—people powerful enough to mediate their own community's beliefs with those of outsiders.[47]

. . . .

By the latter half of the seventeenth century, it wasn't difficult to find missionaries ascribing a judgment of sin to Indigenous cultures of gender and sexuality. Zenobius Membre, a Franciscan friar, wrote that "hermaphrodites are numerous" among the Mississippi tribes. Membre accompanied the French explorer René-Robert Cavalier, Sieur de La Salle, into the Mississippi and Ohio Valleys, in the 1660s, and produced a written account of what he claimed to have seen. His condemnatory description of cross-dressing Native men rose quickly to the level of the sensational. Membre wrote of his shock at seeing Native American men being "lewd, and even unnaturally so, [and] having boys dressed as women, destined for infamous purposes." According to Membre, "boys are employed only in women's work, without taking part in the chase or war." These boys, he surmised, were kept for sodomical acts. They were kept for sinful relations.[48]

The Illinois Country attracted considerable comment from both French missionaries and soldiers about the prevalence of sin among Indigenous communities. Numerous sources reported on instances of "vice" and "cohabitation" among Native women and fur traders. The Jesuit missionary Gabriel Marest, who spent time at the Kaskaskia mission, expressed optimism about these types of sexual relationships. If French authorities could police these relationships, they might offer hope for a future in which Indigenous people would become biologically assimilated into French settler society.[49]

The social engineering of Indigenous-French families stirred considerable debate in the Franco-Atlantic world. In contrast, the subject of cross-dressing, male effeminacy, and "sodomy" drew swift and condemnatory responses from missionaries. The Jesuit Jean-François Buisson de Saint-Cosme was one of these missionaries. Saint-Cosme traveled to the Illinois region in hopes of saving Indian souls. One community—"the village of the Kappas"—caught Father Saint-Cosme's attention. On January 2, 1699, Saint-Cosme wrote that he saw "one of those wretches who from their youth dress as girls." His language was revealing; "one of those" suggests he expected to see Indigenous boys dressed in female attire.

Saint-Cosme's assessment proved equally revealing, if unsurprising. He wrote of pitying "those wretches" as "unfortunate and forlorn" people. A consensus appeared to have emerged among the French on the immorality and sinfulness of Indigenous gender and sexual practices. Even French soldiers, although still superficial in their reflections, wrote of their disdain for Indigenous "sodomites" and effeminate men. Louis Armand de Lorn, who spent almost a decade in North America from 1683, wrote that "some Savages continue Batchelours to their Dying day." These people must surely be "Lunatick or Sickly," de Lorn concluded.[50]

Although French civil and church authorities sometimes clashed over Indian policy, a loose consensus on cross-dressing, effeminate men, and the "sin of sodomy" emerged: Native Americans "pander to the most shameful of all vices."[51] This perspective became so commonplace that it appeared in a variety of written sources, including among the usually mundane reports of European soldiers.[52] Louis-Armand, Baron de Lahontan, was one of those soldiers. Lahontan made a name for himself as an "explorer" of the upper Mississippi region in the 1680s and subsequently became a published author. Lahontan's contemporaries considered his knowledge of the Algonquin language and use of the "noble savage" motif as evidence of a sympathetic attitude toward Indigenous people. A dialogue with Adario, a Huron chief, in which Lahontan appears to question the efficacy of Christianity among Native people solidified this reputation.[53]

Lahontan's writings, however, are punctuated with denigrating remarks about Indigenous practices and morality. A careful reading of them reveals a man who perceived plenty of sin and immorality among the Illinois tribes. "Among the Illinese there are several Hermaphrodites," he wrote. They "go in a Woman's Habit but frequent the Company of both Sexes." Lahontan underscored the prevalence of sin among these people by concluding that "these Illinese are strangely given to Sodomy, as well as the other Savages that live near the River Missisipi [sic]."[54]

Pierre Liette wrote a particularly detailed account of sodomy and sin among the Native communities of Illinois. Born in southern Italy, Liette migrated to France's North American colonies in 1687 where he found employment as a trader and soldier. By 1702 he held the command of a French outpost at Pimétoui (not far from present-day Peoria, Illinois), where he recorded his impressions of the Kaskaskia Indians.[55] Liette's observations included his moral condemnation of Native men, who, he asserted, raped Illinois women. Liette accused Kaskaskia men of scalping women "as punishment for being unfaithful."[56]

The Indigenous people whom Liette observed descended from ancestors who had completed some of North America's most impressive engineering feats. Some built enormous platform mounds that rose high into the sky while others constructed serpent mounds that snaked across the landscape.[57] These stunning architectural achievements constituted material expressions of prosperous communities with rich spiritual beliefs and ceremonial traditions.[58]

Liette didn't see a people who'd inherited proud traditions; instead, he saw Indians who were "cowardly, licentious, and entirely given up to their senses." Men prostituted their daughters and sisters for trade goods—"a pair of stockings or other trifle." Some men did much worse: they partook in the "sin of sodomy."

Liette insisted that sodomy "prevails more among them than in any other nation." These Indigenous sodomites, Liette maintained, were ruled by their passions. They found it almost impossible to satisfy "their passions as much as they would like."[59] Liette explained the existence of these sodomites by claiming that boys "are bred for this purpose from childhood." They received training in women's work—learning to use the spade, spindle, and ax—and wore women's clothes. As Liette understood this training, such boys became women. They grew their hair long and wore "a little skin like a shoulder strap passing under the arm on one side and tied over the shoulder on the other."[60]

By the time Liette preserved his recollections in writing in 1702, Europeans had amassed a substantial archive on Indigenous cross-dressing, hermaphroditism, and sodomy. European letters, diaries, and reports kept filling up with observations from the Aztecs to Kaskaskia and beyond of gender roles and sexual behavior that marked Indigenous souls with "sin."[61] In Liette's account, the mark of sin also proved to be literally a mark. Boys chosen for female roles who engaged in sodomical acts received tattoos. Liette wasn't sure about what these markings meant, but he speculated that the tattooed cheeks and breasts of the boys he observed marked their transition to a feminine status. He concluded that Native men throughout the Illinois territory "assume the garb of women and retain it throughout their lives. There is some mystery in this."[62]

. . . .

Spanish and French sources provide us with traces of gender and sexual fluidity in Indian Country during the sixteenth and seventeenth centuries. The colonizers who created these sources, be they military personnel or missionaries, tried to grasp the meaning of this fluidity. They deployed the confessional, intruded into sacred spaces, and asked questions they had no right to get answers to. Their inquiries resulted in few clear conclusions, leaving some Europeans feeling decidedly unsettled. Others, especially among the ranks of the military and colonial authorities, used this uncertainty—this lack of knowing—as proof that Indigenous people occupied a space beyond the boundaries of Christian civilization. By European logic, they were prime candidates for being declared lawful captives in "just warres."[63]

Beyond the reaches of colonialism's archives and the comprehension of its authors, Indigenous people adapted to the presence of growing numbers of European outsiders. From California to Florida, the Illinois Country to the Gulf Coast, Native communities persisted in and renewed their sacred traditions by infusing everyday life and ceremonial traditions with meaning. Sin, at least in the Christian sense of the word, wasn't originally part of this Indigenous world. Gradually, cautiously, Indigenous people wove the worldviews of Europeans into their understanding of the world. Indeed, the arrival of the English in the late sixteenth century and the establishment of their first successful settler colonies in the early seventeenth meant that Indigenous people would need to be both creative and resilient in navigating the new colonial environments that swirled around them.

CHAPTER 4

EFFEMINACY

Even my grandmother, when I was explaining this [gay identity]
to her, she kind of giggled and thought that I would be dressing
in these flamboyant outfits every day and prancing around,
which is not really what I do.

—CHRISTO APACHE (Mescalero Apache)[1]

I'm still extremely aware of my surroundings.

—J. MIKO THOMAS, aka LANDA LAKES (Chickasaw Nation)[2]

TO READ COLONIALISM'S ARCHIVES is to enter a "New World" in which Indigenous people simultaneously intrigue and disturb Europeans. In the early seventeenth century, these archives began to expand as the Dutch, Swedes, Finns, and English joined the Spanish and French as colonizers in North America. Throughout the Mid-Atlantic region—places we know today as New York, New Jersey, Delaware, and Pennsylvania—the Dutch and Swedes aspired to great wealth by seeking out new trade horizons. In the process, they produced written records in which Indigenous people were generally described in brief and unflattering detail.[3]

This is particularly true of the Dutch. The Dutch colony of New Netherland emerged from a small trading factory known as Fort Amsterdam and the economic ambition of the Dutch West Indian Company. That fort became New Amsterdam, and in 1664, New York, after the English took control of the nascent metropolis. Under Dutch rule, between 1624 and 1664, traders and colonists took what can best be described as only passing interest in local Indigenous populations. The Dutch focus was on trade and acquiring wealth; Native Americans seemed more a hindrance than help in realizing that ambition. Unlike the Swedes, who established the short-lived colony of New Sweden in the Delaware Valley in 1638 and enjoyed generally peaceable relations with the Susquehannocks and the Lenapes, Dutch attitudes toward Indigenous people veered between disinterest and contempt.[4] In 1628, a Dutch minister, Jonas Michaelius, offered a typically dismissive Dutch assessment of Indigenous people, describing the Indians as "entirely savage and wild, strangers to all decency, yea, uncivil and stupid as garden poles, proficient in all wickedness and godlessness." According to Michaelius, Indians were "devilish men, who served nobody but the Devil."[5]

More than a few English colonists shared Michaelius's dismissive views on Indigenous intellectual and moral faculties. In the decades after the first English settler colony took root in Virginia in 1607, English writers speculated about the meaning of Indigenous clothing, hair styles, jewelry, and tattoos. English writing matched in volume the extent of documents produced by the Spanish and French. And like the Spanish and French, English colonial archives reveal latent anxieties about the implications of Indigenous systems of gender and sexuality. For some colonial writers, effeminacy framed these commentaries.[6] Only Indian nakedness was more commented on.[7]

For seventeenth-century Spanish, French, and English writers, the concept of effeminacy offered a way to synthesize observations about cross-dressing, the "transvesti," "hermaphrodites," "sodomites," and the "berdache." However, this seemingly useful framework was belied by its logical sloppiness. Among those who invoked it, the concept of effeminacy obscured the diversity and complexity of gender roles and sexuality throughout Indian Country.

The charge of effeminacy had another purpose: it justified physical and emotional violence against Indigenous people whose gender roles and public presentation belied English norms. That effeminate Native men were also medicine people, elders, and respected members of their communities helped the English rationalize their attacks on Indigenous leaders.[8] Still, Indigenous perspectives found their way into the written records of North American colonialism. In the early 1600s Algonquin-speaking people expressed puzzlement at the sight of English men performing agricultural work—labor typically overseen by Indigenous women. Native people also used gendered tropes to mock Englishmen. In the 1620s, Massachusetts Indians questioned the masculinity of Captain Miles Standish by lampooning his small stature. In the midst of the Pequot War (1636–1638), Pequot warriors questioned the manliness of English soldiers by pointing to their massacring of Indian women and children. In other instances, Pequots taunted the English to "Come out and fight. . . . You are like women."[9]

Accusations of effeminacy and unmanly conduct in battle characterized the mutual disdain in early Anglo-Indian relations. English settlers, however, usually dismissed Native commentaries. They changed the conversation, focusing on effeminate Indigenous men and their tendency to join devilish bands of witches, practice sorcery, or lurk and hunt for human flesh. These sins could be neither tolerated nor endured.[10]

The Spanish, French, and English dominated the race to see which group of colonists could win Indigenous souls while simultaneously dispossessing them of their homelands. During the seventeenth century, European efforts to erode Indigenous sovereignty accelerated as civil and church leaders waged a war against Indian effeminacy and "the foul demon of lust" that seemed to accompany it.

. . . .

European understandings of effeminacy predate colonization in the Americas. In England and Europe, the word "effeminacy" derived etymologically from the Latin *effeminātus*. By the tenth and eleventh centuries, Christian theologians began linking effeminacy to the behavior of sodomites. This is important because in the tenth century, a forgery of a sixth-century letter by Pope Gregory the Great identified the "crime of sodomy," and in the following century the Benedictine monk Peter Damian wrote an influential treatise that described sodomites as people possessed of "a diabolical spirit."[11]

During the twelfth and thirteenth centuries, medieval theologians continued to conflate sodomy with effeminate men. The famous thirteenth-century theologian Thomas Aquinas played a major role in the invention of what is today known as homophobia. Aquinas described sodomy as an "unnatural vice," a characterization that gave shape and meaning to medieval anxieties about homoerotic and homosocial behavior. By the sixteenth century, laws in England and

Europe policed the behavior of sodomites, while the language of "effeminacy" linked boys and men who appeared "soft" or looked like "a woman" as socially suspect.[12]

Occasionally, civil and ecclesiastical authorities labeled effeminate boys and men as hermaphrodites. This usage appears in a number of civil and ecclesiastical contexts across Europe during the late sixteenth and early seventeenth centuries. When used to denote effeminate boys and men the term became another way of describing "softness," womanish behavior, or even "monstrosity." In England, a mythological tradition also developed in which the words "effeminacy," "hermaphroditism," and "sodomy" were sometimes conflated with foul and monstrous acts. For instance, the figure of the ragamuffin—from *ragr*, effeminate, and *baedling*, bad—denoted a demon, "the evil one," or the devil, and one who engaged in effeminate behaviors.[13]

By the time the English started encountering Native Americans on a regular basis in the seventeenth century, a well-established cultural framework for identifying effeminacy among Indigenous men had taken shape. Cultural definitions of effeminacy overlapped with politics and warfare to reinforce a worldview in which humans existed as either a man or woman. Be they English Protestants or Catholics from continental Europe, men perceived women as weaker versions of themselves.[14] Applied in the context of war or in the heat of political debate, effeminacy became a slur, a shorthand for the weak or vanquished.

In North America, two seventeenth-century examples highlight this point. During the first decade of the century, the Spaniard Juan de Torquemada referred to Indigenous men in Florida who performed the work of women as effeminate. Torquemada embedded his accusations in historical precedent—specifically, the historical decline of ancient Greece. The second example comes from the latter half of the century and King Philip's War (1675–1678). In 1676, the Massachusetts Bay Colony struck a peace medal that was presented to Indians who aligned with the British colony. The medal depicts a feminized male warrior, with long hair, breasts, and a skirt made of feathers. Male effeminacy had become not simply a marker of Indigenous subservience, but a predictor of social inferiority and even military defeat. Throughout British colonial America, these gendered perceptions helped to rationalize physical violence and justify political subjugation and empire building.[15]

English men found it difficult to maintain the outer appearance of respect for Indigenous leaders and warriors whom they perceived as "womanly hearted."[16] Indeed, the English also condemned "womanly hearted" men in their own communities. That's why the English quickly identified and prosecuted men accused of cross-dressing in settler-colonial towns and villages. In Virginia, the Englishman Thomas(ine) Hall's gender and sexual ambiguity earned the ire of colonial lawmakers. Hall allegedly admitted to dressing in women's clothing to "get a bitt for my Catt," a euphemism for sexual relations.[17]

Most alarming to colonial officials and church leaders was the ambiguous, perhaps even willfully deceptive, way in which Hall dressed in women's clothing in an attempt to present himself as a woman. Historian Susan Juster refers to such attitudes as reflective of how civil authorities and church leaders disapproved of "social hermaphroditism," the intentional desire of cross-dressers to engage in acts of deception.[18] News of cross-dressing therefore prompted laws to ban it in the English colonies. In the 1690s, Massachusetts passed a law prohibiting cross-dressing. Violence and warfare on the frontiers of settler-colonial society, and the difficulty that settlers had in distinguishing between Indigenous allies and foes, made this an anxious time for colonial officials and church elders throughout New England.[19] In fact, the violence of the late seventeenth and early eighteenth century compounded several generations of colonial anxiety about cross-dressing and its social implications. In 1651, for example, a Massachusetts law prohibited people with annual incomes below £200 from "wearing gold, silver lace or buttons, silk hoods, or 'great boots.'"[20] This type of law aimed to prevent people crossing what we would today understand as class boundaries.

Colonial elites also frowned on cultural and proto-racial cross-dressing. The Puritan minister Cotton Mather wrote disapprovingly about settlers cross-dressing as Indians. Mather's criticism sprang from his perception of Native savagery. He referred to Indians taking "ye girls" captive, having an ear severed, and "ye girls" being forced to roast and eat the removed ear. This cruelty was compounded by Native people reportedly compelling captives to dress in the Indian fashion—a different form of cross-dressing but alarming to colonial authorities nonetheless. Mather condemned these practices, especially the alleged tendencies of Native people to use force and deception in compelling female captives to engage in acts of cannibalism and clothe themselves in "Indian dress."[21]

Cross-dressing that blurred distinctions between men and women, Native and European, sent English settlers like Mather into fits of anxiety. But it was gendered cross-dressing, and fears that such practices concealed sexual desires that transgressed heteronormative sexual intimacy, that prompted officials to take action. Throughout New England, colonial authorities designed laws that prescribed acceptable, and unacceptable, sexual behavior. What we understand today as homosexual sex acts were banned; as the theologian John Cotton put it in relation to the Massachusetts Bay Colony, "carnal fellowship of man with man" was outlawed.[22] Massachusetts's law criminalized sexual behavior that fell outside of heterosexual intercourse, which must occur only between a married couple, and for the purpose of procreation. Legal prescription did not necessarily lead to compliance, however. If the cases of Anne Bonny, the female-bodied pirate who wore men's clothing, or Deborah Sampson, a woman who donned men's attire to enlist for the Patriots in the Revolutionary War, reveal anything, it is that gender fluidity and the policing of human sexuality in the Americas wasn't confined to effeminacy among Indian men.[23]

. . . .

Why do Eurocentric definitions of effeminacy matter?[24] To begin answering that question, I want to briefly return to the Jesuit missionaries. Specifically, a missionary by the name of Joseph-François Lafitau.

Lafitau, the son of "a banker and wine merchant," was born in Bordeaux in 1681. As a teenager he entered the Society of Jesus (the Jesuits) as a novitiate and went on to study philosophy and theology. In 1712, Lafitau was ordained. The new priest wasted little time in getting to work, requesting a post in North America, where he would eventually serve as a missionary among the Iroquois and Mohawk.[25]

When Lafitau sat down to reflect on his experiences among Native Americans, he drew on a familiar vocabulary: sinfulness, savagery, and effeminacy.[26] These qualities weren't gleaned solely from biblical inferences; Lafitau arrived at them through ethnological observation that he considered empirical fact. He published those ethnographic findings in *Moeurs des sauvages ameriquains, comparées aux moeurs des premiers temps* (Customs of the American Indians, compared with the customs of primitive times; 1724).

Moeurs des sauvages ameriquains joined what had become a substantial library of European accounts of the "savages of America."[27] In a particularly revealing section of Lafitau's sprawling narrative, he refers to "special friendships" that Indigenous men form with each other. Lafitau claimed that men contracted these relationships by disguising themselves as women. If the subterfuge works, and a "special friendship" is formed, the relationship results in "much real vice."

Lafitau condemned these "special friendships." He wasn't alone in taking such a stance. The English remained disdainful of Indigenous deceptiveness. And it wasn't just the clergy and the political architects of laws policing sodomy that worried about deception. English writers referred to people who dressed in the clothing of the opposite sex as someone who "transvests" their "true" gender identity. Similarly, the French term for cross-dressing was *transvesti*, the Spanish *transvestis*, and the Portuguese *traviste*.[28]

Lafitau shared this disdain. He wrote that Native people who "transvest" their true gender identity "believe they are honored by debasing themselves to all of women's occupations." Among the American "sauvages," sin passed as virtue; male emasculation was celebrated.[29] If effeminacy existed in European cultures, it paled in significance to the ubiquity of effeminate men throughout Indian Country.

Lafitau also puzzled over Indian men debasing themselves by taking on the roles of women. Were these the "hermaphrodites" that other missionaries reported seeing in North America? Lafitau could understand if a woman tried to elevate herself by displaying "manly courage," but a man assuming "women's occupations" seemed at odds with his definition of a "civilized" society.[30]

Christianity, and the missionary's ethnographic gaze, proved as damaging to Native Americans during the eighteenth century as disease and firearms did in the seventeenth.[31] Missionaries played an active role in this violence by focusing on the men who "debase" themselves by dressing, acting, or performing the work of women. Lafitau claimed that these men "never marry," although they "participate in all religious ceremonies." In an inversion of the Christian patriarchal world he understood, Lafitau wrote that "this profession of an extraordinary life causes them to be regarded as people of a higher order, and above the common man."[32]

These seemingly anomalous gender dynamics remained vexing to most European observers. But in the American wilderness, where "vice slips in everywhere," Lafitau characterized Indian vice as a "species of metamorphosis."[33] That metamorphosis produced sin that was embodied in the "sodomites" and "hermaphrodites" who debauched the "religious spirit" throughout North America. Lafitau insisted that although "the religious spirit which made them embrace this state causes them to be regarded as extraordinary human beings, they have never-the-less really fallen, among the savages themselves, into the contempt in which the priests of Venus Urania and Cybele were held of old."[34]

Lafitau's use of ancient Roman mythology provides us with a clue about why he assessed Native culture and society in explicitly gendered terms. The story of Venus Urania and Cybele centers on the Roman goddess Venus, who is associated with love, beauty, sex, fertility, and prosperity. Roman mythology also positions her as the mother of the Roman people. Curiously, Lafitau pairs her with Urania, a figure in Greek mythology, the patron of astronomy, and one of the nine Muses. And Lafitau's reference to Cybele, "the mistress of wild nature," completes his moral commentary. Cybele mixed gender roles. Cybele was a healer, the goddess of fertility, and a protectress at times of war. The rites Cybele oversaw lacked all restraint and propriety. They were, in a word, orgiastic. The Indigenous "hermaphrodites," "sodomites," and "effeminate men" allegedly indulged in similarly mythic levels of excess.

Lafitau's use of ancient mythology made an explicit point: the social relationships that these people formed needed to be broken, lest they infect all social relations with sin. In taking this position, Lafitau followed the lead of multiple generations of European church and civil authorities. Just as the ancient *athenrosera*, or "warrior pairs," formed "special friendships," so did "young men" in Indian Country, "who are established in nearly the same manner from one end of America to the other," partake in "special friendships."[35] Lafitau insisted that "these bonds of friendship, among the Savages of North America, admit no suspicion of apparent vice, albeit there is, or may be, much real vice."[36]

. . . .

Lafitau's *Moeurs des sauvages ameriquains* provides an insight into the ethnographic imagination of early-eighteenth-century missionaries.[37] Starved of the information that they suspected Native people concealed from them, missionaries made inferences about Indigenous dress, speech, behavior, and tradition by drawing on cultural comparisons and positing conclusions on the basis of historical analogies. This remained a common methodological strategy in ethnological writing for the next century and a half, allowing writers to fill gaps in evidence with sweeping generalizations about the "primitivism" and "savagery" of Native America.[38]

The architects of English settler colonialism in North America also drew on Christianity, mythology, and cultural generalizations to characterize Indigenous people. The irony of this, as the historian Alan Gallay observes, is that the English viewed their mythical traditions as entirely reasonable. Citing the sixteenth-century English mathematician and linguist Thomas Hariot, Gallay notes that Hariot's theorizing presaged the English conviction that "Indian myths must fall beneath the weight of the Christian Bible." And should the English need to act malevolently toward the Indians, well, the ensuing violence would likely reveal the spiritual superiority of the English.[39]

It shouldn't come as a surprise, then, that after the English established their first permanent colonies in North America, during the seventeenth century, they adopted a "scorched earth" approach to colonization.[40] The massacre of Indigenous communities from Virginia to Pennsylvania and New England followed the expansion of settler colonialism throughout eastern North America. By the early eighteenth century, and the Act of Union that brought the English, Scottish, and Welsh together as Britons in 1707, many parts of Indian Country came into closer, and more regular, contact with British traders and settlers. Native power had heretofore confined British colonies to a narrow coastal fringe, but over the course of the eighteenth century the increased contact with Indigenous people spilled into violence, leaving large swathes of Indian Country east of the Mississippi River in ruins.[41]

During the first English forays into North America in the 1580s, few could have imagined the magnitude of the bloodshed that would define their relationships with Indigenous communities over the coming two centuries. Sir Walter Ralegh (which Americans later spelled "Raleigh") attempted to establish settler colonies during the 1580s. Under Ralegh's guidance, the English made two attempts to establish the Roanoke Colony, the first in 1585 under Ralph Lane and the second in 1587, led by John White. The Roanoke failure meant that not until the early seventeenth century did the English successfully establish a permanent settler colony in North America. And even those colonial ventures initially teetered on failure. The Jamestown colony, founded in 1607, endured disease, "starving times," and decades of war with the Powhatan chiefdom. The Jamestown colonists barely survived these early travails, but that survival resulted in no small measure from the agricultural skill and ecological knowledge of Native communities.[42]

Similar dynamics played out in the mid-Atlantic colonies and in New England during the 1620s and 1630s. None of this meant that English cultural chauvinism abated during these early decades of settler colonialism.[43] Quite the contrary. The English viewed Native Americans as unchristian, and therefore savages who were outside the boundaries of Christian civilization.[44] Indigenous gender systems highlighted this savagery. The "idleness" of Native men and the agricultural labor performed by Indigenous women reinforced English perceptions of Indian savagery and their inverted social world.[45] In Virginia, colonial officials acted on their prejudices by confining Native communities to reservations during the middle decades of the seventeenth century.[46] And throughout the colonies of the Atlantic seaboard, the English enslaved Native people on North American and Caribbean plantations.[47]

English property owners and enslavers cared little for the emotions and kinship bonds of enslaved Indians; they simply wanted a tractable labor force so they could establish a stable economic foundation for the colony. In Virginia, these views became explicit as early as the 1620s. Elites in colonial society were already obsessed with the accumulation of laborers to supply nascent tobacco plantations and with an economic system that "treated men as things."[48] Creating emotional distance between the enslaver and enslaved empowered the former to ignore the physical and psychological well-being of Indian slaves so long as they remained cogs in a burgeoning system of production.[49] When those laborers rebelled, worked inefficiently, or showed any signs of human emotion, enslavers turned to violence. Indeed, settler violence toward Native people—be they enslaved Indians, Indigenous diplomats, or Native traders—increasingly spilled into the frontiers and backcountry sections of colonial society during the late seventeenth and early eighteenth centuries. Growing numbers of English people, settlers from all sections of colonial society, embraced the collective conviction that Native Americans needed to be eliminated either by violence or absorption into settler culture. This aggressive, masculine form of colonialism meant that emerging concepts of racial difference overlapped with gendered perceptions of Native effeminacy and sodomy.[50]

The intersection of racialized and gendered concepts of difference sharpened the civilizational divide between settler society and Native America. It also reminded British men of the importance of guarding against effeminacy and "womanish" behavior, lest they themselves degenerate to the savage and effeminate standards that many associated with Indigenous men.[51] In eighteenth-century British culture, the "fop" was known as someone whose obsessive concern for their physical appearance sometimes attracted accusations of effeminacy. An object of ridicule and humor, the fop, like the effeminate and cross-dressing Indigenous male, had no place in a robust settler-colonial culture.[52]

In the British colonies, men needed to act like *men*. Gender and sexual ambiguity were therefore frowned upon, as the famous case of Thomasine Hall and a growing list of anti-sodomy laws revealed. Those who bent, broke, or otherwise flouted European gender conventions were viewed with suspicion, at least in British eyes. Native Americans who changed their physical appearance were thus deemed unreliable military allies and trading partners; those who "lurked" along the trading paths or in the backcountry shadows of settler society became a constant source of colonial anxiety.[53]

According to British church and civil authorities, effeminacy in the American colonies—especially in the hotter, more humid regions—could lead boys and men to "indolence," "cowardice," "luxury," and "effeminacy." Women, too, had to be reminded of the lessons of history's great civilizations—the Assyrians, Persians, Greeks, and Romans—to maintain prescribed feminine standards, lest they slide into robust masculine behaviors unbefitting their gender.[54]

. . . .

Eighteenth-century moral philosophers had a prescription for these anxieties: mastery of one's passions. Men could master their passions by exercising rationality and cultivating their intellects. Retaining a rational mindset empowered one to express love "without effeminacy," and to guard against "a weakness of nature."[55] British men needed to know that "if the passions are acted on without restraint" the mind is injured and the body descends into "effeminacy, Sloth, Supineness, the Disorder and Looseness of a thousand Passions."[56] Stated simply, wise men avoid "excessive venery" if they want to prevent "softness and effeminacy."[57]

In England, individual mastery over emotions was linked to the class system. For elite men of "good breeding," emotional control and rationality were markers of status. In North America, Thomas Jefferson strove to define a theory of good breeding that ordered people according to ranks.[58] Other public figures felt that mastery of emotions should apply equally to all American colonists. So argued Sophia Hume in a sermon published in 1752. Following a trip to England, Hume rejoiced at her return to South Carolina. In Britain, she declared, "Vice, Softness, Effeminacy and Luxury of most Kinds" prevailed. Carolinians—by which she meant Anglo-American settlers—had controlled these "noxious seeds" of sin and were on a path to greatness.[59]

During the latter half of the eighteenth century, a number of political leaders and church ministers in British North America echoed Hume's optimism.[60] They urged continued vigilance to ensure that Anglo-Americans retained mastery over their passions.[61] British colonists needed to ensure that their "friendships" remained sober, rational, measured.[62]

British settlers, like French and Spanish colonizers, monitored friendships. This proved particularly true of British surveillance of friendships among Indigenous men. Reports of effeminate Native men indulging in "special friendships" persisted throughout the eighteenth century and beyond. While Native women did not escape comment, it was the intimate friendships of Indigenous men that attracted the bulk of English and European comment.[63]

The language used to describe friendship in North American colonial settings differed from language to language and culture to culture. For the British, the word "friendship" derived its etymological origins from the Old English word *freonscipe*. Other Europeans brought to North America their own terminology of close relationships. For the French, those terms included *relation amicale* and *amitié*, the latter meaning "friendship, love, kindness, goodwill, concord, correspondency." The Dutch viewed *vriendschap* as the basis for gift-giving traditions, kinship bonds, and community formation.[64] Europeans certainly understood the importance of friendships. From the Pythagorean ideal of friendship in the Greek tale of Damon and Pythias to the "chain of friendship" that bound European settlers and Indigenous polities through treaties, friendship per se didn't automatically equate with effeminacy. Friendships could denote manliness, rationality, or a well-bred body politic.[65]

In North America, Europeans also used friendship as a weapon. For example, Lafitau justified his missionary work in part by writing disapprovingly of the "special friendships" that he witnessed among Indian men. Yet just how common these "special friendships" were remains unclear. John Lawson, an English explorer and naturalist, found little evidence of "effeminacy" among the Native men in the American Southeast. Lawson wrote that during his travels through the Carolinas he didn't see any effeminate Indian men, "sodomites," or "hermaphrodites." Writing in 1709, Lawson contended that "although these People are called Savages, yet Sodomy is never heard of amongst them, and they are so far from the Practice of that beastly and loathsome Sin, that they have no Name for it in their Language."[66]

Half a century later, the French navy captain and explorer Jean Bernard Bossu presented a less sympathetic picture of life in the Native South. Bossu claimed that the Choctaw people "are generally of a brutal and coarse nature." They were intellectually unimpressive, Bossu contended, and "brutal" in their physical appearance. Bossu went on to explain that "you can talk to them as much as you want about the mysteries of our religion," and "they always reply that all of that is beyond their comprehension."[67]

Perhaps the Choctaws found Bossu's questions about their beliefs and ceremonies to be impertinent, feigned ignorance, and hoped the arrogant Frenchman would leave. Eventually he did leave. But before he did, Bossu charged the Choctaws with "very bad morals." He claimed that "most of them [were] addicted to sodomy." Bossu asserted that "those defiled men, wear long hair and a little petticoat like the women, who despise them very much."[68]

Did Choctaw women really despise these "defiled men"?[69] Other than Bossu's assertion, there's little evidence to support the idea that a matrilineal society like the Choctaws would marginalize people identified with female roles or feminine identities. In fact, the Choctaws and neighboring Indigenous communities such as the Chickasaws, Creeks, and Cherokees maintained strikingly flexible and inclusive kinship systems. Europeans didn't seem to want to see this dynamism, and if they did see it, they tried to explain it away, remake it, label it, destroy it. Colonial language—be it legal, religious, or gendered language—both narrowed and distorted the stories that colonizers told about Indigenous people.

As the following chapters reveal, it is possible to see past narratives of erasure, the language of effeminacy, and histories that for too long purported to recount the facts about sexual deviance in Native communities. This work involves us all looking to Indigenous people for leadership and to Native culture and language for a richer understanding of the past and its connection to the present. Across Indian Country today, gendered dynamism lives on and is clearest in language revitalization and the reclaiming of phrases indicative of cultures that nurture gender fluidity. For example, Rebecca Nagle writes that a fellow Cherokee Nation citizen, Wade Blevins, embraces their fluidity by identifying as "ᏇᏞᏗ ᎤᏞᎥᎩ" or "other-spirited" (using the syllabary invented in the early nineteenth century by an autodidact Cherokee, Sequoyah). Building on the Pan-Indian term "Two-Spirit," Blevins is part of a growing movement that is reconnecting with Indigenous languages to gain renewed insights into the tribe-specific gender identities that Bossu, Lafitau, and scores of other European writers dismissed as effeminacy or described euphemistically as "special friendships." As Nagle explains, the "Cherokee language has 10 different pronouns, all of which are gender neutral."[70]

Rebecca Nagle and Wade Blevins are not only decolonizing their sexuality and gender identities; they're challenging the historical distortions about Indigenous cultures that remain embedded in colonial archives. They refuse to allow the obfuscations of written sources to shape their historical consciousness or govern their lives. This is the hard work of decolonization, of being aware of the historical forces and contemporary surroundings that shape one's life and rejecting the colonial knowledge makers who castigated Indigenous culture as savage, evil, strange. That work involves more than the deconstruction of archival silences; it also requires us to dismantle the damaging historical consequences of terms like "sodomite," "hermaphrodite," "sin," and "effeminacy."[71]

CHAPTER 5

STRANGE

*In a lot of Native communities, the child would grow up
and they'd be whoever they were. . . . You're just loved
and protected and nurtured when you grow up.
That's freeing, and it's safe, and it's healthy.*

—ARNOLD DAHL (Leech Lake Band of Ojibwe)[1]

*People have a lot of learning to do. I think sometimes it
can be even harder with folks who think they know.*

—REBECCA NAGLE (Cherokee Nation)[2]

ON HIS SECOND TRIP to North America, the Franciscan missionary
Pedro Font saw something he called "strange."[3] Accompanying Juan
Bautista de Anza on his 1775 expedition into what is today California,
Font kept a journal in which he detailed his thoughts and experiences.[4]
In southern California, Font spotted a small group of Indigenous
women. Nothing strange about that. Font then took a closer look.
Among the group were "men dressed like women." These "men"
seemed to socialize and work alongside the women, "never joining
the men." Perplexed, Font made some inquiries. He wrote that the
"commander called them *amaricados*, perhaps because the Yumas call
effeminate men *maricas*."

Reports of this nature weren't new. Since 1492, Europeans had
been recording their surprise and displeasure at encountering Native
communities with gender systems that breached their own understanding of the increasingly rigid male-female binary. Although Native people nurtured dynamic cultural beliefs and practices, European
traders, soldiers, missionaries, settlers, and others often reduced very

different Indigenous communities to arbitrarily superficial categories. Font, in expressing his shock and moral judgments, contributed to this tradition.

Font made his comments while stationed among the Yuma, or Quechan, people. He described the Quechans as "well formed, tall, robust, not very ugly, and hav[ing] good bodies." That's the closest he came to praise for the Quechans. Much of Font's journal cataloged what he saw as their moral failings and religious inadequacies.[5] The longer he spent among the Quechans the more Font assumed he knew.

Font traveled to North America with all of the prejudices one might expect from an eighteenth-century Catholic. During his time along the Colorado River, he complained about the body odor and constant flatulence of Native people. And Font routinely observed what he called the untrustworthiness of Indigenous people, a character flaw endemic in Indian Country. The Indians, Font insisted, turned from friendliness to "arrogance" in the blink of an eye, their thievery "a characteristic of every Indian."[6]

Font found himself appalled by the Quechans. He wrote about Quechan men painting their bodies in red ochre and black charcoal. When they finished covering their bodies in paint, these men resembled "something infernal."[7] The appearance of Quechan women proved equally disgusting. Font complained that women went about their daily tasks bare breasted, wearing only a flimsy bark skirt to cover their groin and buttocks. The sound that the bark made as it rubbed against the thighs of Quechan women annoyed Font.[8]

At times, Fray Pedro must have wondered why God had sent him to this "savage" place. The Franciscan friar described a cold world—metaphorically and in reality. It was a world barren of Christian culture and miserably cold during the winter months, something Font experienced when he woke up near the banks of the Colorado River one morning only to find the urine in his chamber pot frozen. Font felt decidedly unsafe in this environment, seeing nothing healthy about the Quechans' way of life.[9]

Font's journal is a record of strange people, of even stranger behavior, and an alien landscape. It's a document filled with judgments, of cultural misunderstanding and contempt. It is a hateful relic from colonialism's written archives, but it's a source of information that cannot be ignored. Flawed as it is, the journal provides a window into the colonial encounters of the late eighteenth century. Significantly, Font was not alone in disparaging Native cultures during the so-called Age of Revolutions.[10] The written records of Spanish and French missionaries, European travel writers and armchair ethnologists, and the Founding Fathers of the United States highlight how Christianity, Enlightenment theories, and the logics of settler colonialism dovetailed to obscure knowledge of gender fluidity and sexual diversity in Indian Country. But not all is lost. When we read these documents against Indigenous actions, and filter them through the lens of Native philosophies, linguistics, and culture, the outlines of healthy, nurturing, and sometimes playful systems of gender and sexuality become clearer.

. . . .

When the Quechan people first encountered Spaniards in the mid-sixteenth century, their homelands stretched from the Colorado River to the Gila. Located in what is today southern California and Arizona, the Quechan lived in a particularly dry region of North America. Their system of agriculture, which depended on the annual flooding of local sloughs, formed part of a subsistence economy. These precious sources of water and nutrient-rich silt brought Quechan staples to life. Crops of maize, wheat, beans, melons, and small seeds nourished communities, while the consumption of deer and antelope meat added protein to the diet.[11]

The Quechan spoke a Yuman dialect and lived in small, patrilineal bands. These social ties developed over time into larger tribal groups known as rancherías comprising as many as five hundred people. By the mid-sixteenth century, the Quechan had a history of fighting to preserve their collective identity and provide sustenance for the members of each ranchería.[12] Balancing the subsistence needs of rancherías demanded that Quechans pay attention to the limits of local ecologies. One of the ways they did this was through a flexible system of gendered labor. Quechans lived with local ecosystems, paid attention to environmental changes, and noted fluctuations in the flow of rivers. Binary distinctions—wilderness/civilization, male/female—had little utility in this ever-changing world. People needed to adapt to local ecosystems and embrace a fluid understanding of what it took to ensure the health of their respective communities. Rigidly prescribing which types of labor men and women must perform made little sense to the Quechans; instead, they fostered a dynamic worldview that empowered individuals to take on roles based on evolving skill sets, accomplishment, and communal need. Europeans didn't appreciate this complexity. When they caught their first glimpses of Quechan society their reports suggested that men were employed in menial tasks that required greater physical strength, while people who took on a more feminine appearance engaged in skilled labor involving agriculture and the distribution of food.[13]

Quechan life focused on community collaboration. Individual expression wasn't frowned upon so long as it adhered to the protocols of reciprocity and balanced the needs of everyone who lived within the ranchería. Unlike the Spanish, Quechan people never developed a system of wealth accumulation like those encouraged by the individual or mission-operated encomiendas, a type of estate and system of forced labor in the Spanish settler colonies. An extensive network of trade routes connected communities, facilitating an exchange economy that supported life on the rancherías.[14]

Within this social system Quechan people nurtured blended gender identities and formed intimate relationships that sometimes breached the heteronormative ideals that Europeans brought with them to the Americas. Marriage usually involved a monogamous relationship, although it was not unheard of for a man to have multiple partners. Marriage began with a proposal. The parents of the intended groom usually initiated marriage negotiations with the intended's family, a process that often started shortly after a young woman had her first menses. A dowry was established, and gifts were distributed among the extended family.

Intimate social and sexual relationships in Quechan society also included *kwe'rhame* and *elxa'* people. Male-bodied Quechans who took on women's social roles and wore female clothing were known as kwe'rhame. Female-bodied people who assumed male social roles and dressed like men were known as elxa'. For both kwe'rhame and elxa' people, the adoption of these identities in a Quechan ranchería was as much a spiritual as a physical experience.

Like scores of Native communities throughout the American West, Quechans placed great importance on dreams. Visions that foretold a person's future path were viewed as spiritual messages. For people with gender-fluid identities, teenage dreams held particular importance. Dreams awakened young people to their special identity and, particularly for the elxa', their considerable spiritual powers, which other Quechans both feared and respected.

When Fray Pedro Font arrived in Quechan territory, he found it difficult to see anything spiritually redeeming about kwe'rhame and elxa' people. He saw only their physicality, and it struck him as strange—dangerously and sinfully so. Font claimed that he saw men who constantly stroked their penises in front of other men. He reprimanded these men. They ignored Font and continued engaging in mutual masturbation. At other times, the kwe'rhame laughed at Font's admonishment as they continued stroking their penises. Perhaps this was an act of anticolonial resistance. Font's intrusiveness, like that of the Spanish more generally, was unwelcome to the point of being irritating. Little acts that got under the skin of these foreigners could form part of a larger arsenal of anticolonial resistance.

That resistance boiled over in 1781. As the Anglo settler colonies in the East fought for, and ultimately won, their independence from the British, the Quechan fought their own battle for independence. Missionary intrusiveness in the lives of kwe'rhame and elxa', and reports of Spanish men sexually assaulting Quechan women, resulted in the Quechans fast running out of patience with the Spanish.[15]

The Spanish, though, remained committed to cementing their presence in Quechan territory. Under the leadership of Theodoro de Croix, the general commander of the Provinces of New Spain, two new permanent missions were slated for construction along the Colorado River. The missions aimed to undermine the behaviors that Font found so strange and to convert the Quechan to Catholicism. It was a form of cultural genocide designed to sever Quechan kinship bonds.

The Quechans knew the Spanish were up to no good. They recognized Spanish economic efforts to choke off their communities from exchange networks and complained about Spanish livestock trampling and destroying their crops. Font and other missionaries added to the growing aggravation by trying to change gendered and sexual behaviors that the Quechans saw as both normal and healthy. Relations grew increasingly fraught by 1779 and early 1780. As tensions rose, the Spanish deployed additional troops, effectively establishing "military colonies."

Quechan people refused to be intimidated. In September 1780, de Croix received a warning from the frontlines. Written by Father Garcia, his words could not have been clearer: the Quechans, "already irritated by so many delays and evil influences . . . were becoming every day more restless and could not be controlled except by superior force."[16]

Quechans rebuffed Spanish attempts to restructure their rancherías and rebuffed intrusions into their social life. Months earlier, in July, Quechan warriors had made their intentions clear when they launched a coordinated assault on the Spanish presence in Quechan territory. Quechan offensives against Spanish settlements continued during the summer of 1780, resulting in the deaths of hundreds of Spanish men, women, and children. The Catholic missions were not spared either. Quechan warriors clubbed four Franciscan priests to death and threw religious paraphernalia into the river. The Quechan message to the Spanish was unequivocal: leave.

Eventually the Spanish retreated. Quechan warriors had beaten the colonial invaders, and in the process cut off Spanish land routes to California. European colonizers returned years later, but for the moment the Quechans had won the space to renew their economic, social, and cultural lives. That included renewing the roles of kwe'rhame and elxa' people in Quechan society.

. . . .

The Quechan weren't alone in trying to hold on to their cultural traditions and political autonomy in the face of growing settler intrusions. In California, the Pacific Northwest, the Arctic, and the sub arctic, Indigenous communities continually renewed their traditions. Across this diverse region some Native communities retained a place for gender fluidity in their social structures. Non-Indigenous traders, politicians, missionaries, and anthropologists observed the existence of people with gender-fluid roles and identities. The bulk of these observations were made by anthropological fieldworkers from the late nineteenth century, so caution is needed when reading the labels they used. Over time, the meaning of a word or phrase changes, and usage adapts to new social contexts. Additionally, Indigenous people may decide to resist unwanted questions from outsiders. They can do this by refusing to answer questions deemed overly intrusive, or by giving an answer that conceals the deeper meaning of a word, phrase, or cultural practice.

The result is a contest over meaning that reverberates into our own times. Between the late eighteenth and early twentieth century, scholars, missionaries, traders, settlers, and government officials in the Americas, Europe, and Asia interpreted Indigenous cultural self-preservation as further proof of "Aboriginal" secretiveness and untrustworthiness. Ethnological descriptions of Siberian shamans as sexless, asexual, or given to "perversions"—namely, "transvestitism" and "homosexuality"—further reveal the wild speculations that ethnographic writers indulged in. The invention of this body of knowledge informed empirical fictions about Indigenous people. It was a knowledge system shaped by a revolution in European thought during the Enlightenment of the eighteenth century. Its logics trickled down from an elite few. When applied to the Americas, the enlightened few offered up generalizations about Indigenous communities that were based on scattered assumptions and half-truths.[17]

Enlightenment and post-Enlightenment systems of colonial knowledge placed Indigenous people in fixed, transhistorical categories. They willfully obscured a reality of cultural dynamism and physical movement in a bid to contain, control, and, if necessary, destroy Native people. For example, non-Indigenous linguists attempted to corral gendered pronouns and impose some sort of order on Indigenous cultures. These intellectual labors were in keeping with the empirical thrust of the Western intellectual tradition. In contrast, Native communities operated in worlds in which metaphor and mnemonic devices reminded people of the importance of adaptation and renewal to ensure balance in the overlapping worlds of the physical and the spiritual.

To underscore this point we can use the work of linguists and ethnographers to challenge their own assumptions and reveal dynamic worlds constantly in motion. The Koryak story of how Raven became a woman illustrates this perfectly.[18] The Koryak, whose homelands are located in the present-day Far East of Russia, tell of a time when Quikinnaqu (Big Raven) decided to turn himself into a woman by cutting off his penis. Quikinnaqu turned his penis into a needle case, his testicles into a thimble, and his scrotum into a workbag.

Quikinnaqu thereafter moved to a camp named Chukchee (or Chukchi). Here Quikinnaqu lived for some time, refusing the overtures of young men who offered to make Quikinnaqu their wife. But one day Quikinnaqu met Miti, a woman who had run out of food. Miti needed to adapt to her sudden hardship. She dressed as a man and refashioned her stone maul into a penis. Miti then headed off with a team of reindeer and eventually stopped at Chukchee. A short time passed before the people of Chukchee noticed that Miti worked hard and should have a partner—Raven.

Raven and Miti had changed gender roles prior to their meeting. How should they act toward each other? They debated the question and eventually decided to return to their previous form. They swapped clothes, and in time Raven's penis and testicles grew back.

Native people retained and renewed dynamic storytelling traditions. They did this by retelling stories at the same time and in the same location during the ceremonial cycle. Native knowledge keepers repeated ceremonial practices to ensure the accuracy of their sacred stories and to highlight important morals. In the case of Raven and Miti, the story emphasizes the rebalancing of life. To accomplish their new state of balance Raven and Miti not only moved back and forth along a male-female gender continuum but openly traveled along the gender spectrum in ways that fit their changing circumstances.

Traveling east from Koryak homelands and across the Bering Strait, Yup'ik-speaking people maintained social structures that also included gender-fluid people. On St. Lawrence Island, just south of the Bering Strait, and into what is today Alaska, Yup'ik terms for gender fluidity survived Russian, British, Spanish, and American colonial incursions. However, disentangling Indigenous terms from Eurocentric interpretations and ethnographic studies remains a challenge to any effort to decolonize Native kinship terminology and reclaim gendered traditions.

In Siberia, the Russian Far East, western Alaska, and southern Alaska, the Yup'ik term *uktasik* has been interpreted by non-Indigenous scholars as meaning "soft man" or "womanly man." Anthropologists have ascribed other Yup'ik terms, like *aranu'tiq* and *anasik*, to gender-fluid people in Alaska.[19] As valuable as this language is today, they captured meaning at a particular moment and place in time in the past (and to the extent that Native informants felt comfortable sharing these terms). More challenging is the process of peeling back the cultural filters used in ethnological writing to understand Native cultures and how they change over time.

This challenge becomes even clearer as we move south along the Pacific coastline and into Tlingit communities. Tlingit kinship communities are matrilineal and traditionally included shamans with spiritual powers so great that they could compel a couple to have sexual intercourse. These types of beliefs and practices troubled outsiders—from eighteenth-century missionaries to early twentieth-century psychoanalysts—and were labeled everything from strange to superstitious. But in Tlingit society, shamans and other medicine people played important roles in ensuring the health and balance of society.[20]

When non-Indigenous outsiders asked Tlingit people about shamans and medicine people, they sometimes referred to a small group of people known as *gatxans*.[21] Gatxans reportedly had fluid gender identities. Europeans knew them as "half-men, half-women" who allegedly believed that gatxans possessed spiritual powers and routinely reincarnated themselves. In some cases, gatxans engaged in "homosexual" relationships, although the anthropological record tends to overstate this point.[22] Very little oral or written evidence survives to illuminate how both Tlingits and colonizers viewed the gatxan during the late 1700s and early 1800s, but we have clues. Anthropologists provide one clue: a definition of gatxans as "cowards."[23]

I've uncovered no historical evidence to suggest that Tlingit people viewed gatxans as cowards during the late eighteenth and early nineteenth centuries. That's not surprising, given that the traders, soldiers, and scientists who interacted with the Tlingit weren't focused on deep historical analysis of gender identities or sexual habits among Indigenous people. These outsiders had other objectives, specifically, making money by extracting resources and expanding trade networks. Still, it's possible to trace the outlines of gender and sexual traditions in this region by examining a variety of sources from both Tlingit history and that of their Indigenous neighbors.

The Tlingits' northern neighbors, the Kaska people of the subarctic region, included women who took on male roles or assumed positions of leadership; one of these was "Nahanni Chief," whom early-nineteenth-century fur traders described as "cunning."[24] As with other Athapaskan-speaking people, who forged kinship communities from the subarctic to the Southwest of North America, gender fluidity constituted an important facet of life. Contrary to the opinions of fur traders, there was nothing deceptive about fluid gender identities. Individuals within Kaska society maintained their focus on balancing the needs of local bands and extended family networks.[25]

But what of the gatxan? Did gender fluidity feature in their everyday life, as it did for the Kaska? And what of the association of gatxans with the word "coward"? In early eighteenth-century Anglo-American usage, a coward was "one that has no heart, or Courage." They are "cow-hearted" and were represented on a coat of arms as a lion with its tail between its legs.[26] During the later decades of the eighteenth century and the opening of the nineteenth, a coward was defined in more strident, judgmental terms. A coward was timid (a "poltroon"), "a wretch whose predominant passion is fear," and, according to Noah Webster's 1817 dictionary for school children, "one who wants courage."[27]

These definitions are at odds with the ethnographic source that originally associated gatxan with the word "coward." That association dates back to John Swanton's 1909 book *Tlingit Myths and Texts*. In this ethnological work, written for the Smithsonian Institution, Swanton refers to a story that he recorded in Sitka, Alaska, about a man named Coward (Q!atxa'n). As Swanton relates the story, Coward volunteers to travel into a valley with a figure known as Wolverine-Man (Nu'sgu-qu). Wolverine-Man gives Coward instructions on how to construct a trap to capture groundhogs. After some initial setbacks, Coward successfully captures some groundhogs and trades their skins—skills that help him become exceptionally wealthy.[28]

There's nothing in this story that conforms with Anglo-American definitions of a coward or cowardice. The translation of Q!atxa'n as "Coward" (and the uncritical acceptance of this definition) is curious in light of Q!atxa'n's heading off into an unknown valley, becoming adept at hunting, demonstrating ingenuity, and being enterprising enough to recognize non-Indigenous people who are willing to purchase the skins he's accumulated. Q!atxa'n is the antithesis of a coward.

Still, words have power, and as in much of the material in written historical and anthropological records about Native America, misinformation and misinterpretation conceal deeper truths. This certainly appears true for non-Indigenous interpretations of Tlingit culture. For much of the twentieth century, social scientists combed through old accounts written by fur traders, soldiers, or missionaries, and relied on oral testimonies from the few informants they met during fieldwork trips.

This research elicited a variety of stories about "Coward" being a captive of war forced to wear women's clothing, or the gatxan acting like a woman but not necessarily wearing women's clothing. The different stories are suggestive of the adaptiveness of Native oral traditions and a desire to protect proprietary information from the uninitiated—specifically, non-Native anthropologists and psychologists. They also raise questions about non-Indigenous fieldworkers' impact on oral responses and the interpretative limitations of social scientific methodologies. Undeterred, social scientists lumped gatxans into homogenizing categories like "berdache," "homosexual," or "transvestite."[29] These labels, inventions of the post-1870s Western world, expanded on eighteenth- and nineteenth-century cultural assumptions about certain types of character traits and how those qualities applied to Native Americans. This was (and is) how the cultures of colonialism buttressed the economic, political, and military manifestations of settler imperialism—obscuring Tlingit culture in the process.

. . . .

Colonial writers misrepresented Native people from the Bering Strait to southern California in ways that are painful to recall. Fray Pedro Font's assumptions of knowledge about the Quechan exemplified this trauma. His words also remind us to remain clear-eyed about the motives, biases, and intellectual traditions that informed written historical documents.

If missionaries constructed differences to colonize and transform the bodies and minds of Indigenous people, other colonizers—settlers, land speculators, government officials—aspired to confine, dispossess, or destroy them.[30] They wanted what Native Californians had nurtured for as long as anyone could remember: the land, water, and natural resources of California. This proved especially true of Anglo-Americans, who headed west in growing numbers in the decades after the American Revolution.[31]

Every foreign intruder—traders, soldiers, surveyors, gold-seekers, and ranchers—had an angle for co-opting, containing, removing, or exterminating California Indians. California, home to Native communities that spoke over one hundred distinct dialects and which had experienced wave after wave of European invasion since the sixteenth century, had to figure out how to deal with intrusive and often violent outsiders.

Indigenous people made these calculations amid the constant presence of missionaries. Catholic missionaries like Fray Pedro seeded both antipathy toward and colonial myths about California Indians. Between 1769 and 1833, Franciscans oversaw the establishment of twenty-one missions in California and other Spanish colonies. These missions made some important contributions to anti-Indian racism. In particular, missionaries complained about "abominable vice" and accused Indigenous men of engaging in "sodomy" and behaviors that didn't align with contemporary Spanish gender norms.[32]

Junípero Serra, a contemporary of Font, contributed to California's anti-Indian discourse. Serra is sometimes referred to as California's founding father—he did indeed play a central role in establishing Spanish missions in Mexico and California.[33] At one of those sites, the Mission San Antonio de Padua, located in the territory of the Esselen Indians in modern-day Monterey County, Serra reportedly witnessed two Indian men enter the home of a *neófito*, a neophyte, a recent convert to Christianity. One of the visitors, who went by the name Joya, or Jewell, reportedly wore women's clothing.[34]

This struck Serra as strange. The missionary father sprang into action and alerted a soldier. The representatives of church and state—of God and the Spanish Crown—worked hand-in-glove as they burst into the neophyte's home and caught the suspicious couple "in the act of nefarious sin." The offending lovers were whisked away and promptly punished, although not with the severity befitting their crimes, according to Serra.

If this incident displeased Serra, it enraged the Indian couple. They explained to Serra that they were married and that he should leave them undisturbed in their intimate affections. Serra was unmoved. These "ignorant poor" needed the blessings of the Catholic faith and the "virtues of the greater Glory of God" to rid them of their sinful ways. Serra claimed that these "execrable people" existed at other

Spanish missions, but in California there wasn't a town that didn't have at least two or three people like this. The missionaries had their work cut out for them.

Spanish allegations of effeminate Indigenous men engaged in acts of sodomy date back to the early sixteenth century. And yet, after all that time, Font, Serra, and their contemporaries pointed to the persistence of effeminate Native men "dedicated to nefarious practices." Font maintained that "in this matter of incontinence there will be much to do when the Holy Faith and the Christian religion are established among them." These men "must be hermaphrodites," he added. They, like "some women," needed the "Holy Faith and the Christian religion."[35] Font believed that Indigenous people from the Colorado River to San Francisco were consumed with "ignorance, infelicity, and misery." The "effeminacy" of the "*maricas*," like the "cowardice" of the Tlingit gatxan, were symptoms of superstition and social degradations that seemed endemic throughout Indian Country.

. . . .

During the Age of Revolutions in the Americas and Europe, between 1775 and 1848, a masculine preoccupation with the gendering of personal morality shaped laws, economies, and cultural norms. As a new American republic emerged from the wartime ashes of the former British colonies along North America's Atlantic seaboard, a generation of white men emerged as heroes, founders of a new nation.[36] These men warned against an effeminate citizenry. In a 1764 letter to Charles Thomson, the secretary of the Continental Congress, Benjamin Franklin asserted that "the more effeminate and debauched a people are, the more they are fitted for an absolute and tyranical [sic] Government."[37]

Franklin wasn't alone in this opinion. White men and women of the Revolutionary period and early republic viewed effeminacy as a marker of feebleness in speech and thought. And effeminacy proved a slippery slope for Americans of the late eighteenth and early nineteenth centuries. It led to allegations that men who exposed their genitalia to other men in an attempt "to commit sodomy" were soft of mind.[38] Such incidents prompted military court-martials and a flurry of debate about how the law could inoculate the young republic against this type of debauchery and sin. Sodomy—like atheism, bestiality, incest, indolence, and a host of other sins—needed to be banished from the American republic.[39]

The "sins" that Anglo-Americans and Europeans worried most about seemed to touch every dark corner of Indian Country. In 1797, the Duke of Orleans, later King Louis-Philippe of France, questioned the robustness of Native political society by dismissively referring to the Cherokees as being ruled by "petticoat government"—a criticism of the prominent political and economic roles that Cherokee women played in their respective communities.[40]

Louis-Philippe's dismissiveness of Cherokee gender roles was shared by scores of colonizers, travel writers, missionaries, and government officials. Non-Indigenous observers viewed matrilineal societies as unnatural: the effeminacy and laziness of Native men enabling women to rise to positions of power. Thomas Jefferson, the third president of the United States, held similar views. Jefferson insisted that Native men were weak and impotent. Louis-Philippe and Jefferson projected many of their own masculine prejudices on to Native Americans. Unlike the virile, robust, patriarchal nature of the American republic, Jefferson saw most Native men as idle, effeminate, and lacking in ardency. Indigenous nations were doomed.[41]

Despite the history of such projections and prejudices of men such as Louis-Philippe and Jefferson, complex and complementary gender roles persisted in Native communities. These societies continued renewing their traditions amid the persistent incursions of colonizers, albeit in ways that helped Native communities meet the challenges posed by the United States. In the Southeast, the Five Nations—Cherokees, Muscogee-Creek, Seminoles, Choctaws, and Chickasaws—blended millennia-old gender traditions and social roles in a bid to sustain a collective sense of belonging in a rapidly changing world.

Choctaw people viewed gender as dynamic, complementary, and infused with spiritual power. The Choctaws, whose gendered and sexual practices earned them the ire of Jean Bernard Bossu in the 1750s, understood gender roles as complementary, and critical to a culture of reciprocity. Dynamic gender roles informed a Choctaw's occupation, ceremonial life, politics, and everyday social interactions. Even language underscored the dynamism of gendered traditions. For example, Choctaws used the word *hashi* to refer to a penis or a vagina. Whereas Europeans grafted biological categories on to "men" and "women," Choctaws understood gender as a process in which the physical and spiritual power of individuals blended and worked harmoniously to bring balance to Choctaw society.[42]

The Choctaws' Indigenous neighbors also rejected static understandings of gendered traditions and embraced vibrant, innovative gender practices during the eighteenth century and beyond. For instance, Muskogee speakers didn't use personal pronouns to refer to fixed gender categories. People continued using gender-neutral personal pronouns like *ani* ("I") and *istey* ("who"), indefinite pronouns like *isti* ("someone"), independent possessives (*ca-na:ki*, "mine"), and demonstrative pronouns such as *ma* ("that one").[43]

. . . .

Change began accelerating in the decades after the American Revolution. Muscogee people, like the neighboring Cherokees, suffered terrible losses to life and property during the Revolutionary War. As Native people rebuilt their lives in the 1780s and 1790s, a commitment to the ancestors—to the lessons of the past—persisted among Muscogee people. Tensions did exist about how best to draw on knowledge from the past to inform the future, but those tensions highlighted the continued dynamism within Native cultures.[44]

Settler colonialism had no room for Native dynamism. As the United States expanded its geographical reach, white Americans turned to the law, politics, and popular culture to etch categories of difference relating to gender, sexuality, race, religion, and class into the American psyche. By the early nineteenth century, a new generation of Native leaders in the Southeast had risen to power and were attempting to adapt these American categories to the governance of their own communities. Some also embraced the patriarchal worldview of Anglo-Americans. The men who assumed control of Native nations during this period hoped that these changes would help them protect their lands, their people, and their nations. They were wrong.[45]

White Americans and Europeans, particularly those who bankrolled new businesses, plantations worked by enslaved African Americans, and land speculators, moved aggressively into the Southeast and what is today the Midwest with the goal of replacing Native farms with plantations and settler communities. Most settlers didn't feel the need to justify Indian removal, but those who did pointed to anecdotes about the strange, superstitious, or "wandering" traditions that Native people purportedly clung to.[46]

Charles C. Trowbridge reported something particularly strange among the Cherokees. Drawing on observations made in the 1820s, Trowbridge sat at his desk some thirty years later to write that "there were among them formerly, men who assumed the dress and performed all the duties of women and who lived whole lives in this manner." Who were these people? Trowbridge had no answer. Neither, he insisted, did the Cherokees, writing, "They can give us no reason for this singular fact."[47]

No evidence survives to indicate that Trowbridge ever traveled to Cherokee Country. Born in Albany, New York, in 1800, Trowbridge traveled with Lewis Cass to the Northwest Territory in 1820 and earned minor celebrity for his study of Native languages. He later became a prominent member of Detroit's business community.[48]

Trowbridge was an amateur ethnologist. We should read his writings on Native languages and culture with great care, and a healthy dose of skepticism. His misreading of Cherokee kinship was one glaring case in point. Trowbridge correctly noted that boys and girls inherited the clan affiliation of their mother, a practice commonplace in matrilineal societies like the Cherokees. He erred, however, when trying to explain their education and upbringing. He contended that boys came under the "care of the father and the other [daughters] to obey the mother and receive from her the instruction necessary to their situation and sex."

Trowbridge imposed Western definitions of gender and family onto Cherokee society. His reference to "sex" proved indicative of an empirical tendency to biologize gender according to the genitalia of a person. More significantly, Trowbridge misread Cherokee education. In matrilineal societies throughout the Southeast, boys received an education from matrilineal uncles, not their biological fathers. This type of education nurtured the dynamism of kinship systems by ensuring that young people received the training appropriate to their aptitudes and ability to contribute to the balance and harmony of their respective communities. It also ensured that all Cherokee children received love, care, and guidance. Not until the latter half of the nineteenth century, and as a direct result of federal government policies and settler violence, did orphan children become an issue requiring action from Cherokee lawmakers.[49]

Trowbridge wrote about "men who assumed the dress and performed all the duties of women" in this context. His insinuation that Cherokees "give us no reason for this singular fact" implies that traditions of gender fluidity and blended gender roles once existed in Cherokee society but had fallen into disuse. By the 1820s, few could recall why Cherokee kin once "assumed the dress and performed all the duties of women."

There existed another possibility for Cherokees' coyness about their knowledge of cross-dressing men: they did not want people like Trowbridge to know. Native people had experienced the physical and psychological violence of colonialism for centuries. Avoiding violence and protecting special people—ᏇᏞᏙᎢ ᏍᏞᎾᏫ, "other-spirited" in the Cherokee language and syllabary—and spiritual traditions from the prying eyes and ears of non-Indigenous people constituted a form of resistance to settler colonialism. Cherokees therefore took some of their traditions underground in an effort to preserve them.[50]

Tribal communities across North America adopted a similar strategy. On the opposite side of the continent, Native people used selective silences and misinformation to resist colonial intrusiveness. Illustrative are Shoshone and Crow interactions with the Jesuit missionary Pierre-Jean De Smet. De Smet made some damning observations about Native gender relations in the 1840s.[51] Before embarking on his mission to save the souls of Indian "savages," De Smet had read the journal that the French Jesuit missionary Pierre François Xavier de Charlevoix wrote during his early-eighteenth-century travels through New France. Charlevoix's published accounts included descriptions of "great vices" among Native people, including "lewdness" and "effemines" who dress in women's clothing.[52] Equipped with this knowledge, De Smet arrived in North America fully expecting to encounter strange customs and deep-seated superstitions among Indigenous people. He believed that he could alter the uncivilized path that the Indians were on and set them toward the light of Christian civilization.[53]

De Smet's contemporaries and at least one biographer described him as a "remarkable man," genial, and saintly.[54] He was also part of what the Osage scholar George Tinker refers to as "missionary conquest."[55] De Smet wanted to know why cross-dressing seemed prevalent among the Western tribes. His inquiries led him to conclude that Native people adopted cross-dressing practices after dreams, which De Smet dismissed as superstition. De Smet noted that, as in other sections of Indian Country, the Shoshone and Crow reported being visited by the Great Spirit—the Manitou—and awoke from their dreams with a newfound clarity.[56]

One Shoshone person caught De Smet's attention.[57] It was a woman who had distinguished herself as a great warrior and, according to De Smet, thus had elevated her standing in Shoshone society. De Smet wrote that "there is a woman among the Snakes [Shoshone] who once dreamed that she was a man and killed animals in the chase." After she woke from her dream, De Smet reported that the woman "assumed her husband's garments, took his gun and went out to test the *virtue* of her dream; she killed a deer."[58]

By the early nineteenth century, non-Indigenous people viewed cross-dressing and the blending of occupational roles as evidence of two things. First, they reinforced stereotypes about effeminate, lazy Indigenous men. Second, these effeminate, lazy men allegedly imposed a tyrannical system of drudgery on Indigenous women. From these perceptions the "squaw drudge" stereotype emerged in colonial culture. It was a racist and misogynistic term; it homogenized Native cultures and posited Indian "tradition" as rigid and unchanging. The "squaw drudge" trope did something else: it helped colonizers frame Indian Country as an upside-down world, a world of gendered inversions where no one was as they should be.[59]

Building on two centuries of colonialism, Europeans and Anglo-Americans were telling deeply distorted and damaging stories about Indigenous people. They cast otherwise healthy gender roles and fulfilling sexual relationships as evidence of depravity and sin. These stories became increasingly clinical in tone during the nineteenth century. They diagnosed Native people as "problems," and described their dreams as figments of superstitious imaginations. But the colonizers don't own history. We can, and should, wade through the archival muck they left behind and decolonize their stories. If you're patient, it is possible to yield a richer set of narratives than those bequeathed to posterity by Font, Bossu, Jefferson, Trowbridge, De Smet, and others. But to get to those histories—to reclaim them and renew their meaning—you also have to be resilient. History's strange like that.

PART 2

· · · · · · · · · · · · · · ·

STORIES

CHAPTER 6

RESILIENCE

*Many of our communities suffer from post-traumatic stress
disorder, which happens because of all kinds of things . . . such
as alcohol and substance use, domestic violence, the cultural
genocide of our past, so there are things as a community that
lend themselves to how people shape their identity.*

—CURTIS HARRIS (San Carlos Apache)[1]

*Sometimes I have to tell Native people here that there are so
many variations that Creator made, and that Creator made
them, and they're all related in some way. We have to realize
that we all have something to contribute to each other,
for each other, and for this world.*

—RAVEN HEAVY RUNNER (Blackfeet Nation)[2]

EUROPEANS TRIED TO CHANGE, remake, or destroy Native people.
Fray Pedro Font tried. He failed. Armchair ethnologists, politicians,
traders, and missionaries also tried. Most failed, but in their failures
settlers still inflicted physical, psychological, and intergenerational
pain within Native communities. By the American Revolution (1775–
1783) and the early years of the US republic, colonialism's corrosive-
ness was laid bare across Indian Country. Much of the Native South
lay in ruins, a charred remnant of its former vibrance and prosperity.
In the Ohio and Illinois Valleys, Indigenous warriors steeled themselves to defend their homelands against aggressive Anglo-American
invaders, sparking a Pan-Indian movement that would stand in opposition to settler-colonial expansion. And in the American West, the
ancestors of people who today call themselves Two-Spirit showed resilience to sustain themselves through wars, disease, and genocide.[3]

John Tanner got a unique perspective on Native resilience.[4] Born in Tennessee around 1780, Tanner grew up in uncertain times. Tennessee was home to the Overhill Cherokees and in the 1780s and early 1790s was a site of Anglo-American expansion. Cherokee warriors, known as Chickamaugas, defended their homelands—portions of which include modern-day Tennessee and Kentucky—with violence. The Chickamaugas were fighting an anticolonial war.[5]

If Tanner as a child didn't see these Cherokee warriors, his father, a pastor, certainly had. Everyone on the Tennessee frontier talked about Cherokee violence and Indian "depredations" in the 1780s.[6] When Tanner's family moved up the Ohio River and into Kentucky after his mother died, the theater of Indian "depredations" widened. Tanner was two or three years old when his family settled in Kentucky. There, Shawnee warriors fought to preserve their homelands against Anglo-settler encroachments. John Tanner likely listened to stories about "bad Indians," warriors who muted the voices of the "friendly Indians" and reportedly terrorized homesteads like the one Tanner grew up on.[7] These stories justified the scorched-earth approach to Indian removal that engulfed the Southeast and the Ohio Valley between the 1810s and 1820s.[8]

In the late eighteenth century Native communities still controlled much of eastern North America. As the Tanner family moved west, they went deeper into Indian Country. In 1789, the "bad Indians" struck the Tanner family farm, at the confluence of the Great Miami and the Ohio Rivers. John vanished. Shawnee warriors whisked the boy away into lands that colonizers called Michigan Territory.[9]

Tanner was nine years old. Decades after his initial capture, Tanner recalled that "insults and abuses were heaped upon me." In truth, Tanner was an outsider. A captive. A slave. After traveling with the Shawnee for a short period his captors sold him to the Saulteaux, an Ojibwe people. The Saulteaux shared homelands with other Ojibwe peoples around the Great Lakes. They took the kinless Tanner into their community and began initiating him into the roles and responsibilities required of kin members. Once adopted, Tanner became part of Ojibwe society. He eventually married the first of his two Ojibwe wives, Mis-kwa-bun-o-kwa, and had at least eight children with her. By the early nineteenth century, Tanner enjoyed the protections of the expansive Ojibwe kinship system and performed the responsibilities that came with membership in it.

Tanner returned to settler society in Kentucky for a brief period in 1817, and subsequently wrote a memoir that chronicled his experiences. He described the amorality of fur traders and the efforts of Indigenous chiefs to forge alliances with Native and non-Native leaders, and he wrote about his own experiences in Ojibwe culture. One incident remained embedded in his memory. It involved an *agokwa*.

In the early nineteenth century, Ojibwe people understood an agokwa as a male-bodied person who performed the roles of women.[10] The term translates as "man-woman." During this same period, an individual who possessed female reproductive organs but took on roles associated with men was known as *okitcitakwe*, or "warrior woman."[11] It was during a typically frigid winter's day in the Great Lakes region that Tanner met an agokwa. "This man was one of those who make themselves women," Tanner wrote in his memoir. This was no ordinary agokwa, however. This agokwa was the son of a chief, Weshkobug. The Ojibwe referred to the chief's son as a woman.[12]

Tanner knew the "man-woman"—"this creature"—as Ozawwendib, or "Yellow Head." When the geographer Henry Rowe Schoolcraft traveled through Ojibwe country in 1832, he described Ozawwendib as "one of the principal Chippewas."[13] Ozawwendib was certainly well connected. In addition to Ozawwendib's father being a prominent chief, Ozawwendib seemed well liked in the community.

Tanner guessed Ozawwendib's age as about fifty at the time of their meeting. He added that Ozawwendib "had lived with many husbands." On this winter's day, Ozawwendib had traveled to take a look at John Tanner "with the hope of living with" him. Tanner recalled that Ozawwendib offered their hand to him in marriage. Tanner refused, so Ozawwendib offered again. Tanner declined for a second time.

Ozawwendib's insistence on marrying John Tanner hints at the patrilineal nature of Ojibwe kinship. Ozawwendib, who took on the social role of a woman, sought out a new man to marry to firm up their kinship status.[14] Ojibwes wouldn't have found Ozawwendib's marriage proposal unusual, although they did find Tanner's reaction amusing.[15] Tanner failed to see the humor in the situation; in fact, he recoiled from Ozawwendib's "disgusting advances."

According to Tanner's account, Ozawwendib left the lodge and disappeared for several days. Tanner thought he'd heard the last of Ozawwendib. He was wrong. Ozawwendib had joined another band and after collecting a load of "dry meat" returned to Tanner's lodge to invite him and his kin to join them. "My nephew," Ozawwendib allegedly said, "come to me, and neither you nor my sister shall want any thing it is in my power to give you." Tanner and his small band agreed to accompany Ozawwendib. As they familiarized themselves with their new life, Tanner claimed that Ozawwendib again directed romantic overtures in his direction. This attention stopped, however, after Ozawwendib formed a relationship with an Ojibwe named Wagotote.

Tanner recalled that Ozawwendib and Wagotote married, a match that produced considerable merriment and what he called "some ludicrous incidents." What those incidents entailed Tanner didn't say, but revealingly he wrote that the relationship "was attended with less uneasiness and quarreling than would have been the bringing in of a new wife of the female sex."

Tanner's account, originally published in 1830, provides a rare insight into the spectrum of gendered identities in Ojibwe communities. Tanner is at once an outsider and, by virtue of his adoption, an insider. And yet he never seemed to lose the white man's judgmental stance toward Indigenous gender and sexual practices. Tanner, at least in the printed version of his recollections, felt Ozawwendib's marriage proposal constituted "disgusting advances." Is that what Tanner thought while among the Ojibwe, or did he pen those lines to appeal to white readers' expectations? It's not clear. White readers, especially those from the growing class of bourgeois households who fancied themselves friends of the "Indian race," likely read about those "disgusting advances" and recognized the moral of Tanner's story: the agokwa highlighted the gulf between "American civilization" and the "uncivilized" habits of Native Americans.[16]

Tanner's narrative revealed something else. He drew attention to the resilience of Indigenous gender traditions. His account of Ozawwendib highlighted how agokwas remained part of flexible Ojibwe kinship systems, even after two centuries of colonial intrusion. Native traditions in the Great Lakes, and throughout North America for that matter, changed as a result of sustained contact with Europeans. That didn't mean all Native communities lost the traditions that bound kinship communities together. Those traditions adapted, people innovated, and kinship communities snapped back into place, albeit in modified form. Indigenous people continued adapting to the external pressures of early-nineteenth-century settler colonialism. Sometimes that meant concealing aspects of their culture from the gaze of white Americans, whether these Americans were adopted into kinship systems or were among a growing number of "explorers," artists, and academics.

. . . .

Among the Saulteaux, also called the Plains Ojibwe, cultural practices and ceremonial traditions that transcended Western concepts of male-female gender roles persisted and thrived into the nineteenth century.[17] In the United States and Canada, Cree, Blackfoot, and Native communities across the Plains persisted in their culture of nonbinary gender roles. Gender fluidity continued to characterize a number of traditional roles, like medicine people, warriors, and diplomats, just as they did in other parts of North America. People with gender fluid identities and roles also remained integral to a number of important ceremonial roles, overseeing puberty ceremonies and conducting Sun Dances, a tradition that involved dance, song, and prayers for healing.

European and Euro-American observers generally cast a disapproving eye on Native gender and sexual practices. Before setting off on their own journeys, some non-Indigenous people read "the old writers on America" to prepare them for "the fickleness of the Indian character." Others steeled themselves for the sight of men wearing women's clothing, which missionary and travel writers usually described in "stories of hermaphrodites."[18] One writer typified this sentiment, insisting that "sodomy, onanism, & various other unclean and disgusting practices" existed among tribes on the upper Plains.[19] Indigenous resilience could really irritate nineteenth-century colonizers.

Moral opprobrium became a dominant theme in travel accounts about gender-fluid people in Native communities throughout the American West. Isaac McCoy, a Baptist missionary famed for his proposal to carve out an Indian state in Kansas, Nebraska, and Oklahoma, wrote of a twenty-five-year-old Osage man, "ghost-like" in appearance, who wore women's clothing. Writing in 1828, McCoy claimed that cross-dressing practices were common among "the un-cultivated tribes to the north." He added that "his appearance was so disgusting, and the circumstances of the case so unpleasant, that I spoke not a word to him." McCoy quickly passed over the existence of "so disgusting" a person, cheered by the knowledge that this "relic" of a savage tradition seemed to be "in a declining state of health, and certainly his death would not have been lamented."[20]

The judgmental lens through which McCoy viewed Native com-munities blinded him to the continued importance of gender-fluid people's roles in kin-based communities throughout North America. Among the Blackfeet, for example, a male who "acts like a woman" was known as an *aakíí'skassi*, and *saahkómaapi'aakííkoan* denoted a "boy-girl." Among the Cheyenne, an Algonquian-speaking people, a male who performed some of the social roles of a woman was a *he'eman*, while a woman who took on male roles was a *hetaneman*.

What Europeans and Euro-Americans perceived as "strange" gender roles and affronts to the male-female gender binary, many In-digenous people understood as critical to their kinship communities, and to their health and well-being.[21] The Eastern Dakota, sometimes called the Santee Sioux, viewed gender in this way. They used the term *winkte* to refer to a male-bodied person who assumed the appearance and roles of a woman. Among the Mescalero Apache these people were (and are) *nde'isdzan*; among the Mandan, *mihdacka*; and among the Tohono O'odham, *wik'ovat*. Myriad other terms survived into the nineteenth century and beyond to denote the gender spectrum in Indian Country: the Crow referred to people as *baté* if they were male-bodied but female identified; the Diné referred to gender-fluid persons as *nadleeh* (also spelled *nadleehi* for the singular, *nadleehe* for the plural) to indicate "one in a constant state of change," or "one who changes."[22]

The resilience of these terms underscored their enduring impor-tance to nineteenth-century Indigenous communities. Like the Diné, Crees continued to nurture a sophisticated culture and language that enabled them to maintain a balanced society connected by a spectrum of gender roles and identities. What we would understand today as transgender identities had a place in Cree kinship communities. A man who dressed as a woman was known as *napêw iskwêwisêhot*. Alter-natively, a woman who dressed in male clothing was referred to as *iskwêw ka napêwayat.* A range of other terms denoted specific roles, the ways kin members perceived a person's gender, and whether one's public gender identity was acknowledged and accepted by the Cree community. The word *ayahkwêw*, for instance, referred to a man who lived and dressed like a woman and was accepted by their community as a woman. The term for a woman who wore men's clothes, lived as a man, and was accepted as a male was *înahpîkasoht.* Crees typically looked upon women who took on the roles of men as possessing special skills and medicinal knowledge vital to the community.[23]

The language used to give meaning to gender fluidity during the nineteenth century reflects the valued social roles that these special people performed in scores of other Native communities. The Potawatomi considered men who dressed in female clothes and performed roles associated with women as supernatural and extraordinary. The Otoe thought these people were instructed by the moon and called them *mixo'ge.* The Osage term, *mixu'ga*, had the same meaning: "moon instructed."[24]

Not all terms for people who traversed the gender spectrum were complimentary. A *shainge*, a Ho-Chunk man who dressed and performed work associated with a woman, was considered by their kin as unmanly.[25] This term did not necessarily connote prejudice or result in social marginalization, but it did indicate the diversity of meanings associated with gender roles and identities in Indigenous communities. Native cultures were—and remain to this day—diverse, a historical reality that applied to perceptions of gender and sexuality as much as it held true for other aspects of Indigenous life during the nineteenth century.

In these communities, gender fluidity remained a resilient and adaptive part of Native culture. Indigenous people who didn't conform to heterosexual gender and sexual norms weren't necessarily transgender or homosexual (a term coined later in the nineteenth century)—they were more than that. People like Ozawwendib, whom Tanner described in his memoir, were often viewed by their kin as special.

Like other Ojibwe communities, the early-nineteenth-century Saulteaux viewed gender as an important part of a balanced society. Gender-specific roles existed: Men hunted and trapped game. Women complemented the work of people who identified as men by performing highly skilled occupations like cooking and managing crops. Saulteaux women could also engage in warfare if their community came under attack, but strict prohibitions on their use of weapons like bows and arrows usually existed.

In traditional Ojibwe communities, people possessing Ozawwend-ib's identity united men and women. Known as *ikwekaazo*, "one who endeavors to be like a woman," these people possessed powerful spiritual qualities. Women who performed the roles of men, known as *ininiikaazo*, were similarly honored. The powers that the Ojibwe believed people like Ozawwendib possessed meant that they played leading roles in ceremonies, bringing Anishinaabe men and women together in dance and prayer. And for Ozawwendib it also meant that they transcended male and female roles. While they performed the work of women on a daily basis, Ozawwendib also went into battle, purportedly using bows and arrows against Sioux warriors, which Ojibwe women weren't normally permitted to do.[26]

And what of Ozawwendib's husband, whom Tanner alluded to? The Anishinaabe would not have required Ozawwendib's husband to transition to the status of ikwekaazo. Rather, he was free to live and nurture his relationship with Ozawwendib but was not viewed as ik-wekaazo or burdened with Western labels like "sodomite." In fact, if the relationship ended, or Ozawwendib died, Ozawwendib's husband was free to remarry. And the person he formed that new relationship with could be a man, a woman or an agokwa.[27]

. . . .

The spectrum of blended gender roles and fluid sexual identities that sustained the Ojibwe and scores of other Native societies helped people maintain balance in their family and kinship relationships. The resilience of those connections cannot be understated; they gave meaning to kinship, constituting the foundation of social and spiritual life.

Euro-Americans, on the other hand, were unsettled by persistent examples of gender fluidity in Indian Country.[28] They attacked communities harboring gender-fluid people with armies, with government policies, and with the capitalist culture that dominated nineteenth-century America. Genocidal episodes also swept across the United States—from the federal government's forced removal of Native Americans east of the Mississippi River in the 1820s and 1830s in what became known as the Trail of Tears, to Anglo-American settlers who directed exterminatory violence against California Indians between the 1850s and 1870s. Settler colonists continued to attack Native Americans during the following century with the federal government's policy of removing Indigenous children from their homes and placing them in boarding schools so they could assimilate to white society. The United States' assimilation policy continued the settler-colonial attack on Indigenous gendered traditions well into the twentieth century.[29]

Gendercide, or the deliberate effort to destroy traditions of gender fluidity in Native America, was integral to genocide and ethnocide in nineteenth-century North America. It involved not only physical assaults on Indigenous people and cultures with well-established gender spectrums—be they third, fourth, or fifth genders, in addition to gender-fluid identities—but cultural and psychological assaults on the kinship communities that these adaptive gender traditions supported.[30]

In the United States, gendercide was part of the federal government's ongoing efforts to reduce Native landholdings and undermine Indigenous sovereignty.[31] The removal of entire communities from their homelands and confinement on reservations placed enormous stress on Native people during the latter half of the nineteenth century. The Diné people experienced these stresses, a colonial trauma that haunts citizens of the Navajo Nation to this day. (Diné is the name that the Navajo people have used historically to refer to themselves. It means "the people," whereas the other term associated with the Diné, "Navajo," derives from the Tewa-puebloan word *navu hu*, meaning "place of large planted fields.") Between 1864 and 1866, the federal government targeted the Diné and forcibly removed thousands of people from their ancestral homelands, Dinétah. Dinés were forced to walk hundreds of miles—the "long walk"—to internment camps, like the notorious Bosque Redondo Reservation. The "long walk" was actually no walk at all. It was a forced march, an industrial-scale attempt by the federal government to dispossess a sovereign Native nation of its homelands.[32]

The federal government also used boarding schools to attack and destroy Indigenous cultural and linguistic knowledge. In 1819, federal officials began using the Indian Civilization Act to fund Christian denominations in their efforts to enroll and educate Indigenous children in boarding schools. The Peace Policy adopted by President Ulysses S. Grant's administration in 1869 renewed federal efforts to eliminate

Native culture and social structures through education, the objective being to assimilate Native American children to white society.[33]

Between the 1860s and the 1960s, the federal government removed hundreds of thousands of Native children from their families and communities.[34] Confined in facilities that resembled prisons, Indigenous children endured rigid disciplinary regimes, psychological and sexual abuse, and exposure to disease outbreaks. General Richard Henry Pratt, the architect of the program of off-reservation boarding schools, justified his work by declaring, "A great general has said that the only good Indian is a dead one, and that high sanction of this destruction has been an enormous factor in promoting Indian massacres. In a sense, I agree with the sentiment, but only in this: that all the Indian there is in the race should be dead. Kill the Indian in him, and save the man."[35]

Instead of bullets, Pratt favored education as a more efficient means of eliminating Native American society. By the 1920s, over 350 federal boarding schools existed throughout the United States. Over 80 percent of Indigenous children attended a boarding school during the early twentieth century.

Critical to boarding school curricula was conformity to Western gender norms. Boys and girls received a gender-specific education, boys learning manual skills or trades, girls receiving instruction in sewing and the "domestic arts." No child was permitted to blend gender roles, cross-dress, or alter their physical appearance to resemble that of the opposite gender.

Raven Heavy Runner, a citizen of the Blackfeet Nation, briefly attended a boarding school. He recalls that "there was a lot of sexual abuse that occurred at residential and boarding schools." Heavy Runner is also haunted by stories about school staff and nurses terrorizing children who adopted gender identities that didn't conform to their "biological sex." He recalls the story of a boarding school nurse who discovered that a "little girl was not a little girl." Scandalized, the nurse took immediate action. She cut the child's hair and "dressed her in boy's clothes." When the child returned to a common area where the other children were assembled "the little kids hissed because they knew [what the nurse did] was wrong. What they [nurse] was doing was upsetting the balance."[36]

Experiencing this type of trauma is not easily forgotten. The memories linger, become part of a person's psyche and are integrated into the collective historical consciousness of Native communities. In Canada, a similarly abusive system of boarding schools emerged during the nineteenth century. The formation of the Canadian Confederation in 1867 precipitated a series of treaties with Native people. For the next half century, Canadian officials cajoled and maneuvered First Nations into treaties aimed at legislating Indigenous communities' relocation onto circumscribed reserves. The Indian Act of 1876 became the foundation of the reserve system, giving the Canadian government the legal right to legislate on behalf of Aboriginal people. And in Canada, as in the United States, boarding schools became weapons in coordinated colonial efforts to eradicate Indian cultures and remake Indigenous children in the image of white boys and girls.

For people like Running Eagle, this new era of assimilation and conformity triggered existential crises. Born Otaki around 1800, Running Eagle grew up in the Blackfeet Nation. At an early age, Otaki showed a preference for socializing with boys and wearing male clothing. Her father noticed this and eventually taught Otaki to be a skilled hunter.[37]

Within the Piegan Tribe, one of three tribal communities in the Blackfeet Nation, Otaki took on roles associated with both men and women. Hunting, a skill set traditionally associated with men, became one of Otaki's strengths. At the same time, Otaki's gender fluidity enabled them to seamlessly blend roles typically associated with women. For example, when Otaki's mother became ill, Otaki nursed her until she ultimately died from her illness. Like other members of the Blackfeet Nation, Otaki's focus was on ensuring the health and well-being of the community.

A vision quest provided Otaki with further clarity on the roles they needed to play in Blackfeet society. That vision quest revealed to Otaki the special powers that equipped them for battle. So long as Otaki shunned sleeping with men, Otaki's warrior skills would make an invaluable contribution to their tribe. This Otaki did, receiving the name Running Eagle from a tribal chief, Lone Walker. During their life, Running Eagle honed their warrior skills, engaging Crow warriors in numerous battles. It was in battle, however, that Running

Eagle walked on. In the final years of the 1870s, Flathead warriors killed Running Eagle.[38]

For Native people like Running Eagle, a fluid gender identity constituted an accepted part of Blackfeet life. Their resilience and adaptiveness proved vital to the sovereignty of their community—skills that brought balance and harmony to the Piegan tribe. In the late nineteenth century, the Canadian government had very different ideas. Like the US government, Canadian officials wanted to break apart Native communities. Critical to that endeavor was the targeting of people like Running Eagle.

. . . .

For Native Americans, resilience and renewal meant overcoming some incredible obstacles and immense traumas. In the United States, lawmakers wanted federal Indian policy to have clear and measurable impacts on the bodies of Indigenous people. Surviving the American republic's brand of colonialism meant finding strategies to deal with the mental and medical toll of being separated from homelands, places of ceremony, family, and traditional foodways. The result was chronic diseases such as hypertension, cardiovascular disease, and diabetes. It also included anxiety and depression, which were (and remain) linked to alcoholism and chemical dependency. Native bodies were telling stories about the violent history of colonialism in North America.[39]

Standard history textbooks fail to capture the totality of colonialism's violence among Indigenous communities. The "early republic," "antebellum America," "Civil War era," the "Gilded Age and Progressive Era"—historical epochs American students learn about from a young age—mean little in Native American history. Throughout the nineteenth and twentieth centuries, physical assaults on Indigenous life bled into each other, one massacre followed by another. And the attack on Native culture—language, custom, ceremony, and religion—accelerated as assimilation policies, discriminatory laws, and boarding schools tried to turn Indigenous children into facsimiles of white boys and girls.

The assault on Native America came from all directions, making Indigenous acts of survival and of nourishing and enriching communities both harder and more urgent.[40] Anglo-Canadians in the north,

Anglo-Americans from the east, Mexican colonizers from the south, and Russians in Alaska and the Pacific Northwest all tested the resilience of Native sovereignty and ways of knowing. Importantly, these invasions were as much cultural as they were driven by economic greed and military might. The United States, for example, sent one scientific expedition after another into the American West and beyond. The United States sent Zebulon Montgomery Pike into the West between 1806 and 1807, and Major Stephen Long between 1819 and 1820. John C. Frémont embarked on multiple scientific incursions into the West in the 1840s, and the United States Exploring Expedition received congressional funding to collect (or, more accurately, steal) vast amounts of ethnographic and botanical data from throughout the West between 1838 and 1842. Science and colonial expansion went hand in hand.

By far the most mythologized scientific incursion into the American West was the Corps of Discovery. Led by Meriwether Lewis and William Clark, the expedition relied on Native knowledge to succeed in its mission of exploring, mapping, and recording ethnographic and scientific features of the recently purchased Louisiana Territory. George Drouillard, a mixed-race Shawnee, proved vital to the Corps through his work as an interpreter. So too did a French Canadian by the name of Toussaint Charbonneau and his teenage wife, Sacagawea. Lewis and Clark needed Sacagawea to act as a translator and cultural mediator as they navigated foreign rivers, landscapes, and Native nations. The Corps of Discovery exploited this knowledge while its members maintained condescending opinions of Indigenous people. On Sacagewea's attachment to Shoshone culture and her role in keeping the members of the Corps alive, Lewis wrote dismissively, "If she has enough to eat and a few trinkets I believe she would be perfectly content anywhere."[41]

Lewis appropriated, exploited, and ultimately downplayed Native knowledge. His journals refer to Native men as "savages" and women as "squaws." Corps members viewed some Native people as little more than thieves.[42] But who were the real criminals? Members from the Corps regularly stole food, firewood, and pirogues from Indigenous communities. Joseph Whitehouse, a member of the Corps, justified one of these thefts, writing, "We found some wood on the island covered up with stones where the natives buried salmon every spring. Wood was so scarce that we made use of that which was covered so carefully with stone."[43]

The Corps's theft is overlooked in popular culture. So too are the members' drug use and sexual excesses. Lewis and Clark traveled west with a pharmacopeia: laudanum to treat coughs, opium for pain, calomel for worms. In addition, the Corps was well stocked with penis syringes, salves, and mercury for the treatment of venereal diseases, specifically, syphilis. The white men on this incursion into the West had no intention of keeping their buckskins on, something that members of the Corps later obscured by writing about Indian "prostitution."[44] It was a pattern of deception that continued throughout the nineteenth century. To this pattern white Americans added new means of dispossession; they appropriated Native culture for commercial gain and racially denigrated Indigenous people in the process. This is what George Catlin did as he set about making a career for himself as an artist in the decades after Lewis and Clark's celebrated expedition into the American West.

George Catlin was born in Wilkes-Barre, Pennsylvania, in 1796. After a failed career in law Catlin decided to try his hand at painting. His fascination with the "vanishing race" of American Indians inspired his travels through the western states and territories of the United States during the early nineteenth century. The idea of a race of "noble savages" melting away before the advance of "American civilization" filled the pages of playwrights and novelists during these decades. It was a romantic, idealized, and ultimately racist image of Indigenous people that bore little resemblance to reality. Catlin, like James Fenimore Cooper in his 1826 novel *The Last of the Mohicans*, capitalized on a market for sensational, simplistic portrayals of Native Americans.

Before hucksters and conmen like P. T. Barnum began putting stolen artifacts into hastily constructed glass cabinets and displaying "live" Native American performers in dingy "museums" for the viewing pleasure of a paying public, Catlin tapped into growing consumer demand for ethnographic images of "savage" cultures. His paintings froze Indigenous people in time. The images presented audiences with a visual catalog that fed into the trope of white supremacy, which was buttressed by the short narratives that accompanied Catlin's work.[45]

Catlin's art reflected the temper of his time. He claimed that his work was driven by a desire to capture the "classic beauty" of Native Americans. Critics offered mixed reviews of his work, but those who liked it lavished praise on Catlin as a "native artist." Significantly, Catlin produced art that fed American nationalism. About a decade before the Irish American newspaperman John O'Sullivan wrote about the United States' "manifest destiny," Catlin's art contributed to an emerging mythology in which the Native American "is melting away as the winter snow before the vernal breeze. In a few years more we shall know them only in tradition and song, in painting and history."[46]

Catlin was happy to see some aspects of Native culture wither and die. The *Dance to the Berdash* depicted one of those traditions. Catlin explained that his painting portrayed "a very funny and amusing scene." That "scene" occurred among the Sac and Fox (or Sauk and Meskwaki) people. At the time Catlin made his observations, the Sac and Fox spoke a dialect of the Algonquian language. They shared homelands around Lakes Huron and Michigan and had survived the eighteenth-century incursions of the French. The resilience of the Sac and Fox faced new tests in the early nineteenth century, however. At the time Catlin traveled through the region, American calls for Indian removal had grown louder throughout the eastern half of the United States.[47]

Catlin's *Dance to the Berdash* focused the viewer's attention on "a man dressed in woman's clothes." Who was this "man"? How often did these scenes occur? Catlin wasn't sure, so he speculated. Catlin guessed that the dance "happens once a year or oftener, as they choose, when a feast is given to the 'Berdashe,' as he is called in French (or *I-coo-coo-a*, in their own language)."[48]

It is likely the Sac and Fox limited what Catlin saw. Outsiders uninitiated into the culture and traditions of a kin community were usually kept at arm's length from sacred ceremonies. That did not stop Catlin from pronouncing judgment on what he thought he saw among the Sac and Fox. And he parlayed those judgments into a form of artistic showmanship that sold audiences on the idea that through his art they could glimpse the inner mysteries of "the Indian." Catlin's art reimagined ceremony as a mere dance, transforming the sacred into a consumable object that provided viewers with a window into humanity's past.

Catlin's *Dance to the Berdash* was commercial ethnography. As viewings of Catlin's art traveled around the country, advertisements urged Americans to pay for the privilege of seeing a soon-to-be-extinct race. It was a marketing ploy that played on white America's romanticization of Native people and the conceit of their own racial superiority. And Catlin pandered to it. He had no knowledge of Indigenous languages, and yet broke into Indian tongues when describing scenes that seemed so immoral, so distant from the social controls that ordered white society. Catlin underscored this point when he wrote that the *Dance to the Berdash* "is one of the most unaccountable and disgusting customs that I have ever met in Indian country."

Catlin's wish for the elimination of "disgusting customs" portrayed in *Dance to the Berdash* echoed the eliminationist impulses that millions of Americans harbored for Native Americans. Tapping into the zeitgeist, Catlin declared, "I should wish that it might be extinguished before it be more fully recorded."[49] Well into the twenty-first century, Catlin's racist and misogynistic portrayal of a Two-Spirit ceremony continued to appear in anthropological and scholarly works with little in the way of critique. It wasn't until 2020, and the Cree artist Kent Monkman's painting *Honour Dance*—featuring Miss Chief Eagle Testickle, Monkman's gender-fluid alter ego—that Catlin's piece was simultaneously critiqued, lampooned, and inverted.

. . . .

Catlin's genocidal wish did not materialize, at least not in any uniform way. As hard as white Americans tried to remove Indigenous people and eradicate their culture, the resilience of Native people stood as a bulwark against colonial aggression. Many Indigenous communities held on to their gender traditions, languages, and culture. Others blended Western influences with their own religious and social practices. But the threats to Native survivance never went away. Tradition remained dynamic and adaptive. During the nineteenth century, anthropologists struggled to comprehend this dynamism.[50]

The professionalization of anthropology and a turn to encouraging fieldwork led a new generation of social scientists to leave the comfort of their offices and spend extended periods of time living among Indigenous communities—or, to use anthropological jargon, "primitive" people. For much of the nineteenth century, most ethnological writing didn't involve an author visiting Indigenous communities and gaining permission to speak with elders. Like the British social anthropologist E. B. Tylor, social scientists read folklore, missionary tracts, and travel accounts across a variety of cultures and relied on these as a basis to posit generalizations about Indigenous cultures. These types of commentaries paid scant regard to specific geographical or cultural differences.

That began changing as the twentieth century approached. Scholars from Cambridge University in England, Columbia University in the United States, and the Smithsonian Institution's Bureau of American Ethnology started doing fieldwork among Indigenous communities. By studying other cultures in their own environment, the "field," anthropologists hoped to observe and thereby better understand the function of social and cultural traditions within particular Native communities at specific moments in time.[51] The anthropologists Bronislaw Malinowski, A. R. Radcliffe-Brown, and Franz Boas employed these newer methods to transform Tylor's schema of the stages of "primitive culture" to achieve a deeper appreciation of how cultures functioned in different contexts.[52]

The professionalization of anthropology and the development of fieldwork methodologies coincided with an era in American history in which the majority of non-Indigenous people believed that Native Americans were doomed to extinction. General Nelson A. Miles, who served in the Union Army during the Civil War and fought in the Indian Wars during the late nineteenth century, gave voice to the doomed-race theory. Writing in the popular *North American Review* in 1879, Nelson argued that by "war the natives have been steadily driven toward the setting sun—a subjugated, a doomed race."[53]

Anthropologists understood the implications of such comments. Like their colleagues in archaeology, anthropologists believed that their fieldwork should focus on "salvaging" a catalog of Indigenous cultures and material artifacts before "American civilization" completed its conquest of North America. This racialized perspective on human relations structured the founding of professional anthropology in the United States. For example, Wesley Powell justified the establishment of the Bureau of Ethnography at the Smithsonian Institution in 1879 by emphasizing "ethnographic salvage" work among Native Americans as a core feature of government-funded anthropology.[54]

In her work for the Smithsonian, Frances Theresa Densmore used the phonograph to record songs and preserve stories. Of her work among the Teton, she explained that the ethnographer must approach their work with great care because "Indians become confused, even irritated, if questioned too closely."

Densmore did her best to hide her racial condescension, but it was there, just beneath the questions she posed to the hundreds of Indigenous people who sat in front of her phonograph recorder. Other anthropologists and ethnomusicologists tried to retain the appearance of civility as they conducted their research among Indigenous communities. Their fieldwork informed a body of scholarly writings that exoticized Native cultures. How Indigenous people spoke, dressed, conducted ceremonies, and interacted with one another was frozen in a supposedly precolonial past and became "evidence" for the testing of social scientific theories and the positing of ethnographic categories. Medical doctors, often employed by the military, also added to the growing stores of medical and academic speculation. They, like anthropologists, detached Native communities from the modern world and represented them living by a primitive, "freer," set of moral codes.[55]

Anthropologists wanted to study these "primitive" codes. At the same time, American politicians plotted the extinction of Indigenous people. And among the general public, vivid descriptions of lurid practices and exotic bodies titillated voyeuristic readers. Typical of this sensationalist reporting was one writer who claimed that the "vices found among the Indians are of a kind that usually are found in the most corrupt circles." These anonymous vices were commonplace because "every tribe has its *joyas*, men who dress like women, live with them, share in their work, and enjoy certain privileges, in return for participating in the most infamous debaucheries."[56]

Social scientists and psychoanalysts paid particular attention to these "infamous debaucheries." Specifically, they studied courtship and marital customs, "sodomites," group masturbation, "degenerates," and "squaw-men." That work focused overwhelmingly on western tribes, such as the Apache in the Southwest and the Suquamish in the Pacific Northwest, and began in the decades after the American Civil War and continued into the twentieth century. It caused intergenerational harm to Indigenous communities because it helped shape Indian policies in the United States and Canada, fanned popular prejudices, and distorted the historical record.[57] Take one dictionary definition from 1863. It defines a "Bur-dash" as a "hermaphrodite." The entry continues, "The reputation of hermaphroditism is not uncommon with Indians, and seems to attach to every malformation of organs of generation."[58]

William A. Hammond's writing about "Indian hermaphrodites" echoed these sentiments. Hammond either didn't know about, or ignored, evidence that portrayed the "berdash" as a peacemaker, teacher, or spiritual leader.[59] In an article titled "Disease of the Scythians," Hammond took a global perspective on "Indian hermaphrodites," a topic that he studied as a medical problem.[60]

Hammond served as surgeon general to the United States military for a brief period during the American Civil War. A stout man with short-cropped hair, a full beard, and small puckered mouth, Hammond considered himself a skeptic among scientists. He needed evidence—hard proof—to make any medical recommendations in his papers. Unsurprisingly, Hammond viewed spirituality as a form of mental trickery.

As a founding member of the American Neurological Association, Hammond also had a scholarly interest in human sexuality. More specifically, he studied feminization among men, or what he referred to as sexual "deformities." Hammond started pursuing this interest in the 1850s during a visit to an Indian village called Laguna in New Mexico Territory. When he wrote about his experiences in Laguna some three decades later, Hammond began by referring to the people he examined as the "descendants of the Aztecs." Although many Lagunas converted to Catholicism, Hammond speculated that community members *surreptitiously* engaged in traditional worship of "the Sun."

Laguna culture, as Hammond saw it, was clearly infected with traditional spiritual beliefs. While Hammond took comfort in his belief that the Laguna people "will doubtless disappear ere long before advancing civilization, even if they have not already done so," in the interim he wanted to understand their mental infections. One person caught his attention: a *mujerado*. Hammond believed that *mujerado* was a "corruption" of the Spanish word "*mujeriego*, which signifies 'feminine' or 'womanish.'"

Hammond had stumbled across the type of person that John Tanner recoiled from and George Catlin wanted erased from human history. Hammond began his investigation by interrogating the local chief. Using his position as the Laguna chief's personal physician, Hammond asked for a private audience with the mujerado. The chief expressed reluctance at first. Native people weren't blind to Americans taking their knowledge and misrepresenting it in their writings and lectures. They'd also become well acquainted with American prejudices. Still, Hammond persisted. He wanted to know the mujerado's secrets. After a brief negotiation, Hammond prevailed. Without irony, he wrote that the chief "freely granted" access to the nameless mujerado. Hammond describes how the chief led him from his makeshift surgery to a public area where a large group of women were grinding corn. They zigzagged through the crowd of women as they performed their tasks. Then the chief showed Hammond into a private room. Inside, Hammond saw "about a dozen women" sitting on their knees as they hunched over their work, methodically and expertly preparing corn for the community.

As the chief navigated through the room of busily working women he suddenly paused, then spoke. Hammond didn't record what he said. Whatever it was it caught everyone's attention. The women stopped their work. A short silence fell over the room before one of the women rose to her feet.

"Aqui esta el mujerado," declared the chief. "Here is the mujerado."

Hammond didn't record his immediate reaction to the mujerado. He did note that the chief referred to them with the masculine pronoun *el*. According to Hammond, the chief also said, "You can do what you please with him."

What Hammond did "with him" was conduct an invasive, full-body examination. Hammond guessed that the mujerado was "about thirty-five years old," tall and slim with no facial hair and dressed in women's clothing. Hammond added that the mujerado seemed "cheerful and his face was free from wrinkles, full and rounded, like that of most Indian women of his age."

No written words survive to reconstruct how the mujerado felt during Hammond's intrusive examination. In fact, the remaining description is deceptive, Hammond's detached medical prose providing a facade of objectivity as he voyeuristically gazed upon the mujerado's body. Like other nineteenth-century doctors—including Marion Simms, who conducted gynecological experiments on enslaved women—the "consent" for this medical voyeurism came from the historically constructed power dynamic perpetuated by colonialism. White men exploited the power of their racial and gendered privilege to "explore" the bodies of Indigenous and African American women.

To remind himself of the power that Western science gave him, Hammond never revealed the name of the person he examined. Patient-client confidentiality prohibited these disclosures; it also provided Hammond with psychological distance from his "patient" as he poked, prodded, and measured the mujerado's body. This was a medical subject, not a human being with emotions, kin, and social responsibilities. In Hammond's mind, the person he was examining was, as a mujerado, a biological anomaly.

After completing his preliminary examination, Hammond led the mujerado into a private room. It was just the two of them. Hammond closed a creaky door before asking them to remove "all his clothing." They complied, and the nameless Laguna stood completely still as Hammond examined their limbs and pressed his fingers into the mujerado's protruding stomach. In the course of the examination Hammond jotted down a note about the development of the subject's breasts. His published report explained that he was stunned when he saw the "extraordinary development of the mammary glands, which were as large as those of a child-bearing woman." As Hammond subsequently explained, the mujerado's breasts were so well developed that the mujerado had nursed "several infants whose mothers had died."

Hammond then turned his attention to "the genital organs." He spent much more time detailing this aspect of the examination. Hammond's description was both graphic and reflective of the entitlement he felt in passing judgment. Hammond wrote that "there was no hair on the pubis; the penis was shrunken, but was otherwise normal; the prepuce could be readily retracted and the glans presented a healthy appearance, except that it was not larger than a thimble, which it very much resembled in shape." Hammond didn't explain what constituted "normal" genitals. He did, however, go into extensive detail about the penis in its various states. "The whole organ was, in its flaccid condition, about an inch and a half in length," Hammond explained. "The scrotum was long and pendulous and contained the remains of the testicles, which had almost entirely disappeared." Hammond did not think that was "normal." Hammond wasn't willing to get too close to the mujerado's testicles, although he did get close enough to see that they weren't suffering from cryptorchidism, a condition in which one or both testes don't descend from the abdomen and into the scrotum. Nor did he detect "hermaphroditism." Instead, Hammond reported that one of the mujerado's testicles resembled a "small filbert."

Testicles, like penises, come in different shapes and sizes. Native communities, like other cultures around the world, developed folktales that offered explanations for genital diversity, uses, and misuses. According to Hammond, the mujerado claimed that prior to their transition from male to female he had a large penis and testicles the size of eggs ("grandes como huevos"). This information supported Hammond's argument that the mujerado was a figure in decline. Where the mujerado had once possessed a powerful erection, his penis had atrophied, and his testicles had been reduced to the size of small nuts.

Hammond claimed he saw two mujerados during his time among Pueblo communities in New Mexico. He suggested that their condition was akin to that of Indigenous culture more generally: trapped in a long-forgotten time, the mujerados were embodiments of a backward civilization. Mujerados became habituated to a set of roles that included orgies, "pederastic ceremonies," and passive involvement in group masturbation. These sexual activities reminded Hammond of similar traditions in ancient Greece and Egypt, practices that centered on masturbation and foreshadowed the decline of those once powerful societies.

In Pueblo communities, Hammond saw history repeating itself. The mujerado's lack of courage, acquisition of a passive disposition, and timid nature were all telltale signs of their "deprivation of virility" that "is intentionally produced." The mujerado's physical decline foreshadowed the imminent future of Pueblo communities: they were a "doomed race."

. . . .

Hammond grounded his "science" on the assumption that a feminized male body was a sign of physical weakness and moral decline. He superimposed those cultural stereotypes onto his reading of the human past, a perspective on history that led Hammond to see sexual vices, masturbation, and the feminization of men as an explanation for the decline of once prosperous and powerful civilizations. Like Tanner and Catlin before him, Hammond became convinced that mujerados embodied qualities that would eventually lead to the extinction of Native American people.[61]

Social scientists and medical researchers might convince their white readers about the "disgusting" behavior or physical "degeneracy" of the "berdash," but in Indian Country people knew that Creator made Native people so they could "contribute to each other," in the words of Raven Heavy Runner. Indeed, Indigenous people like Ozawwendib and the mujerado lived fuller lives than white writers were willing to admit (or were allowed to see) and continued to contribute to the fabric of their respective communities. Fleeting and distorted as their appearances were in the memoirs, travel writing, and scholarship produced by non-Indigenous people, their continued existence exposed not only the limits of colonial power but revealed glimpses of how Indigenous actions strained the narrative complacency of non-Native outsiders. Something else is highlighted in the works of people like Tanner, Catlin, and Hammond: the resilience of Indigenous cultures. As the nineteenth century neared its end, that resilience came under renewed pressures.

CHAPTER 7

PLACE

*For me, it's like, why wasn't I taught that? We need to start
talking about bringing back those traditions of accepting
everyone no matter your orientation of your gender expression.*

— SHEILA LOPEZ (Navajo Nation)[1]

We're not all WeWha.

— J. MIKO THOMAS, aka LANDA LAKES (Chickasaw Nation)[2]

AS THE WINTER of 1885 approached, a "debutant" captured the attention of Washington society. The nation's capital was no stranger to
dignitaries, but this "Princess" wowed politicians and their wives like
no other. Described as a "most intelligent young woman of 25 years,
and a Princess and a Priestess in her tribe," the woman graced the
parlors of high society and filled newspaper columns with descriptions
of her activities.[3]

This was no ordinary princess. She reportedly spoke very little English, wore moccasins, and cut her hair in "a short cue."[4] And unlike
other royal visitors to Washington, this princess walked the streets un-
accompanied, day or night, acquainting herself with the city's sights,
sounds, and smells. Standing six feet tall, the princess, a member of
the Zuni tribe, towered over most people she met in Washington. But
this woman's unusual height was not the only physical characteristic that caught the attention of onlookers. While "dignified and self-
possessed," one journalist remarked that the princess was also "very
much larger in frame and more masculine in appearance than is usual
with the Zuni women, who mostly are small and have quite dainty
hands and feet."[5]

The Zuni woman's name was WeWha. Feted as the Zuni "priestess and princess," she remained in Washington City, as it was then called, until the spring of 1886. WeWha became a celebrity, gracing the finest homes, showing off her weaving skills, and meeting a president. But there was more to WeWha than her brief celebrity. Born around 1849, WeWha grew up in the Zuni River Valley.[6] There, in the southeastern corner of the Little Colorado River basin, WeWha's fluid gender identity blended seamlessly into the Zuni social system—a system millennia in the making that had troubled nineteenth-century Americans from George Catlin to William Hammond and others.

The Zunis lived in a matrilineal society defined by ingenuity, creativity, and resilience. They called themselves 'A:shiwi. Zunis made pottery, wove clothing, and painted scenes from daily and ceremonial life on rocks and in caves. The Zuni embedded their culture and religion in the landscape. This attachment to place didn't prevent change and innovation, for example, in Zuni economic life. Traditionally an agricultural people, Zunis responded to the mounting pressures of Anglo-American colonialism by shifting the focus of their economic activity to sheep and cattle herding during the nineteenth century, much as the Diné had done to their north.[7]

An extensive system of overland and riverine trade routes connected Zunis to Native towns, villages, and pueblos throughout the Southwest, the Plains, and the Colorado Plateau. Indigenous people throughout these diverse regions understood that social changes, economic restructuring, and cultural innovation kept kinship identities and communal traditions alive. However, understanding one's place in these Native worlds became increasingly difficult during the nineteenth century.

The destructiveness of colonialism—bringing with it disease, wars, missionaries, and foreign systems of agriculture and economics—vandalized landscapes and disrupted kinship societies throughout the American West. Non-Indigenous scholars kept coming to Indian Country, too. They hoped to map Native culture and languages before they became extinct, as they assumed would occur. As anthropologists, archaeologists, and geologists asked their questions, took material artifacts, and scribbled notes about Native languages, Indigenous gender and sexual practices came under renewed scrutiny. What place did people like WeWha have in a world being studied, parceled off, and fetishized by white Americans? Answering this question requires us to travel back and forth over space and time to appreciate WeWha's life. It also involves a note of caution. As J. Miko Thomas reminds us, not every gender-fluid person to traverse the physical and cultural borderlands of Indian Country and settler society during the nineteenth and early twentieth centuries had the historical experiences of WeWha. Some endured traumas with echoes of the transphobia and homophobia that reverberated through the twentieth century and beyond.

....

The Zuni knew WeWha as a *lhamana*. A lhamana did not conform to Western culture's male-female gender binary. Lhamanas had fluid gender identities, allowing them to play important roles in ensuring the survivance of Zuni kinship society—a concept involving households, religion, and an ethos of adaptiveness.[8]

Nineteenth-century Zuni society was made up of shared households. Matrilineal family groups formed the basis of these households, guiding decisions about the division of labor and social roles among its members: men grew corn, while women stored the corn for household consumption.[9] This social system likely took shape after warming temperatures and a series of droughts precipitated large-scale migrations away from the classic ceremonial sites of Mesa Verde and Chaco Canyon during the twelfth and thirteenth centuries. In response to climate change, the Zuni people renewed their communal traditions in the Zuni River Valley.[10]

These newer Zuni communities bound themselves together in matrilineal households. Religion, based on kachina societies, a belief system focused on ancestral spirit beings (kachinas), strengthened these bonds. Zuni men governed religious life, which revolved around a household's membership in a particular kachina society and the attendant ceremonies. Women participated in kachina ceremonies by "feeding" kachina masks that were stored in households, while men were responsible for assigning to male Zunis membership in one of six kivas, or special rooms—an appointment that occurred randomly.[11]

Zuni households and the kachinas guided decision-making and helped Zuni people renew their place at the center of the cosmos. But traveling the middle "path" was not straightforward: it meant navigating a world comprising six directions—north, south, east, west, up, and down. The Zuni people believed they traveled this world from the center. Staying on the middle path was an ongoing process in which Zuni households and religious traditions helped people navigate the cosmos and renew traditions and social relationships.[12]

Late-nineteenth-century Zunis understood their world as dynamic, changing, and fluid. That fluidity applied particularly to Zuni concepts of gender. In the late 1870s and 1880s, Matilda Coxe Stevenson, the first woman hired by the Smithsonian Institution's Bureau of American Ethnology, wrote that Zuni society included people known as *katsotse* (boy-girl), and male-bodied women referred to as *ko'thlama* and *lha'mana*.[13] The Zunis also told stories about *a'wonawil'ona*. Stevenson recorded these stories using the ethnographic methods she first learned while accompanying her husband, the geologist James D. Stevenson, on a research trip among the Ute and Arapaho in 1878. Stevenson claimed that the Zuni viewed *a'wonawil'ona* as androgynes and "the supreme life-giving bisexual power, who is referred to as He-She, the symbol and initiator of life, and of life itself, pervading all space."[14]

Among other Pueblo communities of the Southwest, fluid social structures and systems of gender identity empowered community members to adapt and change over time: The Keres had a place for gender fluidity in their social system, referring to gender-fluid people as *kokwimu*. Among the Hopi, gender-fluid people were known as *ho'va*; among the Tiwa, as *lhunide*; the Tewa called them *kwido*; and the Pima referred to a boy who acted "like a girl" as a *wik'ovat*.[15]

Traveling northward along the trade routes, Plains tribes continued incorporating gender-fluid people into their social networks during the nineteenth century. Arriving in Mandan country, one might meet a gender-fluid person known as *mihdacka*. The nearby Hidatsa used the word *miati* to refer to gender-fluid people. West across the northern Plains, Crow society, as noted earlier, included people who were known as *batés* (or *badés*). Female-bodied Crows also exercised gender fluidity. One of those people was a prominent warrior and political leader by the name of Bíawacheeitchish.

Bíawacheeitchish was born around 1806. She grew up among the Gros Ventre and showed early signs of her special gifts. In her prairie community, Bíawacheeitchish displayed an aptitude for marksmanship; she also proved highly skilled at killing and butchering buffalo.

As she approached puberty, Bíawacheeitchish was captured by Crow warriors. After initially being brought into Crow society as a captive, Bíawacheeitchish eventually became part of the Crow kinship community and was given her name (her Gros Ventre names are unknown). The Crows encouraged her to pursue her unique skills and placed no prohibitions on her wearing men's clothing. With the support of other Crows, Bíawacheeitchish became an accomplished warrior and chief, a *bacheeítche*. Bíawacheeitchish had found her place in Crow society and remained a prominent member of the community until her untimely death in 1858, when she was killed in battle against Blackfoot warriors.[16]

Bíawacheeitchish occupied a unique place in Crow society. Not unlike the cacica of the Cofitachequi whom the Spanish had encountered in the American South over three centuries earlier, Bíawacheeitchish's fluid gender identity secured for her a special place in the Crow kinship system. Bíawacheeitchish became a warrior, fighting to advance the interests of the people who adopted her into their community. She also became a cultural broker, using her leadership skills and ability to connect men and women, Crows and non-Crows, in alliances, trade, friendship.

. . . .

Across the western half of North America, gender fluidity remained part of daily life in most Native communities during the nineteenth century. However, the historical experiences, cultural roles, and social acceptance of people with fluid gender identities varied from one tribal community to the next.

A few examples from the Great Basin (much of the western US) and the Colorado Plateau (the northwestern US and Canada) regions highlight this point. For the Ute, gender fluidity continued to have a place in their social system. The southern Utes used terms like *tuwasawits* and *tuwasawuts* to refer to male-bodied gender-fluid people. The tuwasawits and tuwasawuts appear to have enjoyed considerable social and economic mobility. In the early twentieth century, one ethnologist claimed to have known a tuwasawits who acquired considerable wealth by maintaining "a great many horses."[17]

Farther north, the place of gender-fluid people in Indigenous communities whose homelands extended from the Cascade Mountains in southeastern British Columbia to the Rockies in the western United States, showed outward signs of change. This proved the case for Kutanei-speaking communities. Like the Crow, Kutanei (or Kootenai) people belong to a language group that linguists refer to as a "language isolate," a language with no clear relationship to other languages. For centuries, Kutenai-speakers traveled with their language. From their ancestral homelands on the Great Plains, some scholars believe that they were driven toward the Rocky Mountains by Blackfoot warriors, by famine, smallpox epidemics, missionaries, greedy settlers, or a combination of all these factors.[18]

The Kutenai eventually migrated to southeastern British Columbia and parts of Idaho and Montana. Here, Kutenais established a new homeland. By the early 1800s, the Kutenai had formed close friendships with the Salish people to their west. Like the Salish, Kutenais nurtured traditions that combined elements of Plains and Plateau Indian cultures, with bison hunting supplementing the fishing and the Kutenais' close attachment to riverine ecosystems. Kutenai-speaking communities formed societies based on a bilateral kinship system in which people traced their ancestry through both male and female lines.[19] Within bilateral kin communities, people who imitated or acted like women were known as *kupatke'tek*. This word appears to have applied to male-bodied women. The Kutenai word for female-bodied men—a "manlike woman"—does not appear to have survived the assault of colonialism. Nonetheless, the kupatke'tek continued to have a place in early-nineteenth-century Kutenai society.[20]

Oral histories have kept the memory of one "manlike woman" alive. Combined with fragments of written archival documents, these oral histories provide insights into the changing place of gender-fluid people in Kutenai society. The bulk of the written and oral sources relate to the Lower Kutenai and the deeds of Ququnok Patke—"One Standing Lodge Pole Woman." Born in the 1790s, Ququnok Patke was the baby name for a Kutenai person whom non-Indigenous fur traders, missionaries, and soldiers referred to as the "Kutenai man-woman." The first written mention of the Kutenai man-woman, or "bowdash," dates to 1811. Over the ensuing decades the Kutenai man-woman made occasional appearances in written documentation. It was the Kutenai, however, who used oral traditions to keep the place of Ququnok Patke and other gender-fluid people alive in collective memory.[21]

According to oral traditions, the Kutenai man-woman grew into a "quite large and heavy boned" young person.[22] Known in her youth as a woman, the Kutenai man-woman's unusually large physical appearance made it difficult for her to secure a husband, something she reportedly tried to do.[23] This misfortune prompted Ququnok Patke to leave the Kutenai community and join a nearby group of fur traders. Around 1808, the Kutenai man-woman appeared in written documentation. Her name was spelled phonetically as Ko-come-ne-pe-ca, and she was purportedly married to a Canadian by the name of Boisverd.[24]

Ququnok Patke seems to have spent several years traveling with fur traders led by David Thompson. During that time, she formed a relationship with and married Boisverd. She separated from Thompson's fur-trading crew in 1808, only to return in 1811. Thompson recorded Ququnok Patke's return in his journal. Writing on July 28, Thompson confessed that he didn't recognize Ququnok Patke at first when he saw her standing at "my tent door." It eventually dawned on him that "in the Man I recognised the Woman who three years ago was the wife of Boisverd, a Canadian and my servant." Thompson added that "her conduct" had become "so loose that I had then requested him to send her away to her friends, but the Kootanaes were also displeased with her."[25]

Thompson did not explain what "loose conduct" entailed. Whatever it was, it proved enough for Ququnok Patke to be banished from the fur-trading crew and led to her eventual return to the Kutenai sometime in 1812. Travel and time spent among fur traders seemed to have changed Ququnok Patke. Once she returned to "her friends," she insisted that her name was Kaúxuma Núpika, Gone to the Spirits, and told fellow Kutenais that she was now a man and possessed spiritual powers.

The fragments of surviving historical evidence provide only glimpses into Kaúxuma Núpika's transition from woman to man. That evidence suggests that Kaúxuma Núpika was not welcomed back by everyone in Kutenai society. Was Kaúxuma Núpika's gender transition some sort of con? Had she, now he, gone mad? Kutenais seemed unsure; more than a few reportedly "came to fear and avoid her."[26]

Kaúxuma Núpika's behavior didn't help. Although he met and married a woman, Kaúxuma Núpika allegedly beat his new wife on a regular basis. Kaúxuma Núpika also gambled excessively. After losing one bet, Kaúxuma Núpika's wife decided she'd had enough and left her "husband." The marriage breakup precipitated another change in Kaúxuma Núpika's life. He turned his attention to becoming a warrior and started honing his hunting and warrior skills.

As Kaúxuma Núpika worked on refining his warrior skills, he continued to struggle to fit in to Kutenai society. When warriors dismounted their horses and disrobed to cross rivers, Kaúxuma Núpika waited behind. On one of these occasions, Kaúxuma Núpika's brother spotted them, naked and alone, in a river. The incident troubled Kaúxuma Núpika. Sometime after this incident, with warriors assembled, Kaúxuma Núpika announced that he'd hereafter be known as Qanqon Kamek Klaula—Sitting-in-the-Water-Grizzly.

The warriors cheered the new name, but Qanqon Kamek Klaula's brother was unimpressed. He refused to use the name, referring to Qanqon Kamek Klaula derisively as Qanqon. Thereafter, the siblings routinely argued in public, the brother reportedly unhappy with the abuse that "Qanqon" dished out to his wife.

Sibling rivalry exists in every culture, but it doesn't explain the apparent marginalization that Qanqon Kamek Klaula experienced among fellow Kutenais. Nor does the influence of non-Indigenous outsiders on Kutenai attitudes about gender fluidity provide an adequate explanation. Before Nupika's wife left him, white travelers and fur traders, regular intruders across the Great Basin and Columbia Plateau since the eighteenth century, mentioned Qanqon Kamek Klaula and his wife—two "strange Indians"—but did not claim that two women living together was uncommon. One writer even paused to comment on Qanqon Kamek Klaula's penchant for wearing leather.[27]

So why did the Kutenais seemingly shun Qanqon Kamek Klaula? Being marginalized by your community was, and remains, a painful experience for Native people. That is what Qanqon Kamek Klaula appears to have experienced during the 1820s and 1830s. The connection between gender and shamanism played a central role in that shunning. Qanqon Kamek Klaula reportedly engaged in shamanism from an early age, a masculine occupation in Kutenai society. If Kutenais looked past Qanqon Kamek Klaula's public declarations about their gender transitions and continued to view "him" as a woman, it would not matter that Qanqon Kamek Klaula wore men's clothes or lived with a wife. What mattered was that Kutenais viewed Qanqon

Kamek Klaula as female. This made Qanqon Kamek Klaula's shamanism a breach of cultural conventions, breaches compounded by their alleged disruptive behavior and regular drunkenness.

In addition to Qanqon Kamek Klaula's gender fluidity, their movement among Native communities across the Plateau and into the Plains transformed them into a person whom Native communities feared. Qanqon Kamek Klaula's prophecies magnified these fears. Some of those prophecies portended the destruction of Native communities, while other prophecies predicted that white people would expel Native people from Indian Country. Indigenous people interpreted these prophecies as signs of a person's immense spiritual power.[28] That power had creative potential; it could also be destructive. In the wrong hands, a powerful shaman could bring ruin to a community.

The Blackfeet evidently took this latter position. Perhaps fearful of Qanqon Kamek Klaula's power, Blackfeet warriors killed her. It reportedly took many shots, and numerous deep knife cuts, to end Qanqon Kamek Klaula's war cries—further evidence of their immense and dangerous powers. When Qanqon Kamek Klaula finally lay on the ground, their chest heaving as they gasped for air, a Blackfoot warrior approached. Taking his knife, he "opened up her chest to get at her heart and cut off the lower portions. This last wound she was unable to heal." Qanqon Kamek Klaula was dead, in body and spirit. However, decades later, the Blackfeet worried that Qanqon Kamek Klaula still haunted them.[29]

. . . .

Warfare had stained North America's western lands and waterways with the blood of Native people since the Spanish started invading the region in the sixteenth century. That violence continued into the latter half of the nineteenth century. Former combatants from the United States' Civil War (1861–1865)—Northerners and Southerners, whites and Blacks—joined together in an effort to clear the American West of Native communities and complete a continental empire that stretched from the Atlantic to the Pacific Ocean. This was the republic's so-called manifest destiny.[30]

This imperial vision had a problem: Indigenous people had never agreed to it. The result was bloodshed. Native resistance fighters emerged, people like the Mescalero-Chiricahua Apache leader Geronimo, who led efforts to repel the insatiable appetite of white (and Black) Americans for Apache lands. Geronimo became a symbol of Native resistance, a hero to Indigenous people and a villain in Hollywood films.

Other Native warriors—resistance fighters—are less well known. The average American knows the name Geronimo, but few have heard of Lozen and Dahteste. Lozen, a Chiricahua Apache, was born into the Chilhenne band in the 1840s. Her brother, Victorio, was a celebrated war chief. Victorio relied on his sister, reportedly saying that Lozen "is my right hand . . . strong as a man, braver than most, and cunning in strategy. Lozen is a shield to her people."[31] One early-twentieth-century anthropologist claimed that Chiricahua Apaches had a long history of incorporating women into their kinship networks who took on "masculine interests," just as the neighboring Pimas included male-bodied women known as *wik'ovat*, according to another early-twentieth-century anthropologist.[32]

If Lozen remained by Victorio's side in daily life and in war, Dahteste proved just as committed to Lozen. Born around 1860, Dahteste was a Choconen Apache. As a child, Dahteste rode with Cochise's band. Dahteste eventually married and fought alongside her husband in defense of the Apache homelands. Dahteste developed into a trusted scout and messenger, skills she honed alongside Lozen, another of her lifelong companions.[33]

The nature of Dahteste and Lozen's relationship is not clear. For decades, ethnographers likened Lozen to other "manly hearted" warrior women in the American West. Like Dahteste, Lozen was a scout and a skilled horsewoman; she also fought bravely and with great intensity, especially after she gathered other women warriors around her to avenge her brother's death in October 1880. Dahteste remained by Lozen's side during this period, but late nineteenth- and early twentieth-century ethnographers tended to discount the possibility of an intimate relationship between the two women on account of Lozen's reputed asexuality. Oral histories recorded by historians in the early twentieth century reveal how Apaches remembered Lozen being able to "ride, shoot, and fight like a man." The recollections also suggested that Lozen possessed special powers, including the ability to determine the location of a wartime enemy.[34]

Irrespective of whether Dahteste and Lozen shared an intimate relationship, they clearly enjoyed a unique bond. Following Geronimo's negotiated surrender in 1880, American troops arrested Dahteste and Lozen, loaded them on a train with other Apache prisoners of war, and sent them to Fort Marion, located in present-day St. Augustine, Florida. A photographer snapped what is now a famous image of the couple when their train stopped en route to Florida. Dahteste spent eight years imprisoned at Fort Marion. After her release she divorced her first husband and later remarried. She lived the rest of her life in quiet dignity, raising sheep on the Mescalero Reservation in south-central New Mexico. She died peacefully in 1955.

Lozen's postwar life ended tragically in June 1889. In fact, it is likely her heart broke earlier, when US troops transferred her from Fort Marion to a prison in Alabama. In Alabama, separated from Dahteste, Lozen sickened. She had contracted tuberculosis and declined rapidly. A skilled warrior and knowledgeable medicine woman, Lozen died in a lonely Alabama prison. She never saw her homeland, or her companion again.[35]

In an era when the US government funded military campaigns to relocate Indigenous communities on geographically remote reservations or to hunt down and kill Native Americans, Dahteste and Lozen's relationship embodied the trauma that American colonialism imposed on Native people. In her declining years, Dahteste had not forgotten her friend and "mourned Lozen." Their relationship was special, characterized by love and respect and a fierce determination to ensure that the Apache people could remain connected to the sacred places that anchored communal life. In working toward what the Anishinaabe writer and scholar Gerald Vizenor calls survivance, the dynamic and creative renewal of Indigenous language and culture, Dahteste and Lozen adopted fluid roles within their communities.[36] It had always been this way; Apaches had not defined themselves according to an abstract gender binary or sexual identity but by the kinship bonds and social roles that they took on to ensure the resilience—the sovereignty—of their community and one's place within that community.

. . . .

Indian Country was not, and is not, a monolithic place. For every example of someone who endured Qanqon Kamek Klaula's fate, or nurtured relationships like that shared by Dahteste and Lozen, scores of other gender-fluid people had yet other experiences. This proved true for WeWha, the Zuni lhamana who attracted momentary celebrity in American popular culture.

The Zuni world that WeWha knew grew out of its Anasazi roots. From roughly 900 CE, Pueblo cultures in the Southwest took shape at the Four Corners area of what is today Arizona, New Mexico, Colorado, and Utah.[37] Pueblo cultures proved innovative and adaptive, qualities that equipped them to meet the challenges posed by climate change and drought during the twelfth century, prepared them to meet rival warriors on the battlefield, and positioned Zunis to repel the aggressiveness of Spanish invaders—most notably during the Pueblo Revolt in 1680.[38] Through the centuries of colonial trauma and intertribal disputes, the nineteenth-century Zuni also remained connected to the outside world through an elaborate web of trading paths and diplomatic and cultural exchanges.[39]

Traveling the middle path in this interconnected world required Zuni people to remain attentive to the social, cultural, political, military, and spiritual forces around them. This was not a static world: Zuni life and culture remained dynamic. Zuni people dedicated and rededicated themselves to renewing religious beliefs and ceremonial traditions. And with cultural commitment came renewed connections to place. This was evident in the introduction of the kachina society.[40] For Zunis, kachinas, or spirit beings, interacted with people during ceremonies. The spirit beings revealed themselves through kachina masks, helping connect Zunis with the spirit world.

WeWha was born in 1849 in what is present-day New Mexico. They entered a Zuni world scarred from ravages of smallpox epidemics and the arrival of Anglo-Americans after the 1840s—outsiders who were pushy, overbearing, and often violent. On a diplomatic and military level, the Anglo-American presence compounded the pressures that Zunis and other Pueblo Indians felt from regular Apache and Diné raids, prompting an unlikely alliance between Zunis and the United States in the 1850s and 1860s.[41]

The Zuni world of WeWha's childhood was one of increasing contact with white Americans. Still, Zuni religious traditions persisted. Zunis remained connected to the kachinas, and they continued raising their children as they always had. For instance, at WeWha's birth, no mention was made of gender. That's because Zunis understood gender as something that a person grew into. Siblings between the ages of four and six didn't refer to each other as brother or sister; instead, they used the nongendered term *hanni* to refer to one another.[42]

As WeWha developed during childhood, gendered interests and the cultivation of specialized skills emerged. WeWha's biographer, Will Roscoe, notes that between the ages of four and eight, WeWha was "initiated into the *chuba:kwe kiwitsinne* or south kiva, the kiva of the husband of the midwife who assisted at his birth." WeWha's religious training began after this initiation. They learned songs, oral traditions, prayers, and kachina lore.[43]

Among the stories WeWha learned was the Zuni tale of creation. Zuni origin stories included accounts of the ancestors traveling through four underworlds and eventually emerging on the surface of the earth. Zunis used stories of earth emergence to remind people of their connection to place. They also shared migration narratives to explain how social differences reinforced the principle of reciprocity in guiding community members along the middle road to balance and harmony. This was the "Zuni way," a code of conduct that connected everything in the universe and in which all life was sacred.

The kachina traditions play a critical role in this journey. They help illuminate key episodes in Zuni creation, from the underworld, to emergence on the surface of the earth, to the development (or "cooking") of social roles and identities. Zuni religion also explained the birth of the gods, war among the gods, and the ongoing quest to find the middle road. The kachina belief system reminded nineteenth-century Zunis of their responsibilities toward one another, provided moral guidance (such as taboos against incest), and explained the spectrum of gender roles.[44]

One narrative, the story of the kachina spirit Ko'lhamana, highlights the dynamism of Zuni gender roles. In a battle between agriculture and hunter spirits, Ko'lhamana, the first of the captive kachinas, is detained by enemy spirits. While in captivity, Ko'lhamana transforms into a "man-woman," a spirit with both male and female qualities. The mixture of these gendered qualities empowered Ko'lhamana with the wisdom to mediate differences between the hunters and farmers— qualities that transcend this particular kachina tale and apply to the broader roles that lhamanas play in weaving together the social fabric of Zuni society.[45]

Zuni storytelling was not reserved solely for ceremonial occasions. Zuni architecture revealed an awareness for how to embed communities into the semiarid landscapes of the Zuni Valley, while Zunis inscribed the lessons of the kachinas on rock art and pottery, thereby contributing to a rich archive of artwork, history lessons, and moral tales.[46]

Zunis believed that rock art—known as petroglyphs—contained messages from the ancestors. The style of Zuni art developed over time, hinting at changes in messages from, and about, the ancestors.[47] The Homol'ovi rock art in the Little Colorado River Valley depicts the importance of the kachina tradition in Zuni and Hopi culture. The art dates from the period between 1250 and 1400 CE. Over seventy petroglyphs provide glimpses into the social and religious importance of the kachinas—what might be called "signs from the ancestors."[48] Zuni petroglyphs also portray the development of localized systems of knowledge that connected people to local ecosystems and tied cultural and religious traditions to the landscapes that the Zunis called home in the centuries after 900 CE.[49]

The Zuni ancestors weren't unique in working to embed their identities in the landscape. From the Timucuan people in Florida to the Chumash in California, European observers commented on the connections that Indigenous communities nurtured with a specific place. Gender-fluid people often played important roles in caring for these places and in mediating the spirit worlds associated with them. This proved especially true in caring for and burying the dead.[50] These were important roles that kept the living connected to the power of the ancestors.

Far to the north of the Zuni communities, archaeological investigations provide further tantalizing clues about the place of gender-fluid people in Native communities. The Hidatsa, for example, used the words *biatti* and *miati* to refer to people with fluid gender identities. When we combine linguistic insights with archaeological evidence, we arrive at some suggestive conclusions about gender in Hidatsa history.

The Hidatsa people lived in earthen lodges on the Northern Plains; most lodges housed between eight and twelve people. These octagon-shaped structures were supported by single-post construction along the exterior walls. In contrast, earthen lodges that included a miati housed fewer people—archaeologists estimate four or five per lodge—and were built using double-post construction along the exterior walls.

What did these differences mean? Unfortunately, the miati didn't leave us with any written words to answer this question, so we can only guess at the reasons for these distinctions. We must return to the cultural traditions and stories that the Hidatsa people passed down from one generation to the next. These clues suggest that the smaller dwellings relate to the more personalized care that a miati provided to the smaller number of residents inside their earthen lodge. The double-post construction is also suggestive, an architectural reminder of the feminine and masculine qualities possessed by the dwelling's principle occupant.[51]

In the Zuni pueblo, plaza architecture and the performance of kachina narratives reveal a similar effort to inscribe the roles of lhamanas in the built landscape. Plazas occupied a central place in the Zuni pueblo. Pathways connected the plaza to the six kivas, located on the ground floor of the pueblo, and faced out onto the plaza where religious ceremonies took place.[52] Zunis constructed plazas as a focal point of their communities. These were the locations where ceremonies occurred, including the reenactment of the kachina spirit Ko'lhamana. Ceremony reminded Zunis of the delicate balance required to walk the middle road. And on a daily basis, lhamanas contributed to the "Zuni way" by caring for the sick and elderly, weaving cloth or using their teaching skills to nurture children, roles that were similar to those performed by miati in Hidatsa communities.

. . . .

In Zuni communities, as in other Native communities across North America, gender-fluid traditions came under sustained assault in the decades after the American Civil War. Those attacks did not come from booming canons or the thunderous advance of approaching cavalry; they arrived in the form of American traders like Douglas D. Graham, eager to infiltrate markets in the pueblos. Attacks also came in the form of anthropologists and their pesky questions. Missionaries and Bureau of Indian Affairs officials also worked to understand some of the most sacred aspects of Zuni culture; ultimately, they tried to extinguish them through their implementation of assimilation policies and boarding schools.

Other non-Indigenous intruders arrived in Zuni society in the 1860s and 1870s. The Smithsonian Institution's Bureau of American Ethnology led the charge into the American West. It sponsored expeditions to "salvage" Indigenous art, archaeology, language, and culture before Western culture swept it away. Leading these efforts was Frank Hamilton Cushing, whom the Zunis remembered as a show-off. Matilda Coxe Stevenson also spent considerable time among the Zunis (she sometimes wrote under the name Tilly E. Stevenson). Although Zunis considered her arrogant, Stevenson managed to develop a relationship with WeWha and was the driving force behind WeWha's Washington tour in 1885. Stevenson hoped to use WeWha's trip east to enhance her scientific reputation. WeWha, as we will see, had an interest in visiting Washington that did not entirely align with Stevenson's aspirations.[53]

Missionaries also continued their assault on Zuni culture and religion. Presbyterian, Baptist, and Mormon missionaries made the most aggressive efforts to proselytize the Zunis. Missionaries had a knack for aggravating virtually everyone they encountered. The US military, Smithsonian ethnologists, and Indigenous people all found missionaries intrusive, judgmental, and downright irritating at times.[54]

Mary DeSette became one of the more polarizing missionary figures among the Zuni. Although she led efforts to combat the spread of smallpox among the Zunis in the 1890s, her commitment to assimilating Zunis into white American culture earned her few friends in Indian Country. DeSette dedicated her missionary career to replacing Indigenous languages with English and making "glad the waste places, and to cause the wilderness to blossom."[55] Zunis recoiled from her "brutal teaching methods" and efforts "to promote rapid and ruthless acculturation." They rejected her accusations of Zuni witchcraft, which she directed toward students who refused to heed her lessons. But what truly angered Zunis was her "sexual bigotry." She waged "war against bestiality" among the Zuni, and she launched a series of attacks on WeWha—"the beloved *lhamana*."[56] WeWha's skill as a cultural broker, a mediator of social and spiritual relationships, and a trusted caregiver to Zuni children endeared her to Zunis. WeWha's "biological sex" was well known, and of little concern, to Zunis. Only outsiders like DeSette seemed to care about WeWha's genitalia.

The Zunis didn't despise every white woman who entered their communities. Although she was ambitious, and willing to exploit Zunis to advance her ethnological career, Zuni people grew to trust Matilda Stevenson. The trust that Stevenson earned from Zunis relates to the close relationship she developed with WeWha. Stevenson met WeWha shortly after arriving at the Zuni Pueblo in 1879. She described WeWha as a "Zuni girl," and over the coming years struck up a friendship of sorts with her. Stevenson described WeWha as "perhaps the tallest person in Zuni; certainly the strongest, both mentally and physically." She added that WeWha's intellectual skills enabled her to store the "lore of her people" in her memory and to inquire after new knowledge.[57]

WeWha tested her skills as a mediator of different worlds when she accompanied Stevenson to Washington in 1885. WeWha's visit proved the talk of the town, garnering Stevenson the attention she craved. But it was the celebrity of WeWha that soared, as did the speculation about her "true" identity. WeWha's masculine features puzzled some onlookers, challenging white American stereotypes about "delicate" Indian "maidens." In the company of Matilda Stevenson, a petite white woman, WeWha's tall and masculine appearance was magnified.[58]

WeWha's visit to Washington in 1885–86 exposed the racial chauvinism of American culture. Seemingly trivial reports of WeWha's introduction to Easter eggs reminded readers of the gulf that existed between their own, superior, form of "civilization," and the exotic appearance and antiquated "superstitions" that journalists ascribed to WeWha. In Washington, the American media fetishized WeWha's every move and word.[59]

Photographs of WeWha demonstrating her weaving skills underlined this point.[60] In the capital city of an imperial, industrialized republic, pictures of WeWha operating a loom on the manicured grounds of the Smithsonian Institution reinforced the apparent gulf between white America and "authentic" Indians. Here, at the heart of American political power, sat a simple Indian, oblivious to the bustle of modernity swirling around them. Seated under a tree, cross-legged, as she performed for the Smithsonian's cameras, WeWha was frozen in time—a human artifact from an era and a culture almost forgotten.

White America's racial conceit blinded journalists and photographers to the roles that WeWha played on behalf of the Zunis in

Washington between the fall of 1885 and the spring of 1886. For WeWha, the Americans themselves were also the objects of ethnographic puzzlement—the subject of one Zuni's ethnological gaze. And what WeWha saw didn't look terribly impressive. Americans were loud and showy. And "Washington women" talk too much, WeWha complained.[61]

WeWha was not in Washington simply to study the strange behavior and foreign traditions of white Americans. WeWha was in the capital city to negotiate. Like any conscientious lhamana, WeWha had a role to play as a mediator on behalf of the Zunis. And so, WeWha sat down to talk with President Grover Cleveland.

The journalists who covered WeWha's visit to Washington couldn't resist reporting on her meeting with Cleveland. In self-congratulatory tones, newspapers ran copy declaring that WeWha "greatly admires President Cleveland" and hoped he would win a "a second term."[62] These superficial reports missed the point of WeWha's visit with the president. WeWha wanted something from Cleveland. She'd seen the problems caused by overzealous missionaries and corrupt Indian agents in Pueblo communities. Therefore, before she returned home in 1886, WeWha asked Cleveland to send an Indian agent who would protect Zuni interests. According to the *New York Herald*'s report of the meeting, WeWha "said the President looked very well and listened to all she had to say, and when she told him her people did not want a Mexican agent, but a Washington one, he said he would remember that." Whatever WeWha said to Cleveland worked; a new agent was dispatched to the Zuni, prompting WeWha reportedly to declare that "the President no lie."[63]

WeWha was more than a curiosity. She was more than an object of racial fetishization—whom Stevenson claimed became lighter skinned in Washington—and more than the labels—cross-dresser, transvestite, masculine, berdache, princess, hermaphrodite—that white Americans used to describe and sometimes denigrate her. WeWha was a much-loved and widely respected keeper of Zuni knowledge, a caregiver to children, and a skilled negotiator. WeWha was neither male nor female, but both. WeWha was a lhamana.

It is why her death was met with deep mourning in the Zuni Pueblo in 1896. Matilda Coxe Stevenson wrote that Zunis rushed to WeWha's aid when they realized she was ill. With her heart failing, family and friends did all they could to ease WeWha's suffering. Their efforts ended in sadness when she breathed her last. Zunis received the news of WeWha's death with "universal regret and distress."[64] She was loved and cherished; now she was gone.

Other lhamanas followed WeWha. They forged their own path in an increasingly hostile world. They navigated a world in which white Americans criminalized Indigenous religion and culture and expressed utter disdain for them. This was an era in which Congress wanted greater control over every aspect of Native American life, establishing the "Indian police" in 1879 and passing the Major Crimes Act in 1885 to undermine Native sovereignty by placing a slew of crimes such as larceny, arson, and murder under federal jurisdiction.[65] As the contours of the federal government's assimilation policies took shape, one thing was certain: a majority of white Americans felt nothing but contempt for Indigenous traditions and spiritual beliefs. General Hugh L. Scott spoke for many when he lampooned the "berdache," writing, "I am satisfied that the berdache is really nothing more than a degenerate and uses the 'spirit' story as an excuse for ignoble actions."[66]

Gender-fluid people in Indian Country faced heightened levels of hostility by the late nineteenth and early twentieth centuries. WeWha's brief celebrity proved an aberration. Over the coming decades, other lhamanas and gender-fluid people from different Native communities found it unsafe to be seen by white Americans. To survive, they had to keep their identities, their traditions, and their place in kinship communities private, lest white Americans try to destroy them. To effectively navigate the assimilation era—to survive—people like WeWha went underground.[67] For some, that meant experiencing the emotional pain of being marginalized from kin. For others, it meant a loss of knowledge that would take decades to reclaim. As the twentieth century dawned, the path into the future was paved with uncertainty.

CHAPTER 8

PATHS

A young man came into my organization back in 1988 or 1989
and he said to me, "Melvin, I just want to be myself today. Can I
dress up here? Can I put on my makeup? Can I put on my dress?"

I said, "Sure."

— MELVIN HARRISON (Navajo Nation)[1]

Cheyenne people, we call God Maheo. Maheo means "I don't
know," because we don't know what it is but it's everything.

— MARLON "MARTY" FIXICO (Southern Cheyenne)[2]

BUZZARDS CIRCLED OVERHEAD. It was 1895, and something, or someone, had died. Hivsu Tupoma and several other Mohave Indians decided to go take a look. They left the little town of Needles, located on the California-Arizona border, and scouted along the Colorado River. The small search party wasn't out long when they stumbled across a body. It was human, partly decomposed, and surrounded by greedy buzzards eager to continue their feast.[3]

Hivsu Tupoma and his fellow Mohaves shooed the buzzards away. They examined the body; lifeless and badly disfigured, the corpse had clearly been exposed to the elements for some time, perhaps two weeks or more. Still, a quick examination revealed to Hivsu Tupoma whose remains lay before him: Sahaykwisa.

Sahaykwisa, or Masahai Amatkwisai, was a *hwame*, a female-bodied person who lived much of their life as a male. Sahaykwisa was a healer, specializing in the treatment of venereal diseases. When Sahaykwisa died in 1895 they were in their mid-forties and displayed no obvious health problems. So how did Sahaykwisa's partly decomposed body end up on a remote riverbank? How did they die? Answering these questions tells us a lot about the changes that a number of Indigenous communities went through during the latter half of the nineteenth century and the beginning of the twentieth. Those changes, the product of centuries of colonial intrusion, sometimes had deadly consequences.

Getting to the bottom of Sahaykwisa's death also exposes the interpretive limits of the white authors who wrote about hwames and other Native people who failed to conform to Western ideals of supposedly normal gender identities and sexual practices. With rare exceptions, these writers were men. The vast majority were anthropologists, although some were also psychiatrists, physicians, or Indian agents employed by the federal government. What they wrote was often offensive, dismissive, wrong. Their writings echoed centuries of colonial writing in its emphasis on "the warm friendship" that some men formed with each other and the "infatuation" that descended into "sexual perversion."[4] Those accounts shaped popular and academic discourses for the next century or more, shrouding the gender and sexual traditions of the Mohave and scores of other Native communities in mystery and misinformation.

White Americans viewed people like Sahaykwisa with a mixture of moral disdain and pity. Sahaykwisa was seen as an exotic remnant of a bygone era, out of step with the modern world encircling them. Other exotic anomalies existed. Ohchiish, a male-bodied Crow, or a baté, who performed the cultural roles of women, and Hosteen Klah, a nadleeh, which means "one who changes," was male-bodied, took on feminine roles, and became an accomplished Diné artist and medicine person. These were just two other gender-fluid people who captured the attention of anthropologists and a voyeuristic American public during the late nineteenth and early twentieth centuries.[5]

Anthropologists referred to other gender-fluid individuals as members of the "berdache cult."[6] The word "cult" is revealing. Derived from the Latin word *cultus*, meaning to worship, "to break ground," or cultivate, by the nineteenth century it was used pejoratively, usually in relation to religious beliefs. By the end of the nineteenth century, the newly professionalized field of anthropology picked up the word and used it to refer to "decadent" practices and "ancient" or "primitive" beliefs, especially among Indigenous people.[7]

"Cult" became a slur. Settlers used it to denigrate Indigenous cultures, to dismiss their religious beliefs and ceremonies as dangerous myths. Settlers spoke about Native America with unearned certainty, even more certainty than Native people spoke about themselves and their beliefs. The growing fixation of anthropologists with cross-dressing further underscores this point. For example, white scholars made much of the cross-dressing of a Tolowa spiritual leader, Old Doctor. To Tolowas, Old Doctor's clothing mattered less than the role the leader played in society.[8]

The scholars, physicians, and psychiatrists of this era were supremely arrogant in their thinking and essentialist in their writings. Late nineteenth- and early twentieth-century scholars wrote about people like Sahaykwisa and Ohchiish as "abnormal."[9] Today, we should read these sources with extreme caution. Anthropology and medical research has come a long way since the early 1900s.[10] The methodological diversity of anthropology, from social and physical methods to linguistic and cultural anthropology, and the growing numbers of Indigenous researchers have slowly altered the tenor and ethical practices of social scientific and scientific research. However, combing through the pages of old anthropology and medical journals is in part an exercise in disentangling an author's prejudices from observational narrative. Too often, those lines blur. Native people knew this then, just as they recognize it now. That's why Indigenous people sometimes went out of their way to avoid nosy anthropologists and intrusive federal government employees.

. . . .

Having to keep a secret can cause ongoing mental and physical pain. But some secrets were (and are) worth keeping. That's especially true when those secrets contain knowledge of a community's traditions, language, and culture that outsiders recast, misrepresent, belittle. For gender-fluid Native Americans, it meant taking different paths to protect sacred knowledge. It meant persisting on a path, especially if white Americans wanted to destroy it.

The Mohave lived in the Southwest of what is today the United States. They nurtured a culture in which gender fluidity was part of daily life. Other Native communities, like the Chiricahua Apaches and Zunis (see chapter 7), also incorporated gender-fluid people into their kinship networks. To the north and east of the Mohave, the Hopi and Diné referred to gender-fluid people as ho'va and nadleeh, respectively. The nadleeh played prominent roles in Diné origin narratives as the first children possessing both male and female spirits; with their industriousness they protected Diné drinking water, built dwellings, and prepared food for the community.[11] The ho'va occupied similarly dynamic gender roles among the neighboring Hopi. But most anthropologists did not see gender fluidity as a virtue. One anthropologist wrote of the Hopi in the 1930s that *ho'va* meant a "hermaphrodite"—a word used in Western culture to indicate abnormality.[12]

During the late nineteenth and early twentieth century, archaeologists joined anthropologists in conducting fieldwork. Small armies of archaeologists fanned out across the United States to collect material fragments of Indian culture. They felt that they were salvaging evidence that was destined to disappear. Like anthropologists, archaeologists focused most of their attention on the western United States. With trowels, shovels, and pickaxes in hand, archaeologists raced toward the mesas and buttes in a desperate search to uncover and preserve as many Native artifacts as they could. Most felt they were in a race against time, as settler communities built over Indigenous homelands and dams flooded ancient ceremonial sites—which was construed as progress. Unfortunately, the practices that archaeologists used to collect, preserve, and write about Native traditions and material artifacts included theft, coercion, and subterfuge. Scholarly practices fell far short of ethical standards of behavior. By the early twentieth century, little had changed. Indigenous people felt justifiably suspicious of these outsiders.[13]

Scholars assumed that the Mohave had remained largely untouched by Western civilization. Consequently, anthropologists, like their archaeology colleagues, viewed the Mohave people as ideal subjects for fieldwork—a unique opportunity to study an authentic Indigenous culture.[14] They couldn't have been more wrong. The Mohave (also spelled Mojave) had experienced a buffeting from European and Indigenous outsiders for several centuries. By the early nineteenth century, the Yuman-speaking Mohaves had managed to renew their communities on both sides of the Lower Colorado River. Numbering between two thousand and three thousand, they shared the desert terrain with Yavapi, Yuma, and other smaller communities to their south and the Walapai, Havasupai, and Paiutes to their north.[15]

The Mohave had not remained outside of human history, untouched and unaffected by the forces of social change, as archaeologists and anthropologists assumed. Their long history of encounters with Europeans proved that. The Spanish, who invaded the Southwest in the centuries before 1800, referred to the Mohave as the *hamakhava*, a mistranslation of the Yuman word *aha'macave*. Late-nineteenth- and early-twentieth-century anthropologists guessed that this word meant "mountain peaks," although there remains uncertainty about this.[16] Today, Mohaves refer to themselves as Pipa Aha Macav, People of the River, a term that reflects the centrality of the Colorado River in Mohave life.[17]

Sahaykwisa entered a Mohave world convulsed by histories of colonial violence and social change. Settler encroachments on Mohave lands had altered the tribe's settled way of life, farming practices, and cultural traditions. Historical interactions with people of European descent, who had been propelled across the landscape by colonial structures of economy, law, and warfare, caused Mohave people intergenerational traumas that reshaped their world. Few events proved as traumatic as the US military's relocation of the Mohave to a reservation in the 1850s. Sahaykwisa lived through that relocation, which also included Chemeheuvi, Hopi, and Diné people. Native people undoubtedly swapped stories about entire villages being relocated and forced to begin life anew on the Colorado River Indian Tribes Reservation or, like Sahaykwisa, struggling to renew communities at the Fort Mojave Reservation in what is now northern Arizona.

Sahaykwisa was born around 1850. Like other Mohave people, Sahaykwisa worked to preserve oral histories and renew traditions through song, dance, and art. By the early twentieth century, professional anthropologists traveled to the Mohave reservations hoping to observe these ceremonies and record the people's origin stories. That anthropologists viewed Mohave knowledge as mere fables with no practical or scientific relationship to the modern world reveals a great deal about the assumptions that these scholars brought to their work.[18]

George Devereux was one of those scholars. Born György Dobó on September 13, 1908, in Hungary, he changed his name in 1932 after converting from Judaism to Catholicism, and first came to the United States in 1933. During the 1930s Devereux came under the influence of the University of California, Berkeley, anthropologist Alfred Kroeber. Under Kroeber's tutelage, Devereux began spending considerable time among the Mohave people.[19]

Devereux's fieldwork informed his theory of ethnopsychoanalysis, a marriage of ethnographic observations with the rapidly expanding fields of psychiatry and psychoanalysis. For Devereux, this approach meant being conscious of his own relationship to the people he studied. It also meant searching for ways to deepen his insights about a given cultural group by applying Sigmund Freud's theory of transference, or the idea that a patient's feelings about their parents are transferred to a present situation. Devereux also drew on the theory of countertransference, whereby a therapist redirects their feelings on to their client.[20] Devereux brought these psychoanalytical insights to his research on Mohave culture, insights he derived largely from his Mohave informant, Nahwera.

This combination of Western theorizing and reliance on a single "informant" is evident in his lengthy summary of the Mohave origin story of Avi-kwame.[21] "Ever since the world began at the magic mountain Avi-kwame," Devereux wrote in 1937, "it was said there would be transvestites." Devereux understood "transvestites" to be people who presented themselves to the world, and took on social roles, that were different from their "true sex." Although this understanding of gender relied on Western culture's male-female binary, Devereux acknowledged that Mohaves believed that the people he labeled transvestites were formed in the mother's womb, their destiny set before birth.

That did not mean that transvestites, to use Devereux's terminology, were welcome in Mohave society. Devereux claimed that their "strange behavior" marked them as different, abnormal. *Hwames*, female-bodied people who identified as male, were viewed by Mohaves in the same light as "lewd women," Devereux claimed. In contrast, Devereux defined an *alyha* as a male transvestite, a male-bodied person who took on the appearance and assumed the roles customarily associated with women.

Devereux also wrote about the hwame and alyha as "types of homosexuals." The alyha, he explained, took on "the role of the woman in sexual intercourse." He added that the sexual proclivities of alyhas was not "normal," they were "unhappy," and their family members generally considered them "crazy."

The drama of Sahaykwisa's story proved compelling to Devereux. From his early twentieth-century vantage point, Devereux reached back in time to present readers with a sad and sordid tale. In Devereux's retelling, Sahaykwisa seduced pregnant women, engaged in prostitution with white men to keep their many wives in comfort, and practiced witchcraft on former lovers to enable Sahaykwisa to have sexual intercourse with their ghosts.[22]

Sahaykwisa's skill as a witch, and their ability to heal venereal diseases, meant that many Mohaves reportedly viewed Sahaykwisa "to be lucky in love." But in private, Sahaykwisa was scorned. Mohaves ridiculed Sahaykwisa, referring to them derisively as "split vulvae." One Mohave, Haqau, took these insults to terrifying levels.

According to Devereux's informant, Haqau's wife left him to become Sahaykwisa's third wife, but the marriage didn't last. The woman wanted to reunite with Haqau, who gave the matter considerable thought because "she had lowered herself by becoming the wife of a transvestite." Haqau and the woman resolved their differences and they resumed married life. But Haqau held a grudge. Still seething from Sahaykwisa's seducing his wife away from him, Haqau never missed an opportunity to mock Sahaykwisa and accuse them of witchcraft.

Haqau's friends urged him not to antagonize Sahaykwisa out of fear they would bewitch him. Haqau was undeterred. "Let her come," he reportedly snapped, "I will show her what a real penis can do." He did. Haqau lay in wait in "the bushes" in order to ambush Sahaykwisa. As they approached, Haqau attacked and raped them.

The assault changed Sahaykwisa's life. According to Devereux's account, Sahaykwisa never married again and was only able to have "intercourse with ghosts" of women they had bewitched prior to the rape. Sahaykwisa turned to alcohol, "became a drunk," and started "craving men." An elderly man, Tcuhum, attracted Sahaykwisa's attention. Tcuhum reportedly refused to have sex with them, prompting Sahaykwisa to pursue other sexual partners while also attempting to bewitch Tcuhum. And then, in 1895, Sahaykwisa disappeared.

Devereux filtered Sahaykwisa's disappearance through multiple generations of Mohave oral history and his own theoretical frameworks. He described his primary informant, Nahwera, as "senile and toothless," bringing into question the accuracy of the elder's recollections.[23] More problematic was Devereux's reliance on Freudian psychological theory to understand Mohave culture. Devereux emphasized human genitalia and sexual acts as primary drivers of Sahaykwisa's behavior and untimely demise.[24] He also assumed that sex—be it fellatio, anal or vaginal penetration, or masturbation—constituted the core expressions of an individual's identity. In all of these respects, Devereux imposed his Freudian framework on to Mohave culture, thereby muting the historically contingent and culturally specific reasons for Mohave behavior.

Like other Indigenous communities in the Southwest, the Mohave enjoyed healthy sex lives and worked hard to renew cultural traditions. During Spanish and Mexican colonial intrusions into the region, the Mohave remained free of intrusive missionaries and grasping settlers. Sexual enjoyment was part of Mohave life, but it also remained tied to a constellation of other daily practices and traditions that needed balancing to ensure that the social and cultural needs of community were met. Mohaves may have perceived Sahaykwisa's actions as causing an imbalance in social and cultural life, but Devereux's singular focus on the "peculiar aspects" of Mohave ceremony, his use of the terms "homosexual" and "transvestite"—both relatively new in Western culture and foreign to Mohave people—and his insistence that in utero impressions led to mental illness, specifically schizophrenia, had consequences that reverberated well into the twentieth century.[25] Devereux's assertions obscured communal kinship identities among the Mohave and contributed to the pathologizing of gender-fluid identities throughout Indian Country by anthropologists and psychologists.[26]

Devereux's fieldwork paints a picture of Mohave people ridiculing those he labeled homosexuals and transvestites. Missing from his portrait of Mohave life is a deeper appreciation of how historical forces reshaped Mohave culture. US military incursions into the Southwest and the federal government's confinement of Mohaves on reservations traumatized multiple generations of Mohave people. So, too, did the oppressive assimilation policies enacted by the US government. All of these factors altered how Mohaves interacted with outsiders like Devereux. A slew of laws—the federal government's establishment of the Courts of Indian Offenses; the Major Crimes Act (1885); the General Allotment Act (1887); General Allotment Act amendments

(1891); the Curtis Act (1898); and the Burke Act (1906)—buttressed an intrusive bureaucratic infrastructure that maintained a sustained assault on every facet of Native American life.[27] Reluctantly, Indigenous communities adapted to these and other external forces. They had to if they wanted to survive.

People like Sahaykwisa did experience persecution, both in Indian Country and in the broader colonial culture. But Native people were not fools; they knew how to tell a good story, how to tell nosy anthropologists and government officials one version of a story while keeping other details private. Sahaykwisa's fate was tied up in these worlds of continuity and change, myth and reality, self-preservation and political expediency.

. . . .

Native Americans told white people stories about witchcraft and deviant sexual behavior while concealing the deeper meaning of spiritual traditions and folklore. Anthropologists and folklorists tried to decipher those hidden meanings. They collected scores of folktales from different racial and ethnic communities during the late nineteenth and early twentieth centuries. Native American folktales proved particularly interesting to scholars and the general reading public. Indigenous stories ranged from the comical to the prophetic. They included a metaphorical tale about a creature with a "drill-shaped penis," the Gros Ventre story about the "talking penis," or, in the case of the Crow, tales of the trickster.[28]

One of the more famous folktales of the 1890s and early 1900s was the Crow story of Old Man Coyote. The story goes something like this: Old Man Coyote saw a "group of good-looking girls picking wild strawberries" and decided to conceal himself. As the girls approached, Old Man Coyote hid in the strawberry patch, with just the "tip of his penis" protruding from the ground. When the girls arrived, they began collecting strawberries. Thinking the tip of Old Man Coyote's penis was a large strawberry, the girls "pulled at" the tip of the penis multiple times until one exclaimed that the strange strawberry has "milk in it."[29]

The story of Old Man Coyote is a trickster tale of coercion and misogyny. While the salaciousness of the story attracted folklorists, it was by no means emblematic of the robust culture of gender fluidity and sexual expression among the Crow. In Crow culture, people with fluid gender identities—"not man, not woman"—were referred to as baté. The baté remained part of Crow kinship communities during the late nineteenth and early twentieth centuries. The Crow, a Siouan-speaking people, did not see these people as "hermaphrodites," "transvestites," or purveyors of "sexual perversion." Instead, batés played important roles in maintaining the cohesion of society.[30] Crows knew batés as charitable people who were "highly regarded." Female-bodied men in Crow society took on leadership roles as diplomats and war chiefs, while male-bodied females wore clothing identified with women.[31]

The unrelenting expansion of American settler colonialism, the frontier wars of the late nineteenth century, and the destructiveness of assimilation policies in the early twentieth meant that Crows tried to shield batés from the prying eyes of outsiders.[32] Given the trauma experienced by tribal communities shunted onto windswept reservations in what became Oklahoma and across the Plains in the decades between the 1850s and World War II, it is not surprising that the Crow and other Native communities turned inward in an effort to preserve their culture. Those who did tell stories about Indian Country focused on issues like poverty, blood-quantum, and oil barons.

Rollie Lynn Riggs, a gay Cherokee playwright, wrote about these issues. Riggs, who was born in 1899, is most famous for his play *Green Grow the Lilacs*, which became the hit musical *Oklahoma!* In another of his plays, *The Cherokee Night*, Riggs tells a modernist story about early-twentieth-century Cherokee society. Riggs's play addresses poverty, mixed-race identity, and murder. Like so many Native writers and storytellers of his era, Riggs did not explore gender fluidity and sexual variance—dangerous topics given the homophobia of early-twentieth-century America—and instead wrote movingly about poverty, the allotment of Indigenous lands, and the importance of social change.[33]

The avoidance of these topics in literature by Native Americans does not mean that people with gender-fluid identities didn't still make contributions to their communities. They did, but those contributions were coded, as Riggs's body of work reveals.[34] According to the Cherokee writer and scholar Daniel Heath Justice, Riggs "furtively explored what it was to be a mixed-blood Indian and a gay man in a society that had no use for either."[35]

People with gender-fluid identities still found nurturing spaces within their respective tribal communities. One of the most celebrated batés in Crow society between the 1850s and World War II was Ohchikapdaapesh, Finds-Them-and-Kills-Them. Born in 1854, the child was known by the abbreviated Ohchiish. In childhood, Ohchiish showed an interest in work that women usually performed. They also began dressing in female clothing at a young age.[36]

Although Ohchiish was often described as "the only berdache left," they were no outsider in Crow society.[37] Ohchiish was part of Crow kinship society. During Ohchiish's lifetime, Crow kinship revolved around extended family networks and ceremonies. Members of kinship groups bound people together culturally and spiritually through traditions like the Sun Dance and sweat lodges.

Central to Crow identity, however, was the clan system, which was (and remains) matrilineal in nature. Historically, Crows organized society around thirteen clans (today eight clans remain active). The Crow clan, or lodge, system, also bore a number of similarities to that of the Hopi and Iroquois, with an individual's affiliation to a clan traced along matrilineal lines. Clan membership was central to identity, determining marriage practices, inheritance, and communal ownership of property and defining responsibilities to other clan members. An ethos of cooperation characterized clan membership. For example, all of the male members of a matrilineal clan addressed each other as "brother." When a man married and had children, those children belonged to the clan of his wife, while the husband's childcare responsibilities focused on the children of his sister (or sisters).

As a baté, "half man, half woman," Ohchiish occupied a special place in the Crow kinship system. Ohchiish moved freely around Crow society and participated in Crow ceremonies. Fellow Crows also addressed Ohchiish as "my sister," a standard kinship term for a Crow woman.[38] According to Pretty Shield, an early-twentieth-century Crow medicine woman, Ohchiish "looked like a man, and yet she wore woman's clothing; and she had the heart of a woman." Pretty Shield added that Ohchiish "was not as strong as a man, and yet she was wiser than a woman."[39]

Ohchiish might have lacked the physical strength of most men, but that did not prevent them from being a skilled warrior. Indeed, Ohchiish wasn't the first gender-fluid Native warrior to go into battle. The Pend d'Oreille woman, Kuilix, earned fame among settlers as a skilled warrior. Sometimes referred to in written documents as a "female berdache," Kuilix distinguished herself in battle, especially against Crow enemies. Missionaries marveled at women like Kuilix, reporting that they participated in war dances, wore the clothing of a warrior, and demonstrated as much skill as male warriors in battle.[40]

Ohchiish displayed all of these qualities, and more. In 1876, Ohchiish joined Shoshone warriors and fellow Crows in working as scouts for General George Crook and the United States Cavalry in their pursuit of Sitting Bull and the Sioux and Cheyenne warriors. For the Crow and Shoshone, aligning with Crook constituted an opportunity to strike a blow against their traditional enemies—the Sioux and Cheyenne.[41]

But who was George Crook, the general whom the Crow and Shoshone partnered with? Crook was born in Ohio in 1828. Standing five feet eight inches, Crook possessed piercing, intense, eyes, and overgrown mutton chops. A decorated soldier, Crook served in the Union Army during the American Civil War and saw action in the Pacific Northwest and Arizona during the late 1860s and early 1870s. Crook became one of the most notorious Indian fighters of the late nineteenth century, but he almost met a sudden, bloody, end at Rosebud Creek in the Montana Territory.[42] On June 17, 1876, after a long day's marching, Crook bivouacked along the creek. Crook's soldiers, exhausted and hungry, set up camp and settled in for an evening of relaxation. But Crow and Shoshone scouts felt uneasy. They worried that Sioux and Cheyenne warriors were massing and preparing an attack.[43]

They were right. As Crook sat playing a game of cards, one of the Indian scouts ran into camp warning of a Lakota Sioux attack. The Battle of the Rosebud had begun. Less than two weeks before General George Armstrong Custer led his men to death and defeat at the Battle of Greasy Grass—what Americans called the Battle of the Little Big Horn—Crook's decision to set a grueling schedule of daily marches through enemy territory imperiled his troops and Native allies.[44]

The Crow and Cheyenne engaged the advancing Sioux and Cheyenne warriors, giving the US cavalry time to gather their weapons and respond to the attack. In the fog of war, Ohchiish remained clear-eyed, repelled a rapidly advancing enemy, and saved General Crook from certain death. Ohchiish also saved the life of a warrior named Bull-snake, who fell from his horse after being badly wounded. Believing that Bull-snake was at risk of being scalped by Lakota warriors, Ohchiish skillfully shot at and repelled the advancing warriors. The-Other-Magpie, another baté warrior, came to Ohchiish's aid, riding around the Lakota "singing her war-song and waving her coup-stick, the only weapons she had." Bull-Snake, like Crook, survived the Battle of Rosebud because of the bravery and skill of Ohchiish and The-Other-Magpie.[45]

In the weeks and months after Crook's near demise, Ohchiish, The-Other-Magpie, and other Crow scouts returned home. In the United States, reports of the Battle of the Rosebud filled American newspapers with accounts of "hostile Sioux" killing and scalping American soldiers.[46] Crook's brush with death on the banks of the Rosebud also led to political recriminations. President Ulysses S. Grant's "ridiculous and pretentious 'peace policy'" attracted growing choruses of criticism, as did the "agents of the Indian bureau" for allegedly supplying Sioux warriors with firearms.[47] These criticisms placed pressure on lawmakers to reform Indian policy—pressures that ultimately led to a federal government push to dissolve tribal governments and allot land to Native people on an individual basis.

Although they were often the targets of public criticism, Indian agents proved critical to the success or failure of the federal government's assimilation policy during the late nineteenth and early twentieth century. On the Crow Indian Reservation, E. P. Briscoe was the government's man. In the 1880s, Briscoe launched a campaign of terror against batés residing on the Crow reservation. Briscoe never enjoyed a good reputation among the Crow. His authoritarian military style and overbearing personality routinely upset Crow people.

Briscoe had cut his political teeth in Mississippi during the bloody years of Reconstruction. In the 1870s he attracted the attention of journalists who reported on his frequent outbursts against carpetbaggers and independent politicians who courted "Negro" voters. One of the politicians Briscoe targeted for appealing to the "prejudices" of Black voters was H. M. Dixon. In 1879, political attacks on Dixon's efforts to build an interracial coalition descended into violence: he fell victim to a political assassination in Yazoo County, Mississippi, which put the Magnolia State on a path toward white supremacist government and Jim Crow segregation.[48]

Briscoe brought the racism and misogyny of post–Civil War Mississippi to his work on the Crow reservation, in Montana. In 1888, a year after Congress passed the Dawes Act—legislation that took Native American lands that tribes owned in common and allotted parcels of land to individuals on the basis of "blood quantum," or the degree of Indigenous ancestry one could prove to government officials—Briscoe urged Congress to reduce the size of individual land allotments available to eligible Crows. Briscoe argued that the Crows' "scattered" farming methods and large "districts" meant the "allotment of land to each Indian is too large." He insisted that "the Crow Indian will never use 40 acres for agriculture, yet he is given 160 acres, with an additional 80 for each child."[49]

Briscoe also voiced his trenchant opposition to interracial marriage. He castigated other Indian agents for allowing Indigenous women to marry white men. In 1889, Briscoe removed four white men from the Crow reservation after he discovered them living with Crow women. Like most white Americans during this time, Briscoe despised miscegenation; he had nothing but contempt for the white men who engaged in racially mixed unions, referring to them derisively as "squaw men."[50]

More even than squaw men, people like Ohchiish really got under Briscoe's skin. Ohchiish stood about five feet seven inches. Stout in frame, Ohchiish wore women's clothing and lived with a Crow man. During the 1880s, the Crow continued to embrace Ohchiish as an important member of their kinship society and celebrated them as a war hero. This infuriated Briscoe. He set out to break Ohchiish.[51]

Crow oral history details Briscoe's obsession with Ohchiish. According to Joe Medicine Crow, the tribal historian, federal officials persecuted all Crow batés: "The agent incarcerated the batés, cut off their hair, made them wear men's clothing. He forced them to do manual labor, planting these trees that you see here on the BIA [Bureau of Indian Affairs] grounds. The people were so upset with this that Chief Pretty Eagle came into Crow Agency, and told [the agent] to leave the reservation."[52]

Briscoe did eventually leave, but not before repeated warnings from Crows to "change your ways and be nice to people like Ohchiish."[53] Unfortunately, Briscoe's departure did not end Ohchiish's torment.[54] During the first years of the 1900s, the Baptist minister W. A. Petzoldt began a decades-long campaign of harassment against Ohchiish. According to the Crow medicine man, Yellowtail, white men like Petzoldt "tried to take the real meaning of the Indian religion away from us because they condemned everything that the Indian did." Ohchiish endured Petzoldt's harassment for the rest of their life.[55]

The Indian agent Evan W. Estep also terrorized Ohchiish. The Crows knew Estep as "a hot-tempered fellow." He began his role as Indian agent at the Crow reservation in 1914. During his three years in the post, Estep never missed an opportunity to continue the decades-long persecution of Ohchiish. What motivated this persecution? Estep's own words suggest a combination of homophobia and anti-Indian racism fueled his harassment of Ohchiish. According to Estep, Ohchiish was not normal.

The Crow people objected to attacks on batés. Crows considered Ohchiish a "good-natured person" who enjoyed participating in ceremonial dances and moved freely around Crow society. As a show of support, Plenty Coups visited Ohchiish to offer support and to tell them to "just keep that way—dress like a woman."[56]

For all of the abuse that outsiders heaped on Ohchiish, Crows remained steadfast in their support. In Crow society, Ohchiish wasn't a "him" or "her"; Ohchiish was "just a person." Ohchiish remained a valued, cherished member of Crow society.

. . . .

Across the western Plains, other Siouan-speaking peoples strove to hold on to their traditions while renewing cultures that would help them meet the challenges posed by settler-colonial policies. The Crows longtime enemies, the Lakota, used the Siouan word *winkte* (a contraction of *winyanktehca*) to refer to gender-fluid people. The Dakota used the word *winkta* to indicate gender fluidity.[57] The Oglala Sioux viewed winktes as gifted, sacred, special. A winkte's spiritual gifts meant that other Oglalas both respected and feared the winkte.

Few reports of Siouan-speaking people ridiculing winktes survive from the period between the 1880s and the Great Depression of the 1930s.[58] That changed as the twentieth century unfolded. Western terminology crept into Oglala life as tribal members started to refer to winktes as hermaphrodites and ridiculed homosexual sex acts. Hearing about these attitudes in tribal communities, academics began subscribing to the idea that winktes "were considered to be very unfortunate."[59] As the midpoint of the twentieth century approached, colonialism was taking a toll on Native communities, testing the resilience of Indigenous culture while also stepping up attacks on Indigenous sovereignty.

In 1977, an eighty-three-year-old Oglala elder echoed this perspective. Reflecting back on the twentieth century, his testimony revealed the degree to which homophobia had filtered into Indian Country. He referred to winktes as "all freaks of some kind." The elder alluded to assimilationist laws when he claimed that winktes were prevented from making "a show" and "Indians have a lot of fun over *winkte*."[60]

A folktale collected from Omaha tribal members reveals how homophobia spread rapidly across the Plains, including in Native communities. Like the Oglala, the Omaha are a Siouan-speaking people. During the late nineteenth and early twentieth centuries anthropologists recorded words like *minquagq*, translated as hermaphrodite, to designate gender diversity among the Omaha. By the early 1900s, that diversity was not celebrated.[61] The Omaha folktale of Iktinike and Rabbit highlights this point. The story begins with Iktinike and Rabbit chasing women. They were always looking for women to have sex with, but one day they decided to try something different.[62]

"Friend," Iktinike said to Rabbit, "bend over. Let me get on top of you. Let's do it the *winkte* way." Rabbit was reluctant to "bend over." Rabbit didn't want to be "the passive."

"You bend over," Rabbit countered, "and I get on top of you."

Iktinike, who was older than Rabbit, asserted his pederastic right to "go first."

"Respect your elders," insisted Iktinike.

Rabbit demurred. He declared that "youth must be served. It is the younger who always goes first."

Iktinike and Rabbit continued arguing until they came to an agreement. Rabbit "went first."

"All right, get on top of me."

Rabbit mounted Iktinike but Iktinike protested "it hurts. Your *che* is very big."

Rabbit was having none of this. He refused to stop thrusting his erect penis into Iktinike's anus and insisted that Iktinike's "*onze* is too tight."

Rabbit took a few seconds to finish with Iktinike and immediately ran off—"Rabbit is very quick at that kind of thing." Annoyed, Iktinike chased after Rabbit insisting that it was "my turn now." Rabbit refused. Instead he raced around telling everyone that he "mounted" Iktinike.

As word spread of Rabbit's exploits, Iktinike became angrier. He decided to give up trying to find Rabbit and return home. As he set off for home he stopped to urinate, only to find that "baby rabbits popped out of his *onze*." Iktinike wasn't happy: "This is really too much," an exasperated Iktinike screamed. But Iktinike's travails weren't over yet. As he trudged into his home, Iktinike's wife greeted him in an "amorous mood." Iktinike rebuffed his wife's advances, insisting, "I've got a headache."

The story of Iktinike and Rabbit is a braggadocious tale, a licentious narrative of sexual subterfuge and manipulation. But above all it is a folktale punctuated by misogyny, bullying behavior, and sexual mockery. The story of Iktinike and Rabbit is a touchstone for the homophobia that settlers introduced into Indian Country and that spread like a virus through one Native town and village after another during the twentieth century.[63]

. . . .

Assimilationist policies devastated scores of Native communities and traumatized generations of people. Ohchiish's resilience helped them navigate this traumatic era. Indian agents terrorized Ohchiish, forcing them to perform manual labor usually associated with men, like planting trees. Just before Ohchiish's death in 1929, an anthropologist asked why they wore women's clothing, continued doing beadwork, and decorated Iron Bull's lodge. Ohchiish answered simply, "That is my road."[64]

Ohchiish was not the last baté, but the roads taken by future batés proved to be labyrinths filled with prejudice. During the twentieth century, batés navigated a world altered by assimilation policies, re-strictive laws, the theft of land, the pollution of rivers, the breaking of treaties, and rising levels of homophobia from white, Black, and Native Americans. Anthropologists and archaeologists pretended to help, but their jargon, their insensible categories, and their arrogance made things worse. Anthropologists coined categories, endless cate-gories—"halfmen-halfwomen," "transvestites," "berdaches," "homo-sexuals," "hermaphrodites," "sexual inversion," and "intermediate" types.[65] By the mid-twentieth century, there were so many categories that meant so little to the people they claimed to describe.

Unlike Ohchiish, Sahaykwisa's path ended violently. Sahaykwisa's behavior may have antagonized other members of their community, but feelings of hostility toward Sahaykwisa were undoubtedly mag-nified by the homophobia that crept into Indigenous homes and com-munities across North America. The settler-colonial world couldn't be avoided, and for some tribal leaders, survival meant embracing the colonizers' prejudices.

But settler colonialism has never had a complete hold over In-dian Country. Traditions survived, ceremonies were reinvented, and identities renewed. In Native America, being wise enough to say "I don't know" became a way to protect tribal cultures. This remains true. Marlon "Marty" Fixico, a Southern Cheyenne Two-Spirit elder captured the essence of this wisdom when he told me that "Cheyenne people, we call God 'Maheo.' Maheo means 'I don't know,' because we don't know what it is but it's everything."

It is a beautiful sentiment. It's an ethos that protects knowledge and makes room for the possible. For hundreds of Indigenous com-munities throughout North America, protecting knowledge and tra-dition means maintaining a space for people whose gender and sexual identities were considered sacred, fluid, special. This is an ethos that endures, a worldview reawakened during the latter half of the twen-tieth century and that made it possible for an LGBTQ2S person "to be myself."

PART 3

. . . .

RECLAIMING

CHAPTER 9

REAWAKENING

A lot of Native practices went underground, severely went underground, and were not spoken of too much.

— CLYDE HALL (Shoshone-Bannock)[1]

The umbrella term has been a way to gather community, but when you get into the views and traditions that the different tribes have, and even get into languages, you find that each tribe has its own set of cultures and traditions and terms.

— REBECCA NAGLE (Cherokee Nation)[2]

BARBARA CAMERON'S GRANDPARENTS knew she was a "special person." Cameron was born on May 22, 1954, at Fort Yates, North Dakota. The eldest of eight children, she grew up in a bilingual world, speaking Lakota and English, on the Standing Rock Sioux Reservation. On lands that once formed part of the Great Sioux Reservation, Cameron's grandparents played a pivotal role in nurturing their "special" granddaughter.[3]

Reservation life was difficult in Cold War America.[4] Barbara Cameron described it as "grim." And yet Cameron's parents and grandparents worked hard to eke out a livelihood as cattle ranchers to ensure the children in their extended family received the best possible start in life. During her formative years, Cameron excelled in the classroom but struggled with suicidal ideation. She dealt with her mental demons by throwing herself into her academic work, recalling that by the ninth grade "I was far ahead of my classmates academically." She credited her success to the "strong and steady influence" of her grandparents. Cameron treasured her grandparents for their enduring impact "on my life and values. They made me feel that I was someone special and that I was capable of accomplishing anything I wanted."[5]

Cameron's gifts as an artist and budding scholar eventually saw her leave the reservation to further her education. After briefly attending the Institute of American Indian Arts in Santa Fe, New Mexico, Cameron did what many other gay, lesbian, and transgender Indians did during the late 1960s and early 1970s: she moved to San Francisco. Cameron arrived in the Bay Area in 1973 to attend the San Francisco Art Institute. At first, San Francisco was a fantasy, an urban dream that "held a future and special place for me."

That idealism soon faded. Feeling culture shock, Cameron recalled the crushing sense of isolation that gripped her. She felt lost, out of place, rootless. These are daunting emotions; in 1973 they crowded out Cameron's creativity. Barbara Cameron began second-guessing her decision to move to San Francisco.

Cameron soon discovered that she wasn't alone in feeling these emotions. In the 1960s and 1970s, gay and lesbian people flocked to California to seek out a college education and economic opportunities and to forge communities free of racism and homophobia. These were heady times in San Francisco. It was a period of social activism and political assertiveness as the gay leader Harvey Milk and the Native American student activist Richard Oakes and others like them enjoyed unprecedented levels of fame and influence.[6] A rising generation of gay, lesbian, and gender-nonconforming Indians used this energy to inspire a politics that addressed their specific needs and aspirations. They advanced a politics that celebrated the resilience of Native people while also working to reclaim the tribally specific traditions and languages that bound people together in community and formed the basis of politically sovereign tribal nations.

Future Two-Spirit leaders emerged during the 1970s. Phil Tingley, a Kiowa, arrived in San Francisco in 1971. Having grown up in rural Oklahoma, in San Francisco Tingley struggled with urban poverty and the type of culture shock that awakened Cameron's political consciousness. In the 1970s, Tingley took a job at the Corporation for American Indian Development that set him on a path to eventually becoming a trusted elder.[7] Beverly Little Thunder also came of age in California. Little Thunder, a Lakota woman who, like Cameron, had family connections at Standing Rock, navigated a childhood characterized by urban poverty, sexual abuse at the hands of relatives, and stints in juvenile facilities. By the late 1960s, Little Thunder reconnected with Indigenous culture. She started attending sweat lodges, became an activist in the American Indian Movement (AIM), and confronted the misogyny in both Native and white America.[8]

Tingley, Little Thunder, and an emerging generation of leaders were renewing Native culture and advancing Indigenous political causes. They added energy to what's sometimes referred to as the decolonial aspirations of "indigenous Third World people" and "Third World lesbian and gay groups."[9] Like Tingley and Little Thunder, Barbara Cameron threw herself into political organizing, activism, and community building. Although Cameron was a "shy and private" person, she became a self-described "avowed political activist." Few of her peers matched her clarity and frankness—qualities that propelled Cameron into a leadership role as cofounder of the Gay American Indians (GAI) in 1975.[10] Randy Burns (Northern Paiute), GAI's cofounder, remembered Cameron as being highly engaged in politics. "She was more political and forthright in her writing," Burns recalled. "I couldn't believe what she was writing about."[11] To her contemporaries, Cameron seemed fearless.

GAI was one of scores of gay and lesbian groups to emerge in San Francisco in the 1970s. Groups like Bay Area Gay Liberation, Gay Action, Save our Human Rights, Black Gay Caucus, and Gay Latino Alliance revealed the growing political assertiveness of gay and lesbian politics.[12] In 1977, novelist Herbert Gold wrote about these changes, asserting that one in three voters in San Francisco was gay.[13] This flurry of organizing and political clout constituted what is sometimes referred to as the "gay identity movement"; its focus was on civil rights.[14]

GAI emerged in this context. On July 23, 1975, GAI was born at the Twin Peaks bar in San Francisco's Castro District. At that founding meeting, Barbara Cameron, Randy Burns, and three other members formed the nucleus of what became an organization of 150 by the end of the year.[15] The reawakening was getting organized.

. . . .

To understand this reawakening—to fully appreciate the overlapping histories that informed the consciousness-raising work of Cameron, Burns, and others—it is necessary to go back and forth in time. It is a complicated story. It is a history of late-twentieth-century political activism, of community and political organizing that occurred at a time when the federal government continued with its policies of terminating Native nations and relocating Indigenous people in urban areas throughout the United States. These policies, initiated in the 1950s, shaped the childhood experiences of Native activists who came of age in the late 1960s and 1970s. With the support of white allies like Harry Hay, one of the most prominent gay rights activists in twentieth-century America, GAI members understood the historical and cultural forces shaping their lives. As a result, GAI supported the nascent political objectives of the modern gay liberation movement—a movement ignited by the Stonewall uprising in New York in 1969—while remaining conscious of the fact that their Indigeneity shaped how they experienced gender and sexuality.

Marlon "Marty" Fixico remembers how this heightened consciousness played out in tensions between white and Indigenous LGBT people. Fixico, who is Southern Cheyenne and the managing editor of *Native Out*, became involved with the Human Rights Campaign (HRC) when he lived in Washington, DC. Fixico was struck by how the HRC comprised "mainly mainstream whites." He adds, "The white people"—long pause—"they were very white."

I asked Fixico to elaborate on what he meant by "very white." He explained: "I was always marginalized and tokenized. I put up with it to a certain extent because I wanted to be a point of education for people, but after a while it gets tiring."[16] Fixico's experiences weren't unique among LGBT Native people during the latter third of the twentieth century. GAI's founding members recognized this and began organizing intertribal connections to advance their political objectives.[17]

During GAI's formative years, members earned a reputation for partying. Burns jokes about those years, referring to the group's early members as "young, dumb, and full of cum." It's fair to say that people enjoyed themselves during those early years. Members hosted gatherings at their apartments and drank and danced together, performed impromptu drag shows, and got to know one another. But the group did more than party; members came together, Burns remembered, to "celebrate our pride as queer Indian people."[18]

If GAI was a social club, it also grew into a collective committed to gender and sexual liberation for Indigenous people. GAI joined a wave of Indigenous organizations that formed in the United States during the late twentieth century to offer sharp critiques of American colonialism, insist that the federal government fulfill its treaty obligations, and champion Native self-determination.[19] As GAI became better organized, its members crystallized the organization's objectives: community outreach, Native sovereignty, cultural renewal. Alongside Indigenous leaders and activists like Phil Tingley and Beverly Little Thunder, GAI strove to achieve its goals by making LGBT Indians visible to the general public and undermining colonialism's homophobia.[20]

. . . .

Randy Burns moved to San Francisco in 1975 to attend San Francisco State College (now San Francisco State University). Burns, a Northern Paiute, grew up on the Pyramid Lake Indian Reservation in Nevada. As early as five years of age, he knew he was gay. Reconciling himself to this realization, much less articulating it, proved challenging. As for so many LGBT Indians of his generation, the pervasive influences of colonialism and Christianity made finding gay Indigenous role models difficult.[21]

When he arrived in the Bay Area, Burns sought out the support he craved by throwing himself into student government and urban life. Small in stature but possessing a magnetic personality and boundless energy, Burns combined a keen sense of humor with genuine compassion. These qualities drew people to him. At San Francisco State, students elected him leader of the Student Council of American Indians. The student council, founded by the Mohawk activist Richard Oakes, earned national attention for the Alcatraz occupation between November 1969 and June 1971.[22] Burns also held a summer job at the American Indian Center on Valencia Street. These positions gave Burns the opportunity to "meet a lot of queer people" and "intertribal people like myself."[23] Away from the reservation, Burns "felt safe to be myself and free from ridicule and harassment for the first time in my life."[24]

Burns, Cameron, and other GAI members wanted to create an organization capable of meeting "the unique needs of the Bay Area's gay Indian community." These included facilitating access to counseling services, addressing housing and healthcare needs, opening employment opportunities, providing introductions to social and legal services, and encouraging "historical and contemporary cultural activities."[25]

Achieving its goals required GAI to connect with the rising Red Power Movement and LGBT Indians throughout the Bay Area.[26] Members pooled their meager resources to offset the cost of printing fliers and hosting events. Slowly a sense of community emerged. So, too, did a sharpened political identity. GAI members believed they'd started to erode the "marginality of the exile" and the loss of "wealth of social and cultural tradition" caused by American colonialism's "assimilation" and "termination" policies.[27]

GAI strove to unite LGBT Indians and nurture "the self-esteem of individual members."[28] Clyde Hall recalls GAI working to empower LGBT Indians, beginning with offering support for people coming out of the "buckskin closet."[29] Hall, an enrolled member of the Shoshone-Bannock Tribes and an active member of GAI during its formative years, recalls that prior to the 1970s, "Indians were just shoved in a corner." GAI helped to change that. As Hall points out, GAI drew attention to how Indigenous people "are contemporary tribal and cultural people, not caricatures from a bygone era." Contemporary tribal people "are always evolving," Hall notes. "That's what makes the culture live and be vibrant."[30]

GAI nurtured Indigenous vibrance. Its members came together to celebrate their unique contribution to Native culture and politics. San Francisco was like that in the 1970s: it drew people together. At least, it seemed to. Randy Burns recalls that GAI operated in a city and a gay culture that was openly racist toward gay and lesbian Indians. This proved particularly true of the gay bar scene, which had a culture of racism that extended back to at least the early twentieth century. This exclusionary culture continued after World War II. In the 1940s and 1950s, people of color were routinely excluded from the vibrant bath house scene and gay and lesbian bars.[31] By the 1960s, and the opening of the Tool Box, located in the South of Market neighborhood, the "Leathermen" scene added a new outlet for overwhelmingly white gay men to party. However, few LGBT people of color had access to these establishments prior to the 1970s.[32] Rodrigo Reyes, a gay Latino man, recalled that racism within San Francisco's gay community in the 1970s meant it "was a difficult bar situation" for gay Latinos.[33] Randy Burns experienced similar difficulties, recalling that the bar scene was "very racist" in the 1970s.[34] In fact, Burns maintained that this racism in San Francisco's gay community continued into the following decade, touching virtually every facet of gay life. In 1989, Burns lamented that the "leadership in the gay community is still very white and exclusionary."[35]

In the 1970s, radical gay liberationists presented gay politics as antiracist and opposed to sexism.[36] In reality, racism segregated LGBT America. Randy Burns recalls how GAI organized large groups—what are today called flash mobs—to turn up at San Francisco's gay bars and demand entry.[37] LGBT Indians also experienced racism within gay communities in other American cities. Marty Fixico remembers that in Washington, DC, during the 1980s, "white lesbians and gay men treated me terribly."[38]

GAI saw racism and homophobia as colonial ideologies that splintered Native communities and fractured cultural traditions. By the late 1970s, this recognition meant that GAI members had started to take their decolonizing mission seriously. They weren't simply fighting for gay liberation; they were in a battle against the fictions of Western "objectivity"—the lifeblood of colonialism in twentieth-century America. Colonial archives and anthropological research had distorted the public's perceptions of Indigenous people. As one GAI document observed, "Objectivity is always the tool of the powerful."[39] A sharper critique of American colonialism was coming into focus.

Barbara Cameron provided GAI with its most sophisticated take on American colonialism. For Cameron, colonialism worked on multiple levels. It impacted her ability to live as both a Lakota and lesbian woman in San Francisco, a city built on the dispossessed lands of the Ohlone people. And it influenced the decolonial strategies that GAI devised. Cameron believed that "the survival of the Indian people isn't just dependent on one thing." It required a multifaceted set of strategies that empower Native people. Cameron and other GAI members worked to articulate these strategies in position papers. One GAI document declared, "Marginality can become a stance which permits us a broader perspective, with input from two or more cultures and, therefore, with the potential for new insights which can produce creative change in the larger society." Addressing the twin scourges of racism and homophobia, GAI members embraced their outsider status in relation to colonial America to decolonize their stories and reclaim their place in Native communities. This approach represented the renewal of a strategy that had sustained Native communities for millennia: a tradition of cultural evolution, adaptation, and innovation.[40]

. . . .

LGBT Indians faced challenges on many fronts. For those who came of age in the late 1960s and early 1970s, the ongoing effects of relocation and termination stiffened their political resolve. In the 1950s, the federal government enacted laws to relocate Native families to American cities and to terminate tribal governments and reservation land holdings.[41] The BIA aimed to relocate thirty thousand Native Americans from reservations to urban areas, a target figure that increased threefold in the 1960s and 1970s. In cities such as Seattle, Los Angeles, and Dallas, Indigenous people encountered racism, underemployment, and poverty. In Denver, Alfred Ziegler, a member of the Lower Brule Sioux, recalled, "Heck, if I wanted to work in a junkyard, I could've stayed at home. . . . There's junked cars at home."[42] Relocation was a cruel part of an ill-conceived policy to assimilate Native Americans to white society. It caused family dislocation, splintered communities, and resulted in the loss of tribal lands as petroleum companies swooped in like vultures to enrich their shareholders.

But the people of Indian Country weren't passive; they couldn't afford to be. Across Indian Country, colonialism threatened people's livelihoods. Some, like Elmer Gage, a gay Mohave man, eked out a living making art. Elsewhere, Diné ranchers kept a watchful eye on federal agents between the 1930s and 1950s as they monitored government plans to seize land that they needed for their livestock. In the Pacific Northwest, Indigenous people led fish-ins in the 1960s in an effort to force the federal government to recognize their fishing rights.[44] For tribes in the Pacific Northwest, as for the Diné and tribal communities across the United States, these battles were about treaty rights and economic survival. They were also about cultural renewal and the sovereignty of Native nations.

By the 1970s, Red Power was attracting national headlines. College students, artists, writers, and activists were organizing. Sometimes they'd stumble, disagree, and trip over their own egos. Revolutionary work isn't glamorous; it requires patience that the young don't always have. Still, young Indigenous people energized Indian Country, drawing inspiration from decolonial movements in the "Third World" as they defined, refined, and asserted their political agendas. They did so at a time when non-Indigenous Americans were "rediscovering" Native Americans.[45] Dee Brown's best-selling book *Bury My Heart at Wounded Knee* (1970) and the film *Little Big Man* (1970) blended romantic stereotypes of Indigenous culture with earnest critiques of American colonialism. *Little Big Man* proved particularly noteworthy for its portrayal of Little Horse, a cross-dressing, male-bodied character with a penchant for "soft furs."[46] Although *Little Big Man* represented Indigenous people with greater depth than standard Hollywood westerns, the portrayal of Little Horse relied on homophobic tropes. As one film scholar argues, Little Horse was "a caricature of a drag queen who bats his eyes and dances coyly away."[47]

Breaking down cultural stereotypes takes time. Maurice Kenny tried to accelerate the process in the 1975–76 winter edition of *Gay Sunshine*.[48] Kenny was a prolific writer and poet. He also had Mohawk heritage, a facet of his identity that he explored in his work.[49] Randy Burns read and kept Kenny's writings, as did other gay and lesbian Indians and their non-Indigenous allies.[50]

In the winter of 1975–76, Kenny's essay "Tinselled Bucks" provided the readers of *Gay Sunshine* with a sweeping historical overview of homosexuality in Native America. That's how most Americans viewed LGBT Indian history in the 1970s: as a matter of sex and sexuality. Kenny began with the Spanish, the first European homophobes in North America. He argued that "male love was destroyed more than ignored in the new Spanish macho world." Kenny's language was provocative, accusatory, and occasionally misleading. On this latter point, he claimed that "homosexuality was found in all American Indian tribes, though perhaps kept to a small number in particular tribes." Kenny erred; homosexuality was not "found in all American Indian tribes." At the time, though, historical and cultural specificity took a backseat to political activism.

Kenny described Indigenous sexuality as "uninhibited." Gay Indian men, the focus of his essay, were both part of a "fetish" culture and "an integral part of ceremony." Kenny's essay offered a simplistic historical comparison between a utopian world of Indigenous libertines and prudish European colonizers. His gendered analysis was also problematic. Kenny presented gender as a binary of feminine and macho powers. He stated that the berdache combined feminine and macho powers and enjoyed an honored status. Kenny concluded that the berdache didn't possess fluid gender roles or identities but constituted a third gender.

Kenny wrote "Tinselled Bucks" for popular audiences who viewed LGBT Indians as part of a larger global history of homosexuality. "Tinsel," denoting showy and sparkly qualities, more aptly described the emerging aesthetic of mainstream gay culture during the late twentieth century. Although it wasn't his intention, Kenny misrepresented LGBT Indians to advance an argument about sexual freedom. That argument no doubt resonated—to a point—with LGBT Indians, but it missed the larger decolonial agenda and somewhat misrepresented activists' efforts to reclaim their place in Native communities.

Robert Lynch shared elements of Kenny's analysis. Born on September 14, 1946, Lynch grew up in rural Halifax County, North Carolina. He attended Harvard Law School and had a successful career as an attorney in New York City.[51] Lynch felt unsettled in New York and returned to North Carolina in the late 1970s. He worked as a writer and photographer and used his New York connections to advance the arts in North Carolina. He also devoted considerable time to personal introspection. Lynch claimed a triracial heritage—African, European, and Native American. His Indigenous lineage included a connection to the Haliwa-Saponi Nation.

Lynch wanted to know more about his Native roots, so he started digging. That research clarified his homosexuality. Like Kenny, Lynch focused on the sexual aspects of his identity. However, he departed from Kenny's "third gender" argument by emphasizing the sexual continuum in Indigenous cultures. Lynch found this insight exhilarating and emancipatory. In his personal writings, Lynch stated that this sexual continuum constituted an important part of communal identities. Colonialism changed that, introducing homophobia to the Americas—a Western disease that he lumped with "Christian or bourgeois petty moralizing, Marxist notions of bourgeois decadence or nationalistic posturing about genocide."[52]

Attacked by colonialism, "the cultural expression of homoeroticism suffered and disappeared" in Native America. Lynch maintained that "there was a sustained effort to eradicate any native homoeroticism." He concluded that the result of centuries of colonial attacks on Native gender and sexual traditions caused social dislocation, homophobia, and even incest.[53] Longing for a return to traditional gender roles and sexual health, Lynch lamented "that some Indian men have adopted Western male chauvinism and try to rationalize anti-feminism as 'traditional.'"[54]

. . . .

Henry "Harry" Hay thought he understood the traditions of LGBT Indians better than most. Hay was born in England on April 7, 1912. As a small child his family relocated to Chile before settling in California. A labor activist, communist, and devotee of Marxist theory, Hay also became one of the most prominent gay rights leaders in Cold War America. According to some Americans, Hay's life as an activist and advocate for the downtrodden appeared foreordained from a young age.

The legend of Harry Hay occupies a prominent place in twentieth-century gay history. To many people, Hay is a hero. A number of Two-Spirit people I've spoken with over the years share this view, valuing Hay as an ally in their cause to reclaim their traditions. Others, like J. Miko Thomas, balk at Hay's romanticization of Native cultures.[55]

The Hay legend begins in Yerington, Nevada, where he vacationed as a child. These visits were like living a tale out of a late-nineteenth-century dime novel. Hay explored the family ranch, rode horses, and enjoyed the great outdoors. Summer vacations at the Yerington ranch also brought Hay into contact with an old Indian prophet, an encounter that sparked a lifelong interest in Native American history.

The story of Hay's encounter with an old prophet circulated for decades. In the mid-1980s, anthropologist Walter Williams put the legend in writing. Allegedly based on correspondence with Hay, Williams wrote that a young Harry "became fascinated by Indians and attended traditional Washo dances." Nothing strange about that. However, Williams's retelling of the Hay legend takes a mystical turn: At age thirteen he was blessed by the elderly Paiute prophet Wovoka, whom Hay remembers as a very old man, blind and with a heavily wrinkled face. The Ghost dance prophet touched the boy and said a prayer in his native language. Hay later recalled that the Indians told him Wovoka had said that "we should be good to this boy, for he will be a friend to us later."[56]

Did the legend bear any resemblance to the facts of Hay's life? Did this mythical event happen?

Answering these questions requires us to go back to the 1930s when Hay began throwing himself into political activism. An active member of the Communist Party, Hay organized meetings, rallies, and pickets. On one of these picket lines Hay met an attractive young woman by the name of Anita Platky. Committed to social justice, and possessing an artistic sensibility, Platky caught Hay's eye. The couple seemed well matched. Hay, whose sexual identity wasn't yet "fixed," married Platky in 1938. For the moment he had quashed concerns about his sexuality within the Communist Party—a virulently homophobic organization.[57]

Wovoka's prophecy was coming to pass. Hay's life appeared on course to aid the downtrodden. In November 1950, Hay took another step on this seemingly foreordained path when he cofounded the Mattachine Society, a gay rights group that viewed homosexual people as a marginalized minority with a distinct history and culture. The scholar and activist Michael Bronski argues that the Mattachine Society held that it was "possible and desirable that a highly ethical homosexual culture emerge, . . . paralleling the emerging cultures of our fellow-minorities—the Negro, Mexican, and Jewish peoples."[58]

The Mattachines, taking their name from a secret fraternal society of unmarried men in Renaissance France, formed as Americans grappled with Alfred Kinsey's reports on human sexuality, *Sexual Behavior in the Human Male* (1948) and *Sexual Behavior in the Human Female* (1953). In the early 1950s, Mattachine Society membership grew rapidly, and branches emerged across the United States.[59] By the end of 1953, though, divisions over tactics and tone splintered the group. One of the Mattachine factions felt the moment had arrived to cultivate an image of respectability and to build coalitions. In contrast, Hay and a number of "old aunties" felt that more radical strategies were vital to attracting new members to homophile societies.[60]

During the turbulence of these foundational years in modern gay liberation, Hay devoted a considerable amount of his time to studying the berdache. In the 1950s, Hay's thinking on the berdache institution mixed mythology with historical materialism. He wondered privately about the gendered division of labor in Native societies and how these divisions were reproduced in society.[61] These concerns framed Hay's search for a "gay origins" story, a quest that conflated questions of sexuality with stereotypes about primitive Indigenous cultures.

Hay's early dalliances with mythology and Native histories proved esoteric. In one of the hundreds of note cards he made for himself, Hay speculated "that man, as a social animal, [is] integrally inclined to warrior-hood."[62] Although he often criticized anthropologists for their tendency to use chauvinistic language and rigid categories, Hay fell back on their work—and their ahistorical categories—in a bid to understand "folk cultures."[63] By the early 1960s these private speculations also incorporated astrology. Hay's marriage of folk cultures and astrology convinced him that the Julian calendar held the key to understanding the global history of the berdache. On a note card titled "Berdache: The Julian Calendar Origins," Hay speculated about the links among the berdache tradition, Christianity, and astrology, writing, "Christianity was heavily under the influence of astrology."[64]

If Hay had set out to fulfill Wovoka's prophecy, he had lost his way burrowing through esoteric rabbit-holes. Hay sought out historical insight, but that search took him far from Indian Country and into the obscure corners of Europe's past. He became fascinated, for example, with the Beth-Luis-Nion alphabet of the Ollaves—poets and spell-casters, magicians and priests—that Hay felt revealed to him the ancient roots of the English alphabet and an international exchange of ideas and sacred traditions. On one note card he scribbled his desire to "adduce additional Berdache culture into the Pythagorian/ Dactyl-Beth-Luis Charm for the letter numbers 9–10–11–12—9 being Huarh, 10 ura, & 11 & 12 D&T the successive times."[65] Robert Graves's treatise on the poet's art, *The White Goddess*, convinced Hay that an ancient Irish priesthood had traveled to Egypt, studied in its esoteric mystery schools, and brought the knowledge they acquired back to Ireland, where it was taught throughout Europe and beyond. Hay's speculations had veered perilously close to full-blown Orientalism—an essentialist understanding of non-Western cultures and the diffusion of language. Orientalist thinking framed European perceptions of Native Americans in the eighteenth century—Indigenous people were often referred to as "Arabs"—and persisted in subsequent centuries as American writers romanticized the "noble savage."[66] Whether intended or not, Hay's speculations fit into this framework.

Hay's speculation about the past also created a flat historical universe where social and cultural differences specific to place and time collapsed under the weight of his romanticism. Turning to ancient Israel and Egypt, Hay indulged his interest in the evolutionary theory of human development, from primitive to civilized, from tribe to state. "In the long transition stage between Matriarchal society and democratic polity," Hay wrote, "the Berdache Institution served as deputies and communally assigned, or devoted, assistants to the Matrons' councils, the hunter-warriors [who] emerged in a new role as defenders not only of the village storehouses but also of their widespread field and flocks."[67]

Hay's flirtation with historical analysis echoed not only nineteenth-century Orientalism but also Enlightenment stadial theory, the idea that human societies evolve through stages of development. A third influence, the historical dialecticism of Marxian theory, remained part of Hay's thinking as he worked to understand human relationships and their material (or economic) connections.

These intellectual influences framed Hay's understanding of the berdache. He speculated that "the Berdache, in contrast to the family household, having no old ones or young ones to care for, could provide for their own needs in one-quarter of time spent by the rest of the village." The material condition of berdaches in a society also gave them a degree of cultural flexibility. According to Hay, berdaches dressed in women's garb and assisted women in their work "or they made many arrows, bows, moccasins, rigs, bowls; tanned leather for thongs, and tepee coverings."

Hay's view of the berdache fit into his larger search for a global "gay origins" story. He made this plain when he wrote that "by nature of their own householding, and by reason of their sharing in women's work, [berdaches] learned the recipes and formulas by which ritual agriculture was maintained." He goes on to state, "In many cultures of Asia, Africa, and South America, the Berdache[s] carried the responsibility as the medicine men, or shamans, of their village and cultures."

The global berdache made things, cared for people, and educated children "through design, story-telling, singing, and organizing the practice of ritual . . . all of these women's prerogatives and inventions."

Hay labeled this versatile figure the "folk-berdache." Berdaches existed everywhere. They were anatomically male but traversed a spectrum of gendered and sexual roles. Hay's berdache theory applied to Native America too. He wrote:

> The Berdache began to dress the everyday moccasin with pictorial designs representing the work-pattern recipe that must accompany its fabrication. He decorated tepee coverings with patterns of social history called wisdom. He began to make signs and designs to record the ritual festivals of dance which were nothing more than the natural imitations by which wind, rain, heat, and cold, were summoned by imitation of natural forces . . . which everyone must know and be able to perform if nature were to respond. He began to teach the children, because the women really didn't have the time, to do the stylized calisthenics which would prepare them for all the needed work patterns of their maturity.[68]

Hay's search for a history of gay origins was understandable given the pervasiveness of homophobia in the United States during the 1950s and 1960s. His global framing of that search, however, took him far from his fabled encounter with Wovoka and obscured what was culturally, socially, and spiritually specific about Native traditions throughout Indian Country.

To Hay's credit, he remained open to new ideas. By the 1960s, Hay dove back into the work of the anthropologists Lewis Henry Morgan, Franz Boas, and Ruth Benedict.[69] He read the canon of early-twentieth-century anthropology for evidence of "Indian communities practicing facsimiles of ritual agriculture." Hay's rereading of these scholars reinforced his "folk culture" theory of the berdache in world history. In fact, Hay remained committed to his materialist perspective on the past. His view of Indian labor reinforced his belief that the "family units called tribes generally lived in large shelters or in closely connected shelters." Within these communities, "women superintended the main production of food which was the yield of husbandry and agriculture. The men were hunters and fishers, but their yield was chancey and seasonal."[70]

The idea that Native cultures practiced a gendered division of labor based on the anatomical sex of a person came not from Indigenous people but from European perceptions of Indian labor. This rigid male-female binary still shapes historical writing about Native America. It is simplistic at best, misleading at worse. It's simplistic because it imposes a European understanding of gender as biology onto Native communities. It is misleading because it relies on what Europeans thought they saw in Indigenous societies between the sixteenth and nineteenth centuries.[71]

Hay accepted the binary trope. Where his views diverged from those of professional anthropologists was on the historical significance of anal sex. Hay gave considerable thought to the "anal sacra" and "ceremonial fellatio." Hay wrote, "It occurs to me that my point on ritual fellatio as a common clan or phratry pattern in Ice Age and subsequent Matriarchal-matrilineal Magic cultures, is not far wrong." Hay had a high opinion of his own intellect, and he felt his self-regard was justified on this point. He continued, "Phala—as seed in Sanskrit, Sperm of the male horse—as *soma* in the RgVeda (sperm, of course, being a late perhaps Ghandarese approximation), Mar—as 'fountainhead' in ritual, all seem to move toward the idea."[72] The evidence for "ceremonial fellatio," in Hay's mind, was clear. Hay's understanding of "ceremonial fellatio" involved a return to his Orientalist speculations and hinted at the Hindu and Buddhist influences that eventually inspired his founding of the Radical Faeries in the late 1970s. This was a group of non-Native gay men who appropriated Indigenous traditions to "liberate an Indigenous gay nature" and promote their "back-to-the-land primitivism."[73]

Hay's historical speculation on this issue connects back to his Marxian understanding of folk cultures, labor, and the importance of ceremony. The "Berdache Institution" was not one of "continual 'ball,'" Hay euphemistically wrote. Instead, it was an institution in which the "ritual of anal intercourse would have been a 'sacra,' . . . that is it was an act permitted *only* when the Berdache was fully purified with proper sanctifications, consecrated to a specific invocational occasion, and robed in the raiment of his patroness AS HER DEPUTY (or substitute) *for the occasion*." On these occasions, the berdache acted as the patroness's sexual surrogate, the berdache bringing their holiness to the most intimate of "invocational" occasions.

Hay viewed the berdache through a Eurocentric lens. His views began changing in the 1970s, but in the decades before that Hay filtered his search for a "gay origin" story through an explicitly Western perspective. He understood everything in Indigenous cultures—from the architecture produced by Native societies in South America to gender roles and sexual behavior—in this way. These intellectual filters led to some embarrassing claims. For example, Hay believed the Cherokee "booger" dance had its origins in sex between men because the word "booger" must surely have been a corruption of "bugger." It was not. Cherokees invented the dance during the eighteenth century to laugh at what they saw as the crudeness of Europeans and African Americans.[74]

If Harry Hay wanted to fulfill the prophecy that Wovoka reportedly envisioned, he hadn't yet found his way back to the path prophesied by the old prophet. Native people valued sex and sexuality—historically and in Hay's time—but concern about sexual issues did not dominate their politics, theories of history, or understandings of kinship in the way it dominated "mainstream" gay politics. Hay eventually tried to understand this. As he grew older, he paid closer attention to Native political and historical consciousness. He listened to Native people, was led by their ideas, and developed an enduring respect for place-based traditions.[75]

As his eyes opened, and his heart softened, Hay began understanding Native cultures on their own terms. Even after his romanticization of Indigenous cultures inspired him to cofound the Radical Faeries, he managed to find room for introspection. Take the legend of his childhood meeting with Wovoka. It never happened, at least not in the way Walter Williams described it. Williams, who served jail time in the early 2010s on child sex charges, ignored a letter from Hay in which he quashed the Wovoka myth. Hay wrote: "At age 13 (1925) I knew Wovoka only as an old sacred man whom everybody in Smith Valley called only 'old Jack Wilson.' He and his family lived on the Wilson Ranch outside Yerington, in Mason Valley to the east of us. I wouldn't have know [sic] that his name was Wovoka, and that he was in fact the great Ghost-Dance Prophet, until the Spring of 1969."

This detail, missing from Williams's 1986 book *The Spirit and the Flesh*, is important. Hay's thinking began changing toward the end of the 1960s when he realized he needed to pay more attention to Native knowledge on its own terms.

. . . .

Remember: 1969 marked a turning point for Native politics. It was the year of the Alcatraz occupation and the beginning of the American Indian Movement.

Red Power had arrived.

Just a few years later, Gay American Indians was founded. GAI, cofounded by Barbara Cameron and Randy Burns, took the lead in addressing issues of identity, correcting the racial romanticism of white activists like Harry Hay, and making the diverse community of gay and lesbian Indians visible to the "mainstream" LGBT movement.

San Francisco proved fertile political ground for GAI to grow and develop. In 1977, GAI members joined over 300,000 LGBT people at San Francisco's Gay Freedom Day parade. That June, Anita Bryant, the singer turned anti-gay activist who led the "Save Our Children" campaign in Dade County, Florida, was the butt of jokes on placards and banners held aloft by paraders.[76] Placards lampooned Bryant for having a "Big Mouth, Small Brain," and banners thanked her for unifying gay people across racial and ethnic lines. The founding generation of GAI soaked up the energy at the parade.[77] They partied, but they were also learning to become better organized. Cameron and Burns led these efforts. Cameron was particularly driven, recalling, "I've never been the kind of person who goes along in the world never questioning, never wondering why certain things are the way they are."[78]

Question she did. In fact, GAI posed lots of questions. Members had a few observations to share with the world, too. One of those was the realization that groups like GAI were vitally important to meeting the specific needs of LGBT Indians. At the National March for Lesbian and Gay Rights in October 1979, a small contingent from GAI made their voices heard, joining over 100,000 people who marched on Washington, DC, to demand civil rights for LGBT people. March organizers wanted to "show good faith and good politics" toward "minority gays" and organized what they called a Third World Conference three days before the march. It was a clumsy attempt at inclusion that left LGBT Indians convinced that they needed to define their own future.[79] Cameron understood this better than most, writing, "In the Lesbian/Gay community, I have been the only Indian political activist for many years. I bring up issues important to Indians so that others will learn and perhaps begin to get a different understanding of this country they are living in."[80]

The 1979 march on Washington underscored the importance of organizing. A number of small groups emerged across Indian Country to represent the interests of both LGBT Indians and Native women. Like gay and lesbian Indians, Native women navigated prejudices, hostility, and violence in their own communities and in mainstream society.

Madonna Thunder Hawk played a pivotal role in forming one of those groups. Women of All Red Nations—WARN—emerged amid the tumultuous Native politics in the 1970s. Born on the Yankton Sioux Reservation in South Dakota in 1940, Thunder Hawk is best known today for coordinating water protectors in opposition to the Dakota Access Pipeline—"the black snake"—in 2016.

Thunder Hawk's activism dates back to the Alcatraz occupation. She emerged from Alcatraz as one of the leading figures in WARN, sometimes referred to as the "sisterhood of AIM," the American Indian Movement. Like her cousin, Russell Means, Thunder Hawk played a leading role as an organizer. WARN drew attention to gender inequality and sexual violence against Indigenous women. Thunder Hawk proved to be a tireless advocate for Native women, as she demonstrated at a gathering in South Dakota in July 1980 that included ranchers, farmers, environmentalists, feminists, and Native Americans. This unlikely coalition joined together to oppose uranium mining in the Black Hills.

Noting the strong Native presence at the gathering, Thunder Hawk made a point of telling reporters, "We have a strong contingent in the gay community."[81] Native women had concerns about legal rights and healthcare accessibility that put their politics in alignment with those of LGBT Indians. With white Americans embroiled in a culture war over abortion following the Supreme Court's 1973 ruling in *Roe v. Wade*, Thunder Hawk reflected on the colonial history of "forced sterilization, zero population growth and contamination" imposed on Indian Country. Thunder Hawk stated that the continuation of that dark history meant "our *very existence* as a people is threatened."[82]

In the 1970s, the existential threats that American colonialism still posed to Native America framed the historical and political consciousness of Indigenous activists. From Balboa setting his attack dogs on

Indigenous "sodomites" in the sixteenth century to the military-style quashing of Native activism in the twentieth, the very existence of Native people, particularly gay and lesbian Indians, meant that a new generation of Native activists were galvanized in advancing cultural renewal and the sovereignty of tribal nations.

For LGBT Indians, AIM looked like the ideal political platform to address the enduring legacies of colonialism. However, like African American organizations during the civil rights movement in the 1950s and 1960s, and Black Power groups in the late 1960s and 1970s, LGBT Indians found that misogyny and sexual double standards existed in both Native communities and in local chapters of AIM. Beverly Little Thunder recalls the misogyny she encountered from Native men when she started attending sweat lodges. She recalls one elder accusing her of spending too much time "listening to too many bra-burning women's libbers." In her memoir, Little Thunder recalls similarly confronting instances of misogyny and makes allegations against AIM members engaging in violent sexual behavior with her son during the "longest walk," a 1978 march from San Francisco to Washington, DC, in support of tribal sovereignty.[83] I've asked former AIM members about these allegations; none are able to corroborate them, and two (who insist on anonymity) deny that the events Little Thunder describes ever happened.[84]

This is not to say that misogyny and sexual assaults didn't happen in activist circles in the 1970s; they did. It does suggest that that history is still emotional and fiercely contested by its participants. Today, Little Thunder is a much-loved and respected Two-Spirit elder. She has remained a staunch defender of women's and Two-Spirit rights.

The members of GAI also remained fierce opponents of misogyny and sexual violence, and advocates for LGBT Indians. Its members linked misogyny and sexual abuse to five centuries of colonialism and the accompanying poverty, loss of land, disease, and genocidal levels of violence. GAI members attempted to help each other overcome these disadvantages, but GAI members were also interested in the present and the future—not in Hay's materialist and often romantic interpretations of the past. They wanted to feel empowered, and they wanted the tools to *be* empowered.

Reclaiming cultures, traditions, and symbols became central to the work of GAI. The group's literature described the "self-validation and empowerment" derived from the "very process of exploration and rediscovery" of Indigenous history and cultures.[85] Maurice Kenny wrote similarly in his essay "Tinselled Bucks," a piece that influenced GAI members. Kenny hoped that if Native Americans regain "their old cultures, languages and ceremonies the berdache will not only be respected but will find a place in his chosen society."[86] Robert Lynch made a similar argument, stating, "Oppression of native homosexuals should be considered part of the overall oppression of Indian culture."[87]

For GAI, empowerment was both psychological and material, cultural and social. By the early 1980s, questions about language renewal, cultural reengagement, and political sovereignty gave further energy to GAI activities. However, the politics of gay liberation, with its emphasis on inclusion of gays in neoliberal society, failed to adequately address the Native-centric issues at the heart of GAI's organizing.

This became clear as Indigenous LGBT people debated what to call themselves. Virtually everyone agreed that the anthropological use of the word "berdache" had to go. Many saw it as a slur. In 1979, an anonymous letter writer from Anadarko, Oklahoma, summed up the emerging consensus on the use of this offensive term in the gay men's magazine *Blueboy*. Recoiling at the continued use of the word "berdache," the letter writer wrote that "true ignorance exists *towards* Native Americans—not *among* them." The anonymous author—likely Phil Tingley, who grew up in Anadarko—went on to explain that the ignorance of non-Native people might actually have helped Indigenous people "survive to this day. If any of you really knew what we were up to, we truly would have breathed our last a hundred years ago."[88]

As the 1980s began, reclaiming practices forced underground by the oppressive structures of colonialism and identifying traces of Indigenous history and culture became a priority for LGBT Indians across North America. Their focus became a search for the language that truly reflected their lived histories and gave coherence to their identities as Indigenous people who happened to be gay, lesbian, bisexual, or transgender. Writing in 1981, Paula Gunn Allen tried to get this process started. She posited her own origin story, placing women at the center of that narrative. Allen had no use for Hay's earlier speculations; instead, she wrote of a world where women once married other women, where lesbians were part of the "tribal consciousness," and in which "manly-hearted women . . . functioned as warriors."[89]

Over the coming two decades, gay, lesbian, bisexual, and transgender Indians harnessed that warrior spirit. Leading gay and lesbian organizers continued to seek out a new umbrella term to combat homophobia, educate the Native and non-Native public, and provide a political space to empower people and reawaken their specific tribal traditions. Just as Barbara Cameron's grandparents saw her as a "special person," Native activists felt that a new unifying term was necessary to convey this sentiment to the world. However, as this reawakening took shape, a new plague emerged.

CHAPTER 10

TWO-SPIRITS

*Until racism, sexism, homophobia have left our earth,
or until I die, I will always have an intimate
daily dialogue with violence.*

—BARBARA CAMERON (Hunkpapa Lakota)[1]

*Trying to come to terms with our Indianness and our
gayness at the same time has meant trying to look back
into our past and trying to understand who we are on
the basis of our own traditional cultures.*

—RON ROWELL (Choctaw)[2]

THE 1980S OPENED with a mixture of trepidation and optimism for
LGBT Indians. Ronald Reagan's election to the US presidency caused
considerable alarm. Barbara Cameron saw what she called the "Reagan regime" as a new phase in an ongoing battle against the bigoted
politics of right-wing reactionaries and activist Christian conservatives. Cameron also identified Anita Bryant, conservative activist
Phyllis Schlafly, and what she called the "Moral Majority clones"
who swept Reagan to power as threats to everything she believed in.
Cameron stated that LGBT Indians needed to keep organizing because
"we have the responsibility to not remain silent."[3]

Other LGBT Indians shared Cameron's anxiety about conservative activism during the Reagan presidency, but tribal leaders adopted
a wait and see approach.[4] They didn't have to wait long to see how
Reagan folded his Indian policies into a larger agenda of reduced government spending on nonmilitary items. Federal support for tribal
self-determination and government-to-government relations initiated

under the Nixon administration continued, but only to advance Reagan's goal of reducing the size of government. To the shock of Native leaders, Reagan proposed draconian cuts in Indian education and health and human services. As the 1980s unfolded, distrust for the Reagan administration grew across Indian Country.[5]

That mistrust remained a constant for LGBT Indians as they worked to build communities.[6] In Minnesota, Lee Staples and Richard LaFortune (aka Anguksuar) nurtured community connections by founding American Indian Gays and Lesbians. In New York, where the American Indian Community House had offered support services to Native people since 1969, Curtis Harris and Leota Lone Dog (Mohawk-Delaware-Lakota) founded the group WeWha and BarCheAmpe in New York City. Named after WeWha, the Zuni lhamana, and BarCheAmpe, a Crow warrior woman, the group provided access to resources and a social space where people could be themselves. Harris, a San Carlos Apache, is today a trusted elder, but shortly after his arrival in New York in 1989 he emphasized WeWha and BarCheAmpe's work in providing support for LGBT Indians and in "educating the Native community."[7] Lone Dog added that the line between WeWha and BarCheAmpe and AICH was so blurred that everyone felt "part of the circle."[8]

LGBT Indians organized in Canada too. In Toronto, Gays and Lesbians of the First Nations emerged, and in Winnipeg, Nichiwakan N.G.S. (for Native Gay Society) became a focal point of community and support for gay and lesbian Indigenous people.[9] Activists, artists, social workers, and healthcare professionals in both Canada and the United States led these organizations, which focused on the social, economic, and political challenges of their time. These leaders also wanted to tell their own stories. For too long anthropologists had misrepresented LGBT Indians and reduced kinship to a narrow set of academic terms, and while academics in a slew of other disciplines made assumptions about the berdache and what community meant to Indigenous people.[10] But did they? Carrie House didn't think so. House, a Diné, believed that "non-Indian people lacked the context for proper interpretation" of gendered traditions in Native communities.[11] Ruth Beebe Hill's *Hanta Yo* (1978), a fictionalized account of the winkte tradition, underscored House's point with its stereotyped portrayal of Indigenous gender and sexuality.[12]

During this period of ferment in Indigenous activism, an even bigger challenge than the colonizing influences of the past emerged, a truly existential challenge: AIDS. Randy Burns remembered warning GAI members that AIDS is "coming our way. We've got to be prepared."[13] AIDS felt like another terrifying foreign invasion.[14] Out of the pain and loss that AIDS caused, LGBT Indians renewed their collective determination to heal communities and tell the world, "We exist."

. . . .

In 1981, reports of a deadly new illness caused alarm across the United States. In Los Angeles, five previously healthy young men were diagnosed with a rare lung infection. At the same time, men in New York were being diagnosed with an aggressive form of cancer known as Kaposi's sarcoma.[15] At first, medical professionals and community leaders weren't sure about the scale and scope of what they were dealing with. What they did know was the illness appeared to target gay and bisexual men, with major outbreaks in cities like New York, Los Angeles, and San Francisco. Straight Americans called it the "gay virus."[16] It was a callous slur. In 1982, the Centers for Disease Control labeled the virus AIDS, for acquired immune deficiency syndrome. An acronym—short, pithy, terrifying.

Media reports filled newspapers, popular magazines, and television news programs. A generation of Americans—not just gay and bisexual men—were shaped by AIDS. In the early years, journalists reported that gay and bisexual men and intravenous drug users were at greatest risk. Americans learned that AIDS was contracted through the exchange of bodily fluids, like semen or blood, or through the sharing of needles. Within a few years of the first reports of the syndrome, cases of women and children contracting AIDS also emerged. No one was safe from a virus that entered the bloodstream and presented flu-like symptoms that quickly manifested into acute infection.[17]

To most Americans, the face of AIDS was white, gay, and male. Television images of previously healthy young men withered by the virus shocked viewers. For white gay men, AIDS undermined the few advances they'd been able to make. Back in the 1970s, their whiteness had propelled some gay men to political gains and economic advances. The specter of the "gay virus" and the "gay fear" it inspired threatened white gay America with a new era of marginalization; it seemed to be wiping out a whole generation of gay men.[18]

AIDS first appeared in the United States in the early 1960s. It was not until the early 1980s, however, that doctors in New York, San Francisco, and Los Angeles began reporting clusters of AIDS patients. Between 1981 and 1987, the Centers for Disease Control estimated that 92 percent of the 50,280 new infections occurred among men, with almost 60 percent of those occurring among whites and 25.5 percent among African Americans.[19] The symptoms of infection included Kaposi's sarcoma, a cancer that typically presents on the skin or lymph nodes, and pneumocystis pneumonia, caused by a fungus that leads to inflammation and fluid accumulation in the lungs. Doctors and medical researchers scrambled to better understand what had become a global pandemic.[20]

The trigger of the disease remained unclear. However, in 1983 researchers reported that AIDS was caused by the human T-lymphotropic virus type III/lymphadenopathy-associated virus, or HTLV-III/LAV. The cumbersome term was soon changed to HIV, for human immunodeficiency virus; its source was traced to West Equatorial Africa. In these parts of Africa, humans had long hunted chimpanzees for their meat. Medical researchers speculated that human hunters likely contracted the virus after coming into contact with infected chimpanzee blood.[21]

During the middle decades of the 1980s, the Reagan administration remained silent on HIV/AIDS, but scientists wanted answers. In 1985, Dr. Anthony Fauci, the director of the National Institute of Allergy and Infectious Diseases, issued a typically forthright, if grim, report. Fauci said that new research revealed that a subset of T4 helper cells went missing or became inactive in infected patients. Fauci claimed that "not only are there not enough cells, but among those that are left, the very important ones that are supposed to respond to antigen are either defective or absent."[22]

Understanding the cause of HIV/AIDS and why it led to this type of immune system response added urgency to the search for effective treatments. As research continued, the human toll of HIV/AIDS reached staggering proportions. As of 2019, the World Health Organization (WHO) estimated that since 1981, seventy-five million people had been infected with HIV/AIDS globally and thirty-two million had died of the disease.[23]

Theodor de Bry, *Balboa Throws Some Indians, Who Had Committed the Terrible Sin of Sodomy, to the Dogs to Be Torn Apart*, 1594

Stirrup Spout Vessel Depicting Fellatio, Moche ceramic, ca. 100–700 CE

Two Women with a Baby, Bahía ceramic, ca. 500 BCE–500 CE

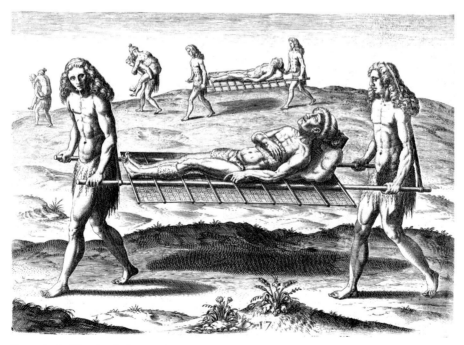

Engraving by Theodor de Bry, *Employments of the Hermaphrodites*, 1591, reputed to depict a scene portrayed by Jacques Le Moyne but lost in the violence at Fort Caroline

Nicholas Point, *Marie Quilax a la bataille contre Les Corbeaux (Août 1846)* (Marie Quilax at War with the Crow [August 1846])

George Catlin, *Dance to the Berdash*, 1835–1837, oil on canvas

Kent Monkman, *Honour Dance*, 2020

"PINE LEAF," THE INDIAN HEROINE, MOUNTED ON HER WAR-HORSE.

Woman Chief, or "Pine Leaf," whom ethnologists speculated was Bíawacheeitchish

Lozen and Dahteste, 1886. Lozen and Dahteste are sixth and fifth from the right, back row.

John K. Hillers, *WeWha Weaving*, ca. 1886

Mary Wheelwright, *Hosteen Klah*

Alexander W. Chase, *Tolowa Man from Taa-'at-dvn Village (Crescent City, Called the "Old Doctor")*

C. H. Asbury, *Ohchiish (Finds-Them-and-Kills-Them)*, 1928

Barbara Cameron, undated photo

Randy Burns, 1984

Raven Heavy Runner at the Seattle Pride Parade, 2018

In Indian Country, the stigma associated with AIDS made it difficult to accurately gauge the scale of the health emergency. According to CDC estimates, Native Americans constituted 0.1 percent of reported HIV/AIDS infections between 1981 and 1987. CDC data for Indian Country likely undercounted the number of HIV/AIDS cases. In one year alone, 1990, the National Native American AIDS Prevention Center (NNAAPC) in Oakland, California, put the number of new cases at 200.[24] CDC data highlighted how large segments of Indian Country believed that HIV/AIDS was a white man's disease. Homophobia and misinformation fueled this belief, hampering treatment efforts and prompting people living with HIV/AIDS to either conceal their illness or seek treatment from non–Indian Health Service providers (the IHS is an agency within the Department of Health and Human Services that provides federal health services to American Indians and Alaska Natives).

For Indigenous people on the frontlines of HIV/AIDS prevention and treatment, the federal government's neglect of Indian Country and seeming lack of interest in tackling HIV/AIDS generally made it difficult to combat misinformation.[25] Nonetheless, healthcare professionals persisted as infection rates increased. During the final four years of the 1990s, the CDC estimated that 0.4 percent of all new HIV/AIDS infections in the United States occurred among Indigenous people. Given the homophobia that persisted in many Native communities, this data likely undercounts infection rates. Still, the numbers made for sober reading. The American Indian and Native Alaskan population constituted 0.8 percent of the total US population in 1990 and 1.5 percent of the total population in 2000. Over that time, few Native communities went untouched by HIV/AIDS, as infection rates reached as high as 25 per 100,000 in this population group.[26]

Treating and preventing HIV/AIDS both in urban America and on rural reservations involved considerable challenges during the 1980s and 1990s. Healthcare professionals felt constrained by homophobia, a strained IHS system, and federal government neglect. Compounding these issues was the persistent denial among Native people that HIV/AIDS afflicted their communities. Cecilia Limberhand, a tribal health worker, found that on the Northern Cheyenne Reservation in Montana people "think it's not going to come to us." According to Limberhand, tribal members believed that AIDS was "a white man's disease" that they didn't need to worry about.[27]

In reality, HIV/AIDS couldn't be ignored. Carole LaFavor, an Ojibwe woman who worked to raise awareness about the virus in the 1980s, insisted that "how we respond to AIDS will tell a lot about us as a people."[28] Barbara Cameron shared LaFavor's concern about AIDS. Cameron felt particularly frustrated about gay and lesbian people who perpetuated stereotypes that harmed prevention and treatment efforts. "It is sickening," Cameron complained in 1983, "that in a time of uncertainty, that we have these individuals who are not AIDS patients but indeed have become AIDS victims. These individuals become ministers of doom in our community, perpetuating lies about our community, invoking stereotypes and myths of the gay lifestyle."[29]

Ron Rowell, a Choctaw, knew that homophobic and racist stereotypes made effective awareness and treatment campaigns in Indian communities additionally challenging. Rowell, a cofounder of the NNAAPC, also turned his attention outward and to criticism of the Reagan administration for "consciously and consistently" failing to adequately address the AIDS crisis in Indian Country.[30]

Rowell and fellow healthcare providers felt frustrated. Rowell often argued that the IHS should have led efforts to prevent and treat AIDS in Indian Country. Formed as a division of the Bureau of Indian Affairs (BIA) in 1955, the IHS was subsequently transferred to the Department of Health and Human Services. Throughout its history, IHS has struggled to receive adequate federal funding and to meet patient needs. This remained true during the early years of the AIDS crisis.[31]

It wasn't until the latter half of the 1980s that the IHS developed a clear set of protocols for effectively treating HIV/AIDS and working to prevent its spread. In 1986 and 1987, IHS policy focused on seven areas: "prevention, infection control, employee education, antibody testing for the Human Immunodeficiency Virus (HIV), contact tracing, community education, and confidentiality."[32]

Confidentiality remained a problem.[33] Patients at risk of contracting AIDS, or those infected, often found they had to navigate an IHS workforce that stigmatized gay and bisexual men. On reservations and in small rural communities, fears about gossipy IHS staff magnified the stress associated with AIDS. Melvin Harrison, a Navajo Nation citizen and Two-Spirit ally, recalls the dual stigma of homophobia and infection that followed people living with HIV/AIDS. Harrison responded by founding the Navajo AIDS Network. Although not medically trained, Harrison worked to provide emotional support and connect people with medical services. Harrison encountered abuse from some Navajo citizens for undertaking this work and was the target of a slur campaign that alleged he had AIDS. He nonetheless persisted. Harrison felt he had to do something, recalling that gay and trans men often sought care outside of the IHS system to avoid being stigmatized. Countless others went untreated.[34] Given that AIDS activists and healthcare professionals wanted to prevent the spread of HIV/AIDS, persistent breaches of confidentiality, homophobia, and attacks on people who provided desperately needed services became impediments to effective treatment and education campaigns well into the 1990s and beyond.[35]

The formation of privately funded clinics in both urban and reservation communities aimed to serve patients who felt IHS couldn't meet their needs. Ron Rowell's cofounding of NNAAPC filled that healthcare need in San Francisco and then, later, in Denver. In Minneapolis, the National Native American AIDS Prevention Center was established to provide a range of services, education programs, and treatment options. In 1989, the Minneapolis center issued a statement urging continued vigilance about HIV/AIDS infection in Indian Country: "We are more than five years into the AIDS epidemic among American Indians and many Indian communities have felt the devastating effects of AIDS. Because of the high drug and alcohol usage among Indian people, we are at a high risk for sexually transmitted diseases such as AIDS."[36]

Centers like those in Oakland and Minneapolis worked to shatter the stigma associated with AIDS and reach people at risk of infection. That work felt urgent. In November 1987, the *Seattle Times* warned that AIDS was a "time bomb" in the urban and rural sections of Indian Country. In response to these concerns, Ron Rowell asked rhetorically: "How much is an Indian life worth?"[37] Rowell continued raising awareness about the impacts of HIV/AIDS as infection rates skyrocketed. By August 1989, Rowell declared that AIDS was "a holocaust among young people."[38]

The AIDS pandemic ravaged communities of color during the 1990s.[39] In Indian Country, the majority of new infections occurred among Native men, with Indigenous women comprising roughly 14 percent of new HIV/AIDS infections. In 1992, the rate of infection among Native Americans was ten times the rate among African American and Latinx communities.[40] Homophobia and gossipy IHS employees continued hampering effective treatment, particularly in rural reservation communities.

Ken Pinkham, an Indigenous gay man, recalled that the stigma was real. He laughed when he remembered straight Indians referring to gay Indians by the slur "he's a bottom." Behind the laughter, though, Pinkham's memories of the 1990s were tinged with pain.[41] For a lot of gay men in the 1980s and 1990s, it was not easy to be gay and Indigenous. Pinkham recalls those decades by remembering a culture in which bars became outlets for socializing and places where you could hook up and "go for a quickie." If you were Indigenous, though, the racism in gay communities meant your nightlife was limited. When AIDS began infecting gay and bisexual Native men, it felt like Indigenous men were again being excluded—this time from the educational materials, prevention resources, and medical treatments available to white gay and bisexual men.

The rapid spread of AIDS in the 1980s gave rise to myths and conspiracy theories.[42] Ken Pinkham still views AIDS as a conspiracy against people of color. When I spoke with Pinkham in February 2019, he recounted a version of the "patient zero" hypothesis popularized by journalist Randy Shilts in his 1987 book *And the Band Played On.* Shilts pandered to homophobia by positing the "gay lifestyle" argument as the driver of the AIDS pandemic.[43] Pinkham didn't share Shilts's position on the "gay lifestyle" slur, and it wasn't clear to me that he'd read Shilts's book. But Pinkham had heard a version of the "patient zero" story. According to Pinkham, the first Native American to contract AIDS was a young boy in 1980. The source of the boy's infection was a gay flight attendant who had sex with a pilot in New York. That pilot, Pinkham recounted, later had sex with, and infected, the Indian boy. Pinkham remembers attending a gathering around 1991 or 1992, where, he claims, he saw FBI documents revealing a government conspiracy to let AIDS wipe out Native men. That same document allegedly detailed a plan to have military doctors inject Indigenous men with the AIDS virus.[44]

There is a long history of medical malpractice and unethical scientific research involving communities of color in the United States.[45] Knowing this, I understood why Pinkham still harbored a belief about an AIDS conspiracy, even if there's no scientific evidence to support his claims. Pinkham certainly isn't alone in questioning the origins of AIDS. A number of prominent journalists—notably Tom Curtis and Edward Hooper—wrote articles and books that linked the origins of HIV/AIDS in the Congo to infected chimpanzee kidneys allegedly used in making Hilary Koprowski oral polio vaccine during the late 1950s and early 1960s. Koprowski, a Polish-born virologist and immunologist, remained steadfast in his denials of malpractice, unethical research practices, and questionable data collection up until his death in 2013. The scientific community agrees, concluding that the link between Koprowski's oral polio vaccine and the origins of HIV/AIDS is little more than a conspiracy theory.[46]

Conspiracy theories, however, have long shelf lives. They outlive factual rebuttals, especially when a government has a history of causing harm to one group of people. This is the case with the origin of HIV/AIDS. It's unsurprising, then, that Pinkham incorporates these theories into his own understanding of the AIDS pandemic, given the Reagan administration's mishandling of it in the early 1980s. At the same time, conspiracy theories proved an impediment to effective education campaigns and treatment during the 1980s and 1990s.[47]

Healthcare workers and social service providers like Ron Rowell took on the work of providing services and raising awareness about HIV/AIDS among Indigenous people. Rowell has devoted his adult life to HIV/AIDS prevention and treatment. In the 1980s and 1990s he successfully acquired grants from private philanthropies and worked to draw attention to the challenges of providing culturally appropriate medical and emotional support to Native people living with HIV/AIDS. The ongoing effects of colonialism, economic marginalization, and social isolation among large segments of the LGBT population in Indian Country meant that the services Rowell provided became lifelines.[48]

Emotional and spiritual support became one of the focal points of HIV/AIDS treatment in Native communities, particularly in urban settings. Historically, Indigenous people believe that healing comes from within. Healing can't begin unless it is connected to a nurturing community. These beliefs inspired a "return to the medicine wheel."[49] In Native communities across North America, the medicine wheel focuses on health and healing. The medicine wheel is represented by the four cardinal directions and also includes Father Sky, Mother Earth, and Spirit Tree. In some cultures, the medicine wheel is also represented by the hoop ("the never-ending circle of life"), embedded in artwork (as it is in Diné sand paintings), or built into the landscape (as it is in the stone medicine wheel located in Bighorn National Forest in Wyoming).[50] Medicine bundles are also incorporated into traditional healthcare practices, particularly among Plains tribes. In treating people living with HIV/AIDS, medicine bundles included ceremonial plants such as sage, tobacco, or sweet grass. These traditional approaches to medicine recognize the interconnectedness of physical, mental, emotional, and spiritual well-being. In the 1980s and 1990s, groups devoted to traditional medicine incorporated the medicine wheel into their treatments. For example, the Shoshone-Bannock elder Clyde Hall used medicine bundles to treat AIDS patients. Then as now, Indigenous healing techniques emphasize the powerful medicine derived from within a person and from connecting—or in some cases, reconnecting—to community.[51]

A new generation of leaders facilitated the reconnection with traditional medicine. Phil Tingley was one of those leaders. A proud Kiowa man, he encouraged Indigenous people to go back to their traditions so they might heal and walk peacefully into the future.[52] Tingley devoted his adult life to enriching Native communities, reclaiming Indigenous cultures and languages, and working to understand the impact of historical trauma among Native Americans.[53] Phillip Tingley was born in Oklahoma in 1951. He grew up in Anadarko, a small town where he began learning the culture and language of the Kiowa people. In high school he ran on the track team, made good grades, and, once he graduated, left Oklahoma and headed to San Francisco. He arrived in the Bay Area in 1971 and wasted no time making connections with the Pan-Indian community. With the support of other gay and lesbian Indians like Barbara Cameron, Tingley played an important role in nurturing a sense of community for all Native people in San Francisco.

Tingley possessed an immense intellect, was a captivating public speaker, and championed social justice. As president of the National Indian Social Workers Association he advocated on behalf of Indigenous child welfare and worked to raise awareness about the traumatic effects of boarding schools, child poverty and sexual abuse, and racial discrimination in adoption practices.

Tingley began his career at a time when Indigenous child welfare policies attracted renewed attention from federal lawmakers. These debates culminated in the passage of the Indian Child Welfare Act in 1978. The legislation aimed to halt the exceedingly high rates at which Indigenous children were forcibly taken from their families and placed in government institutions, or with white foster families. Debate over the act drew national media attention, reminding Americans of the abuses suffered by Indigenous children in federal boarding schools.[54]

For decades, child removal programs had caused physical and emotional pain to children, their families, and communities.[55] That trauma persisted into the 1970s. Tingley focused on addressing the wrongs caused by federal boarding schools and the removal of Indigenous children.[56] Before PTSD—post-traumatic stress disorder—entered the popular vernacular, Tingley sought out historical comparisons to help explain the impact of trauma on Native children. In 1990, in an unpublished manuscript for San Francisco's Indian Health Clinic, "Native American Cultures: Homosexuality & the Family," he argued: "American Indians, like some war veterans and survivors of concentration camps and other severe traumas, suffer from post traumatic stress. American Indians are survivors of from one to five hundred years of the most brutal genocide, ethnocide and forced acculturation the world has ever seen. . . . For the past five generations, we have experienced one cultural and individual trauma after another."[57]

HIV/AIDS opened a new chapter in the history of colonial trauma. Just as he threw himself into research and advocacy on behalf of Indian child welfare, Tingley confronted the AIDS pandemic with wisdom and a determination to mitigate its impact in Native communities.

Tingley approached the AIDS crisis as an existential threat to Native America. He lamented how the weight of European colonial history made it difficult to cut through the dual stigmas of racism and homophobia and reach Native people living with HIV/AIDS. He also believed that the modern European terms "gay," "lesbian," and the deeply offensive "berdache" undermined efforts to decolonize the minds of Native people and move beyond the myth that HIV/AIDS was a "white disease." This language also made it that much harder to reclaim the "alternative genders" and sexual identities that once proved integral to many Indigenous kinship systems. "You can't have a people go through the levels of holocaust that we've been through,"

Tingley argued in 1990, "with levels of genocide and ethnocide that still continues today in many parts of this country, in the hemisphere, without there being significant changes" to Native cultures.[58]

For Tingley, addressing HIV/AIDS meant grappling with colonialism. AIDS, like smallpox and other diseases introduced by colonizers, needed to be understood in the context of European invasion throughout the Americas. These diseases, coupled with the searing levels of physical and psychological violence directed at "alternative gender" Indians since the late fifteenth century, had decimated caregivers, medicine people, and elders—people like Tingley. With HIV/AIDS, Tingley saw history repeating itself.

Tingley stood firm in his belief that the leadership of "alternative genders" was critical to Native people reclaiming their culture and languages. He knew that the rebirth of traditional cultures was a source of spiritual strength for Indigenous people living with HIV/AIDS, but more needed to be done. Native Americans needed allies. They needed "whites to reverse the negative aspects of your culture," while Native medicine people needed more time to understand the AIDS virus. Tingley, like Ron Rowell and other gay and lesbian leaders, knew that medicine people had heard about the AIDS pandemic and wanted to help, just as past generations of medicine people tried to heal those afflicted by smallpox, measles, and a host of other foreign pathogens. Indigenous knowledge keepers faced a difficult challenge, Tingley claimed, because these "viruses are relatively new to us. They came over during colonization." Moreover, "a virus goes into the cell and not outside the cell," Tingley contended. From a "spiritual perspective," that made it "harder to see a virus than a bacteria."[59]

Time was not something that Native people with HIV/AIDS had much of. Tingley didn't have much time either. After he contracted AIDS, his health declined rapidly. He died in September 1991 at just forty years old. Tingley's passing touched people across Indian Country. At his memorial service, Barbara Cameron spoke of continuing Tingley's work: reconnecting with culture, reclaiming traditions, and revitalizing language. Phil "made me proud to know him," Cameron recalled. Her grief was compounded by the fact that "Indian people are fighting a terrible illness. . . . It has taken many Indian lives in San Francisco. And I don't want any Indian person to die alone, unaccepted by their own because of a disease or because of sexual orientation."[60]

AIDS robbed Native communities of creative, insightful, and spiritual people. It could also bring communities together. In 1989, a Kiowa man living in California who used the name Dennis expressed his gratitude for his community. "I always brag about my Kiowa people," Dennis wrote. "They have always supported any tribal member who faces illness . . . no matter what type of illness, they stand by you."[61] Clyde Hall echoed these sentiments several decades later when he told me that "traditionally, no one was ever thrown away."[62]

Phil Tingley knew the healing power of community. Speaking from the grave in a newspaper article that was published posthumously in 1992, Tingley urged Native people to "provide ourselves with something to replace our pain. We must have something to go to." Tingley believed Indian people needed to share and borrow traditions. Tingley left the world with a powerful message: "As a people," he concluded, "by confronting and accepting our history and experiences, we will free the power and strength we have required to suppress our traumas for use in overcoming them and moving forward."[63]

. . . .

Barbara Cameron understood the power of human connection. Like Tingley, she knew that "Indian people do not live in the past." Native Americans have diverse histories and complex identities. Speaking about her own identity, Cameron claimed that being a "lesbian of color" was the weakest part of "my home." Like other Native women, Cameron's sense of home, of safety and family, was routinely threatened by "the heartache that racism creates." The persistence of racism and homophobia magnified the importance of Cameron's Indianness and drove her to cofound GAI.

Cameron's activism also inspired a search for non-Indigenous allies. She felt no less a Lakota warrior and lesbian woman for "stepping out of the boundaries" of racial, gender, or sexual identity prescribed by colonialism to initiate political alliances with non-Indigenous people. Political alliances empowered Cameron's quest to educate Native and non-Native people, gay and straight, about the complexity, richness, and beauty of her identity. She maintained that by "reclaiming family, we are reclaiming humanity and dignity." Her concept of family involved building an adaptive home. She used the metaphor of the adobe home to emphasize the resilience of Native families: "If you've seen adobe homes," Cameron wrote, "you know its design is for multi-dwellings, you can always add to an adobe, it's connected in all its different levels and it is in harmony with the environment."[64]

Cameron's GAI cofounder, Randy Burns, shared her alliance-building ethos. In the early 1980s Burns collaborated with the non-Native historian Will Roscoe to raise awareness among "Indian and non-Indian people about the place of Gay American Indians in our cultural history."[65] That collaboration led to the founding of the GAI history project and the publication of *Living the Spirit*, a history of GAI and an oral history anthology. Burns was a driving force behind the GAI history project. In consultation with GAI, he began collecting stories from LGBT Indians in the hope of raising awareness about their cultural diversity, creativity, and existence. This latter point was no small matter in the 1980s. Burns was acutely aware of the racially exclusive nature of the gay community in San Francisco, marginalization replicated across North America. Burns also wanted to confront homophobia in Native communities. He argued that "many Indian families then and now are very Christian, very influenced by Western thought. Meaning that they're very homophobic in a lot of ways."[66]

Burns recognized the importance of publicity to fundraising efforts. He therefore agreed to appear in photographer Stephen Stewart's 1985 book *Positive Image*, a collection of photographs chronicling the people and struggles of the gay liberation movement.[67] The GAI history project's directors also sent letters to Native people requesting written and artistic contributions that spoke to "traditional gay roles" in tribal communities, and solicited donations from the readers of gay and lesbian periodicals so that Native people could tell their "story in their own words." A $7,000 grant from the Chicago Resource Center helped the GAI offset a number of production and advertising costs, but raising enough money to keep the project afloat proved a continual struggle.[68]

Living the Spirit rolled off the presses in 1988.[69] The anthology brought together historical analysis, contemporary reflections and creative writing, and sections devoted to "Contacts and Resources" and "Berdache and Alternative Gender Roles," which listed tribe-specific names for these individuals in Native American communities.[70] Burns wrote the preface and used the opening pages to set the tone for the anthology. Borrowing from Maurice Kenny, Burns reminded readers: "We are special." As HIV/AIDS gripped communities, this was an important message.

The anthology aimed to undermine homophobia and move LGBT Indians out of history's shadows. Although some sections read like a dry report, the politics of many of the anthology's contributors were unmistakable. Many lambasted terms like "berdache," criticized the racism of gay and straight white Americans, and narrated their own histories.[71] This collaborative exercise in decolonizing LGBT literature and history received positive reviews in the gay press and from Indigenous scholars. Deganawidah-Quetzalcoatl (D-Q) University professor Alfred "Al" Robinson wrote that *Living the Spirit* represented "a deeply moved and moving discovery of identity, [and] a thirst for wholeness and unity."[72]

. . . .

Living the Spirit contributed to a conversation about the offensiveness of colonial labels like "berdache" and inspired debate about a new language that reflected the unique place of LGBT people in Indigenous history and culture.[73] As this conversation gathered momentum in Indian Country, the work of two prominent historians threatened to set these discussions back decades.

In separate publications during the late 1980s and 1990s, historians Ramón Gutiérrez and Richard Trexler sparked intense debates in gay and lesbian communities. The fallout from their work reverberated into the early 2000s and is remembered by numerous Two-Spirit people I've spoken with. In 1989, Gutiérrez published a controversial essay in *Out/Look,* a popular magazine that catered to LGBT readers, that was a precursor to his book *When Jesus Came, the Corn Mothers Went Away* (1991). Trexler took a more academic path, writing the salaciously titled *Sex and Conquest* (1995), and a 2002 essay in an academic journal. Both historians used what LGBT people in Indian Country considered the offensive "berdache" label, and both presented readers with a picture of a violent past in which the berdache was often kinless, a war captive, or sex slave. Gutiérrez and Trexler relied overwhelmingly—and uncritically—on the written sources of European colonial archives. Those sources distorted the past by presenting the berdache in overwhelmingly negative terms, usually as victims of violence, or, as Gutiérrez wrote in *Out/Look*, as someone who provided a "passive sexual service to men."[74]

Gutiérrez and Trexler focused on a narrow academic obsession: refuting the gay "origins" thesis posited by Harry Hay and expanded on by scholars Will Roscoe and Walter Williams. The gay "origins" thesis turned to Native American traditions of gender fluidity to make the case that homosexuality had deep historical roots in North America and that gay men and lesbian women enjoyed a special place in many Indigenous communities.[75] Trexler intervened in this debate by combing through early colonial sources and drawing connections among the use of force, "transvestism," and sodomy in Indian Country. In *Sex and Conquest*, he speculated that Indigenous parents and their local community determined the gendered identities of children shortly after birth.[76] Gutiérrez's take proved more strident. He characterized the search for a gay "origins" story as "romantic obfuscation."[77] It was pure historical fiction, a series of feel-good generalizations lacking historical specificity. For Gutiérrez and Trexler, written evidence provided virtually no evidence of the berdache enjoying an honored place in Native communities. Writing in 2002, Trexler doubled down on this position. Pointing to the history of Plains Indians prior to 1800, Trexler argued that "no evidence exists suggesting that [Native] Americans thought of themselves as choosing to be a berdache, let alone evidence that they in fact had exercised choice in this regard." As a rule, Trexler speculated that force was used to "convert children of one sex to the opposite gender."[78]

Trexler's argument discounted the communal traditions across Indian Country. Like that of Gutiérrez, his analysis put little stock in personal recollections, emotion, or the post-structural theories that informed a newer generation of LGBT Indians who were appropriating terms like "queer"—a previously offensive label that growing numbers of LGBTQ people began adopting to announce their fluid gender and sexual identities.

For Gutiérrez, claims about gay origins and theoretical speculations ran counter to his primary focus: historical specificity. This is understandable given Gutiérrez's academic training. In his book *When Jesus Came, the Corn Mothers Went Away*, Gutiérrez drew on written Spanish sources to argue that violence and coercion characterized the life of a berdache. "Sex with a berdache," Gutiérrez wrote, "served a personal erotic need and a religious (political) end."[79] Gutiérrez had started advancing this argument in his 1989 essay for *Out/Look*, earning the ire of readers. Harry Hay picked up his pen and accused Gutiérrez of "ethnocentrism, indeed racism." An *Out/Look* reader accused Gutiérrez of imposing his personal beliefs onto the past, writing in a letter, "Gutiérrez' ascription of the 'universal' concept of feminization of the enemy of the Native American cultures is only a projection."[80]

Not every letter writer found fault with Gutiérrez's work. One particularly vitriolic letter went after both Hay and Roscoe. Responding to Hay's criticism of Gutiérrez, the correspondent contended that the problem wasn't the arguments advanced by Gutiérrez but white gay men like Hay who have "the temerity . . . to place themselves in the position of speaking for people of color." Turning their wrath on Will Roscoe and the mainstream gay movement's appropriation of Indigenous cultures, the correspondent concluded the letter by expressing their exasperation at white scholars who attempt to "define every Indian that ever cross-dressed or sucked a cock as gay."[81]

. . . .

The debate sparked by the work of Gutiérrez and Trexler reminded LGBTQ Indians of the importance of telling their own stories. They needed their own narratives, their own histories, and a language of their own to talk about the needs of their communities. GAI initiated that process. Other Native people joined them in rejecting the "phallocentrism, androcentrism, and heterosexism" imposed on them by settler culture.[82] As HIV/AIDS continued terrorizing gay communities, other Native groups began forming to advocate for LGBTQ Indians.[83]

The American Indian Gay and Lesbian Center (AIGL) was one of those new groups. Founded in Minneapolis in 1987, the AIGL aimed to build community in the Twin Cities and to forge networks with LGBT Indians throughout the United States and beyond. AIGL's cofounders, Lee Staples and Richard LaFortune, worked to cut through the isolation that LGBT Indians felt in Minneapolis, and in rural reservation communities. Joining the efforts of the Ojibwe community organizer Debra Williams, AIGL began connecting people to "traditional indigenous cultures." Staples and LaFortune also recognized that they needed to work tirelessly to combat homophobia, racism, and historical misrepresentation. They wanted to make AIGL an oasis of support. By the early 1990s, AIGL's mailing list had grown slowly to include just over one hundred people.[84]

Lee Staples inspired AIGL members. In Minneapolis, Staples earned a reputation for being a "special person among 'special people.'" Raised by elders on the Mille Lacs Reservation in Minnesota, Staples experienced homophobia and racism during his youth and into his early adult life. These dual prejudices shaped the course of his life.

Staples did not come out until 1985. In the years prior to that decision, he recalled that his identity felt fragmented. He remembered presenting himself as "Indian" or "gay" depending on the social situation, never a blend of the two. He recalled thinking that "all there was to our lives as gays was the bar scene and sex." That changed after he came out. Staples felt a new lease on life, a freedom that inspired his return to the spiritual grounding that elders had provided him in his youth at Mille Lacs.[85]

With LaFortune, Staples worked to make AIGL an important site of community formation in the Twin Cities. LaFortune, a Yup'ik born in Alaska in 1960, was a tireless advocate for Native people. In addition to his work at AIGL, LaFortune later cofounded the Two Spirit Press Room to raise awareness about Two-Spirit issues and foster a larger sense of community. With the energy and organizing skills of Staples, Williams, and LaFortune, AIGL became to Minneapolis what the American Indian Community House was to New York City: a refuge where Native people could socialize and find desperately needed support services and resources to address the AIDS pandemic.[86] In this context, questions about "self-identity" were debated in a safe and supportive environment.[87]

Defining identity in terms that celebrated the diversity of LGBTQ Indians while also connecting straight and gay Indians were issues of vital importance to AICH, GAI, and AIGL.[88] Claiming an identity that did not marginalize LGBTQ Indians in Native and non-Native settings was not merely an abstract exercise. Between the 1979 March on Washington for Lesbian and Gay Rights and a subsequent march on Washington in 1987, LGBTQ Native Americans continued experiencing the dual discrimination of homophobia and racism. Reflecting on the 1987 March on Washington, the Menominee Two-Spirit writer and activist Chrystos remembers the racism directed at gay and lesbian Indians. In a poem dedicated to Randy Burns, Chrystos wrote: "gay white america same as straight white."[89]

The 1987 March on Washington occurred at a critical moment in LGBTQ politics. It coincided with growing disenchantment with the Reagan administration's mishandling of the AIDS pandemic and the Supreme Court's upholding of Georgia's anti-sodomy law in *Bowers v. Hardwick*. In handing down the court's decision, Chief Justice Warren Burger claimed that laws against homosexuality had "ancient roots." The decision sparked protests on the steps of the Supreme Court building. It also inspired the Mohawk writer Maurice Kenny to pick up his pen and write a searing condemnation of the court, arguing: "When the U.S. Supreme Court cited millennia of moral teaching in support of Georgia's sodomy law they must not have been thinking of American history and American morals. Because, throughout America for centuries before and after the arrival of Europeans, Gay and Lesbian American Indians were recognized and valued members of tribal communities. We were special!"[90]

That's not how most Americans saw things. In 1987, polling data suggested that roughly 70 percent of Americans thought homosexual relationships were "always wrong." For Native LGBTQ people, racism compounded the effects of homophobia, something Chrystos experienced at the 1987 March on Washington. While the 1987 March ultimately proved transformative for LGBTQ Indians, at the time Native people were few in number and were routinely ignored by white gay and lesbian leaders.[91] Randy Burns recalls attending the march with "my warrior brothers and sisters." He remembers a group of Black and Latino gay men fighting over who would lead the parade. Burns wasn't going to stand for this bickering. He approached the group, and scolded them: "Excuse me, please remember whose land you're walking on. It's only appropriate, don't you think, you two fighting communities, that you should honor the American Indian gays and lesbians with our banner."[92] They did. Gay and lesbian Indians led the 1987 march. It was a small victory, but it energized a movement on the cusp of explosive growth.

LGBTQ Indians made themselves increasingly visible in the final years of the 1980s. Poet Janice Gould played her part in raising the profile of LGBTQ Native people with a powerful poem entitled "we exist." The poem's title spoke volumes, while its thoughtfully crafted lines took readers on a journey through the destructive history of colonialism.[93] For thousands of Native people, that history was not in the past: it was their present. Battered women, children suffering unspeakable forms of abuse, and gay Native Americans navigating homophobia and the deadly possibility of AIDS all struggled to "exist" in a world that routinely ignored them.[94] As Phil Tingley often reminded Native people, they could not forget how the past shaped their present, but they also needed to heal to create a meaningful future.

Healing meant different things to different people in Indian Country. For a growing number of LGBTQ Indians, it meant reconnecting with Indigenous culture and tradition. That is what Beverly Little Thunder did. She came out in the mid-1980s after years of involvement with AIM. Little Thunder began leading a Sun Dance ceremony that gave old traditions contemporary meaning. "The dance is simple," she explains. "You pray the whole time for the people, for everyone but yourself. It is your sacrifice. You pledge to pray for Mother Earth, the ill and those in need of help, and you set yourself aside." In an era when HIV/AIDS tore communities apart, the forces of racism and homophobia persisted, and Americans started to become aware of the human impact on global climate change, Little Thunder's innovative turn to tradition constituted a call to community and a prayer for the traditional Native ideal of balance and harmony.[95]

Reclaiming ceremonies at tribal and intertribal gatherings aided the healing process by connecting participants to both tribe-specific and pan-tribal communities.[96] "The Basket and the Bow: A Gathering of Lesbian & Gay Native Americans," first convened in 1988, became a regular event known popularly as the annual American Indian Gay and Lesbian Conference. This conference quickly became the most important gathering for gay and lesbian Indians. After the first gathering in Minneapolis, these events were usually held in quiet, rural settings.[97] The gatherings grew quickly and began attracting LGBTQ Indians from the United States and Canada and also Aboriginal Australians. Writers, artists, community organizers, and future academics attended the international gatherings. Randy Burns and Barbara Cameron appeared on the international gathering's mailing list, as did Joey Criddle, Chrystos, Clyde Hall, Carrie House, Beverly Little Thunder, Richard LaFortune, Michael Red Earth, Ron Rowell,

Wesley Thomas, Craig Womack, and Wayne Davis, an Aboriginal Australian.[98]

After the second annual American Indian Gay and Lesbian gathering, in Wascott, Wisconsin, in late August 1989, Lee Staples declared: "We made history." There was a feeling that these annual gatherings were creating something special. Staples wanted to see LGBTQ Indians continue to organize and come together at the annual gathering. Doing so would facilitate the incorporation of "our traditions and ceremonies" and help communities heal from the ongoing effects of colonialism.[99] Janet Spotted Eagle, an Apache medicine woman, proclaimed the transformative nature of the gay and lesbian annual gathering: "I am here to tell the world that most lesbians and some gay men are a special creation and have [a] special spiritual purpose in this world." She added that they are leaders, healers, medicine people. Spotted Eagle concluded with words that resonate in Native communities today: "As the Mother Earth cleanses Herself of man's pollution, they will be teaching the things we need to know in order to survive."[100] LGBTQ Indians were needed to heal Native America. They would lead in healing the trauma of the past, connecting people in the circle, or hoop, of community.

The gathering that changed the course of modern history for LGBTQ Indians and Native people with gender-fluid identities occurred in early August 1990. It drew a small group of lesbian, gay, bisexual, and transgender Native people to Winnipeg, Manitoba, to discuss a range of issues: "Chemical Dependency, AIDS, Coming Out, Relationships." A "women's pipe ceremony and a Giveaway" was also promised.[101]

This was the gathering where gay and lesbian Indians adopted the term "Two-Spirit," an English translation of the Northern Algonquin *niizh manitoag*, which expresses the existence of feminine and masculine qualities in a single person. The new English-language term advanced the process of decolonizing LGBTQ identities in Indian Country and established a path for greater recognition—which is today recognized in the acronym LGBTQ2S. It also built on the work of GAI and AIGL in recognizing that Indigenous identities added up to more than gender or sexual labels. Their identities were more dynamic than could be expressed in the language of the gay liberation movement.

"Two-Spirit" began restoring that dynamism. It gave people a pan-tribal term that opened a space for organizational unity at a Pan-Indian level. At the same time, the umbrella term "Two-Spirit" inspired people to reengage with tribally specific identities. "Two-Spirit" quickly became a term that empowered Native people who had felt isolated, marginalized, and ridiculed within Indian Country and beyond.

The decolonization of Native gender roles and sexual identities had entered a new phase. Indeed, a new chapter in the reassertion of sovereign Indigenous nations was opening. It is why Two-Spirit people proclaimed to the world in 1990: "We are everywhere. With groups and organizations existing or forming from Winnipeg to San Francisco, Seattle to New York, Minneapolis, Vancouver, Phoenix, Regina, and Saskatoon; we're reappearing with all of our own memories and traditions, our focus on culture and spirituality, sobriety, and political goals."[102]

. . . .

A new dawn had broken over Indian Country. Shortly after the Winnipeg gathering, "Two-Spirit" entered popular usage in Native communities throughout North America. Anthropologists had to catch up. Some scholars tried to gatekeep—they often do—but deep down they knew that "Two-Spirit" was a term by and for Native people, their communities, and their future.[103]

The term "Two-Spirit" became a powerful tool in the fight against homophobia and hate crimes, and in bringing people together.[104] New Two-Spirit organizations formed to educate people and provide resources for LGBTQ Native Americans. In Denver, Sage Douglas Remington formed the Two Spirit Society of Colorado in 1993. Like other societies formed in the 1990s and over the subsequent two decades, the Two Spirit Society of Colorado promoted drug- and alcohol-free gatherings. The society engaged with elders and reclaimed ceremonies like the Wanbi Sina Sundance. They also worked to address contemporary issues of particular interest to Two-Spirit people. "The Society," as an information brochure declared, "is concerned with mending the sacred hoop and re-establishing the roles and responsibilities which Two Spirit people had the honor of serving."[105]

Not everyone got the message. *Lavender* magazine ran a story in 1998 with the headline "Who Were the Berdaches?"[106] Non-Indigenous media outlets in both gay and straight America represented Two-Spirit people as minorities within a minority. Viewing these developments through the lens of late-twentieth-century neoliberalism, one journalist declared that "homosexuality in minority cultures is still taboo. Consequently, there are few political or emotional support groups in communities of color, as there are for white gays and lesbians."[107] Two-Spirit leaders still had work to do.[108]

Combating stereotypes continues today. The battle is never over; each generation inherits a responsibility to never forget, to learn, and to teach. Inverting the historical power of words and phrases that once triggered fear, anxiety, and isolation has been one of the more pronounced contributions of post-structural theories of colonial history. Most famously, the founding of Queer Nation in New York in 1990 promoted a movement to invert language such a "queer" long used to demean and discriminate against LGBTQ people. Queer Nation produced literature and bumper stickers, and purchased billboard space that used irony to proclaim "Homophobia is a social disease," celebrated sexuality with stickers that read "Cock Sucking Faggot," and actively worked to change public discourse by using radio, television, and ultimately the Internet.[109] This provocative, in-your-face turn in LGBTQ activism was at odds with Two-Spirit organizing in the 1990s and their focus on sober, drug-free events, the rejection of homophobic language, and an emphasis on reclaiming traditions.[110]

. . . .

On the streets of urban centers and in rural reservation communities, the reality of HIV/AIDS meant there was not a lot of time for theoretical debates and outlandish political theater. A spike in HIV/AIDS transmission rates in Native communities during the 1990s showed that action was needed. The Campaign for Fairness and other groups worked to educate lawmakers about the enduring impacts of the AIDS pandemic on gay men of color. AIGL, NNAAPC, and other Indigenous organizations worked desperately to acquire much-needed grant funding to stem the wave of infections among Indigenous men.

Hampering these efforts were familiar roadblocks: prejudice, ignorance, and government inertia. Racism remained an issue for Indigenous gay men, just as Native women continued to face sexual violence.[111] The National Task Force on AIDS Prevention, formed in

San Francisco in 1985 as part of the National Association of Black and White Men Together, tried to break down discriminatory barriers and open access to care for poor and racially marginalized gay men. However, the coalition showed signs of fraying in the early 1990s due to racism within the organization. Racial divisions reminded gay men of the tenuousness of interracial coalitions in the fight against HIV/AIDS.[112]

Native people with HIV/AIDS often responded better to treatment when they withdrew from the racism endemic in American society and sought out tribe-specific settings.[113] Melvin Harrison—not gay, but a deeply compassionate and caring man—founded the Navajo Nation AIDS network in 1990 as HIV/AIDS infection rates increased dramatically. Harrison ran a Navajo-centric treatment clinic in the Navajo Nation during the 1990s and early 2000s.[114] Reflecting on this work, Harrison says it "brings tears to my eyes." Among Harrison's memories are the faces of the people who suffered as a result of homophobia in the Navajo Nation. He also acknowledges that his work was hampered by the belief among gay and trans Navajos that no governments—neither Navajo nor white—can be trusted.[115]

Curtis Harris encountered similar assumptions in New York during the 1990s. Harris recalls that AIDS remained a taboo subject, one that many Native people preferred to avoid. And the persistent belief that AIDS was a "settler disease" frustrated his efforts to get preventive tools into Indigenous communities. For Harris, "The struggle for me was to come up with messages and to talk to these communities about HIV and the impact it might have even in small communities."[116]

Harrison's and Harris's experiences highlight the difficulty of raising awareness about HIV/AIDS and encouraging prevention in reservation communities. In urban contexts, a slightly different dynamic existed among intertribal communities. The largest and most successful urban AIDS treatment organization was NNAAPC. Under the leadership of Ron Rowell, NNAAPC provided a range of case management services, AIDS testing, advocacy, and resources. In the 1990s, NNAAPC became national in scope and aimed to build networks around the country that would provide Native-centric care.[117]

NNAAPC proved effective at disseminating information about HIV/AIDS prevention and treatment options, dispelling myths about HIV/AIDS, and raising grant monies to conduct further research into

effective treatments.[118] Rowell used the NNAACP's national footprint
to get the word out about the importance of sexual health among
LGBTQ2S people. Concerned about the growing number of new
AIDS cases among Native men, Rowell worried that "the 1990's could
spell tragedy if we as Indian people don't take the necessary steps to
combat this disease."[119]

For Rowell and others working in the field of HIV/AIDS, prevention was a focal point in Indian Country. In both the United
States and Canada, Two-Spirit leaders recognized the importance of
"aboriginal-specific HIV/AIDS information." This meant expanding
efforts to prevent infection and treat those suffering from the virus
in ways that combined traditional healing and cutting-edge medical
therapies.[120] It also meant launching public awareness campaigns that
urged all Native Americans to practice safe sex. An advertisement in a
popular Native American magazine reminded readers that "no matter
what shape you're in, anyone can get the AIDS virus."[121] A separate
public awareness campaign involved the packaging of condoms em-
blazoned with catchy slogans such as "Do the trick with a rubber on
your dick."[122]

Harrison, Harris, Rowell, and other dedicated healthcare professionals and activists worked tirelessly to prevent the spread of HIV/
AIDS in Indian Country. Challenges remained, though. At a time
when Two-Spirit people were reclaiming their past and defining their
own futures, many Native people with HIV/AIDS continued to feel
disconnected from community and worried about seeking treatment
at inadequately resourced IHS facilities. In other instances, Native
people with HIV/AIDS remained in the "buckskin closet" and worried
that seeking treatment from a reservation clinic might result in gossipy
healthcare workers breaching their confidentiality. In large urban areas, racism exacerbated feelings of isolation.[123]

By the mid-1990s, sustained pressure from activists groups such
as the AIDS Coalition to Unleash Power (ACT UP) led medical researchers and Big Pharma to expedite a treatment regime that became
known as "cocktail therapy," or HAART, highly active antiretrovi-
ral therapy. At the same time, Native AIDS activists and Two-Spirit
leaders reminded Two-Spirit people that they were special and that
organizations exist to support them. Janice Command reflected on
this consciousness. In 1990 she explained that being a lesbian and

a Native person "helped me as a spiritual person and for that I am thankful." Lee Staples had a simple, yet powerful message: "Being gay is a gift."[124]

By the end of the 1990s, Two-Spirit people had found the language to start decolonizing their history, reclaiming their traditions, and renewing their roles in Indian Country. The celebrations, however, were muted. After a generation of HIV/AIDS, Two-Spirit people still needed support. They needed resources. And they needed allies. Chrystos wrote about this reality: "Don't admire what you perceive as our stoicism or spirituality—work for our lives to continue in our own Ways. Despite the books which still appear, even in radical bookstores, we are not Vanishing Americans."[125]

As the twenty-first century opened, a new generation of Two-Spirit people emerged. People like Rebecca Nagle, Candi Brings Plenty, Joshua Whitehead, and many others joined artists like Chrystos and an established generation of organizers that included Marty Fixico, Randy Burns, Richard LaFortune, Debra Williams, and Curtis Harris to tell their own stories and champion their political needs. Older and newer generations of Two-Spirit teachers, knowledge keepers, caregivers, and organizers were determined to address the ongoing challenges confronting their communities—from HIV/AIDS to marriage equality and the ongoing fight against trans- and homophobia.

Far from vanishing, Two-Spirit people declared: "We are everywhere."

CHAPTER 11

LOVE

We lived together as a married couple the last five years.
Nobody has paid any attention to us until we got this license.
Nobody—you know, they could care less what we were doing,
as long as we didn't go to try to get married. And now that we
have this license, they're all up busy in our stuff and want to
know what's going on. And they all have an opinion now.

—DAWN MCKINLEY (Cherokee Nation)[1]

The place where two discriminations meet
is a dangerous place to live.

—RICHARD LAFORTUNE, aka ANGUKSUAR (Yup'ik)[2]

IN MAY 2004, Kathy Reynolds and Dawn McKinley drove from their
Owasso, Oklahoma, home, to the Cherokee Nation Judicial Branch
offices in Tahlequah. Reynolds and McKinley were attempting to become the first same-sex couple in modern Cherokee history to get
married. Paperwork in hand, Reynolds and McKinley walked into
the Judicial Branch offices and handed their application for a marriage license to the clerk. The clerk processed their paperwork but
offered a warning: they'd struggle to find a Cherokee minister willing
to officiate at a wedding ceremony. What followed was thirteen years
of struggle that pitted competing claims to traditional cultural and
marital practices against each other and tested the robustness of Indigenous sovereignty.[3]

Reynolds and McKinley are citizens of the Cherokee Nation. Back
in 2004, neither wanted the attention of the media or the scrutiny that
comes with a high-profile legal case. That is what they experienced,

however, after Darrell Dowty, the chief justice of the Cherokee Judicial Appeals Tribunal, placed a thirty-day moratorium on marriage
licenses for same-sex couples.[4] Todd Hembree, a Cherokee citizen and
tribal attorney (he went on to become the Cherokee Nation's attorney
general, 2012–2019) viewed the moratorium as inadequate. Hembree
filed suit to have the couple's marriage license invalidated. The culture
wars over same-sex marriage had arrived in Indian Country.[5]

Debates about same-sex marriage grew in intensity in Indian
Country and across the United States during the 1990s and early
2000s.[6] News coverage of same-sex marriage reported "culture warriors" competing over the meaning of marriage and family, American
culture, and citizenship. These debates marked a palpable escalation
in the political divide between conservatives and their opposition to a
so-called gay agenda, and liberal and progressive groups who championed an expansive understanding of civil rights.[7] Indian Country was
not immune to shifting cultural sensibilities and competing political
ideologies, magnified during this period by growing access to the Internet and the proliferation of online news sites, many with questionable journalistic standards and poor editorial integrity.[8]

Reynolds and McKinley became ensnared in these larger debates.
At the core of their case was a desire to have the same legal rights and
protections that other married Cherokee citizens took for granted: a
life shared together through good times and bad, and a family they
could nurture knowing that the laws of the Cherokee Nation protected them. Those motives highlighted the stark divide in LGBTQ
politics. Non-Indigenous queer theorists and activists sometimes expressed opposition to marriage equality because it represented assimilation into heteronormative family structures. However, this position
became less common during the first two decades of the twenty-first
century. And in Indian Country, Native trans and Two-Spirit people
viewed marriage equality as a way to build diverse families—the mul-
tidwelling "adobe homes" metaphor that Barbara Cameron wrote
about—and to insist on their reinclusion into the rights and responsibilities of their nation.[9]

The Cherokee Nation chief, Chad Smith, had other ideas. Smith
supported Hembree's suit and insisted that "marriage is only between
a man and woman."[10] Smith wasn't alone in this view: Merritt Young-
deer Sr., a Baptist preacher, warned Cherokees against gay marriage,

exclaiming "It's coming."[11] These types of comments fueled often-acrimonious political and cultural debates.

Reynolds and McKinley felt they had Cherokee tradition on their side. On May 18, 2004, five days after they filed for their marriage license, the couple gathered with family and friends in Mohawk Park, in Tulsa, Oklahoma, to celebrate their marriage. Leslie Penrose presided over a ceremony in which Reynolds and McKinley declared their connection to traditional Cherokee marriage practices. The couple's vows invoked earth, fire, wind, and water: "Creator God, we honor all you created as we pledge our hearts and lives together. We honor earth and ask for our marriage to be abundant and grow stronger through the seasons."[12]

Reynolds and McKinley then reached down to grab a handful of red earth. They threw the red dirt into the wind, declaring: "We honor fire and ask that our union be warm and full of passion."

The couple whisked their hands over a candle, stating: "We honor wind and ask for wisdom as we struggle and grow this marriage together."

Water, carried to the ceremony from a sacred spring in the Cherokee homelands in the Southeast, was then introduced to the ceremony: "We honor water and ask that our marriage may never thirst for commitment and care."

Penrose concluded the ceremony by joining Reynolds's and McKinley's "hearts and lives together" and pronouncing them "cooker and companion," a traditional declaration of love, commitment, and reciprocity that sealed a marital union between two people in Cherokee culture.

News of Reynolds and McKinley's marriage traveled quickly throughout the Cherokee Nation and beyond. For years, the couple had lived quietly in their Owasso home. No one had bothered them, or the child they were raising together. That changed. As McKinley told journalist Amy Goodman in 2005, everyone seemed to "have an opinion now."[13]

Sounding more and more like Christian conservatives and white "culture warriors," the Cherokee opponents of same-sex marriage launched a blistering tirade against marriage equality. Opponents lambasted the promiscuousness of modern life, insisting that outside forces had introduced the "gay agenda" into the Cherokee Nation,[14] eroding traditional values, testing the sovereignty of Indigenous nations, and leading to calls for a reexamination of marriage laws. Everyone in Indian Country seemed to have an opinion on this issue. The Navajo Nation Supreme Court stated that its control over marriage was designed to "enhance Navajo sovereignty, preserve the Navajo marriage tradition, and protect those who adhere to the Navajo tradition."[15]

Throughout Indian Country, Native people expressed strong views on gay marriage. Titus Upham, a member of the Blackfeet Nation, opposed same-sex marriage on the grounds that homosexuality was unnatural. He echoed the views of many Christian conservatives in Indian Country by claiming that LGBTQ Indians "live outside the inner circle."[16] Upham's remarks typified Indigenous opposition to Two-Spirit people and same-sex marriage: what they stood for, and how they lived, was not part of traditional Indigenous cultures.

Tim Giago wasn't buying these types of arguments. As the editor of the *Lakota Journal*, Giago reported on a range of issues impacting Native communities during the 1990s and early 2000s. In 2003 he wrote that if homophobia divided tribal communities it was because colonialism introduced those divisions. People who shared Titus Upham's position had got it all wrong: Europeans brought bigotry and prejudice with them when they invaded the Americas.

At the opening of the twenty-first century, homophobia remained a problem in Indian Country. Giago linked discriminatory attitudes to the continued integration of Native people into colonial institutions. For example, he reported that in the wake of the 9/11 terrorist attacks and the wars in Iraq and Afghanistan, Native participation in the armed services increased. When those Native servicepeople returned to reservation communities, they brought with them homophobic attitudes they had picked up in the military.[17]

Reynolds and McKinley filed for their marriage certificate in this cultural and political context. And they were not the only same-sex couple to test the heteronormative standards of Indian Country's legal and political boundaries. A new generation of Two-Spirit leaders and advocates became increasingly vocal in calling on Native nations to combat trans- and homophobia. Marriage equality represented a political opportunity for Two-Spirit people to advocate for a reclaiming of fluid gender roles and sexual identities, in addition to empowering diverse family structures.[18] Heather Purser, a member of the Suqua-mish Tribe, embodied this new energy. Her brave and skillful political campaign provides another perspective on how marriage equality in Indian Country was helping Two-Spirit people reclaim their past and guide their futures.[19]

The struggle for marriage equality in tribal nations was the most visible part of a larger movement to renew Two-Spirit traditions and gender-fluid roles. It is an issue that remains entangled in questions about the inherent rights of sovereign Indian nations to define their own marriage laws and broader debates about the historical construction of marriage.[20] For Two-Spirit people, marriage equality debates tested the willingness of political authorities to include them under the protections of tribal law. In other words, Two-Spirit people do not want to be "tolerated"; they wanted love, respect, legal rights, and political empowerment. The activism of GAI in San Francisco and AIGL in Minnesota opened a door to these types of connections during the last quarter of the twentieth century, but obstacles remained. At the beginning of the twenty-first century, tribal constitutions and laws in most Native nations prevented same-sex marriage and left Two-Spirit people with no legal protections. For trans and Two-Spirit people, legal changes were not only overdue; they were a matter of life and death.[21]

. . . .

Fred Martinez was just sixteen years old when Shaun Murphy stole his life. On the night of June 16, 2001, Murphy bludgeoned Martinez to death in a canyon just south of Cortez, Colorado.[22] It was a crime of shocking brutality, an attack that evoked the memories of Balboa's attack dogs and centuries of genocidal violence.[23]

Martinez's death occurred just under three years after Matthew Shepard, a white gay student at the University of Wyoming, was murdered. Three years before Shepard was killed, James Byrd Jr., an African American man, was brutally murdered at the hands of white supremacists in Jasper, Texas. These murders touched off a national conversation about hate crimes, culminating in the Matthew Shepard and James Byrd, Jr., Hate Crimes Prevention Act in 2009.[24]

Cathy Renna, director of the Gay and Lesbian Alliance Against Defamation, played an active role in pursuing justice for Matthew Shepard and his family. Renna also aided Martinez's family. In an interview with the *Washington Post,* Renna stated that Martinez's murder was also a hate crime; it was political. "Yeh, of course this is political. No kidding!" Renna exclaimed. "It's also very, very personal. It's about not having this kid die for absolutely no reason."[25]

A decade later, Martinez's death still haunted Renna. She recalled joining "local activists and others who had come from around the country to help" the Martinez family. For Renna, "Seeing the spot where he was killed was a gut-wrenching sight, even for those of us with experience dealing with the horror of a hallmark of hate crimes called 'overkill.'"[26]

Pauline Mitchell, Martinez's mother, was heartbroken by the loss of her son. A softly spoken woman, Mitchell didn't seek out the spotlight. She wanted to mourn her son's loss privately. Eventually, though, Mitchell joined Renna and a growing chorus of parents, family members, and friends in expressing their frustration and grief about the violence being perpetrated against LGBTQ people throughout the Four Corners region of Arizona, Colorado, New Mexico, and Utah. She called her son's murder a hate crime and demanded that lawmakers address the systemic violence faced by LGBTQ people.[27]

Martinez's murder was a reminder of the violence that Native trans and Two-Spirit people routinely encounter.[28] Accurate statistics are hard to obtain, but between 2000 and 2020 an estimated ten thousand trans and Two-Spirit people have gone missing in the United States and Canada. For all trans people of color, these numbers continue rising at a frightening rate.[29] Fred Martinez lived these statistics. He complained to his mother that people were too "nosy," and one of his brothers warned him to "be careful."[30] Martinez lived at "the place where two discriminations meet"—racism and homophobia. As Richard LaFortune acknowledged in the 2010 documentary *Two Spirits,* that's "a dangerous place to live."[31]

In life, Fred Martinez refused to let hatred and bigotry define him. He loved Beyoncé and thought it was "cool" when his mother suggested he was nadleeh. He blended his nadleeh identity with other identities, like gay and transgender. Being a nadleeh meant that gender fluidity felt normal, just as it was normal for Martinez to use the names FC, Frederica, or simply Fred. Martinez dressed in male and female clothing; sometimes he wore makeup, and at other times he didn't. He experienced the sting of hate speech and bullying, was sent home from school for wearing women's shoes, and attempted suicide, but found the strength to walk his path.[32] He was kind, loving, and generous. He was preparing to live a long and beautiful life.[33] And then, Shaun Murphy murdered Fred.

Details of Martinez's murder are chillingly straightforward. On the evening of June 16, 2001, Fred and a small group of his friends went into the border town of Cortez to attend the annual Ute Mountain rodeo and carnival. At some point during the evening Fred and his friends separated. Shaun Murphy, who also attended the rodeo with his friends, spotted Fred walking alone and gave him a ride to a convenience store.

Up to this point, Martinez's interactions with Murphy were mundane. Murphy and his friends left Fred at the convenience store and headed to an apartment where they smoked a couple of joints. Shaun Murphy decided to leave the apartment and tracked down Martinez.

In the 2010 documentary, *Two Spirits*, directed by Lydia Nibley, Fred Martinez's family and friends recall that he was afraid of the dark. But something more terrifying than the dark of night chased Fred on the evening of June 16. Driven by hate and bigotry, Shaun Murphy pursued Martinez down a dark gravel road and into a small canyon known as The Pits.[34] Fred tried to get away from Murphy by climbing up and over a series of limestone rocks less than a quarter mile from his home. Unable to outrun Murphy, Martinez must surely have been gripped by terror and fear as he fought for his life.

Murphy, who had a history of violent crimes, bashed Fred's skull with a small rock, leaving him bloodied and dazed. It is unclear whether Fred crawled down the mountainside, trying to evade his attacker, or was dragged, but in Murphy's vile act of overkill he picked up a much larger rock to strike multiple blows to Martinez's head.

Five days after he was last seen, two little boys found Fred's body by the sewer ponds at the southern edge of Cortez. He was so badly beaten that his teeth were missing, his face unrecognizable. During the five days that Martinez's body lay exposed to the elements, Murphy bragged to friends that he "bug-smashed a hoto"—"hoto" is a slang term for someone who is homosexual.[35] In an era when "gay bashing" was still all too common in the United States, Martinez's family, friends, and allies decided to take a stand. They labeled Martinez's murder a hate crime and demanded justice. In response to questions from a journalist, Cortez police chief Roy Lane responded to the community's grief by declaring, "I don't think we have a problem [with hate crimes] in our area."[36] It was a hollow statement, made all the more painful by Lane's insistence that "all crimes are hate crimes."[37]

Lane's comments did, however, reveal how lived experiences shaped a person's sense of reality. Lane lacked the cultural awareness and historical consciousness necessary to empathize with LGBTQ2S people. His stunning lack of empathy did more than trouble lawyers working on behalf of the Martinez family; his comments revealed the logic (such as it was) on one side of the debate that engulfed Cortez in the weeks after Fred's murder. It was the twenty-first century, but in Cortez many residents remained blithely unaware of how Two-Spirit people experienced the world; and some still believed that "God hates fags!"[38]

Those attitudes didn't go unchallenged. But first the community had to get through the trial of Shaun Murphy, who was charged with second-degree murder (Murphy was not charged with a hate crime). As the police and the prosecution gathered evidence, the glare of the national news media shone on Cortez. News of Murphy's violent past and his expulsion from both middle school and Montezuma-Cortez High School was leaked to the media. As Murphy's scowling face began appearing in newspapers, at first Murphy seemed determined to fight the charges.[39] In fact, he changed his story more than once. He initially entered a not guilty plea. Eventually his lawyer struck a deal with prosecutors that took the death penalty off the table. He received a sentence of up to forty years for second-degree murder. He served only seventeen years and was released in 2019.[40]

Fred Martinez's murder not only "changed the LGBT world," it inspired discussion about the need for systemic changes in Indian Country, the Four Corners region, and throughout the United States.[41] In Cortez, Montezuma-Cortez High School, the school where administrators sent Fred home for wearing women's shoes and where he endured daily bullying, responded to pressure from the Four Corners Parents, Families and Friends of Lesbians and Gays by revising its anti-bullying policies.[42]

For Two-Spirit leaders and advocates, Fred Martinez's death provided the world with a tragic reminder of the dangers that trans and Two-Spirit people face every day. Young people grappling with their gender and sexual identities needed the space, support, and love to feel safe to explore and express their fluid identities. Arnold Dahl, a member of the Leech Lake Band of Ojibwe, works tirelessly to offer support to young people coming to terms with their gender and sexual identities. He views this work as ongoing, as "a struggle to make sure we keep all of our heritage." Dahl adds that "reclaiming what used to be can be a struggle sometimes."[43]

Dahl wants young Two-Spirit people not to feel overwhelmed by the type of "negative information" that he experienced growing up in the late twentieth century. His involvement in education and mentorship is driven by the hunger he sees in young people to "remember our history." Key to providing Two-Spirit youth with the support they need is letting them know that there are people who understand their emotions and are ready to offer support. They are seen. They are part of what Dahl calls a "beautiful history."[44]

Roger Kuhn holds similar views. An enrolled member of the Poarch Band of Creek Indians, Kuhn advocates for "community love." He views this concept as a traditional Muscogee value that can inspire new generations of Two-Spirit people to reclaim their traditions, to support and heal one another, and tell their own stories.

Kuhn, a talented artist who used his music to express his Two-Spirit identity during the first decade of the twenty-first century, completed a PhD in human sexuality in 2021. He understands "gender variance" as the "most natural thing" and moves effortlessly among Two-Spirit, gay, and queer identities. Gender and sexual fluidity, the blending of identities, is important to Kuhn, who recognizes the importance of "being seen and being visible." Social and cultural empowerment makes it possible to not only reclaim "what the ancestors did," but to provide support, community, and love for people grappling with the complexities of their own identities, facing discrimination, or struggling with addiction. As Kuhn so eloquently says, it's "about looking out for each other." It's about community. It's about respecting the ancestors. It is about power.[45]

Kuhn nurtures Two-Spirit community through his involvement with the Bay Area American Indian Two Spirits (BAAITS). Formed in 1998, BAAITS built on the work of a previous generation of organizers, like Randy Burns, the cofounder of GAI. The members of BAAITS set out to provide a space free of alcohol and substance use and to provide a sense of community that reconnected people with

Two-Spirit traditions. Integrating those traditions into contemporary Native culture remains a priority for BAAITS. It is the focal point of their annual powwow, held in February each year, and was the centerpiece of an exhibition that Kuhn curated with fellow BAAITS members Amelia Vigil and Ruth Villaseñor at the GLBT Historical Society. The 2019 exhibition focused on Two-Spirit pride, the history of the BAAITS powwow, Indigenous medicine and HIV/AIDS, and the evolving meanings of Two-Spirit identities in Native communities.[46]

. . . .

Connecting Two-Spirit stories to legal equality and civil rights within tribal nations continues to shape Two-Spirit politics.[47] Since the 1990s political debates about the rights and legal protections for trans and Two-Spirit people in Indian Country have echoed the polarized political discourse in the United States. Few issues attracted as much attention as marriage equality.

In the midst of the culture wars of the 1990s, debate over marriage equality divided Americans. One state, Vermont, permitted civil unions between same-sex couples, and in 1993 the Supreme Court of Hawaii ruled it illegal to prohibit same-sex couples from getting married.[48] Critics were alarmed. Conservative activists bombarded federal lawmakers with mail, resulting in the passage of the Defense of Marriage Act (DOMA) in 1996.[49]

DOMA restricted federal benefits to married couples of the opposite sex. The legislation emboldened opponents of same-sex marriage. When George W. Bush became president, in 2001, conservative groups felt they had an ally in the White House. "I believe marriage is between a man and a woman," Bush declared in a Rose Garden speech in 2003. "I believe we ought to codify that one way or the other, and we have lawyers looking at the best way to do that."[50]

Conservatives suffered a blow the following year when Massachusetts became the first state to legalize same-sex marriage. However, at least thirteen other states adopted laws banning same-sex marriage. The battle lines over same-sex marriage were being drawn. The advocates of marriage equality—the Gay and Lesbian Advocates and Defenders, Lambda Legal, the ACLU's LGBT Project, and the National Center for Lesbian Rights—readied for the coming legal fight over same-sex marriage.

Indian Country could not escape these debates which, in Native communities, were about more than marriage equality; they were also about sovereignty. One Native woman, Heather Purser, recognized the connection between marriage equality and tribal sovereignty. She read news stories about the importance of Indigenous sovereignty, LGBTQ persecution, and the structural discrimination endured by same-sex couples; it all resonated with Purser.

Purser grew up near the Port Madison Reservation in western Washington State. The daughter of a Suquamish father and white mother, Purser is a member of the Suquamish Tribe. At an early age Purser knew she was different. "I knew I was gay when I was seven," Purser told me in 2018.[51] Like scores of other Two-Spirit people, she remembers growing up with the taunts, bullying, and crude jokes that Suquamish and non-Suquamish people felt comfortable directing at her. When she came out at sixteen, her parents reacted badly. By that time, her father had left the family, but her mother responded with violence. Purser went back into the closet and didn't come out again until she was in her early twenties.

To understand Purser's response it's important to remember the pervasiveness of homophobia in the United States during the 1990s and early 2000s. In Indian Country, homophobia persisted in reservation communities and in the lives of urban Two-Spirits. Jaxin Enemy-Hunter (Crow) told the *New York Times*, "I would see friends going through hell over being gay. It was just very sad. They didn't know about our history."[52]

Purser experienced that painful void in her tribal knowledge. She also endured the daily trauma of feeling rejected, not only for her sexuality but also for the way she looked. Purser has red hair, a pale complexion, and freckles. She can pass as white, a source of jokes and mean-spirited comments from some Native people she has crossed paths with over the years. These casual, normalized forms of discrimination have been part of Purser's life. They hurt, but she refuses to let them define her.

At eighteen, Purser took the first steps to following her own path in life. She left Washington and headed to Kansas, where she started college at Haskell Indian Nations University. She didn't stay long; the taunts about her white skin made her feel unwelcome. Purser decided to head back to Washington, where she attended Western Washington

University and began attending gay pride events. It was there, at Western Washington, that Purser embraced her sexuality. Coming out felt liberating.

Still, something was missing. Centuries of colonialism—the memories of genocidal violence, the trauma of boarding school experiences, and the federal government's deliberate splintering of communities— had had a devastating effect on many aspects of Suquamish culture. When we spoke in 2018, Purser talked about the historical and cultural silences that colonialism caused. I asked her if there's a Suquamish word akin to Two-Spirit. "I don't think so," she replied. Her response isn't unusual. It means that Two-Spirit people must nurture new stories.

That's what Purser did when she took up the cause of marriage equality in the Suquamish Tribe. Although she'd felt rejected by her father and her tribe growing up, the elders she spoke with as a young adult assured her that there's a place for everyone. "Everybody's important," the elders instructed.[53]

In the months after she graduated from Western Washington, however, Purser struggled to feel important. She felt lost, lacking in purpose. She responded to these emotions by turning to alcohol and drugs (mostly marijuana). The haze didn't last long. After a party at her cousin's home turned violent, Purser woke up the next morning with the clarity of purpose she had been searching for. With her cousin's encouragement, Heather Purser was going to get the Suquamish Tribe to recognize gay marriage.[54]

Purser prepared. She began reading widely and crafted her strategy. She worried that the tribal council would reject her calls for change, so she approached marriage equality gently, cautiously, at first.[55] She soon realized that there was little opposition to her call for marriage equality. When one councilman declared, "I'm all for it, but how can you guarantee me that non-Indian men won't start marrying tribal men just for their fishing rights or a new boat?" Purser burst into laughter. So too did everyone in the room.[56]

That moment of levity proved an ice breaker. Purser left the meeting with newfound confidence and in the following weeks began preparing to present her case at the annual general council meeting. Three to four hundred Suquamish tribal members showed up, including her father and two brothers. They stood behind Purser as she brought the marriage equality motion to a vote. It passed. The decision was unanimous.[57]

When I asked Purser about this transformative experience in her life, she said she "just wanted what everyone else has. I just wanted the chance to have a family."[58] Purser's modesty belies the magnitude of her accomplishment. The Suquamish, like hundreds of other Native communities, had their sovereignty eroded, their culture attacked, and their people violated by colonizers. Purser wasn't "just" fighting for the right to have a family on her terms; she was rejecting Western gender and sexual norms and standing up for the sovereign right of her tribal community to define family on Suquamish terms. Understood in this way, the marriage equality debate in Indian Country is about more than marriage; it tests the agility of Indigenous lawmakers and the responsiveness of tribal sovereignty to both protect and incorporate transgender and Two-Spirit people into their communities.[59]

Purser's success proved an outlier in Indian Country during the 2000s. Two-Spirit leaders and advocates pressed tribal governments to change their marriage laws, but those efforts met with stern resistance. With the brutal murder of Fred Martinez still fresh in people's minds, in 2005 the Navajo Nation passed the Diné Marriage Act, which specifically prohibited same-sex marriage among members of the nation, over the veto of its president, Joe Shirley. President Shirley's veto was inspired by his belief that same-sex marriage "is not even an issue" in the Navajo Nation. He asserted that the "elderly, the medicine people are not talking about it. . . . Gay people, they're not coming forward to say, we want to get married in tribal courts."[60]

But Navajo lawmakers did see a problem and overrode Shirley's veto. Echoing the language of DOMA, Larry Anderson, the sponsor of the Navajo bill, argued that his legislation was designed "to strengthen traditional Navajo values."[61] Invoking "tradition" is a powerful rhetorical strategy in Indian Country, irrespective of the merits of this language. It's why, once the Navajo law passed, supporters contended that it would "promote strong families and strengthen family values."[62]

The Navajo Nation's 2005 ban on same-sex marriage represented a stinging rebuke to the growing Two-Spirit community and their allies. But Diné opponents of same-sex marriage were overjoyed. They insisted that their stance defended Navajo sovereignty. Borrowing from the language of Christian conservatism, one opponent declared, "We believe in a god who despises same-sex unions."[63]

The Diné Coalition for Cultural Preservation, a group led by gay Navajos, opposed the ban on same-sex marriage. Sherrick Roanhorse issued a statement on behalf of the coalition in which he insisted the ban would not halt calls for "aggressive governmental reforms."[64] Similar messages have become more common across Indian Country in the years since the 2005 law passed. Journalist Julian Brave NoiseCat, a member of the Canim Lake Band Tsq'escen, echoes the thoughts of a growing number of people in Indian Country, arguing that marriage law reforms are vital to protect the social, economic, and cultural well-being of Two-Spirit people.[65]

Trudie Jackson works to make change happen. A Navajo Nation citizen and trans woman, Jackson is an articulate advocate for trans and Two-Spirit rights. "I embrace the tradition of multiple genders," Jackson says, referring to the five gender categories—woman, man, nadleeh, masculine female, and feminine male—described by the Navajo anthropologist Wesley Thomas. "That tradition is sacred."[66]

Roanhorse and Jackson are not alone in believing that supporting fluid gender identities and diverse families is an act of Navajo sovereignty. Throughout Indian Country, Two-Spirit people are insisting on their reinclusion into the circle of community. Marca Cassity, a citizen of the Osage Nation who embraces a Two-Spirit identity, is deeply uncomfortable with the uncritical use of heteronormative language in Native nations. Cassity came to this position after years of emotional turmoil, introspection, and struggles with addiction. She views tribal bans on same-sex marriage as a reiteration of colonial logic, a message that says Two-Spirit people are "deviant or defective."[67] That logic, those words, hurt. They are messages of rejection that sow the seeds of violence and hate crimes.[68] For Cassity, as for Trudie Jackson, the conflation of "tradition" with a conservative Christian definition of "family values" distorts the social and cultural traditions that persist throughout Indian Country. In the early 2000s, this rhetoric echoed the homophobic logic of DOMA.[69]

In the years after DOMA became federal law, individual advocates like Heather Purser and organizations like BAAITS continued to challenge tribal governments to craft laws that honored their ancestors and reflected more inclusive forms of tribal sovereignty and the diversity of their twenty-first-century communities. In Indian Country, though, change occurs slowly. Rebecca Nagle has recognized this in her work. "One thing I don't see talked about is I think Native communities are more conservative than the mainstream US." Nagle understands that colonialism and the oppressiveness of Christian conservatism contributes to the glacial pace at which social and cultural change occurs in Native communities. From Nagle's perspective, it "sometimes feels like we're thirty or forty years behind."[70]

Nagle is not alone in that view. Fellow Cherokee Nation citizen and Two-Spirit writer, Jen Deerinwater, argues that Two-Spirit people must share their stories to raise awareness about the realities of their lives. "We can't change the system if our existence isn't even acknowledged," Deerinwater insists.[71] In reclaiming their traditions and reconnecting with the circle of community, Two-Spirit people recognize the importance of patience, but that doesn't mean they're not persistent in calling for structural political and legal changes that will recognize their existence and protect their rights within Native nations.

The tides of political change began sweeping over the United States and Indian Country during the 2010s. In 2010, President Barack Obama repealed the Defense Department's 1994 "Don't ask, don't tell" directive.[72] The repeal of "Don't ask, don't tell" reflected changing social attitudes. In 2003, only 32 percent of Americans favored same-sex marriages. By 2020, 67 percent of Americans supported same-sex marriage.[73]

US Supreme Court rulings also reflected changes in societal attitudes. In 2013, the court struck down the DOMA as unconstitutional. Two years later, it recognized same-sex marriage as a fundamental right of Americans that is protected by the Fourteenth Amendment's due process and equal protection clauses. The court's ruling followed the legal logic used by the Supreme Court in its 1967 ruling in *Loving v. Virginia*, declaring laws against interracial marriage unconstitutional.[74]

How would tribal governments respond? According to Marty Fixico, they haven't responded well. For Fixico, an enrolled Southern Cheyenne, the absence of legal recognition and protections for same-sex marriage in Indian Country is "heartbreaking." As Two-Spirit people increasingly live openly in reservation and urban communities, contribute to ceremony, and offer their service to their respective tribal communities, few Native nations recognize their basic right to marry same-sex partners and nurture diverse and supportive families.

There are 574 federally recognized tribes in the United States. Of those, just over 40 have legal provisions that recognize same-sex marriages. In 2008, the Coquille Tribe, located in Oregon, became the first tribal nation to legalize same-sex marriage. Only a few others—the Tlingit and Haida Indian Tribes, the Leech Lake Band of Ojibwe, the Oneida Nation (Wisconsin), and Puyallulup Tribe—have followed suit.[75]

The issue of same-sex marriage remains a matter of ongoing debate in Native nations. For gender-nonbinary and sexually fluid people, it is the most visible example of their struggle for legal rights and protections within their respective tribal nations. Like issues of racial exclusion in Native nations—such as the Cherokee Nation's controversial history with African American freedpeople—the issue of same-sex marriage continues to test the robustness of tribal sovereignty.[76] Under the current system of federalism that governs relations between tribal governments and the United States, Native nations have the inherent sovereign right to determine marriage laws, a right that predates colonial invasion. Thus, the US government has not "delegated" this right to tribes and so it cannot be withdrawn by the US government.[77]

However, many of the current marriage laws in Indian Country are the products of two profoundly homophobic eras in American history: the decades after the American Civil War and the Cold War decades of the mid-twentieth century. During both historical periods, Indigenous leaders fought to preserve the sovereignty of their people by passing laws and tribal constitutions that aligned with the laws of the United States. To comply with the whims of federal officials, this sometimes meant passing laws that discriminated against people on racial grounds or on the basis of a person's gender and sexual orientation.[78]

Since the 1990s and the Hawaii Supreme Court's 1993 decision to prohibit bans against same-sex marriages, Two-Spirit people and their allies have refused to remain silent on these issues.[79] They have assailed heteronormative marriage laws. In response, large tribal nations—most prominently, the Cherokee Nation and the Navajo Nation—passed laws that clarified opposition to same-sex marriage. These laws usually mirrored the heteronormative logic of DOMA.

Other Native nations—including the Muscogee (Creek) Nation, Chickasaw Nation, the Sault Tribe of Chippewa Indians, and Iowa Tribe—have followed suit.[80]

The restrictive marriage laws passed by tribal nations in the early 2000s attracted immediate opposition from Two-Spirit leaders and their allies. Alray Nelson, a past president of the Navajo Nation, remains highly critical of Indigenous people who think same-sex marriage is tied to the "white man's way of thinking." Nelson insists that it's wrong "to think of LGBTQ [as] not traditional." Nelson also views the issue of legal recognition and protections for trans and Two-Spirit Native people as an issue of human decency and public health. "It's very clear," Nelson told *High Country News* in 2018, "that if you identify as trans, especially if you're a Navajo trans woman living here on the reservation, it's more likely you're going to see violence within your lifetime because it's become so normalized and it's an issue that no one is really talking about."[81] Almost two decades after Fred Martinez's brutal murder, it felt as though little had changed in the Navajo Nation.

Heather Purser recognizes marginalization. That's why she launched her campaign to change Suquamish marriage laws. She, like Alray Nelson, understands that the law can serve as a tool to combat homophobia and help normalize the traditional place of Two-Spirit people in Native communities. And while hate often does an end run around human decency, much less the law, one can't help but wonder how Fred Martinez's life might have taken a different course in a world without laws that normalized transphobia and homophobia.

These issues have everything to do with tribal sovereignty. Mark Anthony Rolo, a member of the Bad River Band of Ojibwe, recognized this. In 2006, Rolo argued that "tribal governments can help put an end to oppression within our communities by embracing, accepting and legalizing marriage between Indians of the same sex."[82]

. . . .

The marriage of Kathy Reynolds and Dawn McKinley tested the willingness of one of the largest and most visible Native nations to "help put an end to oppression." When Reynolds and McKinley filed their original application for a marriage license, they believed that the Cherokee Nation's constitution did not explicitly outlaw same-sex marriage.[83]

Todd Hembree, the tribal attorney, disagreed. He deployed an "originalist" argument, contending that the framers of the Cherokee constitution intended for marriage to be between a man and a woman. That's what the authors of the Cherokee Nation Code meant when they updated the Nation's laws in 1892 by referring to marriage being between a "companion and cooker." Hembree argued that this proved that "Cherokees have a strong traditional sense of marriage." Hembree suggested that he understood Cherokee tradition and was determined to apply the Nation's laws to defend those traditions. Hembree insisted, "There's never been a tribal recognition of same-sex marriage."[84]

Some Cherokee leaders didn't bother with arguments about tradition and instead voiced personal biases. One of these was Linda O'Leary, a member of the Cherokee Tribal Council. O'Leary was one of nine councilors who, in 2005, filed a restraining order with the Judicial Appeals Tribunal to prevent McKinley and Reynolds from acquiring a marriage certificate from the Cherokee Nation. O'Leary was joined by fellow councilors Bill John Baker, Audra Smoke-Connor, Joe Crittenden, Charles Hoskin, Johnny Keener, Melvina Shotpouch, David Thornton, and Phyllis Yargee, in urging the court to rule "that same-sex marriages are not allowed under Cherokee law and that the respondents' marriage certificate is null and void." Councilor Bill John Baker, who went on to become the principal chief of the Cherokee Nation in 2011, justified his decision to join the petition by stoking fear, claiming that "Cherokee grandmothers out there are very concerned we'll be the only government to have same-sex marriage, and we're trying to protect our constituents." O'Leary didn't bother with dog whistle politics. Her message was unequivocal: "We don't want gay marriages in the Cherokee Nation. It's that simple."[85]

It wasn't "that simple" for McKinley and Reynolds. In the spring of 2004, they had reached a critical juncture in their relationship. They had been together for about five years, were raising a child, and enjoyed a quiet, happy life. However, earlier that year Reynolds was admitted to hospital for emergency care. McKinley was not only barred from visiting Reynolds but "kicked out" of her hospital room because she wasn't a blood relative. It was a painful, frightening moment that added to the anxiety of an already stressful situation. It was a scenario all too familiar to same-sex couples throughout the United States.[86]

Following this incident, a friend told the couple that the Cherokee Nation had no explicit prohibition on same-sex marriage. That
conversation prompted their original application for a marriage certificate from the Cherokee Nation in 2004. In a 2005 interview with
the *Washington Post*, Reynolds explained, "We were told that the
Cherokee law didn't exclude same-sex marriages. . . . We just wanted
recognition for our relationship."[87]

Reynolds and McKinley could not gain that recognition from the
state of Oklahoma because it had had an explicit ban on same-sex
marriages since 1910. No such ban existed in the Cherokee Nation.
Reynolds admitted, though, that they were "very naïve." The couple
did not set out to become activists; they simply wanted to "get married
under Cherokee law and that would be the end of it. We never thought
it would turn into this."[88]

Initially, the couple represented themselves in their legal battle with
the Cherokee Nation. Cherokee lawyers wouldn't touch their case. A
year into their legal battle, David Cornsilk, a writer, historian, human
rights advocate, and Cherokee Nation citizen, offered his assistance.
He introduced Reynolds and McKinley to Lena Ayoub of the National
Center for Lesbian Rights, and Ayoub agreed to represent the couple.
Shortly thereafter, on August 3, 2005, the Cherokee District Court
agreed to an earlier application for a motion to dismiss the injunction
against their marriage on the grounds that Hembree suffered "no in-
dividualized harm and thus lacked standing to proceed."[89]

That decision prompted the September 9 application for a restraining order from O'Leary and eight fellow councilors. The Cherokee
Judicial Appeals Tribunal dismissed the restraining order, but the legal
standing of McKinley and Reynolds's relationship remained in limbo
because the court failed to rule on the legality of their marriage within
the Cherokee Nation.[90] That is where McKinley and Reynolds's marriage stayed—in legal limbo—for over a decade.

In Minneapolis, Richard LaFortune kept a close eye on the fate
of Reynolds and McKinley's case. He believed that "fundamentalist
churches," external pressure groups, and conservative tribal politicians stood in the way of Native nations reclaiming their cultural sovereignty and fully exercising their political sovereignty. After centuries
of "alien religious and cultural traditions" being imposed on Indigenous communities, it was understandable that "some Native people

who were dissected from their cultures and languages" would oppose progressive efforts to reclaim traditional practices. Indeed, LaFortune didn't see the legal struggles of Reynolds and McKinley as simply a matter of marriage equality; he saw it as a test of "how marriage and customs and even sovereignty are being eroded by conservative and Euro-centric trends."[91]

Opponents of same-sex marriage were dealt a major blow on June 26, 2015, when the Supreme Court ruled in the case of *Obergefell v. Hodges*.[92] After decades of legal action and scores of cases, the Supreme Court ruled that bans on same-sex marriages were illegal in the United States. State laws would need to comply with the new federal law, but what about in Indian Country? The journalist Steve Russell pointed out that there was no universal law prohibiting same-sex marriage in Indian Country—indeed, some tribal governments legalized same-sex marriages years before *Obergefell*—but would that trend continue?[93]

That remains an open question as this book goes to press. What is clear is that the Supreme Court ruling creates a precedent for the inherent right of tribal governments to determine their own marriage laws.[94] It's also true that the link between marriage equality and tribal sovereignty routinely plays out in very public and messy ways. As law professor Marcia Zug noted in 2016, the subject is fraught with wider implications:

> Tribal sovereignty remains precarious. Same-sex marriage bans are costly, not only for couples, but for the tribes who impose them. The longer they remain in place, the higher the likelihood that they will negatively impact perceptions of tribes and tribal justice. Historically, when tribal and Anglo-American values were in conflict, non-Indians tended to disparage tribal values as backwards, inferior, and unjust. These instances put tribal sovereignty at risk.[95]

For centuries, the homophobia of colonial societies, legal structures, and Christianity "disparage[d] tribal values as backwards, inferior, and unjust" on the issue of same-sex unions and the role of Two-Spirit people in Native communities. Tribes changed is response to these perceptions. Some adopted homophobic and discriminatory laws in a bid to both assert and hold on to their sovereignty. The *Obergefell* decision reversed the course of settler-colonial history in the United States and raises new questions about how tribal lawmakers will respond.

For a growing number of citizens of the Navajo Nation, marriage equality and legal protections for transgender people remain a priority. In 2016, the Navajo Nation Human Rights Commission observed that LGBTQ2S Navajos still lacked legal protections within the Navajo Nation. Attitudes had changed in the Navajo Nation in the years since Fred Martinez's brutal murder, adding pressure on lawmakers to institute structural changes. Each June, Diné Pride celebrations take over Window Rock, the Navajo capital in Arizona.[96] Growing cultural acceptance isn't political empowerment, however. Two-Spirit leaders and activists insist that laws and political structures still need to change.

In the Navajo Nation, change remains slow. Diné Equality, a Diné organization committed to "Sovereignty, Family, & Traditional Knowledge," aims to accelerate legal changes on behalf of LGBTQ2S Navajos. Diné Equality continues to call for the repeal of the Diné Marriage Act (2005), its official website observing that "long before Stonewall, our Sovereign Nations revered & honored gay, lesbian, bisexual, transgender, queer & two-spirit family members."[97] That type of commitment inspires other Diné people to continue the calls for change. Alray Nelson, a Navajo Nation citizen, has called for Fred Martinez's name to be honored through the retitling of federal anti–hate crime laws and is committed to repealing the Diné Marriage Act. However, repeated calls from Two-Spirit elders and advocates to repeal the Act have so far failed, preventing marriage equality in the Navajo Nation.[98]

LGBTQ2S Dinés continue to advocate for legal protections within the Navajo Nation. As the Navajo Nation Human Rights Commission observed in 2016, too few women and LGBTQ2S people have access to resources and leadership roles.[99] Trudie Jackson tried to change that in 2018 when she ran for president of the Navajo Nation. Although her campaign was unsuccessful, it was by no means a loss; Jackson was seen, and in the process made sure that other LGBTQ2S Navajos knew they had people advocating on their behalf. "I never forget the struggles the Navajo Nation continues to encounter in a society in which they are considered wardens of the federal government," Jackson explained after the election. "My identity as a candidate gave hope and inspiration to many young [and] older Navajo 2SLGBTQ 3rd, 4th, and 5th gender individuals to embrace their identity."[100]

And what of Kathy Reynolds and Dawn McKinley's battle to have the Cherokee Nation recognize their marriage? After feeling unwanted by their tribe in 2004, Reynolds and McKinley successfully filed for their marriage license at the Cherokee Nation Courthouse in January 2017. Their struggle had lasted twelve years.[101]

Ironically, it was Todd Hembree who paved a legal path for Reynolds and McKinley's union to become the first legally recognized same-sex marriage in modern Cherokee history.[102] Having opposed the couple's bid to obtain a marriage-license in 2004, in 2017 and 2018, Hembree oversaw a number of contentious political debates about marriage equality in his role as attorney general of the Cherokee Nation. In December 2016, Hembree successfully argued that the nation's Marriage and Family Act (2004) was contrary to the tribe's Equal Protection and Due Process clauses—so it would be unconstitutional for the Cherokee Nation to deny Reynolds and McKinley a marriage license.[103]

....

What we understand today as marriage has a long history, and is expressed in many forms throughout Indian Country. Culturally, marriage constitutes a visible symbol of belonging, a marker of a community's inclusiveness and vibrance. The Suquamish Tribe, the Cheyenne and Arapaho Tribes in Oklahoma, the Coquille Indian Tribe in Oregon, the Little Traverse Bay Bands of Odawa Indians in Michigan, and other tribal communities have exercised their sovereignty and legalized same-sex marriage. In doing so they head into the future having reclaimed a piece of their culture and traditions.

Not every Native nation has embraced calls for marriage equality since the Supreme Court's 2015 ruling. In addition to the Navajo and Cherokee Nations, the Eastern Band of Cherokee Indians is one of numerous tribal nations that reiterated their opposition to same-sex marriage.[104] It remains to be seen how long these bans will survive.

Members of a younger and more politically engaged generation of Indigenous people, comfortable in expressing their gender fluidity and sexual identities in both subtle and overt ways, seem unlikely to let discriminatory laws stand. They see cultural and social inclusiveness, legal protections, and political and economic empowerment as tests of the sovereignty of their respective tribal nations.

As we head into the digital future, worlds of possibility await.

CHAPTER 12

FUTURES

*Our use and adaptation of the term "Two-Spirit" reflects the
fact that we cannot distill into one word, out of two hundred
languages, a word like "gay." But if we say "Two-Spirit"
in English, it's something that people can wrap their
heads around and understand and respect.*

—RICHARD LAFORTUNE, AKA ANGUKSUAR (Yup'ik)[1]

*FUTURE: In the spirit of this stewardship, we respectfully
acknowledge our generations rising; for it is in their
interest that we carry forward this work, and it
is to them that we entrust it.*

— *Tribal Equity Toolkit 3.0*[2]

TWO-SPIRIT PEOPLE ARE imagining their futures in creative ways.
They are designing futures through their art, and they are organizing
at powwows and in digital spaces. Like Indigenous futurists who use
the visual and literary arts to envision decolonized futures, Two-Spirit
people are drawing inspiration from broader cultural trends, Indigenous philosophies, stories of alternative realities, and narratives of
different Native worlds. Two-Spirit futurists are mindful of colonialism's past and hopeful of finding paths to vibrant futures.[3]

Vibrance is key to Indigenous futures, just as it characterizes Native histories. "We're a very vibrant people," Clyde Hall reminded me
in 2019. I was glad he brought this up because most Americans don't
associate Native Americans with vibrancy. The casual, sometimes callous, nature of American racism means that Indian Country is still
marginalized in political discourse and too often caricatured in pop-

ular culture. "People in this country," said Hall of the United States, "as far as First Peoples go, don't even have an idea that we exist."[4]

Native people do exist. They live, work, and create vibrant lives for themselves, their families, and their communities. Two-Spirit people draw creative energy from these Indigenous spaces. "Two-Spirit" denotes the existence of feminine and masculine qualities in a single person. This English translation was never meant to limit gender and sexual expression, or the connections people make to tradition and community. LGBTQ Native Americans adopted Two-Spirit in the 1990s to provide people with a sense of Pan-Indian unity, to give greater visibility to people made almost invisible by settler colonialism, and to reclaim tribally specific roles and identities. This is what Monique "Muffie" Mousseau wants. Mousseau lives with her wife, Felipa De Leon, on the Pine Ridge Reservation, home to the Oglala Lakota. Mousseau wants Two-Spirit people to feel proud, confident, and empowered; she wants them to know that they are "beautiful, amazing individuals."[5]

Today, "Two-Spirit" continues to empower a sense of Pan-Indigenous community among Native people who identify as trans, queer, and/or Two-Spirited. The term also reveals new paths into the future and toward tribally specific roles and fluid identities within sovereign Native nations. As we head toward the middle decades of the twenty-first century, Two-Spirit futures are focused on decolonizing gender identities and sexual expression—but not only on this. They're about continuing the conversation about the type of language that best defines a fluid, blended sense of identity. They're about reclaiming traditions and telling new stories. And they're about playing a role in meeting the challenges confronting Native communities, including the continued struggle to decolonize virtually every facet of Indigenous life while also identifying ways to address the most pressing existential threat of our time: human-induced climate change.

. . . .

Language is important to Two-Spirit futures. The words that people use to tell stories, sing songs, recite a prayer, or attach a label—all blend together to seed futures of possibility. Language is complex and ever changing. Words are debated, disagreed over, replaced. Some words are invented because the old ones were inadequate. Reclaiming

Native languages—an ongoing process—inspires fresh ways of knowing. Additionally, the ways people embody words and how culture emerges from bodies to inform the ways we present to a lover, to family, to the world are shaped by, and shape, the layers of verbal and bodily language that fill our lives.[6]

Miko Thomas, an enrolled member of the Chickasaw Nation who grew up in Oklahoma, gives a lot of thought to language. "I think a lot of times we're very scripted in how we respond to things," Thomas said in July 2018. I asked Thomas whether the term "Two-Spirit" had become part of a script that some people use to understand their lives. Thomas responded by recalling the questions that swirled in their mind after first hearing the term. "What is it? Is this an actual Native word? Is it the LGBT umbrella? What's meant specifically?" Initially, Thomas was skeptical.[7]

A writer, performance artist, and Two-Spirit activist, Thomas served in the US Navy and was deployed in Desert Shield, Desert Storm, and Desert Recovery between 1989 and 1992 before settling in San Francisco. Thomas grew up political. Their father was involved in the American Indian Movement, and Thomas has remained an active member of BAAITS and the GLBT Historical Society in San Francisco. Thomas is also a successful drag artist, performing under the stage-name Landa Lakes, a parody on the Land O'Lakes brand. Land O'Lakes, a farmer-owned cooperative founded in 1921, until 2020 used a stereotypical image of a Native woman wearing a feathered headdress to market the company's butter.[8]

Thomas eventually embraced the term "Two-Spirit." After initially thinking the term wasn't necessary, Thomas changed their mind after attending a gathering and hearing stories about the first Two-Spirit people. That gathering convinced Thomas that they could identify as a "Two-Spirit person and I could connect back to my spirituality."[9] It was a moment of clarity: Thomas was making new connections with people from the Two-Spirit diaspora while also finding new ways to reengage with Chickasaw philosophies and spiritual traditions.[10]

Two-Spirits feel like "floating words" to Thomas. They're words filled with possibility that help "you feel this bond with other Native people who are seeking out their own connections with traditions and spirituality."[11] Two-Spirit is a term with no fixed meaning; it doesn't separate people into categories. Instead, it's malleable, adaptive, contested. In the decades since it was first used, Two-Spirit has come to mean different things to different people. However, most Two-Spirit people view the term as a way to feel whole. For people who share Miko Thomas's perspective, the term enriches, it decolonizes gender and sexuality.[12] For others, Two-Spirit raises questions about their personal identity and their relationship to their tribal community. For still others, the meaning of the term has changed over time, prompting some people to ask if a newer term is needed.

Few Two-Spirit people would argue that the term has become an important part of decolonial politics in Indian Country. Sheldon Raymore (Cheyenne River Sioux) views the term in this way. Raymore uses "Two-Spirit" to encompass a decolonial politics in which Native people strive for "sexual sovereignty." The decolonization of Indigenous sexuality impacts a range of issues, from enabling Native nations to prosecute people who abduct or murder Indigenous women and trans people, to legalizing same-sex marriage and decoupling sexual desire from heteropatriarchy. As the Cherokee writer Daniel Heath Justice puts this latter point, "Every orgasm can be an act of decolonization."[13]

For many in Indian Country, decolonizing sexuality starts by undoing the harm caused to Native communities by Christianity, the gender binary, and colonial patriarchy. Sexual sovereignty is therefore a vital part of Native sovereignty. Ben Geboe, an enrolled member of the Yankton Sioux Tribe of South Dakota and executive director of American Indian Community House in New York City, explains how decolonization occurs at multiple levels: "It's familial, sometimes it's the tribal unit, sometimes it's the actual interfacing with the United States government."[14] Colonial thinking infiltrated these different levels of experience over the past five centuries, introducing homophobia and the gender binary to Indigenous communities. This interconnection of levels means that the decolonization of Indian Country will remain ongoing for the foreseeable future.

Geo Soctomah Neptune, a Two-Spirit member of the Passamaquoddy tribe in Maine, a basket maker and drag performer, views the decolonization of gender and sexuality as important work that taps into the best aspects of Native cultures. Neptune points out, "We went from a place where women were in charge to a place where women and feminine people and Two Spirits were disrespected because Native identity was almost a direct antithesis to patriarchy."[15] Undoing the damage done to Native communities is a priority for Neptune, just as it is for Cecelia LaPointe, an Ojibway-Métis who identifies as androgynous, gender nonconforming, and Two-Spirit. LaPointe views decolonizing work as essential to the future of sexual sovereignty.[16] In a 2019 blog post for the Weisman Art Museum in Minneapolis, LaPointe argued, "Through decolonization, we can uncover the various meanings that might not align with the definitions of 'lesbian,' 'gay,' 'bi-sexual,' 'transgender,' and 'queer.'" LaPointe, the founder and owner of Native Justice Coalition, concludes, "[The] work of decolonization includes reclaiming identities and restoring gender balance within the Anishinaabe Nation."[17]

Decolonial work is happening across Indian Country, in different spaces, and among a variety of groups. It's occurring at a legal and political level, in the passage of same-sex marriage laws by tribal governments. It is also happening at powwows. Sean Snyder (Navajo and Southern Ute) and Adrian Matthias Stevens (Shoshone Bannock, Ute, and Apache) began making headlines during the 2010s when they pushed through homophobic barriers to compete in Sweetheart Dance contests. In 2020, a PBS documentary, *Sweetheart Dancers*, chronicled Sean and Adrian's journey.[18]

And they're not alone in reclaiming traditions for the future. Other Two-Spirit artists are breaking down prejudices. In the 2019 season of Amazon Prime's fantasy drama *American Gods*, the Kanien'kehá:ka (Mohawk) actor Devery Jacobs brings the Two-Spirit Cherokee character Sam Black Crow to life. In contrast to HBO's *Lovecraft Country*, in which the Two-Spirit character Yahima is portrayed with little humanity and gratuitously murdered, critics noted that Jacobs, who identifies as queer, played Sam Black Crow with a level of depth and compassion that is rarely seen on mainstream television.[19]

Travis Goldtooth is also breaking barriers and declaring "we're still here." Goldtooth, aka Buffalo Barbie, a former Miss Montana Two-Spirit, who identifies with the female pronoun, says that Two-Spirit people are medicine. "Our words have power," Goldtooth declares, adding, "Your words have strength; your words and actions can either build a bridge or tear it down."[20] Scores of younger Two-Spirit artists, singers, dancers, writers, and storytellers continue to strengthen the medicine Goldtooth alludes to, adding depth and diversity to the meaning of Two-Spiritedness.[21]

"Reclaiming" and "restoring" Two-Spirit roles and identities is about constantly striving for balance within Native communities. It is also about renewal and maintaining connections to ancestors so that Indigenous knowledge remains vibrant and alive with meaning. Reclaiming Two-Spirit roles and identities in the twenty-first century and beyond builds on the work of people like Marty Fixico, who began contributing to this decolonizing process in the 1980s and 1990s. Fixico recalls embracing the term "Two-Spirit," which he understood as meaning "there was some combination of male and female spirit in somebody. . . . It didn't matter what body you had."

Fixico was living in Washington, DC, in the early 1990s when he heard this new term. It recentered him. Fixico was born and raised in Oklahoma City. His family included a "long line of spiritual people," a lineage that Fixico initially internalized as "pressure to be something I didn't want to be." He knew he was gay but lacked the language and support networks to openly express this aspect of his identity. After graduating from high school in 1975, Fixico set out to find his path in life. That path involved some wrong turns and tough times. Fixico married and started a family, but the marriage broke down. With legal assistance from Clyde Hall, he divorced his wife, an emotionally draining experience that left Fixico heartbroken after he was separated from his children. As the 1990s dawned, Fixico moved to DC, joined a theater group, and "partied a lot." He shared a house with four other men, one of whom was his Seneca boyfriend. Of the early 1990s, Fixico remembers thinking he "was going to contract AIDS and die." He didn't, but tragically his lover did, passing away from AIDS in 1994.

Fixico grew to realize that he wanted to help people. He recalls meeting Native gay men who were full of "self-loathing." This saddened Fixico, a deeply compassionate and loving person. Through his growing involvement in advocacy work, Fixico tried to make connections and help people disconnected from family and community. He eventually recognized that he had more power than he realized to shape the course of his own life and the lives of those around him. Embracing his own Two-Spiritedness opened his eyes to this reality. Fixico also found inspiration when he learned that in some Native communities Two-Spirit people had never stopped performing roles historically associated with their special identity, knowledge, and skills. This realization felt empowering. Two-Spirit people were "taking care of the elderly, they were taking care of children, they were nurses, they were teachers, doctors, these are the same roles that we always played in our communities." Through decades of oppressive assimilation policies, "it was unconscious" that Two-Spirit people kept performing these roles out of sight of government officials. In the 1990s, those roles, and their associated identities, were again being publicly embraced and celebrated.

Today, Fixico sees a "lot of really good young people coming up." They, like his generation, include some strong personalities. This newer generation isn't the first to grapple with American colonialism, something Fixico's peers also had to recognize in the 1980s and 1990s. Back then, Fixico remembers, "We had to come to terms with our egos" and acknowledge that decolonizing gender and sexuality was bigger, and more important, than any one individual. "What pains me," Fixico told me in 2019, "is people who think they're the only ones doing" decolonial work, "or they're the first ones doing it." That's the hubris of youth. Still, that energy, Fixico reminds me, can, and is, being put to productive use to "create a better world for us to be safe and happy."[22]

Christo Apache shares Fixico's aspiration for a "better world." Apache was born and raised on the Mescalero Apache Reservation, located in south central New Mexico. Like Fixico, Apache knew he was gay from a young age but couldn't find the right words to explain his sexuality to family members. Not until he was in his thirties did Apache "learn about the term Two-Spirit." The pieces of his identity started to fall into place, so Apache went back to his family and told them, "Yeah, I'm gay, but not in the way you think I am. There's this other term, Two-Spirit, which means you want a closer connection to your culture, and you want an identification that is much closer to your tribal affiliation."[23]

Apache is a writer, so words are important to him. How people interact with community is also a form of communication, an unspoken language that involves how people read bodies. Apache came to see that "people who have gender expression or sexuality attached with their nature have always been around." He believes that because of "religious indoctrination," not every family accepts people with nonbinary genders and the roles traditionally associated with fluid identities. However, language has the power to unlock memories of these identities and roles within Native communities. "Somewhere within us," Apache says, "the words that we perpetuate is a kind of memory we are grasping for."

Christo Apache sees an interplay between the English and Apache languages in Mescalero Apache communities. The point at which two languages meet has the power to occlude memories; it can also clarify. One of Apache's aunts provided the clarity he was looking for. When he explained to her that he combined gay and Two-Spirit identities, she offered a cautionary note: "When you're saying the term 'Two-Spirit,' if you were to translate that from English to Apache, you're translating it into somebody who was imbalanced, or somebody who was mentally off. That doesn't sound right."[24] Apache's aunt explained that Mescalero Apaches have their own terms for people who follow nonbinary gender roles. One of the terms to survive the onslaught of colonialism is *nde'isdzan*, which roughly translates as "man-woman" and refers to a person assigned male roles with the community.[25]

Christo Apache's adoption of the umbrella term "Two-Spirit" initiated conversations that made it possible for his aunt to show him the way back to Mescalero Apache traditions. This type of reclaiming process is happening throughout Indian Country. It involves a decolonizing of the mind, of language, and of everyday life. As Apache learned, the term "Two-Spirit" can be used in multiple ways, providing awareness and visibility for gender- and sexually nonconforming people while also connecting a person to their respective Indigenous language, culture, and ways of knowing.

DeLesslin "Roo" George-Warren is making these connections. George-Warren is a member of the Catawba Nation, a Siouan-speaking community with tribal lands along the Catawba River at the present-day South Carolina–North Carolina border. George-Warren is part of a newer generation of artists and storytellers imagining Native futures in exciting ways. He and his family remain active in the Catawba community, where he is hard at work on language revitalization, and his aunt runs the Catawba Cultural Center. His mother served as executive director of the tribe, and his grandfather, Evans M. "Buck"

George, played a major role in Catawba politics during the latter half of the twentieth century.[26]

In fact, Buck George was a pathbreaker. In the 1950s he became the first nonwhite player on Clemson University's football team, earning the nickname "the vanishing Indian" because he was so fast.[27] Injuries curtailed George's professional career, but it didn't slow his involvement in politics and his tireless efforts to make the future a better place for Catawba people. He opposed South Carolina's miscegenation laws, advocated for tribal sovereignty, and played an integral role in the Catawba tribe's receiving state and federal recognition. Buck George also oversaw the settlement, in 1993, of a Catawba land claim in York and Lancaster Counties that had been 150 years in the making.[28]

George-Warren is from a proud Catawba family with a long history of helping community. As a teenager, though, he distanced himself from his Catawba heritage. With hindsight, he recognizes that he lacked the historical context to understand the beauty and the problems confronting Catawbas. That changed during his sophomore year of college. One of his professors introduced him to Vine Deloria Jr.'s *Custer Died for Your Sins*. This iconic book awakened George-Warren's historical consciousness, providing the context he'd been missing as a teen.[29]

Decolonizing his sexuality proved more challenging. In high school George-Warren remained in the closet. When he did "come out as queer" he recalls some "tough conversations in Catawba spaces." Coming out was made more difficult by the discomfort he felt with the term "gay." It just didn't feel right; it still doesn't. When he heard the term "Two-Spirit" he felt a jolt of exhilaration. He remembers that sense of "Oh my gosh, this is the most perfect thing ever." What he found particularly appealing was how the term provided him with a language to articulate the complexity of his identity. He felt whole.

Since that revelatory moment, his relationship with Two-Spiritedness has become, by his own admission, "complicated." In Catawba spaces, people have asked whether the term "Two-Spirit" is an appropriation because no term like it exists in Catawba culture and language. That might be true, but it must be remembered that Catawbas have suffered enormously from cultural and linguistic loss due to colonialism. George-Warren is acutely aware of this. It's why he's reached out to the Two-Spirit diaspora and found inspiration from conversations with Mandan, Hidatsa, and people from other Siouan-speaking cultures. These conversations remind him of the existence of nonbinary gender systems in Siouan-speaking communities and the fact that matrilineal societies, such as the Catawba, tend not to have histories of homophobia. "Would a matrilineal society be conducive to homophobia?" he asks rhetorically. "I tend to think probably not." Instead, he echoes a conversation I had with Clyde Hall, who says that "no one is disposable" in Native cultures.[30]

For George-Warren, the term "Two-Spirit" still raises a lot of questions. He understands the criticisms directed at Pan-Indigeneity but counters them: "I think the benefit of it is, for queer folks, we're always the minority even in our own communities." A term like "Two-Spirit" cuts through that marginalization; it evokes Indigeneity, even if one lacks the language to articulate specific tribal terminology that contributes to the decolonization of gender and sexuality. At the same time, George-Warren is able to feel more than one identity at a time. Outside the Catawba community, he identifies as Two-Spirit. Inside the community, he identifies as queer.

Importantly, the term "Two-Spirit" provides a sense of Pan-Indian solidarity. At the Capital Pride celebrations in Washington, DC, in 2017, the strength derived from Pan-Indigenous unity was needed. George-Warren recalls being part of a group of Two-Spirit people who temporarily locked down the front of the Pride parade and chanted "No pride in genocide." A group of older white gay men took exception; they were "drunk, and also very angry," and began a counter-chant: "We don't care."

Two-Spirit people are all too aware of this type of racism. They know that non-Indigenous LGBTQ people find it hard to extract themselves from colonial thinking. Even well-intentioned groups, such as the Human Rights Campaign, struggle to be good allies and understand the issues that Native trans, queer, and Two-Spirit people grapple with on a daily basis.[31] Young people of George-Warren's generation recognize this reality. It prompts some bold political and cultural stands. George-Warren, for instance, is part of a generational movement that takes previously offensive language and inverts its meaning. In adopting a queer identity in Catawba spaces, he inverts a word that once denoted "disposability" and gives it an affirming, powerful, and special identity.[32]

George-Warren is not alone in this effort. Rebecca Nagle, a Cherokee writer and advocate, uses language in very specific ways. She states that "for me, the term queer is about my sexuality, and then it's also about my political perspective of the world." This doesn't mean that Nagle has no use for the term "Two-Spirit"—she does—but it does underscore Clyde Hall's point about the vitality of popular and political culture throughout Indian Country.[33]

Candi Brings Plenty views her work as an advocate in this light. Brings Plenty says she strives to "empower trans folks by identifying as a cis-woman."[34] Critical to this situational empowerment, and to broader decolonial objectives, is explicitly bringing the diversity of Native roles and identities back into the "sacred circle." Brings Plenty notes that "some folks identify as queer Indigenous, other folks identify as Two-Spirit."[35] Two-Spirit people are able to embrace more than one identity simultaneously, but to do so they need the language and supportive community networks to shape an enriching sense of self.[36]

Two-Spirit people are telling new stories about the pain and the possibilities of community. Although Two-Spirited people traditionally assumed asexual identities in many communities, contemporary artists and writers have effectively explored erotic desire and longing for love.[37] In *Two-Spirit Acts*, Muriel Miguel (Kuna, Rappahannock), Kent Monkman (Fish River Band), and Waawaate Fobister (Anishinaabe), give voice to erotic feelings, invert the power dynamics of historical tropes, and navigate homophobia in reclaiming their tribal language and Two-Spiritedness. Miguel, who founded the Native female performance group Spiderwoman Theater in 1976, adapts the coyote trickster to her play *Hot 'n' Soft*. This powerful play explores a range of physical and psychological feelings. Desire, passion, and a willingness to let go and be vulnerable are beautifully conveyed to the audience. Miguel captures these emotions, these erotic desires with the line: "She can do anything she wants to me as long as she licks under my armpits. Howl. Howl. Howl!!"[38]

The Cree playwright and performance artist Kent Monkman also explores bodies. Monkman does this by inverting the heteropatriachal gaze and the history of categorizing, fetishizing, and commodifying Indigenous bodies. His inversion of George Catlin's painting *Dance to the Berdash* highlights this brilliantly. In 2008, Monkman used multiple video feeds to bring his artwork *Honour Dance* to life. Then, in 2019, he used virtual reality to provide viewers with an immersive experience of *Honour Dance*.[39] Monkman also committed *Honour Dance* to canvas in 2019. The painting, now housed in the Smithsonian's Hirshhorn Museum, features Monkman's alter ego, Miss Chief Eagle Testickle, posing at the center of a dance circle. Miss Chief's sexuality is on full display, her gaze is fixed outward onto settler viewers. From this empowered position the dancers move joyously around Miss Chief. Unlike Catlin's painting, Monkman provides us with a window into the emotions of the individual dancers. We see laughter, joy, hope, and empowerment expressed on the faces of the dancers. *Honour Dance* is full of energy, a striking contrast from the expressionless, out-of-focus face of the "berdash" and the demonic expression of the dancers offered up by Catlin in the 1830s.

Monkman possesses an expansive creativity, and he thinks critically about the past and the role of art in representing Indigenous subjectivities.[40] In an interview with *Smithsonian Magazine* in May 2020, Monkman reflected on how the coronavirus pandemic might impact his art. He explained that the "similarities to some of the themes I'm already exploring in my work that have to do with devastating loss and the resilience of Indigenous people in times of hardship" seemed more urgent than ever as COVID-19 devastated Indigenous communities. "I'm not sure how this experience will shift my work yet," he said, "but I've been thinking a lot about it."[41]

In *Two-Spirit Acts*, Monkman showcases his skill as a writer of satire. Monkman's "Taxonomy of the European Male, Séance," introduces us to Miss Chief. Miss Chief has traveled to Europe to study the "customs and manners of the European male" in their "original state" before they "are obliteratcd completely." This deliciously funny play is a decolonial masterpiece. In Monkman's hands, Miss Chief takes her anthropological specimens of authentic Europeanness and invites them to join the Nation of Mischief—which has no "blood quantum requirements"—so long as they're willing to be satirized.[42]

Waawaate Fobister's *Agokwe* is a story of desire, longing, and homophobia. Like Miguel, Fobister invokes the trickster motif, introducing audiences to Nanabush, "the trickster of tricksters." In a world filled with homophobia and hate—"What do you people call them nowadays? Gays? Queers? Fags? Homo?"—Nanabush challenges the hate imported to Turtle Island by European colonizers.

"Homo," Nanabush chortles, "that word cracks me up. There are many words used for Two-Spirited people in Indian languages—Lhamana from the Zuni, Gatxan from the Tlingit, Nadleeh the Navajo, Mohave the Alyahas, Winkte the Lakota Sioux, Mexoga the Omaha." Nanabush's favorite, though, is "Agokwe," an Ojibwe word. "It means within the man there is a woman; not one spirit, but two." Audiences look up on the stage as Nanabush decolonizes gender and sexuality and offers hope for the future by looking into the past: "Yes, there was a time when the Anishinaabe had no prejudice against a boy who was Agokwe."[43]

Fobister longs for that time, a world without prejudice, a place where they could be an Agokwe and everything else an Anishinaabe could become. Colonialism stole that hope; it still tears at the well-being of Two-Spirit people, gnawing at their minds and terrorizing their bodies. Like Fobister, Joshua Whitehead, an Oji-Cree writer, confronts that pain in his work. Whitehead embraces radical possibilities for future Native identities. Whitehead's writing weaves together Two-Spirit and queer identities, the pain of the past and present, and the anticipation of the erotic. This is urgent, vital, incisive writing. It evokes diverse emotions—pain, longing, anger, frustration, lust, and more—that a previous generation of Native writers like Beth Brant (Bay of Quinte Mohawk), Chrystos (Menominee), Maurice Kenny (noncitizen Mohawk), and Paula Gunn Allen (Laguna Pueblo, Sioux) unlocked with their poetry, prose, zines, and historical analysis. Whitehead's writing is part of a contemporary literary scene that includes the Two-Spirit writers and scholars Daniel Heath Justice (Cherokee Nation), Billy-Ray Belcourt (Driftpile Cree), Gwen Benaway (Anishinaabe, Métis), and many others. The literary scholar Lisa Tatonetti observes, "This new generation of LGBTQ/2S Indigenous intellectuals is on fire."[44]

Speaking on the *All My Relations* podcast in April 2019, Whitehead explained that the term "Two-Spirit" calls them back to their Indigeneity but in ways that feel "not fully developed." Whitehead worries that calls for a return to tradition and ceremony that are often attached to Two-Spiritedness feel like they get wrapped up in neocolonial thinking and an "imprisoned past." To ensure that Native traditions don't become entombed in a static history, Whitehead's writing posits dynamic links among the past, present, and future. The result is radical possibilities in which Whitehead uses "queerness" to open spaces and explore the complexity of Native identities, empowerment, and bodies that are "pained, harmed, removed or dispossessed."

These insights have led Whitehead to embrace the term "Indigiqueer," to combine Two-Spirit and queer identities. It provides a "contemporary way of thinking for Two-Spirit people."[45] It evokes the colonial past and present—"Us ndns sure are some badass biopunks" who've "coalesced, convened, intersected, interwoven"—and it explores the eroticism and transcendence of being.[46] As Whitehead writes in their 2018 novel *Jonny Appleseed*, "Sex does strange things to people—it's like blacking out or going on cruise control. Your body knows what it wants and goes for it. This can be dangerous, as I'd learn later."[47]

Indigiqueer inverts and empowers; it tests the boundaries of vulnerability and inspires new ideas, new ways of seeing and interacting with one's body and the bodies of others. Indigiqueer is, Whitehead writes, about the "past|present|future" because "the spirits of all three strive within me."[48] However, some Two-Spirit elders worry that terms like "Indigiqueer" bear too many of the hallmarks of critical theory. The terms feel detached from reality, jargon-laden, anthropological. They understand the search for new words, new stories, but they wonder whether terms like "Indigiqueer" speak only to a particular generation or a particular group with a specific level of education or type of radical politics.

Debates about cultural meaning and terminology reveal that a lively discussion about language and culture is underway in Indian Country. Sometimes those discussions become tense. In March 2017, I spoke to a Two-Spirit person in Washington, DC, about these debates. Wishing to remain anonymous, they told me, "Two-Spirit politics is awful right now." When I asked them if they'd care to elaborate, the response was curt: "Look, there's just a lot of woke Indians right now. Everyone's talking but no one's really listening." In the heat of discussions, these tense moments can feel overwhelming. Debates about tactics, ideology, and language can develop sharp edges.[49]

I spoke to Curtis Harris about these creative tensions. Harris, now Harris-Davia after he married his partner following the 2015 Supreme Court decision legalizing same-sex marriage, expresses skepticism about the "alphabet soup of our identity." Harris-Davia, a San Carlos Apache, was fifty-eight when we spoke in December 2018.

He understands, and is sympathetic toward, younger people injecting new vitality into Native culture but worries about the political purity demanded by a younger generation of Indigenous advocates and activists. The pronouns, the questions—"Are you cis?"; "Are you cis-hetero?"—it "can get tricky," Harris-Davia says. It can lead to superficial judgments about a person's character, their commitment to decolonial politics. It also leads to "raised eyebrows" from young people—a posture that sometimes springs from the "ego" that Marty Fixico worries about. Questioning the non-Native origins of some of this newer terminology, Harris-Davia asks wryly, "Is there a lexicon I have to buy at Barnes and Noble that will give me all of this?"[50]

Harris-Davia isn't dismissive of the vitality that younger people bring to Native politics. He worries, though, about the uncritical use of academic theories, the inversion of terms like queer, and the superficiality of social media platforms. "I'm not sure that's the way we should do it," Harris-Davia says of the memes and mantras that populate the digital world. "Just because you feel comfortable with that identity doesn't necessarily mean all of us have to buy into using that term."[51]

The discomfort that Harris-Davia shared with me about terminology deserves respect and consideration. Elders like Harris-Davia have earned that. At the same time, there are enormous creative and political possibilities within these debates. Indeed, debate and disagreement are the essence of vital and vibrant communities that seek to reclaim traditions and tell new stories. The urgency and energy of the young will find the patience and reflectiveness of elders frustrating at times, but when has this creative tension not existed? There are many paths to a decolonial future, to a future in which Two-Spirit and Indigiqueer people reclaim their place in the sacred circle.

. . . .

Two-Spirit artists, writers, and academics envision futures through multiple mediums. Tony Enos, a musician and member of the Eastern Band of Cherokee Indians, celebrates Two-Spirit identities through music. Enos emphasizes the diversity of Two-Spirit traditions and the "resilience, strength, and sheer indomitable will of Two Spirit people."[52] There's more than one way to be a Two-Spirit person and to unlock the "soul energy" that is important to Native communities.

Native philosophies are incredibly rich and diverse. Most of these philosophies emphasize the importance of the soul and soul energy, but they do so in different ways. "Soul" is associated with "breath" and the source of life bestowed by Creator. In some cultures, such as the Havasupai, a person is thought to have one soul. Among others, such as the Apache and Diné, the soul is formed of two parts, and in still other cultural communities the soul includes four or as many as six parts. Soul, or souls, are nongendered. They give life. As Tomson Highway, a Cree playwright and enrolled member of the Barren Lands First Nation explains, "A woman, man, dog, tree, rock, and even an ant all have equal status because they all have souls."[53] Souls can leave the body for short periods. If souls depart permanently, death to the physical body ensues and the personal qualities that form human and more-than-human spirits cease to be animated.[54] Colonialism almost destroyed these beliefs. From genocidal violence, the ethnocide and gendercide of the boarding school movement, and government efforts to terminate sovereign Indian nations, the US and Canadian governments implemented policies designed to snuff out the souls and spirits of Indigenous people.

Reclaiming Two-Spirit traditions is part of the resistance to settler colonialism's eliminationist tendencies. It's hard work—work that Enos contributes to through his music, that Rebecca Nagle and De-Lesslin "Roo" George-Warren undertake in revitalizing their respective tribes' languages, that Joshua Whitehead adds to through their exhilarating prose, and Candi Brings Plenty via her tireless advocacy and work for social justice. They all enrich Two-Spirit culture, just as the Mi'kmaq-Ojibwe filmmaker Bretten Hannam makes Two-Spirit stories visible through movies, and Patrick Hunter, Aria Evans, Ryan Young, Asa Wright, Raven John, and many others use art to express Two-Spiritedness and reveal futures of hope and possibility.

Marcy Angeles seeks out possibilities in their art. Angeles uses creative energy to find a path back to their Chiricahua Apache culture. As a trans person, Angeles has endured terrifying levels of prejudice. During their teenage years, Angeles told me, they were almost stoned to death and they were threatened with a Catholic exorcism. Angeles finds refuge in music and the support of friends like Jen Deerinwater. Angeles also feels empowered knowing that there's "no decolonization without Two-Spirit," something that they feel necessitates Native people "going forward to the past."

The bodies of too many Native trans people know the pain of colonialism. Angeles is no exception. "We lost so much," Angeles reflects. It is why it hurts when Native people tell Angeles that being trans is a colonial lie. As Angeles sees things, transphobia feels a lot like a rearticulation of the prejudices experienced by previous generations of Two-Spirit people in Native and non-Native communities. And so, Angeles returns to music. As they told me, "Art is the only way I can survive."[55]

Survivance, defined by the Anishinaabe cultural theorist Gerald Vizenor as "that active sense of presence in remembrance, that trace of creation and natural reason in native stories," also runs through Miko Thomas's creativity. Just as Vizenor renounces "dominance, tragedy and victimry," Thomas's drag ensemble, Brush Arbor Gurls, both critiques settler colonialism and makes Indigenous stories visible to Native and non-Native audiences.[56]

Performing under the stage name Landa Lakes, Thomas founded the Brush Arbor Gurls as a way to fundraise for BAAITS. In addition to giving back to the Bay Area Two-Spirit community, the Brush Arbor Gurls have broken down barriers. Thomas has taken Brush Arbor Gurls into historically white, gay spaces, such as San Francisco's Leather bars—indeed, Randy Burns, the cofounder of GAI, told Thomas that the Brush Arbor Gurls "was the first Native American drag troupe" that he knew of.[57]

Thomas's creativity expands on a previous generation of extraordinarily creative Two-Spirit artists like Judy Tallwing, an elder of Apache, Tewa-puebloan, and African ancestry who survived the boarding school era. Born in Arizona, Tallwing, who has lived and worked as an artist in Baltimore since 2007, blazed a path for Two-Spirit people in the late 1980s and 1990s. In 1987, she became the first International Ms. Leather.[58] In her acceptance speech, preserved on YouTube, Tallwing acknowledges her upbringing on the White Mountain Reservation in Arizona and makes a declaration: "We're here because we have to let the world know we're here."[59]

A generation later, Miko Thomas continues to let the "world know we're here." Thomas draws inspiration from Buffy Sainte-Marie and other Native artists, mixing political and historical commentary, Indigenous stories, and satirical takes on popular culture. Thomas's art represents the panoply of both Native and Two-Spirit experiences. In "Shake the Feathers," the Brush Arbor Gurls pay tribute to the Zuni lhamana WeWha. In a separate performance, the troupe provides a moving meditation on the intergenerational impact of residential boarding schools.[60] Of these and other performances, Thomas says, "I really enjoy being able to take something that is really Indigenous and share it with a wider public," adding, "It's a lot of history that some people are unaware of, and there's sometimes people in the audience whose parents and grandparents experienced it" in boarding schools.[61]

Artistic expression is a creative outlet, a space where Two-Spirit people can both escape a world that often feels cruel or indifferent to their existence, and to confront worlds filled with injustice. Marca Cassity (Osage Nation) told me that she goes into a trancelike state when performing her songs, a place she calls "the pocket, a blissful place of self-expression."[62] George-Warren also finds that sense of fulfillment from self-expression and creativity. At the Smithsonian's National Portrait Gallery in 2016–17, George-Warren led audiences on tours, called the "Indigenous Corps of Discovery," of presidential portraits. His goal was to provide patrons with an Indigenous historical perspective of past American presidents.[63] He took his artistic eye and historical critique to the Utah Museum of Fine Arts in 2017 and 2018, where his "Don't Go West" tour reexamined Euro-American art and the "glorified understanding of the West."[64]

George-Warren openly acknowledges that his historical critiques are subversive: "History is not a listing of facts, it's a mythology with citations."[65] Historians will bristle at such suggestions. In 1973, the historian Hayden White made a similar argument, contending that meaning is not derived solely from reading written documents but is made through narrative. Moreover, cultural assumptions, legends, myths, if cited often enough, became part of our received wisdom—part of our collective historical consciousness. When popularly assumed facts are questioned and found wanting, people often experience cognitive dissonance. George-Warren's work taps into that uncomfortable sensation, transforming official portrait galleries and the unquestioned mythologies of United States history into spaces where people actively critique colonial legends and arrive at new, Indigenized, insights about the past.[66]

By entering public spaces historically reserved for white people, from leather bars to portrait galleries, Two-Spirit artists continue to find creative ways to highlight how history mediates future possibilities. This work has exploded since the early 2000s as Two-Spirit people have gone online and used digital spaces to make connections, tell their own stories, and give Two-Spirit experiences greater visibility. Marty Fixico calls the Internet "Creator's gift to Native people."[67]

The digital age in which we live holds both possibilities and familiar challenges. Access to digital technologies remains patchy in many parts of Indian Country, and ensuring that Native people retain ownership—Indigenous digital sovereignty—of their content is as much an issue for the future as land and water rights.[68] Two-Spirit elders, advocates, and artists have embraced the Internet. In the early 2000s, for example, Richard LaFortune launched the Two-Spirit Press Room (2SPR). As national director of 2SPR, LaFortune hoped to raise the visibility of Two-Spirit people and their political needs.

2SPR received guidance from its inaugural advisory board, which included Ken Harper (Cherokee), Louva Hartwell (Navajo), Larry Kairaiauk (Yup'ik), Kehaulani Kauanui (Hawaiian), Wesley Thomas (Navajo), Karina Walters (Choctaw), and LaFortune. In addition to raising the visibility of Two-Spirit people, 2SPR focused on attracting grants to combat the ongoing HIV/AIDS pandemic in Indian Country. In May 2006 LaFortune lobbied Joe Wilson, the program officer at the Public Welfare Foundation, for a $50,000 grant to assist with HIV/AIDS awareness and treatment. In making his case, LaFortune wrote, "The HIV pandemic has continuously and disproportionately affected Native people, as dramatically as did the smallpox epidemics, the constant treaty violations which caused displacement, disease and trauma, and the death and destruction [caused] by church-run boarding schools designed to Disappear the languages, cultures, spiritual traditions and families of Native children."[69]

2SPR's public outreach also made it possible to attract support from major political figures. In 2008, presidential hopeful Barack Obama sent a letter of congratulations to LaFortune acknowledging the twentieth anniversary of the International Two-Spirit Gathering.

"We welcomed Senator Obama's expression of support," LaFortune wrote, "which we certainly hadn't expected. It is completely appropriate for our tribal participants to have heard from a US presidential candidate, because the Gathering participants represent Sovereign Nations . . . and we have always been known as leaders among other cultures." LaFortune noted that the Republican presidential candidate, John McCain, had not sent a similar statement of support.[70]

Since the early 2000s, a growing number of digital communities have helped to connect the Two-Spirit diaspora. Marty Fixico curates Native Out on Facebook, providing news, updates on events, and profiles of Two-Spirit people. In both the United States and Canada, a bevy of digital resources link people to local Two-Spirit organizations, events, webinars, podcasts, and a growing body of literature.[71] And in 2021, the BAAITS powwow responded to the COVID-19 pandemic by going online.

One of the more prominent examples of digital news media in recent years is the *Two-Spirit Journal*. Edited by Harlan Pruden, an activist and scholar who is a member of the Saddle Lake Indian Reservation's Goodfish Lake Band. Pruden has spent a lifetime raising awareness about Two-Spirit history, culture, and political issues. Pruden's tireless advocacy led him to cofound the NorthEast Two-Spirit Society and play an active role in the American Indian Community House in New York.

Two-Spirit Journal, a multimedia platform for Two-Spirit news, commentary, research, and artistic expression, brings Pruden's work to a larger, digital, audience. When the COVID-19 pandemic began spreading across the United States and Canada in early 2020, *Two-Spirit Journal* provided one of the few sources of news tailored to the needs of Two-Spirit people.[72] *Two-Spirit Journal* also builds community by celebrating the accomplishments of Two-Spirit people. On August 4, 2020, Pruden reminded readers that thirty years had passed since the term "Two-Spirit" was adopted as an umbrella term. *Two-Spirit Journal* marked the anniversary by celebrating the elders Myra Laramee (First Nations Cree), Albert McLeod (Nisichawayasihk Cree Nation and Métis), Sandy Laframboise (Métis), Edward Lavalle (Cree), and others. As the article showed, the people who attended the international gathering in Winnepeg in 1990 continue to produce art, tell stories, and provide leadership.

The historical importance of the 1990 gathering endures.[73] Future generations will define Two-Spiritedness in ways most relevant to them. Some may abandon the term altogether, preferring to identify as Indigiqueer, or with tribe-specific identities. Then again, terms not yet imagined may emerge. The future is full of possibilities.

. . . .

Without sustainable and resilient climate systems there will be no future, at least no human future. The Anthropocene—our current era of climate change, mass extinctions, and the collapse of ecosystems—is caused by human activity that releases warming greenhouse gases into the atmosphere. Climate change presents us all with the possibility of a dystopian future.[74]

In recent decades a new generation of Native futurists, scientists, and scholars has made major contributions to climate change debates. Some imagine future worlds of rising sea levels, warmer temperatures, extreme weather events, and shortages of food and fresh water—what one sci-fi writer refers to as the world "going to shit."[75] In 2017, Robin Kimmerer, Rosalyn LaPier, Melissa Nelson, and Kyle Powys Whyte offered a different perspective. They coauthored the "Indigenous Science Statement for the March on Science," in which they implored the wider scientific community to "engage the power of both Indigenous and Western science on behalf of the living earth."[76]

Indigenous science is part of a larger decolonial movement. Like efforts to decolonize gender and sexuality, Native science is about sovereignty, community, and imagining worlds in which human and more-than-human beings relate to the past, to one another, in nurturing and sustainable ways. Indigenous people have long histories of telling these types of stories. Indigenous spaces and bodies—past, present, and future—are not empty, vacant, or disposable frontiers. They are sacred spaces, farms that feed communities, homes that provide comfort to loved ones. Aja Couchois Duncan's *Restless Continent* reminds readers that the earth remembers; like human bodies, the earth feels; it emotes, moves, and changes.[77] Through dreams and prophecies, other Native storytellers build on the knowledge of their ancestors as they strive to meet the challenges of today to ensure a healthy tomorrow. The lyricism of the stories in the recent anthology

Love Beyond Body, Space, and Time and Daniel Heath Justice's trilogy, *The Way of Thorn and Thunder*, exemplify this beautifully.[78]

Getting to a future worth living in means holding on to pieces of the past. Knowledge of the pain that comes through knowing history will make the future a more enriching place.[79] As the Cherokee author and scholar Daniel Heath Justice writes in *The Way of Thorn and Thunder*, "If we fulfill our duty, future generations will look upon us with both respect and love, as we will have been the steadfast champions who made an unhappy choice in dark times for the good of all."[80] These lines offer a reminder of the connections and the responsibilities that Native people continue to respect in their human and more-than-human relations. However, to get to a resilient and sustainable future requires faith in those connections, and trust in the wisdom and power of the ancestors. It also requires resources. *Tribal Equity Toolkit 3.0* outlines the types of relationships, knowledge, and resources needed for sustainable futures. Se-ah-dom Edmo and Aaron Ridings's acknowledgments in the *Tribal Equity Toolkit* establish what is at stake for Native people: "Since time immemorial, Indigenous Nations of what now is known as the United States have been Sovereigns; been responsible for the health and wellbeing of our citizenry, an endeavor that is intergenerational and connects each generation to the work of our ancestors. In the spirit of this kinship connection, we respectfully acknowledge the collective wisdom and traditions of our ancestors."[81]

The *Tribal Equity Toolkit* recognizes the importance of strong, adaptive, and diverse families and communities. Marriage equality is essential to the future of Indian Country. It allows Native communities to build on traditions that enrich people's lives and include homes with "mothers, fathers, grandparents, aunts, uncles, and cousins, as well as more extended or adopted relatives—all of whom may assume childcare responsibilities." Two-Spirit people must be part of futures that support diverse families and sustainable environments: "Two Spirit/LGBTQ people have historically played an important role in tribal communities, including as caretakers and medicine givers." Edmo and Ridings urge extending these roles into the future to ensure that Native people "continue to honor the wisdom that Two Spirit/LGBTQ people have to offer all children in our tribal communities." They emphasize the importance of education, antidiscrimination laws, and Native-centric health services that combine the best aspects of Western medicine and Indigenous healing practices—care that remains important to people living with HIV/AIDS.[82]

The future health and well-being of Native communities will require equitable access to affordable healthcare. In addition to ongoing HIV/AIDS prevention and treatment, care for chronic conditions like diabetes and hypertension and the capacity of tribal health networks to respond to future pandemics will remain vital to healthy and vibrant communities.

If healthcare is to facilitate the well-being of Native people it must also support efforts to mitigate climate change. The United Nations has shown that Indigenous communities are at an elevated risk of being adversely impacted by climate change over the next century.[83] The impacts of a rapidly changing climate are already being felt by Native communities along the Gulf Coast, in the Pacific Northwest, in Alaska, in the Great Lakes region, and elsewhere. Two-Spirit people who experience marginalization within their tribal communities are particularly vulnerable to the social, cultural, and economic impacts of climate change. To meet the multifaceted challenges posed by the climate emergency, and to ensure the resilience of Native nations, the ecological knowledge and political engagement of Two-Spirit people must be included in effective climate policies.[84]

Human-induced climate change has the potential to compound the well-established consequences of environmental racism. In 1990, the United Nations encouraged governments and multinational corporations to adopt practices that would mitigate social and environmental harm to Indigenous communities.[85] In the decades since, the climate crisis has worsened. Indigenous futurists, writes Danika Medak-Saltzman, an enrolled member of the Turtle Mountain Chippewa, warn about "dystopian possibilities" and draw on Native traditions to "call forth better futures."[86] Native writers dedicated to combating environmental racism, promoting social justice, and advancing decolonization share this concern.[87] Nick Estes, a member of the Lower Brule Sioux Tribe, addresses these issues in his scholarship and activism, writing, "Indigenous notions of time consider the present to be structured by our past and our present. . . . There is no separation between past and present, meaning that an alternative future is also determined by our understanding of our past. Our history is the future."[88]

Two-Spirit elders like Sharon Day, an Ojibwe woman who helped establish the Mother Earth Water Walks, and younger Two-Spirit people like Candi Brings Plenty and the Mescalero Apache–Rarámuri artist and activist Celestino Crow recognize that "our history is the future."[89] Two-Spirit land and water protectors are, in the words of the Potawatomi philosopher Kyle Powys Whyte, "always in a dialogue with our ancestors as dystopianists and fantasizers." They are forming alliances, devising political strategies, and imagining paths through the climate crisis so they and their communities can reach "better futures."[90]

Two-Spirit advocacy for sustainable futures came of age at the Standing Rock Sioux Reservation between April 2016 and February 2017. In early 2016, Two-Spirit people from across the United States and Canada traveled to Oceti Sakowin, People of the Seven Council Fires (also known as the Sioux Nation). Their goal was to support elders LaDonna Brave Bull Allard, Debra White Plume, and thousands of other water protectors in the Standing Rock Sioux Tribe's fight against the proposed Dakota Access Pipeline (DAPL). Guided by the principle "water is life"—*mní wičóni*—Two-Spirit water protectors remained steadfast in their opposition to the Dakota Access Pipeline— the "black snake"—that threatened the lands and the health of Lake Oahe on the Missouri River.[91]

Energy Transfer Partners, a corporation with over $98 billion in assets, was responsible for constructing the pipeline. It proposed a construction route that took the pipeline through the unceded lands of Oceti Sakowin. The Standing Rock Sioux charged that the proposed construction would contravene the Fort Laramie Treaty of 1868.[92] The fight to stop DAPL was on. The social media hashtag #NoDAPL went viral, and a new chapter in the ongoing battle to defend Native sovereignty and protect their climate futures began.[93]

Since its founding at the end of the Revolutionary War in 1783, the United States has forcibly removed Indigenous peoples from their homelands so it could exploit their land, control waterways, and extract resources buried in the ground. During the twentieth century, dam construction also wiped out Native communities, farms, and sacred sites to make way for large reservoirs that provided hydroelectricity, reliable water supplies for agribusiness, and recreational spaces for urban and suburban communities throughout North America.[94]

In the early 2010s multinational oil and gas interests attracted coverage in mainstream news outlets when Indigenous people began opposing Trans-Canada's proposed Keystone XL (KXL; XL stands for "export limited") Pipeline. In a portent of #NoDAPL, an unlikely coalition of farmers, ranchers, environmentalists, libertarians, and Native communities came together to oppose the KXL. The proposed pipeline, which would transport oil extracted from Canada's tar sands to refineries on the Gulf Coast of Texas and elsewhere in the United States, was seen by opponents as a pollution threat to groundwater supplies. Lakota elder Debra White Plume, who was born and raised on the Pine Ridge Indian Reservation, recalled getting some money together for "a delegation of activists, singers, speakers, warriors, elders" to stop the KXL. White Plume wrote about being joined by other Native women, all determined to halt the pipeline to ensure a future for their "children, grandchildren, nieces, nephews."[95] With the exception of the tribal chairman and council of the Lower Brule, Oceti Sakowin stood in opposition to the KXL. It was a grassroots movement, something White Plume emphasized when she declared, "We sought spiritual guidance and were told that the spirit of Unci Maka will awaken people to protect her. For us it has always been about protecting sacred water, whether it's [from] uranium mining or KXL."[96]

That motivation, that spirit, inspired Native water protectors and their non-Indigenous allies to rally around #NoDAPL in 2016 and set up a camp to serve as a focus for their protest. Water protectors endured freezing cold, clothing that smelled of smoke from campfires, and the unrelenting surveillance of law enforcement. The members of the Two Spirit Nation were at the forefront of this movement. The group's website states, "The Two Spirit Nation was planted as a seed at Oceti Sakowin and is now bearing fruit as a nationwide movement of visibility for the Indigenous spectrum of LGBTQ2S+ warriors and healers."[97] Candi Brings Plenty, one of the founding members of Two Spirit Nation, led the camp at Oceti Sakowin. The camp attracted elders like Beverly Little Thunder, who traveled from her home in Maine to join the Two Spirit Nation camp, and a younger generation of Two-Spirit water protectors including Rebecca Nagle, Tony Enos, and DeLesslin "Roo" George-Warren.[98]

Two Spirit Nation members understand that a decolonial future requires action on multiple fronts, which they proclaim at the group's website: "The Two Spirit Nation has reclaimed our place at the front of this fight to protect our Mother from greed and corruption. We are here and won't be invisible again. We honor our strong leaders and ALL the many ways that two spirits must be in this fight to keep our land safe and our water clean for the next seven generations."

At Oceti Sakowin, the members of Two Spirit Nation drew power from their ancestors, standing together to honor them. Candi Brings Plenty honored her ancestors through her leadership of the Two Spirit Nation camp.

Brings Plenty shared with me a story that highlighted her skill as a leader and commitment to the water protectors' cause. It was November 24, 2016, Thanksgiving morning, or as some Native people view it, a day of mourning more aptly referred to as "Thankstaking." The day dawned with feelings of hope and determination as people stirred from their sleep and greeted the crisp morning air.

By now, water protectors had taken up residence at a sprawling camp complex. On this morning, people gathered to honor their ancestors. Deep in ceremony, people fasted, offered prayers, and applied paint for the coming day's battle. News outlets eventually beamed the violent images of the day's events to audiences around the world as Native people locked arms, became peaceful warriors, and stood firm in their collective determination to protect the waters of Lake Oahe on the Missouri River from the black snake.

But before the day's violent confrontation took place, an elderly white woman bounded into one of the camps, a picture of health and vitality that belied her seventy-nine years. Her name? Jane Fonda, movie star, fitness guru, and political activist. Fonda's celebrity meant that her presence at Standing Rock attracted immediate media attention. But what the media throngs failed to report was that Jane Fonda had not bounded into just any camp; she found herself in the middle of the Two Spirit Nation.

Brings Plenty, raised in ceremony, saw Fonda and her assistant approaching through the Two Spirit Nation's camp and made a beeline for them. Brings Plenty is articulate, insightful, and generous. People who know her have only positive, loving things to say about her. She's a magnetic leader who describes herself as carrying "both the masculine and feminine identity" within her.

On the morning of November 24, Brings Plenty's leadership skills were on full display. Brings Plenty told me, "Jane Fonda came to our camp right in the middle of us having a ceremony . . . when we were painting, which is one of the most sacred ceremonies, and she walked right in the middle of us." An intervention was urgently needed.

"Have you been through camp orientation," Brings Plenty inquired, determined to stop Fonda from further disrupting the Two Spirit Nation's morning ceremonies.

"No," Fonda replied, "no one told me that I had to."

Recalling this initial encounter, Brings Plenty explained that Fonda marched into the middle of a ceremonial space "still holding the mentality of a white cis-person coming into a sacred place. . . . Her voice and her entitlement gave her authority to speak louder."

Brings Plenty quickly changed that power dynamic by offering Fonda an impromptu history lesson. She started by asking Fonda to rethink the "Thanksgiving feast" she wanted to prepare—a well-intentioned, if culturally insensitive, gesture. Brings Plenty reminded Fonda that for millions of Indigenous people Thanksgiving is a day of great pain and anguish, a day dominated by memories of Europeans "raping and stealing and killing our ancestors."[99]

Fonda listened. "I didn't think of it that way," she exclaimed. "What can I do today to remedy this?"

"When we come back you can bring us the food and you can serve us," Brings Plenty told her.

According to Brings Plenty, Fonda replied, "That's exactly what I'll do." True to her word, Fonda worked alongside the Two-Spirit people who stayed back at the camp to offer prayers and prepare food for the Two-Spirit water protectors after a day of fasting and facing down law enforcement officers, tear gas, and rubber bullets.

Media reports later dismissed Fonda's "Thanksgiving feast" as a cynical attempt to attract publicity. That's the problem with celebrities attaching themselves to grassroots movements: their fame provides a movement with much needed visibility but risks shifting media attention away from the cause and on to them. This happened when Joan Baez, Mark Ruffalo, Patricia Arquette, and Shailene Woodley visited

Oceti Sakowin.[100] But Candi Brings Plenty was not star struck. The fact that Jane Fonda stopped, listened, and took cues from Brings Plenty—ultimately providing transportation and accommodation for gender-nonconforming members at the Two Spirit Nation camp—reflects Brings Plenty's skill as a leader and organizer.

Brings Plenty's involvement with Fonda and the leadership role she took on at Oceti Sakowin reveals how Two-Spirit people continue to reclaim "our place at the front of this fight to protect our Mother from greed and corruption." The fight, as I've mentioned, is about decolonizing gender and sexuality; it's also about tribal sovereignty and decolonizing the strategies and proposed solutions to the climate crisis. It's about a collective recognition that human and more-than-human relations are, in the words of the Apalech man Tyson Yunkaporta, "interdependent and interpersonal."[101]

Rebecca Nagle gets this. She knows that more resources are needed to support Two-Spirit futures and their connections to community. Resources for the climate crisis must be part of that future. During her second visit to the Two Spirit Nation camp, Nagle felt inspired by a sense of connection to a larger community and by Brings Plenty's leadership. Nagle saw Brings Plenty "work with the leadership of the camp to make sure Two-Spirit people were recognized and had a place in the culture and workings of the camp." Those connections—that interdependence—proved nurturing at Oceti Sakowin. It was certainly needed: "Cops were lined up in full riot gear," said Nagle, their guns pointed straight at water protectors. At all hours of the day and night, helicopters and drones whirred overhead, and spotlights turned night into day. Interpersonal connections provided a sense of community, giving members of the Two Spirit Nation camp the strength to resist this latest iteration of settler-colonial terrorism.[102]

DeLesslin "Roo" George-Warren was drawn to the Two Spirit Nation camp after seeing social media posts from Oceti Sakowin. He explained to a journalist, "I'm from the Catawba Indian Nation in South Carolina. We are people of the river so I felt strongly connected to this struggle, this prayer."[103] Like Nagle and other water protectors, he found strength in community and in the responsibilities members felt for present and future human and more-than-human relations. One member of the Two Spirit Nation camp noted, "Since I've been here I've felt the strongest sense of family that I've had in a long time."[104]

That interpersonal commitment to building a better climate future sustained the Two Spirit Nation camp, just as it sustained other water protectors. Together, they shared stories, pooled resources, and fought for a decolonized future.[105] Two Spirit Nation not only reclaimed their place in the circle; they were taking on traditional leadership roles. It wasn't perfect, but the water protectors at Oceti Sakowin provided a glimpse of the possible.

. . . .

None of us knows what tomorrow will look like, but the past and the present provide clues. For many Two-Spirit people, the past is a dark place, filled with physical violence, emotional trauma, and the theft of land, water, language, family. The trauma of the past, the struggles of the present, they can suffocate hope.[106]

It doesn't have to be that way. If, as Nick Estes suggests, history is the future, Two-Spirit people will undoubtedly keep reaching back into the past and reclaiming their place in the circle.[107] Not everyone will agree on what the past means, and people will argue about politics—they always do. What will it mean to be a Two-Spirit person in the future? No one knows. What is known, Raven Heavy Runner told me, is that "there's a responsibility that goes with that term." That term is "much more than just a word. It's historical significance, and the experiences of Two-Spirit people, they are encased in that word."[108]

In that word are traditions, knowledge, stories of community, and love. There are also stories of terror borne of colonialism, and fear caused by homophobia and transphobia in both Indian Country and beyond. In the future, some Two-Spirit people will find that their communities will embrace them as "a gift to the world," others will encounter prejudice, and still others will search inside themselves and find they don't need the term Two-Spirit to accept their non-gendered identity.[109] History isn't always pretty, and the future comes with no guarantees. But that's the thing about history's future: it's not written yet.

ACKNOWLEDGMENTS

RECLAIMING TWO-SPIRITS is the culmination of many years of research, collaboration, and friendships. I have many wonderful people,
institutions, and communities to thank. First, let me extend my heart-
felt appreciation to the librarians and archivists who work so hard to
preserve Indigenous histories. These include the Arizona Historical
Society; Autry Museum of the American West; Bancroft Library at
the University of California, Berkeley; Division of Rare and Manuscript Collections at Cornell University; GLBT Historical Society,
San Francisco; Jean-Nickolaus Tretter Collection in GLBT Studies,
University of Minnesota; Lambda Archives of San Diego; Lavender
Library, Sacramento; Library of Congress; Museo Antropológico y de
Arte Contemporáneo, Guayaquil, Ecuador; Smithsonian Institution's
National Anthropological Archives, American Art Museum, and Hirshhorn Museum; Pennsylvania Historical Society; ONE Archives at
the USC Libraries, Los Angeles; Archives and Manuscripts Division at
the Sterling Memorial Library and the Beinecke Rare Book and Manuscript Library, Yale University; Library of Virginia; Special Collections
and Archives departments at James Branch Cabell Library at Virginia Commonwealth University; Manuscripts, Archives, and Special
Collections at Washington State University, Pullman; San Francisco
Public Library; Archives and Special Collections at the University of
Manitoba; State Archives of Florida; University of Houston Libraries;
and Wheelwright Museum of the American Indian, Santa Fe.

Early drafts of this book benefited enormously from the feedback
of trusted colleagues and friends. In particular, I am grateful to Denise
Bossy, Andrew Frank, Paul Chaat Smith (Comanche), Carolyn East-
man, Rachel Hope Cleves, Susan Stryker, Ann McGrath, Elizabeth

Reis, Ethan Blue, and Brian Behnken. I was helped in thinking through some of the themes in the book by Diana Di Stefano, Catherine Franklin, Carol Higham, Celeste Menchaca, Dee Garceau, and James Brooks, all of whom participated in a fruitful roundtable discussion at the 2017 Western Historical Association conference. I thank them for their generous insights. I am especially indebted to Alan Gallay for his careful reading and detailed comments of my earlier drafts. There are few in the historical profession I trust more than Alan. As ever, I thank him from the bottom of my heart and aspire to be the type of historian he is. This book was completed while I was a British Academy Global Professor at the University of Hull. I wish to extend my gratitude to Joy Porter, Charles Prior, and Susannah Hopson for their support, friendship, and energy. I am also grateful to the Humanities Research Center at Virginia Commonwealth University and the then director Richard Godbeer for the financial support that made travel and research for this book possible. Richard is a wonderful historian and trusted friend; I'm lucky to have him in my life.

Over the years it took me to write this book I have been guided by some incredible people. I am in awe of the work of Kyle Mays (Black, Saginaw Chippewa), Kent Blansett (Cherokee, Creek, Choctaw, Shawnee, and Potawatomi descendant), and David Martinez (Akimel O'odham, Hia Ced O'odham, Mexican), and thank them for taking the time to read the manuscript in its entirety. Similarly, to the generous and insanely talented Georgina Lightning (Samson Cree Nation), thank you for your support. What an incredible storyteller you are; may you enrich all our lives for many years to come. Ambassador (ret.) Keith Harper (Cherokee Nation), former US representative to the United Nations Human Rights Council, graciously gave of his time to read the manuscript and offer his support. To Ambassador Harper, I say, "Wado." Lynette Allston, chief of the Nottoway Indian Tribe of Virginia, also warrants a special note of appreciation for her leadership, kindness, and knowledge. My thanks also go to Don Fehr, my agent at Trident Media Group. Don helped me organize my ideas into a coherent narrative and reminded me of the importance of language. Michael Bronski, the editor of Beacon's Queer Action/Queer Ideas series, also offered much needed advice and encouragement, which I treasure. I am especially indebted to the wonderful team at Beacon

Press. I'm particularly grateful to Susan Lumenello and Katherine Scott for their outstanding copyediting work and to Gayatri Patnaik for supporting the book. Gayatri's skill as an editor and her insights and good humor have improved the book and made working on it a pure joy. Thank you, Gayatri.

This book would not have been written without the support, counsel, and guidance of members of the Two-Spirit community. My commitment to decolonizing American history and expanding our collective understanding of the past first drew me to writing this book, but it is the knowledge of Two-Spirit people that drives the narrative. When I started this journey, I did not set out with a prescriptive set of questions. Instead, I wrote this book acutely aware of the fallible nature of colonialism's written archives and made a conscious decision to let conversations I had with Two-Spirit people lead and shape the contours of the book. *Reclaiming Two-Spirits* is meant to be a living history inspired by the stories Two-Spirit people shared with me, the themes that came out of many conversations, and the questions that Two-Spirit people challenged me with and the feedback they offered. There are many people to thank. I begin with my gratitude for the work and wisdom of Candi Brings Plenty (Oglala Lakota Sioux). Candi is owed a special thanks because she inspired the book's title. The wisdom of Trudie Jackson (Navajo Nation), Clyde Hall (Shoshone-Métis), Marlon "Marty" Fixico (Southern Cheyenne), Curtis Harris-Davia (San Carlos Apache), Christo Apache (Mescalero Apache), and Arnold Dahl (Leech Lake Band of Ojibwe) helped guide the book to the form it now takes. My thanks also go to Roger Kuhn (Poarch Creek), Heather Purser (Suquamish), Marca Cassity (Osage Nation), and DeLesslin "Roo" George-Warren (Catawba Indian Nation) for sharing their knowledge with me. There are many other people to acknowledge, some of whom preferred to remain anonymous. I hope this book does your stories justice.

Two special people warrant particular acknowledgment. First, Ken Harper (Cherokee Nation): words don't adequately describe how indebted I am to him. Ken's warmth, his amazing intellect, and his infectious laughter are treasured by all who've had the good fortune to cross paths with him. Ken has shown incredible patience with me, always being there when I've had a question or felt the need to bounce an idea off him. Wado, Ken. I must also extend my sincerest thanks to Raven Heavy Runner (Blackfeet Nation). Like Ken's, Raven's warmth, his knowledge, and his generous spirit are a blessing for us all. Thank you, Raven.

Finally, and most important, to the three people closest to me in the world: Brooke, Gwyneth, and Simone. Life couldn't possibly be dull in a pandemic-induced quarantine with the three of you! I love you all.

NOTES

A NOTE ABOUT LANGUAGE

1. Joshua B. Nelson, *Progressive Traditions: Identity in Cherokee Literature and Culture* (Norman: University of Oklahoma Press, 2014), 88.

PROLOGUE

1. Posted on Native Out, "Two Spirit Natives are sacred," Facebook, June 3, 2019, www.facebook.com/nativeout.

2. Roger Kuhn, interview with author, Feb. 22, 2019.

3. Identity, Chickasaw anthropologist Jenny Davis observes, is dynamic, changing, and context dependent. Davis notes that an individual's identity "is comprised of numerous components including ethnicity, socioeconomic class, sexual orientation, gender identity, and occupation." Jenny L. Davis, *Talking Indian: Identity and Language Revitalization in the Chickasaw Renaissance* (Tucson: University of Arizona Press, 2018), 17–18.

4. Jenny Davis refers to this as the "'both/and' approach to gender and sexuality" in Indigenous communities. Jenny L. Davis, "More Than Just 'Gay Indians': Intersecting Articulations of Two-Spirit Gender, Sexuality, and Indigenousness," in *Queer Excursions: Retheorizing Binaries in Language, Gender, and Sexuality*, ed. Lal Zimman, Jenny L. Davis, and Joshua Raclaw (New York: Oxford University Press, 2014), 63. See also Megan L. MacDonald, "Two-Spirit Organizing: Indigenous Two-Spirit Identity in the Twin Cities Region," in *Queer Twin Cities*, ed. Kevin P. Murphy, Jennifer L. Pierce, and Larry Knopp (Minneapolis: University of Minnesota Press, 2010), 151.

5. An example of this worldview can be found in Umek (E. Richard Atleo), *Tsawalk: A Nuu-chah-nulth Worldview* (Vancouver: UBC Press, 2004), 87–88.

6. Ken Pinkham, interview with author, Feb. 2, 2019.

7. Speech at the memorial of Phil Tingley, 1991, folder 17, Barbara Cameron Papers (GLC 63), Gay and Lesbian Center, San Francisco Public Library.

8. Two controversial historical titles from the 1990s were Ramon A. Gutierrez, *When Jesus Came, the Corn Mothers Went Away: Marriage, Sexuality, and Power in New Mexico, 1500–1846* (Stanford, CA: Stanford University Press, 1991), and Richard C. Trexler, *Sex and Conquest: Gendered Violence, Political Order, and the European Conquest of the Americas* (Ithaca, NY: Cornell University Press, 1995). I address the critiques of these books in the final section of this book.

9. In 1990, the United Nations identified the deleterious impacts of corporations and extractive industries on Indigenous nations as the major obstacle to self-determination and community development. UN Secretary-General, *Global Consultation on the Right to Development as a Human Right* (1990), https://digitallibrary.un.org/record/100164?ln=en#record-files-collapse-header.

10. Jorge A. Suarez, *The Mesoamerican Indian Languages* (Cambridge: Cambridge University Press, 1983), 86–89; Paul Manhart, *Lakota Dictionary: Lakota-English/English-Lakota* (Lincoln: University of Nebraska Press, 2002), xx.

11. Aleksandra IUr'evna Aîkhenval'd, *Classifiers: A Typology of Noun Categorization Devices* (Oxford: Oxford University Press, 2000), 80.

12. Theda Perdue, *Cherokee Women: Gender and Culture Change, 1700–1835* (Lincoln: University of Nebraska Press, 1998), 40; Marianne Mithun, *The Languages of Native North America* (Cambridge: Cambridge University Press, 1999), 94–98; Waziyatawin Angela Wilson, *Remember This! Dakota Decolonization and the Eli Taylor Narratives*, trans. Walipetunwin Carolynn Schommer (Lincoln: University of Nebraska Press, 2005), 221.

13. Sabine Lang, "Various Kinds of Two-Spirit People: Gender Variance and Homosexuality in Native American Communities," in *Two-Spirit People: Native American Gender Identity, Sexuality, and Spirituality*, ed. Sue-Ellen Jacobs, Wesley Thomas, and Sabine Lang (Urbana: University of Illinois Press, 1997), 101.

14. Carolyn Epple, "A Navajo Worldview of the Nadleehi: Implications for Western Categories," in Jacobs, Thomas, and Lang, *Two-Spirit People*, 175–91.

15. Wesley Thomas, "Navajo Cultural Constructions of Gender and Sexuality," in Jacobs, Thomas, and Lang, *Two-Spirit People*, 156–73. For "Most of them were asexual," see Thomas's comments in Chadwick Moore, "Joining the Annual Gathering of the Two Spirit Society in Montana," *Out*, Nov. 24, 2016, https://www.out.com/news-opinion/2015/9/22/joining-annual-gathering-two-spirit-society-montana. See also Epple, "A Navajo Worldview of the Nadleehi," 182.

16. Many Native Americans distinguish between "settlers" and their own tribal identity when talking about colonial relations. This binary becomes clearest in the final section of this book.

17. My analysis departs from that of Qwo-Li Driskill, who questions the connection of Two-Spirit people to history. Contrary to Driskill's speculations, my research suggests that Two-Spirit people, and Native people generally, remember, interpret, and understand the past through a variety of sources, from oral and artistic sources to the written documents they find in archives and on websites like Ancestry.com. Indigenous history is full of ruptures and colonial-inspired trauma, and how people connect to tribal and colonial histories differs. History, though, was and remains a domain that many Two-Spirit people have taken and redefined on their own terms, as the efforts of the Gay American Indians and other groups have demonstrated since the 1970s. Understanding the diversity of historical perspectives—how the past is mediated and understood in the context of the ever-changing present—is vital in reclaiming and rearticulating tradition, culture, and individual and communal identities. For Driskill's argument see Qwo-Li Driskill, "Shaking Our Shells: Cherokee Two-Spirits Rebalancing the World," in *Beyond Masculinity: Essays by Queer*

Men on Gender and Politics, ed. Trevor Hoppe (n.p., 2008), http://www.beyond masculinity.com/articles/driskill.php.

18. Daniel Heath Justice, "Fear of a Changeling Moon," in *The Broadway Anthology of Expository Prose: Third Canadian Edition*, ed. Laura Buzzard, Don LePan, Nora Ruddock, and Alexandria Stuart (Peterborough, ON: Broadview Press, 2017), 443.

19. Judith Butler, *Bodies That Matter: On the Discursive Limits of "Sex"* (New York: Routledge, 1993), 228–29; Carla Freccero, *Queer/Early/Modern* (Durham, NC: Duke University Press, 2006), 15–16.

20. Michael D. McNally, *Defend the Sacred: Native American Religious Freedom Beyond the First Amendment* (Princeton, NJ: Princeton University Press, 2020), 21, 31; J. Miko Thomas, interview with author, July 13, 2018.

21. Benjamin Madley, *An American Genocide: The United States and the California Indian Catastrophe* (New Haven, CT: Yale University Press, 2016).

22. Joseph P. Gone, "Alternative Knowledges and the Future of Community Psychology: Provocations from an American Indian Healing Tradition," *American Journal of Community Psychology* 58 (2016): 314–21. Gone has posed questions about the concept of historical trauma and warned against "recency," or what historians refer to as presentism—that is, imposing contemporary concerns, ideas, and experiences onto the past. See Gone, "Reconsidering American Indian Historical Trauma: Lessons from an Early Gros Ventre War Narrative," *Transcultural Psychiatry* 5, no. 3 (2014): 387–406.

23. Jade Yamazaki Stewart, "Stolen Labor and Stolen Land," *Eugene Weekly*, July 2, 2020, https://www.eugeneweekly.com/2020/07/02/stolen-labor-and-stolen-land.

24. Amnesty International, *Maze of Injustice: The Failure to Protect Indigenous Women from Sexual Violence in the USA* (New York: Amnesty International USA, 2007), 4; Coalition to Stop Violence Against Native Women, "Missing and Murdered Indigenous Women," https://www.csvanw.org/mmiw/; Nick Estes, *Our History Is the Future: Standing Rock Versus the Dakota Access Pipeline, and the Long Tradition of Indigenous Resistance* (New York: Verso, 2019), 31–32.

25. Jenna M. Calton, Lauren Bennett Cattaneo, and Kris T. Gebhard, "Barriers to Help Seeking for Lesbian, Gay, Bisexual, Transgender, and Queer Survivors of Intimate Partner Violence," *Trauma, Violence, and Abuse* 17, no. 5 (2016): 585–600; Rebecca Nagle, interview with author, June 4, 2018.

26. Karen Lehavot, Karina L. Walters, and Jane M. Simoni, "Abuse, Mastery, and Health Among Lesbian, Bisexual, and Two-Spirit American Indian and Alaska Native Women," *Cultural Diversity and Ethnic Minority Psychology* 15, no. 3 (2009): 175–84.

27. Sarah Deer, *The Beginning and End of Rape: Confronting Sexual Violence in Native America* (Minneapolis: University of Minnesota Press, 2015), 31–32.

28. Jack Healy and Adam Liptak, "Landmark Supreme Court Ruling Affirms Native American Rights in Oklahoma," *New York Times*, July 9, 2020.

29. NCAI Policy Research Center, "A Spotlight on Two Spirit (Native LGBT) Communities," http://www.ncai.org/policy-research-center/research-data/prc-publications/A_Spotlight_on_Native_LGBT.pdf.

30. Linda Alcoff, "Cultural Feminism Versus Post-Structuralism: The Identity Crisis in Feminist Theory," *Signs* 13, no. 3 (Spring 1988): 405–36; Lanita Jacobs-Huey, "The Natives Are Gazing and Talking Back: Reviewing the Problematics of Positionality, Voice, and Accountability Among 'Native' Anthropologists," *American Anthropologist* 104, no. 3 (September 2002): 791–804; Felecia M. Briscoe, "A Question of Representation in Educational Discourse: Multiplicities and Intersections of Identities and Positionalities," *Educational Studies* 38, no. 1 (2005): 23–41.

31. In 2015, Native studies scholar Andrea Smith became embroiled in controversy over accusations that she faked her Cherokee identity. See Scott Jaschik, "Fake Cherokee?," *Inside Higher Ed*, July 6, 2016, https://www.insidehighered .com/news/2015/07/06/scholar-who-has-made-name-cherokee-accused-not -having-native-american-roots. In politics, Elizabeth Warren has received widespread criticism for many years for laying claim to a Cherokee identity. Rebecca Nagle, "I'm a Cherokee Woman. Elizabeth Warren Is Not," *Think Progress*, November 30, 2017, https://thinkprogress.org/elizabeth-warren-is-not-cherokee -c1ec6c91b696/. For exposure of Terry Tofoya's claim to being a Taos Pueblo Indian, see Ruth Teichroeb, "Masking the Truth: False Claims on Tribal Ties, Degrees Tarnish Counselor," *SeattlePi*, June 20, 2006, https://www.seattlepi.com /local/article/Masking-the-Truth-False-claims-on-tribal-ties-1206723.php.

32. Ken Harper, interview with author, May 20, 2018.

33. Candi Brings Plenty, interview with author, May 25, 2018.

34. Katherine Ellinghaus and Barry Judd, "Writing as Kin: Producing Ethical Histories Through Collaboration in Unexpected Places. Researching F. W. Albrecht, Assimilation Policy and Lutheran Experiments in Aboriginal Education," in *Questioning Indigenous-Settler Relations*, ed. Sarah Madison and Sana Nakata (Singapore: Springer, 2020), 61.

35. Judith V. Jordan and Harriet L. Schwartz, "Radical Empathy in Teaching," *New Directions for Teaching and Learning* 153 (Spring 2018): 25–35; James Lowry, "Radical Empathy, the Imaginary and Affect in (Post)colonial Records: How to Break Out of International Stalemates on Displaced Archives," *Archival Science* 19 (May 2019): 185–203. The approach I outline does not mean, as some historians mistakenly assume, that critical analysis or historical studies of uncomfortable topics are ignored and replaced with politically inspired hagiographies or feel-good histories. It does mean that historians have to relinquish that sense of themselves as the historical expert in the room, a prospect that no doubt makes many uncomfortable. This is a lively debate. For some recent articulations of the respective arguments see David J. Silverman, "Living with the Past: Thoughts on Community Collaboration and Difficult History in Native American and Indigenous Studies," *American Historical Review* 125, no. 2 (April 2020): 519–27. Responses to Silverman's critique are provided by Christine M. DeLucia, Alyssa Mt. Pleasant, Philip J. Deloria, and Jean M. O'Brien. See also Alyssa Mt. Pleasant, Caroline Wigginton, and Kelly Wisecup, "Materials and Methods in Native American and Indigenous Studies: Completing the Turn," *William and Mary Quarterly* 75, no. 2 (April 2018): 207–36.

36. Aida Hurtado, "Multiple Lenses: Multicultural Feminist Theory," in *Handbook of Diversity in Feminist Psychology*, ed. Hope Landrine and Nancy

Felipe Russo (New York: Springer, 2010), 29–54; E. Patrick Johnson, "Put a Little Honey in My Sweet Tea: Oral History as Quare Performance," *Women's Studies Quarterly* 44, nos. 3–4 (Fall–Winter 2016): 51–67, especially 51, 57; Michelle Caswell and Marika Cifor, "From Human Rights to Feminist Ethics: Radical Empathy in the Archives," *Archivaria* 81 (Spring 2016): 23–43.

37. This account of the Cuchendado draws on Thomas N. Campbell, *Ethnic Identities of Extinct Coahuiltecan Populations: Case of the Juanca Indians* (Austin: Texas Memorial Museum, 1977); Frederick Webb Hodge, ed., *Handbook of American Indians North of Mexico*, 2 vols. (Washington, DC: Government Printing Offices, 1907, 1910; repr., New York: Pageant, 1959); David La Vere, *The Texas Indians* (College Station: Texas A&M University Press, 2004); William C. Foster, *Historic Native Peoples of Texas* (Austin: University of Texas Press, 2008), 110; Donald E. Chipman and Harriett D. Joseph, *Spanish Texas, 1519–1821*, rev. ed. (Austin: University of Texas Press, 2010), 17.

38. Rolena Adorno, "The Negotiation of Fear in Cabeza de Vaca's *Naufragios*," in *New World Encounters*, ed. Stephen Greenblatt (Berkeley: University of California Press, 1993), 61–62.

39. De Vaca quoted in Jonathan N. Katz, ed., *Gay American History: Lesbians and Gay Men in the U.S.A.* (New York: Meridian Books, 1992), 285. An early-twentieth-century translation of this passage reads slightly differently: "During the time I was among them I saw something very repulsive, namely, a man married to another. Such are impotent and womanish beings, who dress like women and perform the office of women, but use the bow and carry big loads. Among these Indians we saw many of them; they are more robust than other men, taller, and can bear heavy burthens." See Álvar Núñez Cabeza de Vaca, *The Journey of Álvar Núñez Cabeza de Vaca*, trans. Fanny Bandelier (New York: A. S. Barnes & Company, 1905), 126.

40. John L. Kessell, *Spain in the Southwest: A Narrative History of Colonial New Mexico, Arizona, Texas, and California* (Norman: University of Oklahoma Press, 2002), xii.

41. Barbara Weissberger, "'¡A tierra, puto!': Alfonso de Palencia's Discourse of Effeminacy," in *Queer Iberia: Sexualities, Cultures, and Crossings from the Middle Ages to the Renaissance*, ed. Josiah Blackmore and Gregory S. Hinton (Durham, NC: Duke University Press, 1999), 291.

42. The dictionary definition dates the first use of "berdache" to 1806, however, the word appears in written documents long before this. See footnote to "berdache" in Meriam-Webster, https://www.merriam-webster.com/dictionary/berdache.

43. Sarah Hunt and Cindy Holmes, "Everyday Decolonization: Living a Decolonizing Queer Politics," *Journal of Lesbian Studies* 19, no. 2 (2015): 154–72; Anita Hemmila, "Ancestors of Two-Spirits: Historical Depictions of Native North American Gender-Crossing Women Through Critical Discourse Analysis," *Journal of Lesbian Studies* 20, nos. 3–4 (2016): 408–26.

44. Nevzat Soguk, "Indigenous Peoples and Radical Futures in Global Politics," *New Political Science* 29, no. 1 (2007): 1–22; Leanne Betasamosake Simpson, *As We Have Always Done: Indigenous Freedom Through Radical Resistance* (Minneapolis: University of Minnesota Press, 2017); Estes, *Our Past Is the Future*.

45. Candi Brings Plenty interview.

46. Jason Jackman, "Jason Mraz Has Been Slammed for Appropriation After Coming Out as Two Spirit," *Pink News*, July 23, 2018, https://www.pinknews.co.uk/2018/07/23/ja.son-mraz-slammed-appropriation-coming-out-two-spirit.

CHAPTER 1: INVASION

1. Raven Heavy Runner, interview with author, Oct. 17, 2019.
2. Marca Cassity, interview with author, Dec. 21, 2018.
3. On the Cueva (or Cuna) Indians, see Herbert W. Krieger, *Material Culture of the People of Southeastern Panama, Based on Specimens in the United States National Museum* (Washington, DC: Smithsonian Institution, 1926); Sol Tax, *Indian Tribes of Aboriginal America: Selected Papers of the XXIXth International Congress of Americanists* (Chicago: University of Chicago Press, 1952); Carl Ortin Sauer, *The Early Spanish Main* (Cambridge: Cambridge University Press, 1966); Neil L. Whitehead, "The Crisis and Transformation of Invaded Societies: The Caribbean (1492–1580)," in *South America, Vol. 3, Part 1,* of *The Cambridge History of the Native Peoples of the Americas,* ed. Frank Saloman and Stuart B. Schwartz (Cambridge: Cambridge University Press, 1996), 864–903.
4. Martin Austin Nesvig, *Promiscuous Power: An Unorthodox History of New Spain* (Austin: University of Texas Press, 2018), 178.
5. Allan Greer, *Property and Dispossession: Natives, Empires and Land in Early Modern North America* (New York: Cambridge University Press, 2018), 7–9, 99.
6. Nesvig, *Promiscuous Power,* 133, 151.
7. Kelly L. Watson, *Insatiable Appetites: Imperial Encounters with Cannibals in the North Atlantic World* (New York: New York University Press, 2015), 112–13; Richard C. Trexler, *Sex and Conquest: Gender Violence, Political Order, and the European Conquest of the Americas* (Ithaca, NY: Cornell University Press, 1995), 65.
8. Kathleen Romoli, *Balboa of Darién: Discoverer of the Pacific* (1953; repr., New York: Doubleday, 2008), 200; Lewis Hanke, *The Spanish Struggle for Justice in the Conquest of America* (Boston: Little, Brown, 1965), 31–36; Patricia Seed, *Ceremonies of Possession in Europe's Conquest of the New World, 1492–1640* (New York: Cambridge University Press, 1995), 76.
9. The speed and brutality of many Spanish attacks is described by eyewitnesses in other contexts. See, for example, Miguel Leon-Portilla, ed., *The Broken Spears: The Aztec Account of the Conquest of Mexico* (Boston: Beacon Press, 1992); Judy Grahn, "Strange Country This: Lesbianism and North American Indian Tribes," *Journal of Homosexuality* 12, nos. 3–4 (May 1986): 43–57.
10. Pietro Martire d'Anghiera, *De Orbe Novo, the Eight Decades of Peter Maryty d'Anghera,* trans. Francis Augustus MacNutt, 2 vols. (New York: G. P. Putnam's Sons, 1912), 1:284–85. See also Alice Rio, *Slavery After Rome, 500–1100* (Oxford: Oxford University Press, 2017), 11, 13, 121; Fernando Operé, *Indian Captivity in Spanish America: Frontier Narratives,* trans. Gustavo Pellón (Charlottesville: University of Virginia Press, 2008), 4.

11. Barnard Shipp, *The History of Hernando de Soto and Florida; or Records of the Events of Fifty-Six Years, from 1512 to 1568* (Philadelphia: Robert M. Lindsay, 1881), 5; Donald R. Hopkins, *The Greatest Killer: Smallpox in History* (Chicago: University of Chicago Press, 2002), 208.

12. Maureen Ahern, "'Llevando el norte sobre el ojo izquierdo': Mapping, Measuring, and Naming in Castañeda's 'Relación de la jornada de Cíbola' (1563)," in *Mapping Colonial Spanish America: Places and Commonplaces of Identity, Culture, and Experience*, ed. Santa Arias and Mariselle Meléndez (Lewisburg, PA: Bucknell University Press, 2002), 30.

13. James Dougal Fleming, "Introduction: The Invention of Discovery, 1500–1700," in *The Invention of Discovery, 1500–1700*, ed. James Dougal Fleming (Surrey, UK: Ashgate, 1988), 1–14; David Arnold, *The Age of Discovery, 1400–1600*, 2nd ed. (London: Routledge, 2002), 1–4.

14. Anthony Pagden, *The Fall of Natural Man: The American Indian and the Origins of Comparative Ethnology* (New York: Cambridge University Press, 1986); Christian Schafer, "*Conquista* and the Just War," in *A Companion to Early Modern Spanish Imperial Political and Social Thought*, ed. Jorg Alejandro Tellkamp (Boston: Brill, 2020), 202–4.

15. David E. Stannard, *American Holocaust: Columbus and the Conquest of the New World* (New York: Oxford University Press, 1992), 73, 83; John L. Kessell, *Spain in the Southwest: A Narrative History of Colonial New Mexico, Arizona, Texas, and California* (Norman: University of Oklahoma Press, 2002), 7–8; Karen F. Anderson-Cordova, *Surviving Spanish Conquest: Indian Fight, Flight, and Cultural Transformation in Hispaniola and Puerto Rico* (Tuscaloosa: University of Alabama Press, 2017), 125.

16. Pagden, *The Fall of Natural Man*, 88; Steve Jones, *The Darwin Archipelago: The Naturalist's Career Beyond Origins of Species* (New Haven, CT: Yale University Press, 2011), 101.

17. Kessell, *Spain in the Southwest*, 166–70; Watson, *Insatiable Appetites*, 96–98.

18. John H. Elliot, *Empires of the Atlantic World: Britain and Spain in America, 1492–1830* (New Haven, CT: Yale University Press, 2006), 20.

19. Rudolf M. Dekker and Lotte C. van de Pol, *The Tradition of Female Transvestism in Early Modern Europe* (Basingstoke, UK: Macmillan Press, 1989), 55–56.

20. Will Roscoe, "Strange Craft, Strange History, Strange Folks: Cultural Amnesia and the Case of Lesbian and Gay Studies," *American Anthropologist* 97, no. 3 (September 1995): 448–53, esp. 450. Kinship is critical to understanding the meaning of community and modern concepts like sovereignty in Native American history. See Anne Christine Taylor, "The Soul's Body and Its States: An Amazonia Perspective on the Nature of Being Human," *Journal of the Royal Anthropological Institute* 2, no. 2 (June 1996): 201–15, esp. 206; Sabine Lang, *Men as Women, Women as Men: Changing Gender in Native American Culture* (Austin: University of Texas Press, 1998), 248–51.

21. Margaret Visser, *Since Eve Ate Apples Much Depends on Dinner: The Extraordinary History and Mythology, Allure and Obsessions, Perils and Taboos*

of an Ordinary Meal (New York: Grove Press, 1986), 69; Rictor Norton, *Myth of the Modern Homosexual: Queer History and the Search for Cultural Unity* (London: Bloomsbury, 2016), 104.

22. Francois Soyer, *Ambiguous Gender in Early Modern Spain and Portugal: Inquisitors, Doctors and the Transgression of Gender Norms* (Leiden, NL: Brill, 2012), 46.

23. In some parts of sixteenth- and seventeenth-century Europe, sodomy and infanticide had much higher rates of conviction and execution than witchcraft. A. F. Soman, "The Parliament of Paris and the Great Witch Hunt, 1565–1640, *Sixteenth-Century Journal* 9 (1978): 31–44; E. W. Monter, "Sodomy and Heresy in Early Modern Switzerland," *Journal of Homosexuality* 6, nos. 1–2 (Fall–Winter 1980–81): 41–55; Lawrence Stone, *The Family, Sex and Marriage in England, 1500–1800* (New York: Harper and Row, 1977), 398, 466; Lyndal Roper, *Oedipus and the Devil: Witchcraft, Sexuality and Religion in Early Modern Europe* (London: Routledge, 1994), 118; William Naphy, *Sex Crimes: From Renaissance to Enlightenment* (Stroud, UK: Tempus Publishing, 2002), ch. 5; Katherine Crawford, *European Sexualities, 1400–1800* (Cambridge: Cambridge University Press, 1977), 159.

24. Pete Sigal, "Gendered Power, the Hybrid Self, and Homosexual Desire in Late Colonial Yucatan," in *Infamous Desire: Male Homosexuality in Colonial Latin America*, ed. Peter Sigal (Chicago: Chicago University Press, 2003), 102–3.

25. Sigal, "Gendered Power, the Hybrid Self, and Homosexual Desire in Late Colonial Yucatán," 103; Garthine Walker, "Sexual Violence and Rape in Europe, 1500–1750," in *The Routledge History of Sex and the Body: 1500 to the Present*, ed. Sarah Toulalan and Kate Fisher (New York: Routledge, 2013), 437.

26. Mary E. Perry, "The 'Nefarious Sin' in Early Modern Seveille," in *The Pursuit of Sodomy: Male Homosexuality in Renaissance and Enlightenment Europe*, ed. Kent Gerard and Gert Hekma (New York: Harrington Park Press, 1989), 67–89; Sigal, "Gendered Power, the Hybrid Self, and Homosexual Desire in Late Colonial Yucatán," 103–4; Laura R. Bass and Amanda Winder, "The Veiled Ladies of the Early Modern Spanish World: Seduction and Scandal in Seville, Madrid, and Lima," *Hispanic Review* 77, no. 1 (Winter 2009): 97–144; Adrienne Laskier Martin, *An Erotic Philology of Golden Age Spain* (Nashville: Vanderbilt University Press, 2008), 44.

27. Raphael Lemkin, the legal thinker who coined the term "genocide," began his historical definition of genocide by focusing on Spanish violence against Native people in the Americas. See Michael A. McDonnell and A. Dirk Moses, "Raphael Lemkin as Historian of Genocide in the Americas," *Journal of Genocide Research* 7, no. 4 (2005): 501–29.

28. Pete Sigal, "The Politicization of Pederasty Among the Colonial Yucatecan Maya," *Journal of the History of Sexuality* 8, no. 1 (1997): 1–24; Sigal, "Gendered Power, the Hybrid Self, and Homosexual Desire in Late Colonial Yucatán," 102–33; J. F. Chuchiak IV, "The Sins of the Fathers: Franciscan Friars, Parish Priests, and the Sexual Conquest of the Yucatec Maya, 1545–1808," *Ethnohistory* 54, no. 1 (2007): 69–127; Roger M. Carpenter, "Womanish Men and Manlike Women: The Native American Two-Spirit as Warrior," in *Gender*

and Sexuality in Indigenous North America, 1400–1850, ed. Sandra Slater and Fay Yarbrough (Columbia: University of South Carolina Press, 2011), 147.

29. Pete Sigal, *The Flower and the Scorpion: Sexuality and Ritual in Early Nahua Culture* (Durham, NC: Duke University Press, 2011), 11.

30. Sigal, *The Flower and the Scorpion*, 181–85.

31. Ramon A. Gutierrez, *When Jesus Came, the Corn Mothers Went Away: Marriage, Sexuality, and Power in New Mexico* (Stanford, CA: Stanford University Press, 1991), 212, 243–45; Trexler, *Sex and Conquest*, 71.

32. Jeffrey Quilter, "Moche Politics, Religion, and Warfare," *Journal of World Prehistory* 16, no. 2 (June 2002): 145–95.

33. Margaret Ann Jackson, *Moche Art and Visual Culture in Ancient Peru* (Albuquerque: University of New Mexico Press, 2008), 37; Donna McClelland, "Ulluchu: An Elusive Fruit," in *The Art and Archaeology of the Moche: An Ancient Andean Society of the Peruvian North Coast*, ed. Steve Bourget and Kimberly L. Jones (Austin: University of Texas Press, 2008), 56–58.

34. Lynn A. Meisch, *Costume and History in Highland Ecuador* (Austin: University of Texas Press, 2012), 40–41; Yumi Park, *Mirrors of Clay: Reflections of Ancient Andean Life in Ceramics from the Sam Olden Collection* (Oxford: University Press of Mississippi, 2012).

35. Pete Sigal, "Queer Nahuatl: Sahgagun's Faggots and Sodomites, Lesbians and Hermaphrodites," *Ethnohistory* 54, no. 1 (2007): 9–34.

36. *The De Soto Chronicles: The Expedition of Hernan de Soto to North America in 1539–1543*, ed. Lawrence A. Clayton, Vernon James Knight Jr., and Edward C. Moore, 2 vols. (Tuscaloosa: University of Alabama Press, 1993), 2:288.

37. Other prominent chroniclers included Luys Hernandez de Biebma and Rodrigo Rangel, de Soto's private secretary. George E. Lankford, "How Historical Are the De Soto Chronicles?," in *The Search for Mabila: The Decisive Battle Between Hernando de Soto and Chief Tascalusa*, ed. Vernon James Knight Jr. (Tuscaloosa: University of Alabama Press, 2009), 31–44.

38. Edward G. Bourne, ed., *Narratives of the Career of Hernando de Soto*, 2 vols. (New York: A. S. Barnes and Company, 1904), 1:45; Chester B. DePratter, "Cofitachequi: Ethnohistorical and Archaeological Evidence," *Anthropological Studies* 9 (1989): 133–56; David Lavender, *De Soto, Coronado, Cabrillo: Explorers of the Northern Mystery* (Washington, DC: National Park Service, Division of Publications, 1992), 41; Gregory A. Waselkov, "What Do Spanish Expeditionary Artifacts of Circa 1540 Look Like and How Often Are They Preserved?," in Knight, *The Search for Mabila*, 96.

39. Chester B. DePratter, "The Chiefdom of Cofitachequi," in *The Forgotten Centuries: Indians and Europeans in the American South, 1521–1704*, ed. Charles Hudson and Carmen Chaves Tesser (Athens: University of Georgia Press, 1994), 198–99 (Cofitachequi was also spelled Cufitachiqui; see 82). See also Robbie Ethridge, "The European Invasion and the Transformation of the Indians of Tennessee, 1540–1715," in *Before the Volunteer State: New Thoughts on Early Tennessee, 1540–1800*, ed. Kristofer Ray (Knoxville: University of Tennessee Press, 2014), 8.

40. John H. Hann, "Political Leadership Among the Natives of Spanish Florida," *Florida Historical Quarterly* 71, no. 2 (Oct. 1992): 188–208; Sven Loven, *Origins of the Tainan Culture, West Indies* (1935; repr., Tuscaloosa: University of Alabama Press, 2010), 503–6.

41. Soyer, *Ambiguous Gender in Early Modern Spain and Portugal*, 18.

42. Perico, or Pedro, an Indigenous guide in his late teens, is recorded in *The De Soto Chronicles* (86) as offering a somewhat confused account of the cacica's power and position.

43. Michael Hardin, "Altering Masculinities: The Spanish Conquest and the Evolution of the Latin American Machismo," *International Journal of Sexuality and Gender Studies* 7 (Jan. 2002): 1–22; Shifra Armon, *Masculine Virtue in Early Modern Spain* (London: Routledge, 2016), 5–14.

44. Dian Fox, *Hercules and the King of Portugal: Icons of Masculinity and Nation in Calderon's Spain* (Lincoln: University of Nebraska Press, 2019), 11–12.

45. *The De Soto Chronicles*, 83–84, 88–92, 286.

46. Robin Beck, *Chiefdoms, Collapse, and Coalescence in the Early American South* (New York: Cambridge University Press, 2013), 68.

47. Gene Waddell, *Indians of the South Carolina Lowcountry, 1562–1751* (Columbia: University of South Carolina Press, 1980), 59; Susan Richbourg Parker, "Chief Francisco Jospogue: Reconstructing the Paths of a Guale-Yamasee Indian Lineage Through Spanish Records," in *The Yamasee Indians: From Florida to South Carolina*, ed. Denise I. Bossy (Lincoln: University of Nebraska Press, 2018), 287.

48. Waddell, *Indians of the South Carolina Lowcountry*, 72, 75; John E. Worth, *The Struggle for the Georgia Coast* (Tuscaloosa: University of Alabama Press, 2007), 100–103.

49. *The De Soto Chronicles*, 286; Christina Snyder, "The Lady of Cofitachequi: Gender and Political Power Among Native Southerners," in *South Carolina Women: Their Lives and Times*, 3 vols., ed. Majorie J. Spruill, Valinda W. Littlefield, and Joan Marie Johnson (Athens: University of Georgia Press, 2009), 1:20.

50. Marvin T. Smith, *Coosa: The Rise and Fall of a Southeastern Mississippian Chiefdom* (Gainesville: University Press of Florida, 2000).

51. *The De Soto Chronicles*, 85.

52. *The De Soto Chronicles*, 266–67.

53. Luys Hernández de Biedma, *A Translation of a Recently Discovered Manuscript Journal of the Expedition of Hernando de Soto in Florida*, trans. B. F. French (Historical Collections of Louisiana, 1850), 100.

54. *The De Soto Chronicles*, 86–87.

55. Matthew Biberman, *Masculinity, Anti-Semitism and Early Modern English Literature: From the Satanic to the Effeminate Jew* (New York: Routledge, 2016), ch. 1; Ruth Gilbert, *Early Modern Hermaphrodites: Sex and Other Stories* (Basingstoke, UK: Palgrave Macmillan, 2002), 14; Cathy McClive, *Menstruation and Procreation in Early Modern France* (New York: Routledge, 2015), 7; Robert Bonfil, "A Cultural Profile," in *The Jews of Early Modern Venice*,

ed. Robert C. Davis and Benjamin Ravid (Baltimore: Johns Hopkins University Press, 2001), 173; Sherry C. M. Lindquist, "Introduction to Gender and Otherness," in *Gender, Otherness, and Culture in Medieval and Early Modern Art*, ed. Carlee A. Bradbury Michelle Moseley-Christian (London: Palgrave Macmillan, 2017), 7.

56. Roxanne Dunbar-Ortiz, *An Indigenous Peoples' History of the United States* (Boston: Beacon Press, 2014), 8.

57. Andrea Smith, "Queer Theory and Native Studies: The Heteronormativity of Settler Colonialism," in *Queer Indigenous Studies: Critical Interventions in Theory, Politics, and Literature*, ed. Qwo-Li Driskill, Chris Finley, Brian Joseph Gilley, and Scott Lauria Morgansen (Tucson: University of Arizona Press, 2011), 43–44. The concerns informing these questions also existed among other European colonizers. See, for example, Karen Ordahl Kupperman, *Indians and English: Facing Off in Early America* (Ithaca, NY: Cornell University Press, 2000), 33, 59.

CHAPTER 2: "HERMAPHRODITES"

1. Cecily Hilleary, "Native American Two-Spirits Look to Reclaim Lost Heritage," *Voice of America*, June 17, 2018, https://www.voanews.com/a/native -american-two-spirits-look-to-reclaim-lost-heritage/4440354.html.

2. Paula Gunn Allen, *The Sacred Hoop: Recovering the Feminine in American Indian Traditions* (Boston: Beacon Press, 1986), 61.

3. René Goulaine de Laudonnière, *L'Histoire Notable de la Floride* (Paris: Chez P. Jannet, Libraire, 1853), 82; for an English translation of this incident, see René Laudonnière, *Three Voyages*, trans. Charles E. Bennett (Tuscaloosa: University of Alabama Press, 2001), 69–70.

4. Aileen Ajootian, "Monstrum or Daimon: Hermaphrodites in Ancient Art and Cultures," in *Greece and Gender*, ed. B. Berggreen and N. Marinatos (Bergen: Norwegian Institute at Athens, 1995), 93–108; Hans Licht, *Sexual Life in Ancient Greece* (London: Routledge, 2000).

5. Celine Carayon, *Eloquence Embodied: Nonverbal Communication Among French and Indigenous Peoples in the Americas* (Chapel Hill: University of North Carolina Press, 2019), 168.

6. Christopher B. Rodning, Robin A. Beck Jr., and David G. Moore, "Conflict, Violence, and Warfare in La Florida," in *Native and Spanish New World: Sixteenth-Century Entradas in the American Southwest and Southeast*, ed. Clay Mathers and Jeffrey M. Mitchem (Tucson: University of Arizona Press, 2013), 231–50.

7. Laudonnière, *Three Voyages*, 13.

8. Laudonnière expressed condemnation for what he saw as Native warriors desecrating the corpses of their victims. Laudonnière, *Three Voyages*, 11. On "just war," see Armstrong Starkey, *European and Native American Warfare, 1675–1815* (London: UCL Press, 1998); Wayne E. Lee, "Peace Chiefs and Blood Revenge: Patterns of Restraint in Native American Warfare, 1500–1800," *Journal of Military History* 71, no. 3 (July 2007): 701–41.

9. Laudonnière, *Three Voyages*, 13.

10. E. F. J. Tucker, "Ruggle's Ignoramus and Humanistic Criticism of the Language of the Common Law," *Renaissance Quarterly* 30, no. 3 (Autumn 1977): 341–50; Jonathan Rose, "Of Ambidexters and Daffidowndillies: Defamation of Lawyers, Legal Ethics, and Professional Reputation," *University of Chicago Law School Roundtable* 8, no. 2 (2001): 423–67.

11. Ruth Gilbert, "'Strange Notions': Treatments of Early Modern Hermaphrodites," in *Madness, Disability and Social Exclusion: The Archaeology and Anthropology of "Difference,"* ed. Jane Hubert (London: Routledge, 2000), 153; Lorraine Daston and Katherine Park, "The Hermaphrodite and the Orders of Nature," in *Premodern Sexualities*, ed. Louise Fradenburg and Carla Freccero (London: Routledge, 1996), 117–36; Richard Cleminson and Francisco Vazquez Garcia, *Sex, Identity and Hermaphrodites in Iberia, 1500–1800* (London: Routledge, 2013).

12. Joan Cadden, *Meanings of Sex Difference in the Middle Ages: Medicine, Science, and Culture* (New York: Cambridge University Press, 1993), 170, 200, 212; Alice Domurat Dreger, *Hermaphrodites and the Medical Invention of Sex* (Cambridge, MA: Harvard University Press, 1998), 32.

13. Lutz Alexander Graumann, "Monstrous Births and Retrospective Diagnosis: The Case of Hermaphrodites in Antiquity," in *Disability in Roman Antiquity: Disparate Bodies*, ed. Christian Laes, C. F. Goodey, and M. Lynn Rose (Leiden, NL: Brill, 2013), 181–210; Anthony Corbell, *Sexing the World: Grammatical Gender and Biological Sex in Ancient Rome* (Princeton, NJ: Princeton University Press, 2015), 123, 158, 162; Susan Stryker, *Transgender History: The Root of Today's Revolution*, 2nd ed. (New York: Seal Press, 2017), 28–29.

14. Cadden, *The Meanings of Sex Difference in the Middle Ages*, 225; Kathleen P. Long, *Hermaphrodites in Renaissance Europe* (Burlington, VT: Ashgate, 2006), 52, 237.

15. Cathy McClive, "Masculinity on Trial: Penises, Hermaphrodites and the Uncertain Male Body in Early Modern France," *History Workshop Journal* 68, no. 1 (Oct. 2009): 45–68.

16. Leah DeVun, "The Jesus Hermaphrodite: Science and Sex Difference in Premodern Europe," *Journal of the History of Ideas* 69, no. 2 (Apr. 2008): 193–218; Richard Cleminson and Francisco Vázquez García, "Subjectivities in Transition: Gender and Sexual Identities in Cases of 'Sex Change' and 'Hermaphroditism' in Spain, c. 1500–1800," *History of Science* 48, no. 1 (2010); 1–38; Cleminson and García, *Sex, Identity and Hermaphrodites in Iberia, 1500–1800*, 2–8.

17. Francois Soyer, "Androgyny and Fear of the Demonic Intervention in the Early Modern Iberian Peninsula: Ecclesiastical and Popular Responses," in *Ordering Emotions in Europe, 1100–1800*, ed. Susan Broomhall (Leiden, NL: Brill, 2015), 245–62; Kathleen P. Long, Introduction, *Hermaphrodites in Renaissance Europe*.

18. Marie Delcourt, *Hermaphrodites: Myths and Rites of the Bisexual Figure in Classical Antiquity* (London: Studio Books, 1950), 4–8.

19. Mark A. Johnston, *Beard Fetish in Early Modern England: Sex, Gender, and Registers of Value* (London: Routledge, 2011), 239.

20. Fabian Krämer, "Die Individualisierung des Hermaphroditen in Medizin und Naturgeschichte des 17. Jahrhunderts" [The individualization of the hermaphrodite in medicine and natural history of the 17th century], *Berichte zur Wissenschaftsgeschichte* [*Reports on the history of science*] 30 (2007): 53.

21. Krämer, "Die Individualisierung des Hermaphroditen," 55–56; Matthew Johnson, "This Is Not a Hermaphrodite: The Medical Assimilation of Gender Difference in Germany Around 1800," *Canadian Bulletin of Medical History* 22, no. 2 (2005): 247.

22. James Parsons, *A Mechanical and Critical Enquiry into the Nature of Hermaphrodites* (London: Printed by J. Walthoe, 1741), xix.

23. Vine Deloria Jr., *The World We Used to Live In: Remembering the Powers of the Medicine Men* (Golden, CO: Fulcrum, 2006); Walter L. Williams, *The Spirit and the Flesh: Sexual Diversity in American Indian Culture* (Boston: Beacon Press, 1986), 17, 21; Christopher Vecsey, *Imagine Ourselves Richly: Mythic Narratives of the North American Indians* (San Francisco: HarperCollins, 1991); Sabine Lang, *Men as Women, Women as Men: Changing Gender in Native American Culture* (Austin: University of Texas Press, 1998), 12; Joel W. Martin, *The Land Looks After Us: A History of Native American Religion* (New York: Oxford University Press, 1999), ix–x.

24. Deloria, *The World We Used to Live In*; C. Riley Snorten, *Black on Both Sides: A Racial History of Trans Identity* (Minneapolis: University of Minnesota Press, 2017), 2, 5.

25. John H. Hann, *Mission to the Calusa* (Gainesville: University Press of Florida, 1991), 280–300; Charles E. Bennett, *Laudonnière and Fort Caroline* (Tuscaloosa: University of Alabama Press, 2001), 28, 40, 168; John H. Hann, *Indians of Central and South Florida, 1513–1763* (Gainesville: University Press of Florida, 2003), 141; Andrew K. Frank, *Before the Pioneers: Indians, Settlers, Slaves, and the Founding of Miami* (Gainesville: University Press of Florida, 2017), 35–42.

26. Alan Gallay, *Walter Ralegh: Architect of Empire* (New York: Basic Books, 2019), 185, 189, 195–96.

27. The Intersex Society of North America maintains statistical estimates on its website. See "How Common Is Intersex?," www.isna.org/faq/frequency.

28. Jacques Le Moyne de Morgues, *Narrative of Le Moyne, an Artist Who Accompanied the French Expedition to Florida under Laudonniere*; 1564, trans. Frederick B. Perkins (Boston: James R. Osgood, 1875), 7–8. In 1566, an allegedly treasonous and sodomitical French Lutheran was murdered by Spanish Catholics in Florida. The Lutheran had lived with the local chief's two sons, and one of these sons is said to have "loved" the Frenchman "very much" (see part 1, 1566: Gonzalo Soliz de Meras).

29. Jerald T. Milanich, *The Timucua* (Oxford: Blackwell Publishers, 1996), 150–54.

30. John R. Swanton, *Terms of Relationship in Timucua* (Washington, DC: Government Printing Office, 1916), 460–61; Milanich, *The Timucua*, 163; Daniel W. Stowell, *Timucuan Ecological and Historic Preserve: Historic Resource Study* (Atlanta: US Department of the Interior, National Park Service, Southeast

Field Area, 1996), http://npshistory.com/publications/timu/hrs.pdf, 82; David J. Hally, *King: The Social Archaeology of a Late Mississippian Town in Northwestern Georgia* (Tuscaloosa: University of Alabama Press, 2008), 17.

31. On Indian slavery, see Alan Gallay, *The Indian Slave Trade: The Rise of the English Empire in the American South, 1670–1717* (New Haven, CT: Yale University Press, 2002); James F. Brooks, *Captives and Cousins: Slavery, Kinship, and Community in the Southwest Borderlands* (Chapel Hill: University of North Carolina Press, 2002); Christina Snyder, *Slavery in Indian Country: The Changing Face of Captivity in Early America* (Cambridge, MA: Harvard University Press, 2010); Brett Rushforth, *Bonds of Alliance: Indigenous and Atlantic Slaveries in New France* (Chapel Hill: University of North Carolina Press, 2013); Andrés Reséndez, *The Other Slavery: The Uncovered Story of Indian Enslavement in America* (Boston: Houghton Mifflin Harcourt, 2016).

32. Milanich, *The Timucua*, 164.

33. Laudonnière, *L'Histoire Notable de la Floride*, 3; Le Moyne, *Narrative of Le Moyne*, 7; Gregory D. Smithers, "Cherokee Two-Spirits: Gender, Ritual, and Spirituality in the Native South," *Early American Studies* 12, no. 3 (2014): 639–40.

34. Will Roscoe, *Changing Ones: Third and Fourth Genders in Native North America* (New York: St. Martin's Griffin, 1998), 120; Sabine Lang, "There Is More Than Just Women and Men," in *Gender Reversals and Gender Cultures: Anthropological and Historical Perspectives*, ed. Sabrina Petra Ramet (London: Routledge, 1996), 185–86; Bill Brown, "Thing Theory," *Critical Inquiry* 28, no. 1 (Winter 2001): 1–22; Dana Oswald, "Monstrous Gender: Geographies of Ambiguity," in *The Ashgate Research Companion to Monsters and the Monstrous*, ed. Asa Simon Mittman with Peter J. Dendale (Burlington, VT: Ashgate, 2012), 358.

35. H. Angelino and C. L. Shedd, "A Note on the Berdache," *American Anthropologist* 57, no. 1 (February 1955): 121–26; Sue-Ellen Jacobs, "Berdache: A Brief Review of Literature," *Colorado Anthropologist* 1, no. 1 (1968): 25; D. L. Davis and R. G. Whitten, "The Cross-Cultural Study of Human Sexuality," *Annual Review of Anthropology* 16 (1987): 84; Lang, *Men as Women, Women as Men*, 6–7; William Benemann, *Men in Eden: William Drummond Stewart and Same-Sex Desire in the Rocky Mountain Fur Trade* (Lincoln: University of Nebraska Press, 2012), 106.

36. Allen, *The Sacred Hoop*, 223.

37. Allen, *The Sacred Hoop*, 196.

38. Allen, *The Sacred Hoop*, 3; Kathleen Perry Long, "Sexual Dissonance: Early Modern Scientific Accounts of Hermaphrodites," in *Wonders, Marvels, and Monsters in Early Modern Culture*, ed. Peter G. Platt (Newark: University of Delaware Press, 1999), 148; Elizabeth Reis, *Bodies in Doubt: An American History of Intersex* (Baltimore: Johns Hopkins University Press, 2009), ch. 1.

CHAPTER 3: SIN

1. Quoted in Mike Garrido and Tarek Tohme, directors, *As They Are: Two-Spirit People in the Modern World* (University of Southern California, Department of Anthropology, 2012), video, available on YouTube.

2. Paula Gunn Allen, *Off the Reservation: Reflections on Boundary-Busting, Border-Crossing Loose Cannons* (Boston: Beacon Press, 1999), 116.

3. Joel W. Martin, *The Land Looks After Us: A History of Native American Religion* (New York: Oxford University Press, 1999), ix, xxii, 10, 16.

4. Robert R. Gonzales Jr., *Where Sin Abounds: The Spread of Sin and the Curse in Genesis with Special Focus on the Patriarchal Narratives* (Eugene, OR: Wipf and Stock, 2009), 60. For further analysis of the etymology of "sin," see Gary A. Anderson, *Sin: A History* (New Haven, CT: Yale University Press, 2009).

5. Jill Lepore, *The Name of War: King Philip's War and the Origins of American Identity* (New York: Vintage Books, 1998), 7; Joanna Brooks, "Hard Feelings: Samson Occom Contemplates His Christian Mentors," in *Native Americans, Christianity, and the Reshaping of the American Religious Landscape*, ed. Joel W. Martin and Mark A. Nicholas (Chapel Hill: University of North Carolina Press, 2010), 33.

6. Chester B. De Pratter and Marvin T. Smith, "Sixteenth Century European Trade in the Southeastern United States: Evidence from the Juan Pardo Expeditions (1566–1568)," *Notebook* 19, nos. 104 (1987): 53.

7. Herbert E. Ketcham, "Three Sixteenth Century Spanish Chronicles Relating to Georgia," *Georgia Historical Quarterly* 38 (1954): 74.

8. Charles M. Hudson and Paul E. Hoffman, eds., *The Juan Pardo Expeditions: Exploration of the Carolinas and Tennessee, 1566–1568* (Tuscaloosa: University of Alabama Press, 2005), 256–57.

9. A. M. Brooks, *The Unwritten History of Old St. Augustine*, trans. Annie Averette (St. Augustine, FL: Record Company, 1909), 8.

10. The Spanish notary Juan de la Bandera recorded the names of the other caciques present at this exchange as Neguase Orata, Estate Orata, Tacoru Orata, Utaca Orata, and Quetua Orata.

11. Hudson and Hoffman, *The Juan Pardo Expeditions*, 267.

12. Hudson and Hoffman, *The Juan Pardo Expeditions*, 267.

13. Hernando de Alarcon, *The Relation of the Navigation and Discovery which Captaine Fernando Alarchon Made*, Vol. 4 of *The Principal Nauigations, Voiages, Traffiqves & Discoveries of the English Nation*, ed. Richard Hakluyt, 12 vols. (Glasgow: J. MacLehose; NY: Macmillan, 1903–1905), 4:286.

14. Eric Jay Dolin, *Fur, Fortune, and Empire: The Epic History of the Fur Trade in America* (New York: W. W. Norton, 2010), 94–95; Ann M. Carlos and Frank D. Lewis, *Commerce by a Frozen Sea: Native Americans and the European Fur Trade* (Philadelphia: University of Pennsylvania Press, 2010), 1–5. When soldiers commented on effeminacy among Indigenous men, on cross-dressing, or, like the Italian soldier Henri de Tonti in 1697, on "sodomy," the specter of sin and social marginality was conveyed through the language of "horrid vice," "excess," and "wretches." De Tonti's superficial observations of Indigenous life in the Illinois country relied on this language, and on a reflexive inclination to condemn Native cultures through popular Christian ethics. See Henri de Tonti, *An Account of Monsieur de La Salle's Last Expedition and Discoveries in North America: Presented to the French King*, Collections of the New-York Historical Society, ser. 1, vol. 2 (1814): 237–38.

15. Christopher M. Parsons, *A Not-So-New World: Empire and Environment in French Colonial North America* (Philadelphia: University of Pennsylvania Press, 2018).

16. Valerie R. Hotchkiss, *Clothes Make the Man: Female Cross Dressing in Medieval Europe* (New York: Garland, 1996), 6; Elizabeth B. Davis, *Myth and Identity in the Epic of Imperial Spain* (Columbia: University of Missouri Press, 2000), 187.

17. Mary Elizabeth Perry, "From Convent to Battlefield: Cross-Dressing and Gendering the Self in the New World of Imperial Spain," in *Queer Iberia: Sexualities, Cultures, and Crossings from the Middle Ages to the Renaissance*, ed. Josiah Blackmore and Gregory S. Hutcheson (Durham, NC: Duke University Press, 1999), 422; Vern L. Bullough and Bonnie Bullough, *Cross Dressing, Sex, and Gender* (Philadelphia: University of Pennsylvania Press, 1993), 45–46; Anna Klosowska, *Queer Love in the Middle Ages* (New York: Palgrave Macmillan, 2005), 90–91; Mehl Allan Penrose, *Masculinity and Queer Desire in Spanish Enlightenment Literature* (London: Routledge, 2016), 73–74. On European perceptions of gendered divisions of labor in Native societies, see Ruth Gilbert, "'Strange Notions': Treatments of Early Modern Hermaphrodites," in *Madness, Disability and Social Exclusion: The Archaeology and Anthropology of "Difference,"* ed. Jane Hubert (London: Routledge, 2000), 153; Lorraine Daston and Katherine Park, "The Hermaphrodite and the Orders of Nature," in *Premodern Sexualities*, ed. Louise Fradenburg and Carla Freccero (London: Routledge, 1996), 117–36.

18. *The Catholic Church in the United States of America*, 3 vols. (New York: Catholic Editing Company, 1914), 3:236; John E. Worth, "Timucuan Missions of Spanish Florida and the Rebellion of 1656," PhD diss., University of Florida, 1992, 50–57; Maynard Geiger, *The Franciscan Conquest of Florida, 1573–1618* (Washington, DC: Catholic University of America, 1937), 227–32.

19. Roderick Wheeler, "A New Document on the Missions and Martyrs of Spanish Florida," *Franciscan Studies* 1, no. 2 (June 1941): 23–34; Stephen Haliczer, *Sexuality in the Confessional: A Sacrament Profaned* (New York: Oxford University Press, 1996), 9.

20. Jerald T. Milanich and William C. Sturtevant, eds., *Francisco Pareja's 1613 Confessionario: A Documentary Source for Timucuan Ethnography*, trans. Emilio F. Moran (Tallahassee: Department of State, Division of Archives, History, and Records Management, 1972). See also Kathleen A. Deagan, "Spanish-Indian Interaction in Sixteenth-Century Florida and Hispaniola," in *Cultures in Contact: The European Impact on Native Cultural Institutions in Eastern North America, A.D. 1000–1800*, ed. William W. Fitzhugh (Washington DC: Smithsonian, 1985), 281–318; Alejandra Dubcovsky and George Aaron Broadwell, "Writing Timucua: Recovering and Interrogating Indigenous Authorship," *Early American Studies* 15, no. 3 (Summer 2017): 409–41.

21. Milanich and Sturtevant, *Francisco Pareja's 1613 Confesionario*, 39, 43, 48, 75, 76.

22. Erika Pérez, *Colonial Intimacies: Interethnic Kinship, Sexuality, and Marriage in Southern California, 1769–1885* (Norman: University of Oklahoma Press, 2018), 58n35, 316. See also Karen V. Powers, *Women in the Crucible of*

Conquest: The Gendered Genesis of Spanish American Society, 1500–1600 (Albuquerque: University of New Mexico Press, 2005).

23. Ramon A. Gutierrez, "A History of Latina/o Sexualities," in *Latina/o Sexualities: Probing Powers, Passions, Practices, and Politics*, ed. Marysol Asencio (New Brunswick, NJ: Rutgers University Press, 2010), 19; Roberto A. Valdeon, *Translation and the Spanish Empire in the Americas* (Philadelphia: John Benjamins Publishing Company, 2014), 129–30.

24. De Ledesma quoted in Gutierrez, "A History of Latina/o Sexualities," 18–19.

25. The link between reproductive sex and Indigenous dispossession in settler-colonial spaces is well established across a number of historical contexts. See Andrea Smith, *Conquest: Sexual Violence and American Indian Genocide* (Durham, NC: Duke University Press, 2005); Gregory D. Smithers, *Science, Sexuality, and Race in the United States and Australia, 1780–1940*, rev. ed. (Lincoln: University of Nebraska Press, 2017); J. Kehaulani Kauanui, *Paradoxes of Hawaiian Sovereignty: Land, Sex, and the Colonial Politics of State Nationalism* (Durham, NC: Duke University Press, 2018).

26. Jerald T. Milanich, *Florida Indians and the Invasion from Europe* (Gainesville: University Press of Florida, 1998), 166. The mission to the Timucuans also faced the constant struggle of maintaining supplies. See John H. Hahn and Bonnie G. McEwan, *The Apalachee Indians and Mission San Luis* (Gainesville: University Press of Florida, 1998), 28.

27. Milanich and Sturtevant, *Francisco Pareja's 1613 Confesionario*, 29, 48; Amy Turner Bushnell, *Situado and Sabana: Spain's Support System for the Presidio and Mission Provinces of Florida* (Athens: University of Georgia Press, 1994), 71–72; Nicholas P. Cushner, *Why Have You Come Here? The Jesuits and the First Evangelization of North America* (New York: Oxford University Press, 2006), 12, 15, 68.

28. Milanich and Sturtevant, *Francisco Pareja's 1613 Confesionario*, 25.

29. Samuel de Champlain, *Voyages of Samuel de Champlain, 1604–1618*, ed. W. L. Grant (New York: Charles Scribner's Sons, 1907), 272–76; Charles Garrad, *Petun to Wyandot: The Ontario Petun from the Sixteenth Century* (Gatineau, QC: University of Ottawa Press, 2014), 167–68; Scott Weidensaul, *The First Frontier: The Forgotten History of Struggle, Savagery, and Endurance in Early America* (Boston: Houghton Mifflin Harcourt, 2012), 105; Daniel J. Weeks, *Gateways to Empire: Quebec and New Amsterdam to 1664* (Bethlehem, PA: Lehigh University Press, 2019), 297.

30. Micah True, *Masters and Students: Jesuit Mission Ethnography in Seventeenth-Century New France* (Montreal: McGill-Queens University Press, 2015), ch. 2; Bronwen McShea, *Apostles of Empire: The Jesuits and New France* (Lincoln: University of Nebraska Press, 2019), 9–10, 36–7, 54, 135–36.

31. Reuben Gold Thwaites, ed., *The Jesuit Relations and Allied Documents*, 71 vols. (New York: Pageant Books, 1959), 41:183, 185. See also Laura M. Chmielewski, *Jacques Marquette and Louis Jolliet: Exploration, Encounter, and the French New World* (New York: Routledge, 2018), ch. 4; Robert Launey, *Savages, Romans, and Despots: Thinking About Others from Montaigne to Herder* (Chicago: University of Chicago Press, 2018), 95.

32. Richard White, *The Middle Ground: Indians, Empires, and Republics in the Great Lakes Region, 1650–1815* (New York: Cambridge University Press, 1991), 25, 50; Michael A. McDonnell, *Masters of Empire: Great Lakes Indians and the Making of America* (New York: Hill and Wang, 2015), 10, 12, 15, 31.

33. McDonnell, *Masters of Empire*, 31.

34. Chmielewski, *Jacques Marquette and Louis Jolliet*, 121.

35. Jacques Marquette, "Of the First Voyage Made by Father Marquette Toward New Mexico, and How the Idea Thereof Was Conceived," in Thwaites, *The Jesuit Relations and Allied Documents*, 5:59, 213.

36. Marquette, "Of the First Voyage," 127.

37. Chmielewski, *Jacques Marquette and Louis Jolliet*, 24

38. Thwaites, *The Jesuit Relations and Allied Documents*, 59:129.

39. Susan Sleeper-Smith, *Indian Women and French Men: Rethinking Cultural Encounter in the Western Great Lakes* (Amherst: University of Massachusetts Press, 2001), 21–22.

40. Bert Anson, *The Miami Indians* (Norman: University of Oklahoma Press, 2000), 11–17; David Costa, *The Miami-Illinois Language* (Lincoln: University of Nebraska Press, 2003), 10, 25–28.

41. Ernest L. Schusky, *The Forgotten Sioux: An Ethnohistory of the Lower Brule Reservation* (Chicago: Nelson Hall, 1975), 12; Robert V. Dodge, *Which Chosen People: Manifest Destiny Meets the Sioux* (New York: Algora Publishing, 2013), 14; Pekka Hämäläinen, *Lakota America: A New History of Indigenous Power* (New Haven, CT: Yale University Press, 2019), 14–40.

42. Donald Ricky, *Encyclopedia of North Dakota Indians* (Santa Barbara: Somerset Publishers, 2001), 186, 214; Jessica Dawn Palmer, *The Dakota Peoples: A History of the Dakota, Lakota and Nakota Through 1863* (Jefferson, NC: McFarland, 2008), 12–18.

43. Marquette, "Of the First Voyage," 129.

44. Basil Johnston, *The Manitous: Supernatural World of the Ojibway* (New York: HarperCollins, 1996).

45. Reuben Gold Thwaites, *Father Marquette* (New York: D. Appleton & Company, 1910), 181; James Axtell, "The Power of Print in the Eastern Woodlands," *William and Mary Quarterly* 44, no. 2 (Apr. 1987): 300–309.

46. Neal Salisbury, "Religious Encounters in a Colonial Context: New England and New France in the Seventeenth Century," *American Indian Quarterly* 16, no. 4 (Autumn 1992): 501–9; R. Todd Romero, "'Ranging Foresters' and 'Women-Like Men': Physical Accomplishment, Spiritual Power, and Indian Masculinity in Early-Seventeenth-Century New England," *Ethnohistory* 53, no. 2 (Spring 2006): 281–329.

47. Elisabeth Tooker, "Introduction," *Native North American Spirituality of the Eastern Woodlands: Sacred Myths*, ed. Elisabeth Tooker (Mahwah, NJ: Paulist Press, 1979), 17; John A. Grim, *The Shaman: Patterns of Religious Healing Among the Ojibway Indians* (Norman: University of Oklahoma Press, 1983), 150; Catherine L. Albanese, *Nature Religion in America: From the Algonkian to the New Age* (Chicago: University of Chicago Press, 1990), 29.

48. Thwaites, *The Jesuit Relations and Allied Documents*, 59:129. See also Allan Greer, ed., *The Jesuit Relations: Natives and Missionaries in Seventeenth*

Century North America (Boston: Bedford St. Martin's, 2000), 201; John Gilmary Shea, *Discovery and Exploration of the Mississippi Valley; with the Original Narratives of Marquette, Allouez, Membré, Hennepin, and Anastase Douay* (Albany, NY: Joseph McDonough, 1903), 155.

49. Jennifer M. Spear, *Race, Sex, and Social Order in Early New Orleans* (Baltimore: Johns Hopkins University Press, 2009), 27–28.

50. Kathy Peiss, ed., *Major Problems in the History of American Sexuality: Documents and Essays* (New York: Houghton Mifflin, 2002), 30.

51. Louise Philips Kellogg, ed., *Early Narratives of the Northwest, 1634–1699* (New York: Scribner, 1917), 360, 244.

52. See, for example, Andrés González de Barcia Carballido y Zúñiga, *Barcia's Chronological History of the Continent of Florida . . . from the year 1512, in Which Juan Ponce de Leon Discovered Florida, Until the Year 1722*, trans. Anthony Kerrigan (Westport, CT: Greenwood, 1951), 306.

53. Oliver Gloag, "Représentations Coloniales de Lahontan à Camus" [Colonial representations from Lahontan to Camus], PhD diss., Duke University, 2012, 8.

54. Reuben Gold Thwaites, ed., *New Voyages to North-America*, 2 vols. (Chicago: A. C. McClurg, 1905), 2:462.

55. Robert M. Morrissey, "Kaskaskia Social Network: Kinship and Assimilation in the French-Illinois Borderlands, 1695–1735," *William and Mary Quarterly* 70, no. 1 (Jan. 2013): 114.

56. Milo Milton Quaife, ed., *The Western Country in the Seventeenth Century: The Memoirs of Lamothe Cadillac and Pierre Liette* (Chicago: Lakeside Press, 1947), 118–19.

57. Donald R. Ricky, ed., *Indians of Missouri: Past and Present* (St. Clair Shores, MI: Somerset Publishers, 1999), 153; Biloine Whiting Young and Melvin L. Fowler, *Cahokia: The Great North American Metropolis* (Urbana: University of Illinois Press, 2000), 2; Robert L. Hall, *An Archaeology of the Soul: North American Indian Belief and Ritual* (Urbana: University of Illinois Press, 1997), 16, 18,

58. Meghan C. L. Howey, *Mound Builders and Monument Makers of the Northern Great Lakes, 1200–1600* (Norman: University of Oklahoma Press, 2012).

59. James Neill, *The Origins and Role of Same-Sex Relations in Human Societies* (Jefferson, NC: McFarland, 2009), 235.

60. In early modern Europe, when the gendered binary supposedly prescribed by nature was breached, public denunciation followed. In cases of sodomy, a death sentence often ensued. Liette's attitudes about the "sin of sodomy" align with these cultural attitudes. See N. S. Davidson, "Sodomy in Early Modern Venice," in *Sodomy in Early Modern Europe*, ed. Tom Betteridge (Manchester, UK: Manchester University Press, 2002), 75–76; George Rousseau, "Policing the Anus: Stuprum and Sodomy According to Paolo Zacchia's Forensic Medicine," in *The Science of Homosexuality in Early Modern Europe*, ed. Kenneth Borris and George Rousseau (London: Routledge, 2008), 86–87.

61. Francisco Guerra, *The Pre-Columbian Mind: A Study into the Aberrant Nature of Sexual Drives, Drugs Affecting Behaviour and the Attitude Towards Life and Death, with a Survey of Psychotherapy in Pre-Columbian America* (New York: Seminar Press, 1971), 23, 162; Christian Berco, *Sexual Hierarchies,*

Public Status: Men, Sodomy, and Society in Spain's Golden Age (Toronto: University of Toronto Press, 2007); Zeb Tortorici, *Sins Against Nature: Sex and Archives in Colonial New Spain* (Durham, NC: Duke University Press, 2018).

62. Greer, *The Jesuit Relations*, 201; Quaife, *The Western Country in the Seventeenth Century*, 112–13.

63. Mark Breitenberg, *Anxious Masculinity in Early Modern England* (Cambridge: Cambridge University Press, 2003), 160; *The Oxford Handbook of Early Modern European History, 1350–1750*, vol. 1, *Peoples and Place* (2015), s.v. "Cultures of Peoples."

CHAPTER 4: EFFEMINACY

1. Christo Apache, interview with author, November 6, 2017.

2. J. Miko Thomas, interview with author, July 13, 2018.

3. Staffan Brunius, "Some Comments on Early Swedish Collections from the Northeast," in *New Sweden in America*, ed. Carol E. Hoffecker, Richard Waldron, Lorraine E. Williams, and Barbara E. Benson (Newark: University of Delaware Press, 1995), 150–70.

4. Charles T. Gehring, trans. and ed., *New York Historical Manuscripts: Dutch, Volumes XVIII–XIX: Delaware Papers (Dutch Period): A Collection of Documents Pertaining to the Regulation of Affairs on the South River of New Netherland, 1648–1664* (Baltimore: Genealogical Publishing, 1981), 291; Karen Ordahl Kupperman, "Scandinavian Colonists Confront the New World," in Hoffecker et al., *New Sweden in America*, 89–90. See also Cynthia Jean Van Zandt, "Negotiating Settlement: Colonialism, Cultural Exchange, and Conflict in Early Colonial Atlantic North America, 1580–1660," PhD diss., University of Connecticut, 1998.

5. Cynthia J. Van Zandt, *Brothers Among Nations: The Pursuit of Intercultural Alliances in Early America, 1580–1660* (New York: Oxford University Press, 2008), 60–61.

6. Karen Ordahl Kupperman, *Indians and English: Facing Off in Early America* (Ithaca, NY: Cornell University Press, 2000), 46, 74, 107; Kelly L. Watson, *Insatiable Appetites: Imperial Encounters with Cannibals in the North Atlantic World* (New York: New York University Press, 2015), 99–100; Zeb Tortorici, *Sexuality and the Unnatural in Colonial Latin America* (Berkeley: University of California Press, 2016), 133, 152–53.

7. John McIntosh, *The Origins of the North American Indians* (New York: Nafis & Cornish, 1850), 71; Lucien Carr, *Dress and Ornaments of Certain American Indians* (Worcester, MA: Press of Charles Hamilton, 1897), 5–6, 23, 33, 28–29, 48; José Rabasa, *Inventing America: Spanish Historiography and the Formation of Eurocentrism* (Norman: University of Oklahoma Press, 1993), ch. 1; Kupperman, *Indians and English*, 49, 52, 78; Alden T. Vaughan, *Transatlantic Encounters: American Indians in Britain, 1500–1776* (New York: Cambridge University Press, 2006), 138, 155.

8. Paula Gunn Allen, *The Sacred Hoop: Recovering the Feminine in American Indian Traditions* (Boston: Beacon Press, 1986), 4; Renya Ramirez, "Healing, Violence, and Native American Women," *Social Justice* 31, no. 4 (2004): 103–16; Sarah Deer, *The Beginning and End of Rape: Confronting Sexual Violence in Native America* (Minneapolis, University of Minnesota Press, 2015).

9. John W. De Forest, *History of the Indians of Connecticut* (Hartford, CT: Wm. Jas. Hamersley, 1851), 110; Helen C. Rountree, *Pocahontas's People: The Powhatan Indians of Virginia Through Four Centuries* (Norman: University of Oklahoma Press, 1990), 5; Nancy Shoemaker, "An Alliance Between Men: Gender Metaphors in Eighteenth-Century American Indian Diplomacy East of the Mississippi," *Ethnohistory* 46, no. 2 (Spring 1999): 239–63; Kupperman, *Indians and English*, 227.

10. "Address of Thanks, Sent to the King of Spain by His Loyal Subjects, the Chiefs of the Timucua People, dated the 28th of January, 1688," *Proceedings of the American Philosophical Society* 28 (July 1878–Mar. 1880): 499; David R. Galindo, *To Sin No More: Franciscans and Conversion in the Hispanic World, 1683–1830* (Stanford, CA: Stanford University Press, 2018).

11. K. Renato Lings, *Love Lost in Translation: Homosexuality and the Bible* (Bloomington, IN: Trafford Publishing, 2013), 297–300.

12. Lings, *Love Lost in Translation*, 300–305.

13. David F. Greenberg, *The Construction of Homosexuality* (Chicago: University of Chicago Press, 1988), 249; Anatoly Liberman, *An Analytical Dictionary of the English Etymology: An Introduction* (Minneapolis: University of Minnesota Press, 2008), 181.

14. Lings, *Love Lost in Translation*, 302.

15. Leonard Swidler, *Biblical Affirmations of Woman* (Philadelphia: Westminster Press, 1979), 293; Polly Ha, *English Presbyterianism, 1590–1640* (Stanford, CA: Stanford University Press, 2011); R. Todd Romero, *Making War and Minting Christians: Masculinity, Religion, and Colonialism in Early New England* (Amherst: University of Massachusetts Press, 2011), 181–83; Lisa T. Brooks, *Our Beloved Kin: A New History of King Philip's War* (New Haven, CT: Yale University Press, 2018), 8, 328.

16. Carolyn Williams, "'This Effeminate Brat': Tamburlaine's Unmanly Son," *Medieval & Renaissance Drama in England* 9 (1997): 70–71.

17. Elizabeth Reis, *Bodies in Doubt: An American History of Intersex* (Baltimore: Johns Hopkins University Press, 2009), 16.

18. Susan Juster, "'Neither Male Nor Female': Jemima Wilkinson and the Politics of Gender in Post-Revolutionary America," in *Possible Pasts: Becoming Colonial in Early America*, ed. Robert Blair St. George (Ithaca, NY: Cornell University Press, 2000), 367; Elizabeth Reis, "Hermaphrodites and 'Same-Sex' Sex in Early America," in *Long Before Stonewall: Histories of Same-Sex Sexuality in Early America*, ed. Thomas C. Foster (New York: New York University Press, 2007), 152.

19. John Demos, *Entertaining Satan: Witchcraft and the Culture of Early New England* (New York: Oxford University Press, 1982), 381–85.

20. Bennett Capers, "Cross Dressing and the Criminal," *Yale Journal of Law and Humanities* 20, no. 1 (2008): 7.

21. Cotton Mather, *Decennium Luctuosum. An History of Remarkable Occurrences, in the Long War, which New-England Hath had with the Indian Salvages, from the year, 1688. To the Year 1698* (Boston: B. Green, 1699), 224; Ann M. Little, "'Shoot that Rogue, for He Hath an Englishman's Coat On!': Cultural Cross-Dressing on the New England Frontier, 1620–1760," *New England Quarterly* 74, no. 2 (June 2001): 257.

22. Cotton included women in his formulation of same-sex "carnal fellowship," but the law he helped write in 1636 ultimately excluded women. See Richard Godbeer, *Sexual Revolution in Early America* (Baltimore: Johns Hopkins University Press, 2002), 105.

23. Kathleen Brown, "'Changed into the Fashion of a Man': The Politics of Sexual Difference in a Seventeenth-Century Anglo-American Settlement," *Journal of American History* 6, no. 2 (Oct. 1995): 171–93; Mary Beth Norton, "Communal Definitions of Gendered Identity in Colonial America," in *Through a Glass Darkly: Reflections on Personal Identity in Early America*, ed. Ronald Hoffman, Mechal Sobel, and Fredrika J. Teute (Chapel Hill: University of North Carolina Press, 1997), 40–66; Rudolf M. Dekker and Lotte C. van de Pol, *The Tradition of Female Transvestism in Early Modern Europe* (London: Macmillan, 1997); Elizabeth Reis, "Impossible Hermaphrodites: Intersex in America, 1620-1960," *Journal of American History* 92, no 2 (Sept. 2005): 411–41; Susan Stryker, *Transgender History: The Root of Today's Revolution*, 2nd ed. (New York: Seal Press, 2017), 46; Jen Manion, *Female Husbands: A Trans History* (New York: Cambridge University Press, 2020), 55.

24. Richard A. Posner, *Sex and Reason* (Cambridge, MA: Harvard University Press, 1992), 301–2.

25. Michael Sievernich, "Comparing Ancient and Native Customs: Joseph-Francois Lafitau and the 'Sauvages ameriquains,'" in *European Missions in Contact Zones: Transformation Through Interaction in a (Post-)Colonial World*, ed. Judith Becker (Göttingen: Vanderenhoeck and Ruprecht, 2015), 196.

26. Joseph-Francois Lafitau, *Moeurs des sauvages ameriquains, comparées aux moeurs des premiers temps*, 2 vols. (Paris: Saugrain, 1724).

27. Lafitau, *Moeurs des sauvages ameriquains*, 2:203–4.

28. Jason Cromwell, *Transmen and FTMs: Identities, Bodies, Genders, and Sexualities* (Urbana-Champaign: University of Illinois Press, 1999), 160–61n3.

29. Lafitau, *Moeurs des sauvages ameriquains*, 2:52–54, 603–4, 608–10. See also Sievernich, "Comparing Ancient and Native Customs," 198; Jonathan N. Katz, ed., *Gay American History: Lesbian and Gay Men in the U.S.A.: A Documentary History* (New York: Crowell, 1976), 288–90.

30. Lafitau, *Moeurs des sauvages ameriquains*, 2:306

31. Paula Gunn Allen, "Lesbians in American Indian Culture," *Conditions* 3, no. 1 (Spring 1981): 67–87; Thomas A. Foster, *Women in Early America* (New York: New York University Press, 2015), 67.

32. Lafitau, *Moeurs des sauvages ameriquains*, 2:52.

33. Lafitau, *Moeurs des sauvages ameriquains*, 2:263; Laura Ammon, "Work Useful to Religion and the Humanities: A History of the Development of the Comparative Method in Religion from Bartolome Las Casas to Edward Burnett Tylor," PhD diss., Claremont Graduate University, 2005, 110.

34. Lafitau, *Moeurs des sauvages ameriquains*, 2:53.

35. Ammon, "Work Useful to Religion and the Humanities," 5–12; Joseph-Francois Lafitau, *Moeurs, Coutumes et Religions des Sauvages Americains. Extrait* (Lyon and Paris: Librairie D'Education de Perisse Freres, 1845), 2:603 ("L'Aihenrofera, ou les amitiés particulières entre les jeunes gens, qui se trouvent

établies à peu près de la même manière d'un bout de l'Amérique à l'autre, sont un des points les plus intéressants de leurs mœurs").

36. Lafitau quoted in Katz, *Gay American History*, 289; Greenberg, *The Construction of Homosexuality*, 70.

37. John Gilmary Shea and Louis Hennepin, *A Description of Louisiana* (New York: John G. Shea, 1880), 334; Reuben Gold Thwaites, *A New Discovery of a Vast Country in America*, 2 vols. (Chicago: A. C. McClurg, 1903), 1:167–68; Paul Hallam, *The Book of Sodom* (London: Verso, 1993), 200; Kim M. Phillips, *Before Orientalism: Asian Peoples and Cultures in European Travel Writing, 1245–1510* (Philadelphia: University of Pennsylvania Press, 2014), 138.

38. David A. Harvey, "Living Antiquity: Lafitau's *Moeurs des sauvages amériquains* and the Religious Roots of the Enlightenment Science of Man," *Journal of the Western Society of French History* 35 (2008): 75–92; Marc-André Bernier, Clorinda Donato, and Hans-Jürgen Lüsebrink, introduction, *Jesuit Accounts of the Colonial Americas: Intercultural Transfers, Intellectual Disputes, and Textualities*, ed. Marc-André Bernier, Clorinda Donato, and Hans-Jürgen Lüsebrink (Toronto: University of Toronto Press, 2014), 12.

39. Alan Gallay, *Walter Ralegh: Architect of Empire* (New York: Basic Books, 2019), 179, 182.

40. Gregory D. Smithers, "A 'Spreading Fire': Understanding Genocide in Early Colonial North America, 1607–1790s," in *Genocide in the Indigenous, Early Modern, and Imperial Worlds, from c. 1535 to World War One*, ed. Ben Kiernan, Benjamin Madley, Ned Blackhawk, and Rebe Taylor (New York: Cambridge University Press, 2021).

41. Pekka Hämäläinen, "The Shapes of Power: Indians, European, and North American Worlds from the Seventeenth Century to the Nineteenth," in *Contested Spaces of Early America*, ed. Juliana Barr and Edward Countryman (Philadelphia: University of Pennsylvania Press, 2014), 31–68.

42. Ethan A. Schmidt, *The Divided Dominion: Social Conflict and Indian Hatred in Early Virginia* (Boulder: University Press of Colorado, 2015), 32, 77–80.

43. John A. Sainsbury, "Indian Labor in Early Rhode Island," *New England Quarterly* 48, no. 3 (Sept. 1974): 378–93; Joshua M. Marshall, "'A Melancholy People': Anglo-Indian Relations in Early Warwick, Rhode Island, 1642–1675," *New England Quarterly* 68, no. 3 (Sept. 1995): 402–28; Michael Guasco, "To 'Doe Some Good Upon Their Countrymen': The Paradox of Indian Slavery in Early Anglo-America," *Journal of Social History* 41, no. 2 (Winter 2007): 389–411; Margaret E. Newell, *Brethren by Nature: New England Indians, Colonists, and the Origins of American Slavery* (Ithaca, NY: Cornell University Press, 2015).

44. Roy Harvey Pearce, *Savagism and Civilization: A Study of the Indian and the American Mind*, rev. ed. (Berkeley: University of California Press, 1988); Francis Jennings, *The Invasion of America: Indians, Colonialism, and the Cant of Conquest*, rev. ed. (Chapel Hill: University of North Carolina Press, 2010).

45. The concept of Native men's "idleness" had its antecedents in the English colonization of Ireland and the education of "Irish brutes" through English labor systems. See Nicholas P. Canny, "The Ideology of English Colonization: From Ireland to America," *William and Mary Quarterly* 30, no. 4 (Oct. 1973):

588. In Virginia, reservations and enslavement became a means of vanquishing Native Americans and containing enslaved Africans. See Anthony S. Parent Jr., *Foul Means: The Formation of a Slave Society in Virginia, 1660–1740* (Chapel Hill: University of North Carolina Press, 2003), 208.

46. Helen C. Rountree, *The Powhatan Indians of Virginia: Their Traditional Culture* (Norman: University of Oklahoma Press, 1992), 88; Bernard Sheehan, *Savagism and Civility: Indians and Englishmen in Colonial Virginia* (Cambridge: Cambridge University Press, 1980), 94.

47. Wesley F. Craven, "Indian Policy in Early Virginia," *William and Mary Quarterly* 1, no. 1 (Jan. 1944): 65–82; Kathleen M. Brown, "The Anglo-Algonquian Gender Frontier," in *Negotiators of Change: Historical Perspectives on Native American Women,* ed. Nancy Shoemaker (New York: Routledge, 1995), 26–48.

48. Schmidt, *Divided Dominion,* 86.

49. Edmund S. Morgan, "The Labor Problem at Jamestown, 1607–18," *American Historical Review* 76, no. 3 (June 1971): 595–611; Rebecca A. Goetz, "Indian Slavery: An Atlantic and Hemispheric Problem," *History Compass* 14, no. 2 (February 2016): 59–70; Kristalyn Marie Shefveland, *Anglo-Native Virginia: Trade, Conversion, and Indian Slavery in the Old Dominion, 1646–1722* (Athens: University of Georgia Press, 2016), 2, 16, 32, 68.

50. Alfred A. Cave, *Lethal Encounters: Englishmen and Indians in Colonial Virginia* (Santa Barbara: Praeger, 2011); Godbeer, *Sexual Revolution in Early America,* 104–5; Richard Godbeer, "'The Cry of Sodom': Discourse, Intercourse, and Desire in Colonial New England," in Foster, *Long Before Stonewall,* 100.

51. Thomas A. Foster, *Sex and the Eighteenth-Century Man: Massachusetts and the History of Sexuality in America* (Boston: Beacon Press, 2006), 111; Peter Hennen, *Faeries, Bears, and Leathermen: Men in Community Queering the Masculine* (Chicago: University of Chicago Press, 2008), 34–35.

52. Susan S. Parrish, *American Curiosity: Cultures of Natural History in the Colonial British Atlantic World* (Chapel Hill: University of North Carolina Press, 2006), 93, 139, 183.

53. Torias B. Hug, *Impostures in Early Modern England: Representations and Perceptions of Fraudulent Identities* (Manchester, UK: Manchester University Press, 2009), 27, 36, 38, 40, 118; Kathryn Wichelins, "From *The Scarlet Letter* to Stonewall: Reading the 1629 Thomas(ine) Hall Case, 1978–2009," *Early American Studies* 12, no. 3 (Fall 2014): 500–523.

54. "The Then Dedication to the Lord Thomas Manners, Third Son of the Late Duke of Rutland; and one of the Author's Scholars," in *The Inn-Play Cornish-Hugg Wrestler* (London: Thomas Weeks, 1727), xi; Count John Baptista Comazzi, *The Morals of Princes* (London: T. Worrall, 1729), 202; Third Earl of Shaftesbury, *Characteristicks,* 3 vols. (London: n.p., 1732), 3:23; *Britain's Remembrancer,* 4th ed. (London: G. Freer, 1747), 9, 12; Michael J. Rozbicki, *The Complete Colonial Gentleman: Cultural Legitimacy in Plantation America* (Charlottesville: University of Virginia Press, 1998), 68.

55. Comazzi, *The Morals of Princes,* 13, 113.

56. Third Earl of Shaftesbury, *Characteristicks,* 2:154.

57. John Norris, *Christian Blessedness: Or, Practical Discourses Upon the Beatitudes of our Lord and Saviour Jesus Christ*, 10th ed. (London, 1724), 96; on "excessive venery," see M. Tissot, *On-Anism: Or, a Treatise upon the Disorders Produced by Masturbation*, trans. A. Hume, 3rd ed. (London: W. Wilkinson, 1767), 16. Mastering emotions equipped one to govern the masses. See Huffumbourghausen Baron, *The Congress of the Beasts*, 5th ed. (London: W. Webb, 1748), vii. In 1755, the English philosopher John Locke referred back to the ancient Greeks to find a society that became corrupted for its "softness and effeminacy." See *The Continuum Companion to Locke*, ed. S. J. Savonius-Wroth, Paul Schuurman, and Jonathan Walmsley (London: Continuum, 2010), 267.

58. Gregory D. Smithers, *Science, Sexuality, and Race in the United States and Australia, 1780–1940*, rev. 2nd ed. (Lincoln: University of Nebraska Press, 2017), ch. 1.

59. Sophia Hume, *An Exhortation to the Inhabitants of the Province of South-Carolina* (London: Luke Hinde, 1752), 91.

60. Peter Clark, *Christian Bravery. A Sermon Preached before the Honourable Artillery Company in Boston, June 7th, 1736* (Boston: S. Kneeland and T. Green, for D. Henchman in Corn Hill, 1736). See also *A Sermon Preached at the Anniversary of the Three Choirs of Gloucester, Worcester, and Hereford, Cathedral Church at Hereford, on Wednesday Sept. 12, 1753* (London: James Fletcher, 1753), 22; Thomas Ruggles, *The Usefulness and Expedience of Souldiers as Discovered by Reason and Experience, and Countenanced and Supported by the Gospel* (New London, CT: T. Green, 1737).

61. The colonial discourse borrowed liberally from debate in eighteenth-century England about the naturalization of foreign Protestants. See, for example, Anglo-Nativus, *A Letter to Sir John Phillips, Bart., Occasion'd by a Bill brought into Parliament to Naturalize Foreign Protestants* (London: M. Cooper, 1747), 5; Samuel Richardson, *The History of Sir Charles Grandison: In a Series of Letters Published from the Originals*, 7 vols. (London: S. Richardson, 1754), 3:14.

62. Richard Godbeer, *The Overflowing of Friendship: Love Between Men and the Creation of the American Republic* (Baltimore: Johns Hopkins University Press, 2009).

63. John Brown, *An Estimate of the Manners and Principles of the Times*, 6th ed. (London: L. Davis and C. Reymers, 1757), 181; John Archdeacon of Lincoln Gordon, *A New Estimate of Manners and Principles [. . .] and to this Kingdom in Particular* (Cambridge: J. Bentham, 1760), x; William Falconer, *Remarks on the Influence of Climate, Situation, Nature of Country, Population, Nature of Food, and Way of Life* (London: C. Dilly, 1781), 407, 534; Lord Henry Home Kames, *Sketches of the History of Man*, 2 vols. (Edinburgh: W. Creech, 1774), 2:63; William Guthrie, *A New Geographical, Historical, and Commercial Grammar; and Present State of the Kingdoms of the World* (Dublin: James Williams and John Exshaw, 1780), 46, 51, 54, 513; John Langhorne, *The Effusions of Friendship and Fancy*, 2 vols. (London: T. Becket and P. A. D. Hondt, 1763), 2:41; Ezra Stiles, *The United States Elevated to Glory and Honor: A Sermon . . ., May 8th 1783* (New Haven, CT: Thomas and Samuel Green, 1783), 19.

64. James Howell, *A French and English Dictionary, Composed by M'Randle Cotgrave* (London: Anthony Dolle, 1733); Willem Frijhoff and Marijke Spies, *Dutch Culture in a European Perspective: 1650, Hard-Won Unity* (Basingstoke, UK: Palgrave Macmillan, 2004), 215.

65. Timothy D. Willig, *Restoring the Chain of Friendship: British Policy and the Indians of the Great Lakes, 1783–1815* (Lincoln: University of Nebraska Press, 2008); Amanda E. Herbert, *Female Alliances: Gender, Identity, and Friendship in Early Modern Britain* (New Haven, CT: Yale University Press, 2014), 24; Cassandra A. Good, *Founding Friendships: Friendships Between Men and Women in the Early American Republic* (New York: Oxford University Press, 2015), 3.

66. John Lawson, *Lawson's History of North Carolina*, ed. Frances Latham Harris (Richmond, VA: Garrett and Massie, 1937), 208.

67. Rene L. Bossu, *Travels Through that Part of North America Formerly Called Louisiana . . . Translated from the French, by John Reinhold Forster*, 2 vols. (London: T. Davies, 1771), 1:169.

68. Bossu, *Travels Through that Part of North America Formerly Called Louisiana*, 1:303.

69. Theda Perdue, *Cherokee Women: Gender and Culture Change, 1700–1835* (Lincoln: University of Nebraska Press, 1998), 17, 40; Rountree, *Pocahontas's People*, 132.

70. Rebecca Nagle, "The Healing History of Two-Spirit, a Term That Gives LGBTQ Natives a Voice," *Huffington Post*, June 30, 2018, https://www.huffpost.com/entry/two-spirit-identity_n_5b37cfbce4b007aa2f809af1.

71. Vern L. Bullough and Bonnie Bullough, *Cross Dressing, Sex, and Gender* (Philadelphia: University of Pennsylvania Press, 1993), 3–9; Michel-Rolph Trouillot, *Silencing the Past: Power and the Production of History* (Boston: Beacon Press, 1995), 27.

CHAPTER 5: STRANGE

1. Arnold Dahl, interview with author, November 14, 2017.

2. Rebecca Nagle, interview with author, June 4, 2018.

3. The following account draws on Pedro Font, *With Anza to California, 1775–1776, the Journal of Pedro Font, O.F.M.*, ed. and trans. Alan K. Brown (Norman, OK: Arthur H. Clark, 2011), 75–109; *The California Indians: A Source Book*, compiled and ed. R. F. Heizer and M. A. Whipple, 2nd ed. (Berkeley: University of California Press, 1973), 247–54.

4. Donald T. Garate, *Juan Bautista de Anza: Basque Explorer in the New World* (Reno: University of Nevada Press, 2005); Carlos R. Herrera, *Juan Bautista de Anza: The King's Governor in New Mexico* (Norman: University of Oklahoma Press, 2015).

5. Heizer and Whipple, *The California Indians*, 249.

6. Robert A. Kittle, *Franciscan Frontiersmen: How Three Adventurers Charted the West* (Norman: University of Oklahoma Press, 2017), 113.

7. Heizer and Whipple, *The California Indians*, 251.

8. Kittle, *Franciscan Frontiersmen*, 49, 111.

9. Herrera, *Juan Bautista de Anza*, 68.

10. David Armitage and Sanjay Subrahmanyam, "Introduction: The Age of Revolutions, c. 1760–1840—Global Causation, Connection, and Comparison," in *The Age of Revolutions in Global Context, c. 1760–1840*, ed. David Armitage and Sanjay Subrahmanyam (Basingstoke, UK: Palgrave Macmillan, 2010), xii–xxxii.

11. Edward F. Castetter and Willis H. Bell, *Yuman Indian Agriculture: Primitive Subsistence on Lower Colorado and Gila Rivers* (Albuquerque: University of New Mexico Press, 1951), 3–7, 100, 215.

12. Harold E. Driver, "Estimation of Intensity of Land Use from Ethnobiology: Applied to the Yuma Indians," *Ethnohistory* 4, no. 2 (Spring 1957): 174–97; Robert L. Bee, "Changes in Yuma Social Organization," *Ethnology* 2, no. 2 (Apr. 1963): 207–27.

13. C. Daryll Forde, *Ethnography of the Yuma Indians* (Berkeley: University of California Press, 1931), 94–97.

14. Lesley Byrd Simpson, *The Encomienda in New Spain: The Beginnings of Spanish Mexico* (Berkeley: University of California Press, 1950), 1–28; Albert L. Hurtado, *Indian Survival on the California Frontier* (New Haven, CT: Yale University Press, 1988), 24; David J. Weber, *The Spanish Frontier in North America* (New Haven, CT: Yale University Press, 1992), 125.

15. Bárbara O. Reyes, *Private Women, Public Lives: Gender and the Missions of the Californias* (Austin: University of Texas Press, 2009), 103.

16. R. Douglas Hurt, *The Indian Frontier, 1763–1846* (Albuquerque: University of New Mexico Press, 2002), 69; Mark Santiago, *Massacre at the Yuma Crossing: Spanish Relations with the Quechans, 1779–1782* (Tucson: University of Arizona Press, 1998), 87–89.

17. Marie Antoinette Czaplicka, *Aboriginal Siberia: A Study of Social Anthropology* (Oxford: Clarendon Press, 1914), 253–54; Harvie Ferguson, *Self-Identity and Everyday Life* (London: Routledge, 2009), 50–51.

18. Peter Goodchild, *Raven Tales* (Chicago: Chicago Review Press, 1991), 94–95.

19. Jane M. Murphy, "Psychotherapeutic Aspects of Shamanism," in *Magic, Faith, and Healing: Studies in Primitive Psychology*, ed. Ari Kiev (New York: Free Press of Glencoe, 1964), 75; Mihály Hoppál and Otto J. von Sadovszky, *Shamanism: Past and Present* (Budapest: Ethnographic Institute, Hungarian Academy of Sciences), 108.

20. On Tlingit kinship, see George Thornton Emmons, *The Tlingit Indians*, ed. Frederica de Laguna (Seattle: University of Washington Press, 1991), 8; *Haa Tuwunáagu Yís, for Healing Our Spirit: Tlingit Oratory*, ed. with an introduction by Nora Dauenhauer and Richard Dauenhauer (Seattle: University of Washington Press, 1993), 6–7.

21. Frederica de Laguna, "Tlingit Ideas about the Individual," *Southwestern Journal of Anthropology* 10, no. 2 (Summer 1954): 172–91.

22. Frederica de Laguna, *Under Mount Saint Elias: The History and Culture of the Yakutat Tlingit* (Washington, DC: Smithsonian Institution Press, 1972), 796, 863, 874; John R. Swanton, *Tlingit Myths and Texts* (Washington, DC: Government Printing Office, 1909), 16; Sabine Lang, *Men as Women, Women as Men: Changing Gender in Native American Cultures* (Austin:

University of Texas Press, 1998), 224. The term "transvestite" is also misused in twentieth-century descriptions of gender fluidity in Tlingit society.

23. De Laguna, "Tlingit Ideas about the Individual," 178; Lang, *Men as Women, Women as Men*, 224–25, 250.

24. Miriam G. Ellis, "Deadman's Valley," *Hunter, Trader, Trapper* 46, no. 5 (Aug. 1923): 43

25. John J. Honingman, "The Kaska Indians: An Ethnographic Reconstruction," *Yale Publications in Anthropology* 51 (1954): 130; Theodore J. Karamanski, *Fur Trade and Exploration: Opening the Far Northwest, 1821–1852* (Norman: University of Oklahoma Press, 1983), 146.

26. On "coward," see John Kersey, *Dictionarium Anglo-Britannicum: Or, A General English Dictionary* (London: J. Wilde, 1708), p. CR; Nathan Bailey, *Dictionarium Anglo-Britannicum: Or, A More Compleat Universal Etymological English Dictionary* (London: T. Cox, 1730), p. CO.

27. On "courage," see Samuel Johnson, *A Dictionary of the English Language*, 3rd ed. (Dublin: W. G. Jones, 1768), p. CRA; Noah Webster, *A Dictionary of the English Language, Compiled for the Use of Common Schools in the United States* (Hartford, CT: George Goodwin & Sons, 1817), 77.

28. Swanton, *Tlingit Myths and Texts*, 38. The anthropological argument that the gatxan was a coward is replicated in de Laguna, *Under Mount Saint Elias*, 875, 895.

29. De Laguna, *Under Mount Saint Elias*, 874, 895–97, 596. Although one informant told de Laguna that gatxans never compare themselves to transvestites or homosexuals, this information was marginalized in favor of sweeping generalizations about Tlingit gender and sexuality.

30. Nicholas Thomas, *Colonialism's Culture: Anthropology, Travel and Government* (Princeton, NJ: Princeton University Press, 1994), 136.

31. Brendan C. Lindsay, *Murder State: California's Native American Genocide, 1846–1873* (Lincoln: University of Nebraska Press, 2012); Benjamin Madley, *An American Genocide: The United States and the California Indian Catastrophe* (New Haven, CT: Yale University Press, 2016).

32. Walter L. Williams, *The Spirit and the Flesh: Sexual Diversity in American Indian Culture* (Boston: Beacon Press, 1986), 87.

33. Steven W. Hackel, *Junipero Serra: California's Founding Father* (New York: Hill and Wang, 2013).

34. The following account is drawn from Francisco Palou, *Relacion historica de la vida y apostolicas tareas del Venerable Padre Fray Junipero Serra* (Impresa en México: en la Imprenta de Don Felipe de Zúñiga y Ontiveros, 1787), 222. The Esselen defined identity according to bilateral (matrilineal and patrilineal) lineages. See Philip B. Lavery, "Recognizing Indians: Identity, History, and the Federal Acknowledgement of the Ohlone/Costanoan-Esselen Nation," PhD diss., University of New Mexico, 2010, 2–3.

35. Font, *With Anza to California*, 250.

36. Linda K. Kerber, *Women of the Republic: Intellect and Ideology in Revolutionary America* (Chapel Hill: University of North Carolina Press, 1980), 36; Carla Hesse, *The Other Enlightenment: How French Women Became Modern*

(Princeton, NJ: Princeton University Press, 2001), 62; Karen O'Brien, *Women and Enlightenment in Eighteenth-Century Britain* (Cambridge: Cambridge University Press, 2009), 10, 73.

37. Benjamin Franklin, *The Papers of Benjamin Franklin, January 1, 1764, through December 31, 1764*, ed. Leonard W. Labaree, 43 vols. (New Haven, CT: Yale University Press, 1967), 11: 521.

38. George Washington, *The Papers of George Washington, Revolutionary War Series, 1 March 1778–30 April 1778*, ed. Philander D. Chase, 29 vols. (Charlottesville: University of Virginia Press, 2004), 14: 171–73.

39. John Adams, *Diary of John Adams, Volume 1*, "Tuesday [January 1759]," Adams Papers, Digital Edition, Massachusetts Historical Society, http://www.masshist.org/publications/adams-papers/index.php/view/ADMS-01-01-02-0004-0001-0002#sn=0; Thomas Jefferson, *The Papers of Thomas Jefferson, Vol. 2, 1777–18 June 1779*, ed. Julian P. Boyd, 45 vols. (Princeton, NJ: Princeton University Press, 1950), 2: 663–64; Gordon S. Wood, *The Radicalism of the American Revolution* (New York: Vintage Books, 1993), 104–5; Susan Stryker, *Transgender History: The Roots of Today's Revolution*, 2nd ed. (New York: Seal Press, 2017), 50–51; Jen Manion, *Female Husbands: A Trans History* (New York: Cambridge University Press, 2020), 99–100.

40. Gregory D. Smithers, "The 'Pursuits of the Civilized Man': Race and the Meaning of Civilization in the United States and Australia, 1790s–1850s," *Journal of World History* 20, no. 2 (Spring): 245. See also Michelle LeMaster, *Brothers Born of One Mother: British-Native American Relations in the Colonial Southeast* (Charlottesville: University of Virginia Press, 2012), 159.

41. Thomas Jefferson, *Notes on the State of Virginia*, ed. Frank Shuffleton (1785; repr., New York: Penguin Books, 1999), 98–108; Ari Helo, *Thomas Jefferson's Ethics and the Politics of Human Progress: The Morality of a Slaveholder* (New York: Cambridge University Press, 2014), 60–61.

42. Greg O'Brien, *Choctaws in a Revolutionary Age, 1750–1830* (Lincoln: University of Nebraska Press, 2002), 5–6.

43. Jack B. Martin, *A Grammar of Creek (Muscogee)* (Lincoln: University of Nebraska Press, 2011), 142.

44. Joel Martin, "Rebalancing the World in the Contradictions of History: Creek/Muskogee," in *Native Religions and Cultures of North America: Anthropology of the Sacred*, ed. Lawrence E. Sullivan (New York: Continuum, 2003), 86.

45. Donna L. Akers, *Living in the Land of Death: The Choctaw Nation, 1830–1860* (East Lansing: Michigan State University Press, 2004), 34; Claudio Saunt, *A New Order of Things: Property, Power, and the Transformation of the Creek Indians, 1733–1816* (New York: Cambridge University Press, 1999); Andrew Denson, *Demanding the Cherokee Nation: Indian Autonomy and American Culture, 1830–1900* (Lincoln: University of Nebraska Press, 2004), ch. 1.

46. Gregory D. Smithers, *The Cherokee Diaspora: An Indigenous History of Migration, Resettlement, and Identity* (New Haven, CT: Yale University Press, 2015), 44.

47. Charles C. Trowbridge, "Cherokee," box 7, folder 16, 7/6/1852, John Gilmary Shea Papers, Special Collections Library, Georgetown University.

48. Gregory D. Smithers, "Cherokee 'Two-Spirits': Gender, Ritual, and Spirituality in the Native South, 1770s–1840s," *Early American Studies* 12, no. 3 (Fall 2014): 627–28.

49. Theda Purdue, *Cherokee Women: Gender and Culture Change, 1700–1835* (Lincoln: University of Nebraska Press, 1998), 147, 178, 188–94. On orphans, see Julie L. Reed, *Serving the Nation: Cherokee Sovereignty and Social Welfare, 1800–1907* (Norman: University of Oklahoma Press, 2016).

50. Gregory D. Smithers, *Native Southerners: Indigenous History from Origins to Removal* (Norman: University of Oklahoma Press, 2019), 130–31.

51. Anita Hemmilä, "Ancestors of Two-Spirits: Historical Depictions of Native North American Gender-Crossing Women Through Critical Discourse Analysis," *Journal of Lesbian Studies* 20, nos. 2–3 (2016): 408–26.

52. Pierre Francois Xavier de Charlevoix, *Journal of a Voyage to North-America*, 2 vols. (London: R. and J. Dodsley, 1761), 2:74, 79–81.

53. Hiram Martin Chittenden and Alfred Talbot Richardson, eds., *Life, Letters and Travels of Father Pierre-Jean De Smet, S.J., 1801–1878*, 4 vols. (New York: Francis P. Harper, 1905), 3:1017; Albert Antrei, "Father Pierre Jean DeSmet," *Montana: The Magazine of Western History* 13, no. 2 (Spring 1963): 24–42; George Bishop, *Black Robe and Tomahawk: The Life and Travels of Father Pierre-Jean de Smet, SJ (1801–1873)* (Herefordshire: Gracewing, 2003), 92, 127.

54. C. C. Royce, *John Bidwell: Pioneer, Statesman, Philanthropist* (Chico, CA: n.p., 1906), 18; Frank McLynn, *Wagons West: The Epic Story of America's Overland Trails* (New York: Grove Press, 2002), 58.

55. George E. Tinker, *Missionary Conquest: The Gospel and Native American Cultural Genocide* (Minneapolis: Fortress Press, 1993).

56. Pierre Jean De Smet, Letter Book, box 4, folder 4, Pierre Jean De Smet Papers, Washington State University Libraries, Manuscripts, Archives, and Special Collections, Pullman, WA; Hemmilä, "Ancestors of Two-Spirits," 418–20.

57. *Marie Quilax a la bataille contre Les Corbeaux*, series 5, box 7, folder 37, Pierre Jean De Smet Papers.

58. Quoted in Hartley Burr Alexander, *The Mythology of All Races*, 13 vols. (Boston: Marshall Jones Company, 1916), 10: 309; Hemmilä, "Ancestors of Two-Spirits," 417.

59. C. Richard King, "De/Scribing Squ*w: Indigenous Women and Imperial Idioms in the United States," *American Indian Culture and Research Journal* 27, no. 2 (2003): 1–16.

CHAPTER 6: RESILIENCE

1. Curtis Harris-Davia, interview with author, Dec. 5, 2018.

2. Raven Heavy Runner, interview with author. Oct. 17, 2019.

3. Gregory Evans Dowd, *A Spirited Resistance: The North American Indian Struggle for Unity, 1745–1815* (Baltimore: Johns Hopkins University Press, 2008), 45, 115, 191; Michael Witgen, *An Infinity of Nations: How the Native New World Shaped Early North America* (Philadelphia: University of Pennsylvania Press, 2012), 115, 219.

4. John Tanner, *The Falcon: A Narrative of the Captivity and Adventures of John Tanner* (1830; repr., New York: Penguin, 1994).

5. Colin Calloway, *The American Revolution in Indian Country: Crisis and Diversity in Native American Communities* (New York: Cambridge University Press, 1995), 44, 201, 288–89; Natalie R. Inman, *Brothers and Friends: Kinship in Early America* (Athens: University of Georgia Press, 2017), 47.

6. Stanislaus M. Hamilton, ed., *The Writings of James Monroe, 1778–1794*, 7 vols. (New York: Putnam, 1898–1903), 1:lvi; William Knox, *Three Tracts Respecting the Conversion and Instruction of the Free Indians and Negroe Slaves in the Colonies*, 2 vols. (London: J. Debrett, 1789), 2:8–10.

7. Charles H. Arnold, *The New and Impartial Universal History of North and South America* (London: Alex Hogg, 1781), 81; *The Narrative of the Honorable John Byron, Written by Himself* (Wigan, UK: Printed by W. Bancks, 1784), 68; Jonathan Carver, *Three Years Travels Through the Interior Parts of North-America* (Philadelphia: Key & Simpson, 1796), 58.

8. Claudio Saunt, *Unworthy Republic: The Dispossession of Native Americans and the Road to Indian Territory* (New York: W. W. Norton, 2020); Tai S. Edwards and Paul Kelton, "Germs, Genocides, and America's Indigenous Peoples," *Journal of American History* 107, no. 1 (June 2020): 52–76.

9. George C. Tanner, *William Tanner of North Kingstown, Rhode Island, and His Descendants* (Faribault, MN: Published by the Author, 1905), 6–8; John Fierst, "Return to 'Civilization': John Tanner's Troubled Years at Sault Ste. Marie," *Minnesota History Magazine* 50, no. 1 (1986): 23–36; Laura Peers, *The Ojibwa of Western Canada, 1780–1870* (Winnipeg: University of Manitoba Press, 1994), 31–44.

10. Anton Treuer, *The Assassination of Hole in the Day* (St. Paul: Borealis Books, 2011), 25–29; Rebecca Kugel, *To Be the Main Leaders of Our People: A History of Minnesota Ojibwe Politics, 1825–1898* (East Lansing: Michigan State University Press, 1998), 71–73.

11. Harlan Pruden and Se-ah-dom Edmo, *Two-Spirit People: Sex, Gender & Sexuality in Historic and Contemporary Native America*, National Council of American Indians, http://www.ncai.org/policy-research-center/initiatives/Pruden -Edmo_TwoSpiritPeople.pdf.

12. Thomas L. McKenney, *Sketches of a Tour to the Lakes, of the Character and Customs of the Chippeway Indians, and of Incidents Connected with the Treaty of Fond du Lac* (Baltimore: Fielding Lucas Jr., 1827), 315–16.

13. Henry Rowe Schoolcraft, *Narrative of an Expedition Through the Upper Mississippi to Ithaca Lake* (New York: Harper & Brothers, 1834), 21.

14. Anton Treuer, *Ojibwe in Minnesota* (St. Paul: Minnesota Historical Society Press, 2010), 3.

15. Marriage traditions varied across Indian Country. In tribal communities throughout North America, male-bodied people who identified as women could, and did, marry female-bodied people who identified as women. The choice of sexual partners did not automatically correlate with gender identity. See, for example, "The Unpublished Journal of William H. Gray from December 1836 to October 1837," *Whitman College Quarterly* 26 (June 1913): 46–47.

16. Chris Dixon, *Perfecting the Family: Antislavery Marriages in Nineteenth-Century America* (Amherst: University of Massachusetts Press, 1997), 90; Jay Gitlin, *The Bourgeois Frontier: French Towns, French Traders and American Expansion* (New Haven, CT: Yale University Press, 2010), 10, 70, 76.

17. The name Saulteaux likely derives from the French word *saulters*, meaning "people of the rapids."

18. John Franklin, *Narrative of a Journey to the Shores of the Polar Sea, in the Years 1819, 20, 21, and 22* (London: John Murray, 1823), 151–52; William H. Keating, *Narrative of an Expedition to the Source of St. Peter's River*, 2 vols. (London: George B. Whittaker, 1825), 1:216.

19. Jonathan N. Katz, ed., *Gay American History: Lesbian and Gay Men in the USA: A Documentary History* (New York: Meridian, 1992), 299.

20. Isaac McCoy, *History of Baptist Indian Missions* (Washington, DC: William M. Morrison, 1840), 360–61

21. Judy Grahn, "Strange Country This: Lesbianism and North American Indian Tribes," *Journal of Homosexuality* 12, nos. 3–4 (May 1986): 43–57.

22. The rendering of *baté* has changed over time and includes *boté* and *bade*. Hiram Martin Chittenden and Alfred Talbot Richardson, eds., *Life, Letters and Travels of Father Pierre-Jean De Smet, S.J., 1801–1878*, 4 vols. (New York: Francis P. Harper, 1905), 3:1018; Reginald and Gladys Laubin, *Indian Dances of North America: Their Importance to Indian Life* (Norman: University of Oklahoma Press, 1989), 366–68; Claire R. Farrer, "A 'Berdache' by Any Other Name . . . Is a Brother, Friend, Lover, Spouse: Reflections on a Mescalero Apache Singer of Ceremonies," in *Two-Spirit People: Native American Gender Identity, Sexuality, and Spirituality*, eds. Sue-Ellen Jacobs, Wesley Thomas, and Sabine Lang (Urbana: University of Illinois Press, 1997), 236–51; Elizabeth Prine, "Searching for Third Genders: Towards a Prehistory of Domestic Space in Middle Missouri Villages," in *Archaeologies of Sexuality*, ed. Robert A. Schmidt and Barbara L. Voss (New York: Routledge, 2000), 197–219; Sabine Lang, *Men as Women, Women as Men: Changing Gender in Native American Culture* (Austin: University of Texas Press, 1998), 68–74, 103, 203, 224, 341.

23. Kai Pyle, "Naming and Claiming: Recovering Ojibwe and Plains Cree Two-Spirit Language," *Transgender Studies Quarterly* 5, no. 4 (2018): 574–88; Jane Scudeler, "'The Song I Am Singing': Gregory Scofield's Interweavings of Metis, Gay and Jewish Selfhoods," *Studies in Canadian Literature/Études En littérature Canadienne* 31, no. 1 (2006): 129–45.

24. Lang, *Men as Women, Women as Men*, 222–26.

25. Frederica de Laguna, "Tlingit Ideas about the Individual," *Journal of Anthropological Research* 10, no. 2 (Summer 1954): 172–91; Sabine Lang, "Lesbians, Men-Women and Two-Spirits: Homosexuality and Gender in Native American Cultures," in *Female Desires: Same-Sex Relations and Transgender Practices Across Cultures*, ed. Evelyn Blackwood and Saskia E. Wieringa (New York: Columbia University Press, 1999), 91–116.

26. Elliott Coues, ed., *New Light on the Early History of the Greater Northwest: The Manuscript Journals of Alexander Henry and of David Thompson, 1799–1814*, 3 vols. (Cambridge: Cambridge University Press, 2015), 1:260–65;

Walter L. Williams, *The Spirit and the Flesh: Sexual Diversity in American Indian Culture* (Boston: Beacon Press, 1986), 66–70.

27. Treuer, *The Assassination of Hole in the Day*, 27.

28. John T. Irving Jr., *Indian Sketches, Taken During an Expedition to the Pawnee and Other Tribes of American Indians*, 2 vols. (London: John Murray, 1833), 1: ch. 3 ("The Metamorphosis"); Edward Thompson Denig, *Of the Crow Nation*, Anthropological Papers No. 33 (Washington, DC: Smithsonian Institution, Bureau of American Ethnology, 1953), 64–68.

29. Øystein Gullvåg Holte, "A Theory of Gendercide," *Journal of Genocide Research* 4, no. 1 (2002): 11–38; Deborah A. Miranda, "Extermination of the Joyas: Gendercide in Spanish California," *GLQ: A Journal of Lesbian and Gay Studies* 16, nos. 1–2 (Apr. 2010): 253–84.

30. For other cross-cultural examples, see Sharyn G. Davies, *Challenging Gender Norms: Five Genders Among Bugis in Indonesia* (Belmont, CA: Thomson Wadsworth, 2007); Anuja Agrawa, "Gendered Bodies: The Case of the 'Third Gender' in India," *Contributions to Indian Sociology* 31, no. 2 (1997): 273–97; Deborah A. Elliston, "Negotiating Transnational Sexual Economies: Female Māhū and Same-Sex Sexuality in 'Tahiti and Her Islands,'" in Blackwood and Wieringa, *Female Desires*, 232–52.

31. Gerald Vizenor, *The People Named Chippewa: Narrative Histories* (Minneapolis: University of Minnesota Press, 2002), 32–34; William W. Warren, *History of the Ojibway People*, 2nd ed. (St. Paul: Minnesota Historical Society Press, 2009).

32. Roger L. Nichols, *Indians in the United States and Canada: A Comparative History* (Lincoln: University of Nebraska Press, 1998), 9, 38, 91, 116, 149; Peter Iverson, *Diné: A History of the Navajo* (Albuquerque: University of New Mexico Press, 2002), 51–57.

33. Margaret Connell Szasz, *Indian Education in the American Colonies, 1607–1783* (Lincoln: University of Nebraska Press, 1988); Francis Paul Prucha, ed., *Documents of United States Indian Policy*, 3rd ed. (Lincoln: University of Nebraska Press, 2000), 33, 128.

34. David Wallace Adams, *Education for Extinction: American Indians and the Boarding School Experience, 1875–1928* (Lawrence: University of Kansas Press, 1995), 121, 161.

35. Ronald Niezen, *Spirit Wars: Native North American Religions in the Age of Nation Building* (Berkeley: University of California Press, 2000), 46.

36. Raven Heavy Runner interview.

37. The following analysis draws on James W. Schultz, *Running Eagle: The Warrior Girl* (Boston: Houghton Mifflin, 1919); John C. Ewers, "The Blackfoot War Lodge: Its Construction and Use," *American Anthropologist* 46, no. 2 (Apr.–June 1944): 182–92; James W. Schultz, *Blackfeet and Buffalo: Memories of Life Among the Indians* (Norman: University of Oklahoma Press, 1962).

38. Schultz, *Blackfeet and Buffalo*, 348.

39. Karina L. Walters, Selina A. Mohammed, Teresa Evans-Campbell, Ramona E. Beltrain, David H. Chae, and Bonnie Duran, "Bodies Don't Just Tell Stories, They Tell Histories," *Du Bois Review: Social Science Research on Race* 8, no. 1 (2011): 179–89.

40. Gerald Vizenor, "Aesthetics of Survivance," in *Survivance: Narratives of Native Presence*, ed. Gerald Vizenor (Lincoln: University of Nebraska Press, 2008), 1–24.

41. Carlos A. Schwantes, *In Mountain Shadows: A History of Idaho* (Lincoln: University of Nebraska Press, 1991), 23.

42. Meriwether Lewis and William Clark, *Journals of the Lewis and Clark Expedition*, is available online and is searchable: https://lewisandclarkjournals .unl.edu.

43. Thomas P. Slaughter, *Exploring Lewis and Clark: Reflections on Men and Wilderness* (New York: Vintage Books, 2003), 169.

44. Thomas P. Lowry, *Venereal Disease and the Lewis and Clark Expedition* (Lincoln: University of Nebraska Press, 2004); Gray H. Whaley, "'Complete Liberty'? Gender, Sexuality, Race, and Social Change on the Lower Columbia River, 1805–1838," *Ethnohistory* 54, no. 4 (Fall 2007): 669–95.

45. Sarah Burns and John Davis, *American Art to 1900: A Documentary History* (Berkeley: University of California Press, 2009), 439.

46. John James Audubon quoted in Benita Eisler, *The Red Man's Bones: George Catlin, Artist and Showman* (New York: W. W. Norton, 2013), 170.

47. Russell David Edmunds, "The Prairie Potawatomi Removal of 1833," *Indiana Magazine of History* 68, no 3 (Sept. 1972): 240–53; William T. Hagan, *The Sac and Fox Indians* (Norman: University of Oklahoma Press, 1958), 5–12, 102; Michael D. Green, "'We Dance in Opposite Directions': Mesquakie (Fox) Separatism from the Sac and Fox Tribe," *Ethnohistory* 30, no. 3 (Summer 1983): 129–40; Russell David Edmunds and Joseph L. Peyser, *The Fox Wars: The Mesquakie Challenge to New France* (Norman: University of Oklahoma Press, 1993), ch. 6.

48. George Catlin, *Letters and Notes on the Manners, Customs and Conditions of the North American Indians*, 2 vols. (New York: Wiley and Putnam, 1841), 2:214–15.

49. Paula Gunn Allen, *The Sacred Hoop: Recovering the Feminine in American Indian Traditions* (Boston: Beacon Press, 1986), 199–200.

50. Linda Tuhiwai Smith, *Decolonizing Methodologies: Research and Indigenous Peoples*, 2nd ed. (London: Zed Books, 2012), 70.

51. This fieldwork led to the anthropological distinction between *emic* (fieldwork conducted from within a culture) and *etic* analysis (nonparticipatory observations). See Alan Dundes, "From Etic to Emic Units in the Structural Study of Folktales," *Journal of American Folklore* 75 (1962): 95–105; Marvin Harris, "History and Significance of the Emic/Etic Distinction," *Annual Review of Anthropology* 5 (1976): 329–50.

52. Edward B. Tylor, *Primitive Culture: Researches into the Development of Mythology, Philosophy, Religion, Art, and Custom*, 2 vols., (London: John Murray, 1920), 1:26; Bronislaw Malinowski, *Crime and Custom in Savage Society* (1926; repr., New Brunswick, NJ: Transaction, 2013), 14, 78; Franz Boas, *Anthropology and Modern Life* (New York: W. W. Norton, 1928), chapters 7 and 9; A. R. Radcliffe-Brown, *The Andaman Islanders* (Cambridge: Cambridge University Press, 1933), 407–8.

53. Nelson A. Miles, "The Indian Problem," *North American Review* 128, no. 268 (March 1879): 306. On how the "doomed race" theory influenced early

museum collections in the United States, see Shephard Krech III, "Introduction," *Collecting Native America, 1870-1960*, ed. Shephard Krech III (Washington, DC: Smithsonian Books, 1999), 11.

54. Jacob W. Gruber, "Ethnographic Salvage and the Shaping of Anthropology," *American Anthropologist* 72, no. 6 (December 1970): 1295. See also Robert E. Bieder, "The Representations of Indian Bodies in Nineteenth-Century Anthropology," *American Indian Quarterly* 20, no. 2 (Spring 1996): 165–79.

55. Adam Kuper, *The Invention of Primitive Society: Transformations of an Illusion* (London: Routledge, 1997), 1–7. During the late nineteenth and early twentieth centuries, the work of military doctors among Native Americans was superseded by a growing body of scholarship by physical anthropologists. Scholars such as Earnest Hooten and Aleš Hrdlička used physical anthropology to reinforce popular beliefs about racial hierarchies (many of them linked to eugenics) and white supremacy. See Robert Wald Sussman, *The Myth of Race: The Troubling Persistence of an Unscientific Idea* (Cambridge, MA: Harvard University Press, 2014).

56. *Duflot de Mofras' Travels on the Pacific Coast*, 2 vols., trans. and ed. Marguerite E. Wilbur (Santa Ana, CA: Fine Arts Press, 1937), 2:192.

57. Mark Baldwin to Capt. H.L. Scott, Apr. 20, 1897, box 46, Lenox Scott Papers; on "Apaches," see Caleb Henry Carlton Papers, 1831–1954, box 5, MSS 15073, Manuscripts Division, Library of Congress, Washington, DC; Hugh Lenox Scott to the Commissioner of Indian Affairs, Mar. 12, 1894, box 46, Hugh Lenox Scott Papers, 1582–1981, MSSS39297, Manuscripts Division, Library of Congress, Washington, DC; Smith, *Decolonizing Methodologies*, 8; Paul Conrad, *The Apache Diaspora: Four Centuries of Displacement and Survival* (Philadelphia: University of Pennsylvania Press, 2021), 109–10. For a typical example of anthropological analysis among the Suquamish during these decades, see Hermann Haeberlin and Erna Gunther, "The Indians of Puget Sound," *University of Washington Publications in Anthropology* 4, no. 1 (September 1930): 1–84.

58. George Gibbs, *A Dictionary of the Chinook Jargon, Or Trade Language of Oregon* (New York: Cramoisy Press, 1863), 2.

59. Alexander Henry, *The Manuscript Journals of Alexander Henry*, ed. Elliott Coues, 3 vols. (New York: Francis P. Harper, 1897), 1:97, 164–65.

60. The following account is drawn from William A. Hammond, "The Disease of the Scythians (Morbus Feminarum) and Certain Analogous Conditions," *American Journal of Neurology and Psychiatry* 1 (Aug. 1882): 339–55.

61. To this list of "Others" white Anglo-Saxon and Protestant Americans added Mormons. Patrick Q. Mason, *The Mormon Menace: Violence and Anti-Mormonism in the Postbellum South* (New York: Oxford University Press, 2011); Ellen Wayland-Smith, *Oneida: From Free Love Utopia to the Well-Set Table* (New York: Picador, 2016).

CHAPTER 7: PLACE

1. Lopez quoted in Katherine Davis-Young, "For Many Native Americans, Embracing LGBT Members Is a Return to the Past," *Washington Post*, Mar. 29, 2019.

2. J. Miko Thomas, interview with author, July 13, 2018.

3. *Indianapolis Journal,* Apr. 4, 1886, 12; *News and Citizen,* May 13, 1886, 1; *National Tribune,* May 20, 1886, 2.

4. *Kansas City Star,* Apr. 14, 1886, 2; *National Tribune,* May 20, 1886, 2.

5. *National Tribune,* May 20, 1886, 2.

6. *St. Paul Daily Globe,* Apr. 19, 1886, 5. The best and most complete biography of WeWha remains Will Roscoe's *The Zuni Man-Woman* (Albuquerque: University of New Mexico Press, 1991).

7. T. J. Ferguson, *Historic Zuni Architecture and Society: An Archaeological Application of Pace Syntax* (Tucson: University of Arizona Press, 1996), 28–33; Marsha Weisiger, *Dreaming of Sheep in Navajo Country* (Seattle: University of Washington Press, 2009).

8. David F. Greenberg, "Why Was the Berdache Ridiculed?," *Journal of Homosexuality* 11, nos. 3–4 (Summer 1985): 180.

9. Roscoe, *The Zuni Man-Woman,* 18–19.

10. I. Goldman, "The Zuni Indians of New Mexico," in *Cooperation and Competition Among Primitive Peoples,* ed. Margaret Mead, McGraw-Hill Publications in Sociology (New York: McGraw-Hill, 1937), 313–53; Linda K. Watts, "Zuni Family Ties and Household-Group Values: A Revisionist Cultural Model of Zuni Social Organization," *Journal of Anthropological Research* 53, no. 1 (Spring 1997): 17–29.

11. Charles H. Hewitt, "The Kachina Cult of the Pueblo Indians," *KIVA: Journal of Southwestern Anthropology and History* 9, no. 1 (Nov. 1943): 2–6; Roscoe, *The Zuni Man-Woman,* 16–19; Barbara Tedlock, "Zuni Sacred Theater," *American Indian Quarterly* 7, no. 3 (Summer 1983): 93–110; Will Roscoe, "The Semiotics of Gender on Zuni Kachinas," *KIVA: Journal of Southwestern Anthropology and History* 55, no. 1 (1989): 49–70.

12. Roscoe, *The Zuni Man-Woman,* 10–21; *Finding the Center: The Art of the Zuni Storyteller,* trans. Dennis Tedlock, 2nd ed. (Lincoln: University of Nebraska Press, 1999), 26, 213, 283.

13. Mathilda Coxe Stevenson, "The Zuñi Indians: Their Mythology, Esoteric Societies, and Ceremonies," *Annual Report of the Bureau of American Ethnology, Smithsonian Institution* 23 (1904): 1–634, esp. 37; Elsie Clews Parsons, "The Zuñi Ła'mana," *American Anthropologist* 18, no. 4 (Oct.–Dec. 1916): 521–28.

14. Stevenson, "The Zuñi Indians," 22.

15. Willard W. Hill, "Note on the Pima Berdache," *American Anthropologist* 40, no. 2 (Apr.–June 1938): 339.

16. Edwin Thompson Denig, *Five Indian Tribes of the Upper Missouri,* ed. John Ewers (Norman: University of Oklahoma Press, 1961), 195–201; John Ewers, "Deadlier than the Male," *American Heritage* 16 (June 1965): 10–13; Rudolph J. Kurz, *Journal of Rudolph Friedrich Kurz: An Account of His Experiences among Fur Traders and American Indians on the Mississippi and Missouri Rivers during the Years 1846–1852* (Lincoln: University of Nebraska Press, 1970); Benjamin Capps, *Woman Chief* (Garden City, NJ: Doubleday, 1979)

17. Robert H. Lowie, "Notes on Shoshonean Ethnography," *Anthropological Papers, American Museum of Natural History* 20, no. 3 (1924): 185–324. The tuwasawits referred to in this passage invited social discord when they made unwanted sexual advances toward a boy whom she'd cooked for. See 282–83.

18. Franz Boas, "Kinship Terms of the Kutenai Indians," *American Anthropologist* 21, no. 1 (Jan.–Mar. 1919): 98–101; Claude E. Schaeffer, "Early Christian Mission of the Kutenai Indians," *Oregon Historical Quarterly* 71, no. 4 (Dec. 1970): 325–48; Robert H. Ruby and John Arthur Brown, *Indians of the Pacific Northwest: A History* (Norman: University of Oklahoma Press, 1988), 68–9; Robert M. Utley, *A Life Wild and Perilous: Mountain Men and the Paths to the Pacific* (New York: Henry Holt, 1997), 73, 77, 165–68, 186.

19. Harry H. Turney-High, *Ethnography of the Kutenai* (1941; repr., Fairfield, WA: Ye Galleon Press, 1998); Michael P. Malone, Richard B. Roeder, William L. Lang, *Montana: A History of Two Centuries*, rev. ed. (Seattle: University of Washington Press, 1991), 15; Robert J. Muckle, *The First Nations of British Columbia: An Anthropological Survey*, 2nd ed. (Vancouver: UBC Press, 2007), 7, 36–37, 126; James W. Daschuk, *Clearing the Plains: Disease, Politics of Starvation, and the Loss of Aboriginal Life* (Regina: University of Regina Press, 2013), 23–24.

20. Leslie Spier, *The Prophet Dance of the Northwest and Its Derivatives: The Source of the Ghost Dance* (Menasha, WI: George Banta Publishing Company, 1935), 26–27; Claude E. Schaeffer, "The Kutenai Female Berdache," *Ethnohistory* 12, no. 3 (1965): 193–236; Sabine Lang, *Men as Women, Women as Men: Changing Gender in Native American Cultures* (Austin: University of Texas Press, 1998), 159.

21. O. B. Sperlin, "Two Kootenay Women Masquerading as Men? Or Were They One?" *Washington Historical Quarterly* 26 (1913): 120–30; Will Roscoe, "Sexual and Gender Diversity in Native America and the Pacific Islands," in *Identities and Place: Changing Labels and Intersectional Communities of LGBTQ and Two-Spirit People in the United States*, ed. Katherine Crawford-Lackey and Megan E. Springate (New York: Berghahn Books, 2020), 58–88. It's important to also note that Kutenai-speaking people filtered their oral histories through the trauma of disease, which in the early 1900s ravaged Indigenous communities across southeastern British Columbia, Montana, and Idaho. See Larry Cebula, *Plateau Indians and the Quest for Spiritual Power, 1700–1850* (Lincoln: University of Nebraska Press, 2003), 37.

22. Schaeffer, "The Kutenai Female Berdache," 195.

23. Christian missionaries struggled to gain a foothold among the Lower Kutenai, making their impact on Kutenai gender identities questionable. See, for example, *They Call Me Father: Memoirs of Father Nicolas Coccola*, ed. Margaret Whitehead (Vancouver: University of British Columbia Press, 1988), 24.

24. J. Neilson Barry, "Ko-Come-Ne Pe-Ca, the Letter Carrier," *Washington Historical Quarterly* 20, no. 3 (July 1929): 201–3; Alexander Ross, *Adventures of the First Settlers on the Oregon or Columbia River* (London: Smith, Elder and Co., 1849), 85; Sylvia Van Kirk, *Many Tender Ties: Women in Fur-Trade Society, 1670–1870* (Norman: University of Oklahoma Press, 1983), 78; James P. Ronda, *Astoria and Empire* (Lincoln: University of Nebraska Press, 1984), 231.

25. David Thompson, "Narrative of His Explorations in Western America, 1784–1812," boxes 1 and 2, David Thompson Papers, MS COLL 00021, Thomas Fisher Rare Book Library, University of Toronto.

26. Schaeffer, "The Kutenai Female Berdache," 199.

27. Laura Peers, "Trade and Change on the Columbia Plateau, 1750–1840," *Columbia Magazine* 10, no. 4 (Winter 1996–97): 6–12.

28. Lee Irwin, *Coming Down from Above: Prophecy, Resistance, and Renewal in Native American Religions* (Norman: University of Oklahoma Press, 2008), 241–42.

29. "The Unpublished Journal of William H. Gray from December 1836 to October 1837," *Whitman College Quarterly* 26 (June 1913): 46–47.

30. Jeffrey Ostler, "Empire and Liberty: Contradictions and Conflicts in Nineteenth-Century Western Political History," in *A Companion to the American West*, ed. William Deverell (Malden, MA: Blackwell Publishing, 2004), 200–20.

31. Glenda Riley, "Apache Chief Victorio: Seeker of Peace and Master Strategist," in *Chiefs and Generals: Nine Men Who Shaped the American West*, ed. Richard W. Etulain and Glenda Riley (Golden, CO: Fulcrum, 2004), 36.

32. Hill, "Note on the Pima Berdache," 338–40.

33. H. Henrietta Stockel, *Chricahua Apache Women and Children: Safekeepers of the Heritage* (College Station: Texas A&M University Press, 2000), 69–70.

34. Bobbalee Ann Shuler, "More Sin Than Pleasure: A Study of Culture Conflict," PhD diss., University of Wyoming, 1994, 71, 74, 85; Sherry Robinson, *Apache Voices: Their Stories of Survival as Told to Eve Ball* (Albuquerque: University of New Mexico Press, 2003), 1–5.

35. Stockel, *Chricahua Apache Women and Children*, 71.

36. Gerald Vizenor, "Aesthetics of Survivance," in *Survivance: Narratives of Native Persistence*, ed. Gerald Vizenor (Lincoln: University of Nebraska Press, 2008), 19.

37. David H. Thomas, *Exploring Ancient Native America: An Archaeological Guide* (New York: Routledge, 1999), 96; David E. Stuart, *Anasazi America: Seventeen Centuries on the Road from Center Place*, 2nd ed. (Albuquerque: University of New Mexico Press, 2014), ch. 2.

38. Brian Fagan, *The Great Warming: Climate Change and the Rise and Fall of Civilizations* (New York: Bloomsbury Press, 2010); David Roberts, *The Pueblo Revolt: The Secret Rebellion That Drove the Spaniards Out of the Southwest* (New York: Simon & Schuster, 2004).

39. Nancy Y. Davis, *The Zuni Enigma* (New York: W. W. Norton, 2000), 48; Arthur W. Vokes and David A. Gregory, "Exchange Networks for Exotic Goods in the Southwest and Zuni's Place in Them," in *Zuni Origins: Toward a New Synthesis of Southwestern Archaeology*, ed. David A. Gregory and David R. Wilcox (Tucson: University of Arizona Press, 2007), 318–58; Natale A. Zappia, *Traders and Raiders: The Indigenous World of the Colorado Basin, 1540–1859* (Chapel Hill: University of North Carolina Press, 2014), 18, 35–45, 48; Samantha G. Fladd et al., "To and From Hopi: Negotiating Identity Through Migration, Coalescence, and Closure at the Homol'ovi Settlement Cluster," in *The Continuous Path: Pueblo Movement and the Archaeology of Becoming*, ed. Samuel Duwe and Robert W. Preucel (Tucson: University of Arizona Press, 2019), 124–48.

40. Alfred L. Kroeber, "Thoughts on Zuni Religion," in *Holmes Anniversary Volume: Anthropological Essays Presented to William Henry Holmes in Honor of His Seventieth Birthday, December 1, 1916*, ed. F. W. Hodge (Washington,

DC: J. W. Bryan, 1916), 269–77; A. L. Kroeber, *Zuñi Kin and Clan, Anthropological Papers of the American Museum of Natural History*, vol. 18, pt. 2 (New York: American Museum of Natural History, 1917), 100, 138–39; Ruth L. Bunzel, *Zuni Ceremonialism* (Albuquerque: University of New Mexico Press, 1932); Roscoe, *The Zuni Man-Woman*, 17.

41. Margaret D. Jacobs, *Engendered Encounters: Feminism and Pueblo Cultures, 1879–1934* (Lincoln: University of Nebraska Press, 1999), 31; Virgil Wyaco, *A Zuni Life: A Pueblo Indian in Two Worlds* (Albuquerque: University of New Mexico Press, 1998), 141; Eliza McFeely, *Zuni and the American Imagination* (New York: Hill and Wang, 2001), 1–6.

42. Roscoe, *The Zuni Man-Woman*, 32–33, 132; David L. Shaul, *A Prehistory of Western North America: The Impact of Uto-Aztecan Languages* (Albuquerque: University of New Mexico, 2014), 117.

43. Roscoe, *The Zuni Man-Woman*, 38, 132–34.

44. Similarities in ceremonial traditions can be found from the Southwest to California, especially in the narrative interplay between creator characters and the dead. See Linda Heidenreich, *This Land Was Mexican Once: Histories of Resistance from Northern California* (Austin: University of Texas Press, 2007), 27.

45. Roscoe, *The Zuni Man-Woman*, 147–58; Walter L. Williams, *The Spirit and the Flesh: Sexual Diversity in American Indian Culture* (Boston: Beacon Press, 1986), 18.

46. David G. Saile, "Many Dwellings: Views of a Pueblo World," in *Dwelling, Place and Environment: Towards a Phenomenology of Person and World*, ed. David Seamon and Robert Mugerauer (Malabar, FL: Krieger, 2000), 159–81.

47. M. Jane Young, "'Images of Power and the Power of Images': The Significance of Rock Art for Contemporary Zunis," *Journal of American Folklore* 98, no. 387 (Jan.–Mar. 1985): 3–48.

48. M. J. Young, *Signs from the Ancestors* (Albuquerque: University of New Mexico Press, 1988), 152.

49. This chronology highlights the unique developments in style and motifs used in rock art among Zunis and other communities of the Anasazi region between 900 and 1300 CE. See Sally C. Cole, "Katsina Iconography in Homol'ovi Rock Art," *Kiva* 54, no. 3 (1989): 313–29; Sally J. Cole, "Roots of Anasazi and Pueblo Imagery in Basketmaker II Rock Art and Material Culture," *Kiva* 60, no. 2 (1994): 289–311; Polly Schaafsma and M. Jane Young, "Rock Art of the Zuni Region: Cultural-Historical Implications," in Gregory and Wilcox, *Zuni Origins*, 247–69.

50. Sandra E. Hollimon, "Sex, Gender and Health Among the Chumash: An Archaeological Examination of Prehistoric Gender Roles," *Proceedings of the Society for California Archaeology* 9 (1996): 205–8.

51. Elizabeth P. Prine, "Searching for Third Genders: Towards a Prehistory of Domestic Spaces in Middle Missouri Villages," in *Archaeologies of Sexuality*, ed. Robert A. Schmidt and Barbara L. Voss (New York: Routledge, 2000), 197–219; Sandra E. Hollimon, "The Archaeology of Nonbinary Genders in Native North American Societies," in *Handbook of Gender in Archaeology*, ed. Sarah M. Nelson (Lanham, MD: AltaMira Press, 2006), 443.

52. T. J. Ferguson and Barbara J. Mills, "Settlement and Growth of Zuni Pueblo: An Architectural History," *Kiva* 52, no. 4 (Summer 1987): 243–66.

53. McFeely, *Zuni and the American Imagination*, 7.

54. Frederick Webb Hodge, ed., *Handbook of American Indians North of Mexico*, 2 parts (Washington, DC: Government Printing Office, 1910), 2:1017.

55. Mary DeSette, "Report from the Classroom," *Ramona Days* 1, no 2 (1887): 25.

56. On "war against bestiality," see Mary DeSette to Miss Willard, Mar. 3, 1924, reel 40, collection 1523, Indian Rights Association Records, ca. 1830–1986, Historical Society of Pennsylvania; on "the beloved *lhamana*," see Wyaco, *A Zuni Life*, 141.

57. Matilda Coxe Stevenson, *The Zuni Indians: Their Mythology, Esoteric Fraternities, and Ceremonies* (Washington, DC: Government Printing Office, 1904), 20, 310; Roscoe, *The Zuni Man-Woman*, 47.

58. Roscoe, *The Zuni Man-Woman*, 53–55; Darlis A. Miller, *Matilda Coxe Stevenson: Pioneering Anthropologist* (Norman: University of Oklahoma Press, 2007), 80–81.

59. *Sunday Herald*, May 2, 1886, 1.

60. *Sunday Herald*, June 13, 1886, 4.

61. *News and Citizen*, May 13, 1886, 1; *Hocking Sentinel*, Feb. 9, 1888, 1; *Hocking Sentinel*, May 3, 1888, 1.

62. *Daily Gazette*, May 5, 1886, 3; *Morning News*, June 16, 1887, 4.

63. *New York Herald*, June 14, 1887, 3.

64. Stevenson, *The Zuni Indians*, 310, 311–12.

65. Sidney L. Harring, *Crow Dog's Case: American Indian Sovereignty, Tribal Law, and United States Law in the Nineteenth Century* (New York: Cambridge University Press, 1994), 140–42, 173, 175; David E. Wilkins, *American Indian Sovereignty and the U.S. Supreme Court: The Masking of Justice* (Austin: University of Texas Press, 1997), ch. 3.

66. Hugh L. Scott, "That Is My Road: General Hugh L. Scott and the Crow Berdache," MS 2932, National Anthropological Archives, Smithsonian Institution.

67. Herbert Welsh to Goodwin Elliot, Aug. 2, 1923, box 253; "Indian dances, Pueblo-Hopi: papers and documents urging their suppression," ca. 1915–ca. 1921, box 300, Indian Rights Association Records, ca. 1830–1986, Historical Society of Pennsylvania; Tisa Wenger, *We Have a Religion: The 1920s Pueblo Indian Dance Controversy and American Religious Freedom* (Chapel Hill: University of North Carolina Press, 2009).

CHAPTER 8: PATHS

1. Melvin Harrison, interview with author, Dec. 12, 2018.

2. Marlon "Marty" Fixico, interview with author, Mar. 13, 2019.

3. The following account draws on George Devereux, "Institutionalized Homosexuality of the Mohave Indians," *Human Biology* 9, no. 4 (Dec. 1937): 498–527; Will Roscoe, *Changing Ones: Third and Fourth Genders in Native North America* (New York: St. Martin's Press, 1998), 92–97; Walter Williams, *The Spirit and the Flesh: Sexual Diversity in American Indian Culture* (Boston: Beacon Press, 1986), 239–41.

4. H. Clay Trumbull, *Friendship the Master-Passion: Or the Nature and History of Friendship, and its Place as a Force in the World* (Philadelphia: John D. Wattles, 1894), 165 ("the warm friendship"); A. B. Holder, "The Bote: Description of a Peculiar Sexual Perversion Found Among North American Indians," *New York Medical Journal* 1 (1889): 623–25.

5. Williams, *The Spirit and the Flesh*, 19, 50–51; Sabine Lang, *Men as Women, Women as Men: Changing Gender in Native American Culture* (Austin: University of Texas Press, 1998), 117, 122, 149; Roscoe, *Changing Ones*, ch. 2.

6. Clark Wissler, "Societies and Ceremonial Associations in the Oglala Division of the Teton-Dakota," *Anthropological Papers of the American Museum of Natural History*, volume 11, ed. Clark Wissler (New York: American Museum of Natural History, 1916), 92.

7. David Amigoni, *Colonies, Cults and Evolution: Literature, Science and Culture in Nineteenth-Century Writing* (New York: Cambridge University Press, 2007), 11.

8. Linda Tuhiwai Smith, *Decolonizing Methodologies: Research and Indigenous Peoples*, 2nd ed. (London: Zed Books, 2012), 9, 23, 76; Arnold R. Pilling, "Cross-Dressing and Shamanism Among Selected Western North American Tribes," in *Two-Spirit People: Native American Gender Identity, Sexuality, and Spirituality*, ed. Sue-Ellen Jacobs, Wesley Thomas, and Sabine Lang (Urbana: University of Illinois Press, 1997), 69–99.

9. R. Landes, "A Cult Matriarche and Male Homosexuality," *Journal of Abnormal and Social Psychology* 35, no. 3 (1940): 386–97; Claude E. Schaeffer, "The Kutenai Female Berdache: Courier, Guide, Prophetess, and Warrior," *Ethnohistory* 12, no. 3 (Summer 1965): 193–236; James S. Thayer, "The Berdache of the Northern Plains: A Socioreligious Perspective," *Journal of Anthropological Research* 36, no. 3 (Autumn 1980): 287–93; Jay Miller, "People, Berdaches, and Left-Handed Bears: Human Variation in Native America," *Journal of Anthropological Research* 38, no. 3 (Autumn 1982): 274–87.

10. As late as 1969, Vine Deloria Jr. famously wrote that the anthropologist "ALREADY KNOWS" what he was going to find" during research trips to Indigenous communities. Deloria's polemic against anthropologists angered those in the field, some complaining that Deloria unfairly generalized about the methods and work of professional scholars. Vine Deloria Jr., *Custer Died for Your Sins: An Indian Manifesto* (1969; repr., Norman: University of Oklahoma Press, 1988), 80. For analysis, see David Martinez, *Life of the Indigenous Mind: Vine Deloria, Jr., and the Birth of the Red Power Movement* (Lincoln: University of Nebraska Press, 2019), 185–87.

11. Irvin Morris, *From the Glittering World: A Navajo Story* (Norman: University of Oklahoma Press, 1997), 7–10; Raymond F. Locke, *Sweet Salt: Discovering the Sacred World of the Navajo* (Santa Monica: Roundtable, 1989), 83–91.

12. Willard W. Hill, "The Status of the Hermaphrodite and Transvestite in Navaho Culture," *American Anthropologist* 37, no. 2 (Apr.–June 1935): 273–79; E. W. Gifford, "Culture Element Distributions 12: Apache-Pueblo," *Anthropological Records* 4, no. 1 (1940): 66. For the Hopi ho'va, see Ernest

Beaglehole and Pearl Beaglehole, "Hopi of the Second Mesa," *Memoirs of the American Anthropological Association* 44 (1935): 1–65.

13. Robert Silverberg, *Men Against Time: Salvage Archaeology in the United States* (New York: Macmillan, 1967); Don D. Fowler, *A Laboratory for Anthropology: Science and Romanticism in the American Southwest, 1846–1930* (Albuquerque: University of New Mexico, 2000), 28, 178, 190.

14. These assumptions echoed the observations and amateur ethnography of a previous generation of writers. See, for example, Robert Brown, *The Races of Mankind*, 4 vols. (London: Cassell, Petter, & Galpin, 1873), 1:149–56; *Reports of the Peabody Museum of American Archaeology and Ethnology, 1876–79* (Cambridge: Peabody Museum, 1880), 93–94; Stephen D. Peet, "Idols and Images," *American Antiquarian and Oriental Journal* 14, no. 4 (July 1892): 197–220.

15. Alfred L. Kroeber, *Handbook of the Indians of California* (New York: Dover, 1976), 594–601; Sarah A. Davis and Mary Hill, *The Mojave of the Colorado: The Story of the Mojave Indians of the Colorado River and Their Meetings with the Explorers of the Southwest* (Whitefish, MT: Literary Licensing, 2012); Lawrence R. Walker and Frederick H. Landau, *A Natural History of the Mojave Desert* (Tucson: University of Arizona Press, 2018), 180–92.

16. A. L. Kroeber, "Yuman Tribes of the Lower Colorado," *American Archaeology and Ethnology* 16, no. 8 (Aug. 1920): 475–85; Jack D. Forbes, *Native Americans of California and Nevada* (Happy Camp, CA: Naturegraph, 2003), 63; Frederic Hicks, "The Influence of Agriculture on Aboriginal Socio-Political Organization in the Lower Colorado River Valley," *Journal of California Archaeology* 1, no. 2 (Winter 1974): 133–44.

17. Nancy J. Davidson, "Making the Connections: An Archaeological Survey of Prehistoric Trails and Trail Markers Along the Lower Colorado River," master's thesis, California State University, Fullerton, 2009, 21.

18. University of California, Berkeley, anthropologist Alfred Kroeber played an influential role in shaping the tone of anthropological study among the Mohave people. See his "Preliminary Sketch of the Mohave," *American Anthropologist* 4, no. 2 (Apr.–June 1902): 276–85.

19. Atwood D. Gaines, "Ethnopsychiatry: The Cultural Construction of Psychiatries," in *Ethnopsychiatry: The Cultural Construction of Psychiatries*, ed. Atwood F. Gaines (Albany: SUNY Press, 1992), 3–24.

20. See, for instance, George Devereux et al., *Psychoanalysis and the Occult* (London: Souvenir Press, 1953).

21. George Devereux, "Ever Since the World Began: Berdache Myths and Tales," in *Living the Spirit: A Gay American Indian Anthology*, ed. Will Roscoe and Gay American Indians (New York: St. Martin's Press, 1988), 77.

22. Devereux, "Mohave Homosexuality," 501–3, 514, 516, 525. Devereux expands on the idea of sexual intercourse with ghosts in George Devereux, "Mohave Soul Concepts," *American Anthropologist* 39 (1937): 417–22. Mohave people reportedly associated people like Sahaykwisa with special powers of fertility and love. See Gilbert H. Herdt, *Same Sex, Different Cultures: Exploring Gay and Lesbian Lives* (Boulder, CO: Westview Press, 1997), 95–96; Indian Health Service, "Two Spirit," https://www.ihs.gov/lgbt/health/twospirit.

23. Devereux, "Mohave Homosexuality," 505, 516, 523, 525.

24. Sabine Lang, "Various Kinds of Two-Spirit People: Gender Variance and Homosexuality in Native American Communities" in Jacobs, Thomas, and Lang, *Two-Spirit People*, 100–118.

25. The term "homosexual" was first used in 1869, and the German physician and sexologist Magnus Hirschfeld coined the term "transvestite" in 1910. See Susan Stryker, *Transgender History: The Roots of Today's Revolution*, 2nd ed. (New York: Seal Press, 2017), 53–55.

26. Devereux, "Mohave Homosexuality," 500, 510, 516; John B. Randell, "Transvestitism and Trans-Sexualism," *British Medical Journal* 2 (Dec. 1959): 1448–52; Mary McIntosh, "The Homosexual Role," *Social Problems* 16, no. 2 (Autumn 1968): 182–92; Gary J. Mihalik, "More than Two: Anthropological Perspectives on Gender," *Journal of Gay and Lesbian Psychotherapy* 1, no. 1 (1988): 105–18; Gilbert Herdt, "Introduction: Third Sexes and Third Genders" in *Third Sex, Third Gender: Beyond Sexual Dimorphism in Culture and History*, ed. Gilbert Herdt (New York: Zone Books, 1993), 34.

27. David E. Wilkins, *American Indian Sovereignty and the U.S. Supreme Court: The Masking of Justice* (Austin: University of Texas Press, 1997), 64–65.

28. Richard Erdoes and Alfonso Ortiz, eds., *American Indian Myths and Legends* (New York: Pantheon Books, 1984), 161, 369.

29. Erdoes and Ortiz, *American Indian Myths and Legends*, 314.

30. Holder, "The Bote," 623–25.

31. S. C. Simms, "Crow Indian Hermaphrodites," *American Anthropologist* 5 (1903): 580–81; Robert H. Lowie, "Social Life of the Crow Indians," *Anthropological Papers of the American Museum of Natural History*, volume 9, part 2 (New York: American Museum of Natural History, 1912), 226. These descriptions contrast sharply with the nineteenth-century observations of the fur trader Edward Thompson Denig. The Smithsonian Institution republished his accounts in the mid-twentieth century. Of the Crow and their gender fluidity, Denig mused that "most civilized communities recognize but two genders, the masculine and feminine. But strange to say, these people have a neuter." See Edward Thompson Denig, *Of the Crow Nation*, Anthropological Papers No. 33 (Washington, DC: Smithsonian Institution, Bureau of American Ethnology, 1953), 58–59.

32. Robert H. Lowie, *The Crow Indians* (Lincoln: University of Nebraska Press, 1935), 48.

33. Craig S. Womack, *Red on Red: Native American Literary Separatism* (Minneapolis: University of Minnesota Press, 1999), 279; Daniel Heath Justice, *Our Fire Survives the Storm: A Cherokee Literary History* (Minneapolis: University of Minnesota Press, 2006), 95–6; Kirby Brown, *Stoking the Fire: Nationhood in Cherokee Writing, 1907–1970* (Norman: University of Oklahoma Press, 2018), 120.

34. Womack, *Red on Red*, 273.

35. Justice, *Our Fire Survives the Storm*, 107.

36. Hugh Lenox Scott, "Berdache," Notes on Sign Language and Miscellaneous Ethnographic Notes, MS 2932, National Anthropological Archives, Smithsonian Institution, Suitland, MD.

37. Lillian Bullshows Hogan, *The Woman Who Loved Mankind: The Life of a Twentieth-Century Crow Elder* (Lincoln: University of Nebraska Press, 2012), 124.

38. Hogan, *The Woman Who Loved Mankind*, 128.

39. Frank B. Linderman, *Pretty-Shield: Medicine Woman of the Crows* (1932; repr., Lincoln: University of Nebraska Press, 2003), 228.

40. Roscoe, *Changing Ones*, 76–78.

41. Paul Magid, *The Gray Fox: George Crook and the Indian Wars* (Norman: University of Oklahoma Press, 2015).

42. Paul Magid, *George Crook: From the Redwoods to Appomattox* (Norman: University of Oklahoma Press, 2011); Peter Aleshire, *The Fox and the Whirlwind: General George Crook and Geronimo: A Paired Biography* (New York: Wiley & Sons, 2000), 55.

43. Charles M. Robinson III, *General Crook and the Western Frontier* (Norman: University of Oklahoma Press, 2001), 181–85; Paul L. Hedren, *Rosebud, June 17, 1876: Prelude to the Little Big Horn* (Norman: University of Oklahoma Press, 2019).

44. *Chicago Daily Tribune*, July 7, 1876, 4; *Grange Advance*, July 19, 1876, 10; *Worthington Advance*, July 20, 1876, 1; *National Republic*, July 25, 1876, 1.

45. Frank B. Linderman, *Red Mother* (New York: John Day, 1932), 227–31.

46. *Helena Weekly Herald*, July 6, 1876, 5; *Fair Play*, June 29, 1876, 6; *New York Herald*, July 13, 1876, 2; *Daily Dispatch*, July 26, 1876, 1; *Superior Times*, Aug. 4, 1876, 2.

47. *New York Herald*, July 11, 1876, 6; US Senate, *Message from the President of the United States, 44th Congress, 1st Session* (Washington, DC: Government Printing Office, 1876), 1–3; H. W. Brands, *The Man Who Saved the Union: Ulysses Grant in War and Peace* (New York: Anchor Books, 2013), 501, 561–64; Mary Stockwell, *Interrupted Odyssey: Ulysses S. Grant and the American Indians* (Carbondale: Southern Illinois University Press, 2018), 165, 171, 174.

48. *Clarion*, June 18; June 30; Aug. 6; Aug. 20; Aug. 27, 1879; *Times-Picayune*, Feb. 13, 1888, 4; *Duluth Daily News*, Mar. 6, 1888, 1; *The Livingston Enterprise*, July 13, 1889, 1. Briscoe was a member of Mississippi's Democratic Party, a political party dedicated to white supremacy during the late nineteenth and early twentieth centuries. *Clarion*, Sept. 8, 1886, 2; *Clarion Ledger*, July 18, 1889, 1.

49. *Fifty-Seventh Annual Report of the Commissioner of Indian Affairs, 1888* (Washington, DC: Government Printing Office, 1888), 153.

50. Charles C. Bradley, *After the Buffalo Days: An Account of the First Years of Reservation Life for Crow Indians, Based on Official Government Documents from 1880 to 1904 A.D.* (Crow Agency, MT: Crow Central Education Commission, 1977), 153.

51. Lowie, "Social Life of the Crow Indians," 226.

52. Quoted in Will Roscoe, "Sexual and Gender Diversity in Native America and the Pacific Islands," in *Identities and Place: Changing Labels and Intersectional Communities of LGBTQ and Two-Spirit People in the United States*, ed. Katherine Crawford-Lackey and Megan E. Springate (New York: Berghahn Books, 2020), 74.

53. Hogan, *The Woman Who Loved Mankind*, 126.

54. Roscoe, *Changing Ones*, 34–5.

55. Thomas Yellowtail, with Michael Oren Fitzgerald, *Yellowtail: Crow Medicine Man and Sun Dance Chief* (Norman: University of Oklahoma Press, 1991), 21–22; Williams, *The Spirit and the Flesh*, 183.

56. Hogan, *The Woman Who Loved Mankind*, 125, 126.

57. James Owen Dorsey, *"Berdaches" Among the Omaha, Dakota, Kansa, Teton, and Hidatsa tribes*, in *Eleventh Annual Report of the Bureau of American Ethnology to the Secretary of the Smithsonian Institution 1889–90*, ed. J. W. Powell (Washington, DC: Government Printing Office, 1894), 378–79, 467.

58. Sue-Ellen Jacobs, "Berdache: A Brief Review of the Literature," *Colorado Anthropologist* 1, no. 1 (1968): 25–40; William K. Powers, *Oglala Religion* (Lincoln: University of Nebraska Press, 1975), 58; David F. Greenberg, "Why Was the Berdache Ridiculed?," *Journal of Homosexuality* 11, nos. 3–4 (1986): 179–88; Walter L. Williams, "Persistence and Change in the Berdache Tradition Among Contemporary Lakota Indians," *Journal of Homosexuality* 11, nos. 3–4 (1986): 191–200.

59. James O. Dorsey, "A Study of Siouan Cults," in Powell, *Eleventh Annual Report*, 467; Patricia Albers and Beatrice Medicine, *The Hidden Half: Studies of Plains Indian Women* (Lanham, MD: University Press, of America, 1983), 243.

60. See Thomas H. Lewis, letter, *Journal of the American Medical Association*, July 16, 1973, 312.

61. Dorsey, *A Study of Siouan Cults*, 379; Alice Fletcher and Francis La Flesche, *The Omaha Tribe*, Twenty-Seventh Annual Report of the Bureau of American Ethnology to the Secretary of the Smithsonian Institution (Washington, DC: Government Printing Office, 1911), 132.

62. The following account is drawn from Richard Erdoes and Alfonso Ortiz, *American Indian Trickster Tales* (New York: Penguin, 1998), 133–35.

63. Anna H. Gayton, *Yokuts and Western Mono Ethnology* (Berkeley: University of California Press, 1929), 106; Nancy O. Lurie, "Winnebago Berdache," *American Anthropologist* 55 (1953): 708–12.

64. Scott, "Berdache," 51; Roscoe, *Changing Ones*, 27. See also Carolyn R. Riebeth, *J. H. Sharp Among the Crow Indians 1902–1910: Personal Memories of His Life and Friendships on the Crow Reservation in Montana* (El Segundo, CA: Upton and Sons, 1985).

65. Alfred L. Kroeber, "The Arapaho," *Bulletin of the American Museum of Natural History* 18 (1902): 19; Edward Carpenter, *The Intermediate Sex: A Study of Some Transitional Types of Men and Women* (London: Allen and Unwin, 1908); Robert H. Lowie, "The Assiniboine," *Anthropological Papers of the American Museum of Natural History* 4 (1910): 42; Ruth Benedict, "Anthropology and the Abnormal," *Journal of General Psychology* 10 (1934): 59–82.

CHAPTER 9: REAWAKENING

1. Clyde Hall, interview with author, Feb. 18, 2019.

2. Rebecca Nagle, interview with author, June 4, 2018.

3. Barbara Cameron, Biographical Information, undated, folder 2, box 1, Barbara Cameron Papers (GLC 63), Gay and Lesbian Center, San Francisco Public Library (hereafter cited as Cameron Papers).

4. Paul C. Rosier, "'They Are Ancestral Homelands': Race, Place, and Politics in Cold War Native America, 1945–1961," *Journal of American History* 92, no. 4 (Mar. 2006): 1300–26; Valerie L. Kuletz, *The Tainted Desert: Environmental and Social Ruin in the American West* (New York: Routledge, 1998). For more recent reflections, see David Treuer, *Rez Life: An Indian's Journey Through Reservation Life* (New York: Atlantic Monthly Press, 2012).

5. Cameron, Biographical Information.

6. Randy Shilts, *The Mayor of Castro Street: The Life and Times of Harvey Milk* (New York: St. Martin's, 1982); Kent Blansett, *A Journey to Freedom: Richard Oakes, Alcatraz, and the Red Power Movement* (New Haven, CT: Yale University Press, 2018); Lillian Faderman, *Harvey Milk: His Lives and Death* (New Haven, CT: Yale University Press, 2018).

7. Cheryl Sullivan, "Indians in the City," *Christian Science Monitor*, June 26, 1986, https://www.csmonitor.com/layout/set/amphtml/1986/0626/znat3-f.html.

8. Beverly Little Thunder, with Sharron Proulx-Turner, *One Bead at a Time: A Memoir* (Toronto: Ianna, 2016), 23, 25, 26–30, 37, 49, 52, 55.

9. *Gaysweek*, Apr. 2, 1979, 12; *Moja: Gay & Black*, Apr. 3, 1979, 3; Sandie Johnson and Loraine Hutchins, "Black Hills Gathering: The Ties That United and Divide Us," *Off Our Backs* 10, no. 9 (Oct. 1980): 4.

10. Will Roscoe, "Gay American Indians: Creating an Identity from Past Traditions," *Advocate*, Oct. 29, 1985, 48; Megan L. MacDonald, "Two-Spirit Organizing: Indigenous Two-Spirit Identity in the Twin Cities Region," in *Queer Twin Cities*, ed. Kevin P. Murphy, Jennifer L. Pierce, and Larry Knopp (Minneapolis: University of Minnesota Press, 2010), 150.

11. "Ep. 19, Part 2: Randy Burns's Trips Out East and Back," *Storied: San Francisco*, March 2018, https://open.spotify.com/episode/49kUi1DmwAXrZbq JqaUWFd.

12. Fred Fejes, *Gay Rights and Moral Panic: The Origins of America's Debate on Homosexuality* (New York: Palgrave Macmillan, 2011), 181–212; Emily K. Hobson, *Lavender and Red: Liberation and Solidarity in the Gay and Lesbian Left* (Berkeley: University of California Press, 2016), 11–12, 82, 85.

13. Herbert Gold, "A Walk on San Francisco's Gay Side," *New York Times*, Nov. 6, 1977, Section SM, 17.

14. Elizabeth A. Armstrong, *Forging Gay Identities: Organizing Sexuality in San Francisco, 1950–1994* (Chicago: University of Chicago Press, 2002), 2.

15. "Ep. 19, Part 1: Randy Burns's Work Starting Gay American Indians," *Storied: San Francisco*, Feb. 7, 2018, http://storiedsf.libsyn.com/ep-19-part-1 -randy-burnss-work-starting-gay-american-indians.

16. Marty Fixico, interview with author, Mar. 13, 2019.

17. Jenny L. Davis, "More Than Just 'Gay Indians'": Intersecting Articulations of Two-Spirit Gender, Sexuality, and Indigenousness" in *Queer Excursions: Retheorizing Binaries in Language, Gender, and Sexuality*, ed. Lal Zimman, Jenny L. Davis, and Joshua Raclaw (New York: Oxford University Press, 2014), 62–80, espec. 64; Michael Red Earth, "Traditional Influences on a

Contemporary Gay-Identified Sisseton Dakota," in Jacobs, Thomas, and Lang, *Two-Spirit People*, 213–24; "Ep. 19, Part 1: Randy Burns's Work."

18. "Ep. 19, Part 1: Randy Burns's Work"; Curtis Harris-Davia, interview with author, Dec. 5, 2018; Clyde Hall interview.

19. Donald L. Fixico, *Termination and Relocation: Federal Indian Policy, 1945–1960* (Albuquerque: University of New Mexico Press, 1986); Gay American Indians to National Gay Task Force, July 18, 1978, folder 43, box 165, series IV, National Gay and Lesbian Taskforce Records, 1973–2000, Archives of Sexuality and Gender, Cornell University Archives.

20. "Ep. 19, Part 1: Randy Burns's Work"; Cameron, Biographical Information; Barbara Cameron, "How I Got into Politics," folder 3, box 1, Cameron Papers; Susan Lobo, *Oakland's American Indian Community: History, Social Organization, and Factors that Contribute to Census Undercount*, Ethnographic Exploratory Research Report #12 (Washington, DC: US Bureau of the Census, 1990), 2.

21. *San Francisco Sentinel*, June 24, 1988, 15.

22. Paul Chaat Smith and Robert Warrior, *Like a Hurricane: The Indian Movement from Alcatraz to Wounded Knee* (New York: New Press, 1996), 19; Blansett, *A Journey to Freedom*, ch. 3.

23. "Ep. 19, Part 1: Randy Burns's Work."

24. Randy Burns, "Gay Native Americans Find a Safe Harbor," *San Francisco Examiner: Pride 2000*, folder 1, Randy Burns Papers, B1049, LGBT Historical Society. On this point, see also Brian J. Gilley, "Gay American Indian Men's Mobility and Sexual Sedentarism in the United States Census Rules of Residence," *Human Organization* 71, no. 2 (Summer 2012): 151.

25. Burns, "Gay Native Americans Find a Safe Harbor"; Gay American Indians, folder 1999–54, Burns Papers; Clyde M. Hall, "You Anthropologists Make Sure You Get Your Words Right," in Jacobs, Thomas, and Lang, *Two-Spirit People*, 275.

26. Jack D. Forbes, "The Native Struggle for Liberation: Alcatraz," in *American Indian Activism: Alcatraz to the Longest Walk*, ed. Troy Johnson, Joane Nagel, and Duane Champagne (Bloomington: University of Illinois Press, 1997), 129–35.

27. Gay American Indians, folder 1999–54, Burns Papers. On genocide, see Raphael Lemkin, *Axis Rule in Occupied Europe: Laws of Occupation, Analysis of Government, Proposals for Redress* (Washington, DC: Carnegie Endowment for International Peace, 1944), xi–xii, chap. 9; Benjamin Madley, "Reexamining the American Genocide Debate: Meaning, Historiography, and New Methods," *American Historical Review* 120, no. 1 (Feb. 2015): 98–139; Jeffrey Ostler, *Surviving Genocide: Native Nations and the United States* (New Haven, CT: Yale University Press, 2019).

28. Gay American Indians, folder 1999–54, Burns Papers.

29. Clyde Hall interview.

30. Clyde Hall interview.

31. Chong-suk Han, "They Don't Want to Cruise Your Type: Gay Men of Color and the Racial Politics of Exclusion," *Social Identity* 13, no. 1 (2007): 51–67; Karen Krahulik, "Remembering Provincetown: Oral History and

Narrativity at Land's End," in *Bodies of Evidence: The Practice of Queer Oral History*, ed. Nan Alamilla Boyd and Horacio N. Roque Ramírez (New York: Oxford University Press, 2012), 46–47; Mikelle Street, "Gay Bars Can Be Mind-Bogglingly Racist," *Vice*, Apr. 21, 2017, https://www.vice.com/en_us/article /d7bd9k/gay-bars-can-be-mind-bogglingly-racist; Arwa Mahdawi, "It's 100% Segregated: Does Georgia's LGBT Haven Have a Race Problem," *Guardian*, Oct. 24, 2018, https://www.theguardian.com/cities/2018/oct/24/its-100 -segregated-does-georgias-lgbt-haven-have-a-race-problem.

32. Allan Bérubé, "The History of Gay Bathhouses," *Journal of Homosexuality* 44, nos. 3–4 (2003): 33–53; Christopher Agee, "Gayola: Police Professionalization and the Politics of San Francisco's Gay Bars, 1950–1968," *Journal of the History of Sexuality* 15, no. 3 (Sept. 2006): 462–89. For contemporary reflections on bath houses, see Craig M. Loftin, ed., *Letters to ONE: Gay and Lesbian Voices from the 1950s and 1960s* (Albany: SUNY Press, 2012), 66, 73, 77; Gayle Rubin, "Sites, Settlements, and Urban Sex: Archaeology and the Study of Gay Leathermen in San Francisco, 1955–1995," in *Archaeologies of Sexuality*, ed. Robert A. Schmidt and Barbara L. Voss (London: Routledge, 2000), 62–88.

33. Horacio N. Roque Ramírez, "'That's My Place!': Negotiating Racial, Sexual, and Gender Politics in San Francisco's Gay Latino Alliance, 1975–1983," *Journal of the History of Sexuality* 12, no. 2 (April 2003): 232.

34. "Ep. 19, Part 1: Randy Burns's Work."

35. Randy Burns, "Non-Indians Forget Whose Land This Is," *Gay Community News* 16, no. 46 (June 11–17, 1989), 15. Allan Bérubé made a similar observation about whiteness and gay culture in "How Gay Stays White and What Kind of White It Stays," in *Race and Racialization: Essential Readings*, 2nd ed., ed. Tania Das Gupta, Carl E. James, Chris Anderson, Grace-Edwards Galabuzi, and Roger C. A. Maaka (Toronto: Canada Scholars, 2018), 626.

36. Armstrong, *Forging Gay Identities*, 81.

37. "Ep. 19, Part 1: Randy Burns's Work."

38. Marty Fixico interview.

39. Gay American Indians, folder 1999–54, Burns Papers.

40. Clyde Hall interview.

41. In 1953, House Concurrent Resolution 108 led to the termination of over one hundred tribes in the United States. Public Law 280, also passed by Congress in 1953, transferred federal law enforcement authority over Indian Country to the states. See Fixico, *Termination and Relocation*.

42. Larry W. Blunt, "Roots of the Native American Urban Experience: Relocation Policy in the 1950s," *American Indian Quarterly* 10, no. 2 (Spring 1986): 85, 90; Alfred Ziegler, oral history, AIRP 802, American Indian Research Project, South Dakota Oral History Center, University of South Dakota.

43. Marsha Weisiger, *Dreaming of Sheep in Navajo Country* (Seattle: University of Washington Press, 2009); Andrew Needham, *Power Lines: Phoenix and the Making of the Modern Southwest* (Princeton, NJ: Princeton University Press, 2014), 42–44, 128–31; Bob Waltrip, "Elmer Gage: American Indian," *One: The Homosexual Viewpoint* (March 13, 1965): 6–10.

44. Joane Nagel, *American Indian Ethnic Renewal: Red Power and the Resurgence of Identity and Culture* (New York: Oxford University Press, 1996).

45. Bradley G. Shreve, *Red Power Rising: The National Indian Youth Council and the Origins of Native Activism* (Norman: University of Oklahoma Press, 2011); Sherry L. Smith, *Hippies, Indians & the Fight for Red Power* (New York: Oxford University Press, 2012).

46. W. Bryan Rommel Ruiz, *American History Goes to the Movies: Hollywood and the American Experience* (New York: Routledge, 2011), 120.

47. Jacquelyn Kilpatrick, *Celluloid Indians: Native Americans and Film* (Lincoln: University of Nebraska Press, 1999), 92.

48. The following quotations are taken from Maurice Kenny, "Tinselled Bucks: An Historical Study in Indian Homosexuality," *Gay Sunshine*, no. 26–27 (Winter 1975–76): 16–17, 15, box 6, Burns Papers. The final paragraphs in Kenny's essay appeared in reverse order, on p. 15.

49. Penelope M. Kelsey, ed., *Maurice Kenny: Celebrations of a Mohawk Writer* (Albany: SUNY Press, 2011).

50. "Two-Spirits, Berdache, Homosexuality and American Indians, c. 1876–2000," folder 6, Burns Papers, GLBT Historical Society.

51. Biographical Note, Robert Lynch Papers, 1963–1989, Division of Rare and Manuscript Collections, Cornell University Library, Collection No. 7320.

52. "Shamanism, Berdache, and Homoeroticism in Amerindian Culture," n.d., series 2, folder 25, box 2, Lynch Papers.

53. "Shamanism, Berdache, and Homoeroticism in Amerindian Culture," unaddressed letter, Aug. 4, 1977, Lynch Papers.

54. "Shamanism, Berdache, and Homoeroticism in Amerindian Culture," Lynch Papers.

55. J. Miko Thomas, interview with author, July 13, 2018.

56. Walter L. Williams, *The Spirit and the Flesh: Sexual Diversity in American Indian Culture* (Boston: Beacon Press, 1986), 202.

57. Stuart Timmons, *The Trouble with Harry Hay: Founder of the Modern Gay Movement* (Boston: Alyson, 1990), 98; Lillian Faderman, *The Gay Revolution: The Story of the Struggle* (New York: Simon & Schuster, 2015), 53–54.

58. Michael Bronski, *A Queer History of the United States* (Boston: Beacon Press, 2011), 179–80.

59. Nicholas Edsall, *Toward Stonewall: Homosexuality and Society in the Modern Western World* (Charlottesville: University of Virginia Press, 2003), ch. 6; James T. Sears, *Behind the Mask of the Mattachine: The Hal Call Chronicles and the Early Movement for Homosexual Emancipation* (New York: Routledge, 2011), section 3.

60. Harry Hay, *Radically Gay: Gay Liberation in the Words of Its Founder Harry Hay*, ed. Will Roscoe (Boston: Beacon Press, 1996), 139, 167; Martin Meeker, "Behind the Mask of Respectability: Reconsidering the Mattachine Society and Male Homophile Practice, 1950s and 1960s," *Journal of the History of Sexuality* 10, no. 1 (Jan. 2001): 78–116.

61. Hay, *Radically Gay*, 101–2, 161.

62. "Berdache," folder 11, box 19, Harry Hay Papers, San Francisco Public Library (hereafter cited as Hay Papers).

63. See various note cards on this topic in folder 11 and "Berdache: My Theory of History," folder 12, box 19, Hay Papers.

64. Harry Hay, "Notes on Astrology and the Julian Calendar," folder 1, box 19, Hay Papers.

65. Unsigned letter to Harry Hay and untitled note card, folder 1, box 19, Ser. 7, Research & Note Files Sub-Series A. Berdache/Native Americans, Hay Papers.

66. Lawrence A. Peskin, *Captives and Countrymen: Barbary Slavery and the American Public, 1785–1816* (Baltimore: Johns Hopkins University Press, 2009); Matthew H. Pangborn, *Enlightenment Orientalism in the American Mind, 1770–1807* (New York: Routledge, 2019).

67. Harry Hay, "The Homophile in Search of an Historical Context and Cultural Continuity," One Institute, Sept. 1957, folder 3, Box 19, Hay Papers. Hay eventually embraced the idea of the berdache as social mediator. Harry Hay, "Radical Faerie Proposals to the 'March on Washington' Organizing Meeting," in Hay, *Radically Gay,* 272–73.

68. Harry Hay, "The Homosexual and History . . . an invitation for further study," folder 2, box 19, Hay Papers.

69. Harry Hay, unsigned letter to "Mr. Dutton," Sept. 14, 1959, folder 3, box 19, Hay Papers.

70. Hay, "The Homosexual and History . . . an invitation for further study," Hay Papers.

71. Christopher Castiglia, *Bound and Determined: Captivity, Culture-Crossing, and White Womanhood from Mary Rowlandson to Patty Hearst* (Chicago: University of Chicago Press, 1996), 75–78; Patricia Seed, *American Pentimento: The Invention of Indians and the Pursuit of Riches* (Minneapolis: University of Minnesota Press, 2001), 45–47.

72. Harry Hay, "Berdache: Shamanism," folder 8, box 19, Hay Papers; "Berdache: Ritual Fellatio vs. Homophilia," folder 11, box 19, Hay Papers.

73. Scott Lauria Morgensen, *Spaces Between Us: Queer Settler Colonialism and Indigenous Decolonization* (Minneapolis: University of Minnesota Press, 2011), 127–29.

74. Harry Hay, "Cherokee Booger Dance," folder 3, box 20, Hay Papers.

75. On the importance of place-based cultures and belief systems in Native America, see Soren C. Larsen and Jay T. Johnson, *Being Together in Place: Indigenous Coexistence in a More Than Human World* (Minneapolis: University of Minnesota Press, 2017).

76. Bryant opposed the county's ordinances preventing discrimination of people on the basis of sexual orientation. See Anita Bryant, *Save Our Children from Homosexuality! Vote for Repeal of Metro's "Gay" Blunder* (Miami: Save Our Children, 1977).

77. *Out,* July 29, 1977, 4.

78. Cameron, "How I Got into Politics."

79. *Big Mama Rag* 7, no. 10 (1979): 6.

80. Cameron, "How I Got into Politics."

81. Johnson and Hutchins, "Black Hills Gathering," 5.

82. Johnson and Hutchins, "Black Hills Gathering," 4.

83. "'Our Red Nation' (1978)—Diné, Lakota, and Haudenosaunee Traditional Leaders," in *Say We Are Nations: Documents of Politics and Protest in*

Indigenous America Since 1887, ed. Daniel M. Cobb (Chapel Hill: University of North Carolina Press, 2015), 180.

84. Little Thunder, *One Bead at a Time*, 61, 68; Smith and Warrior, *Like a Hurricane*, 212.

85. Gay American Indians, Burns Papers, folder 1999–5427.

86. Kenny, "Tinselled Bucks," box 6, Burns Papers.

87. "Shamanism, Berdache, and Homoeroticism in Amerindian Culture," Lynch Papers.

88. *Blueboy*, Feb. 1980, 7.

89. Paula Gunn Allen, "Lesbians in American Indian Cultures," *Conditions* 3, no. 1 (Spring 1981): 67, 74, 80–81.

CHAPTER 10: TWO-SPIRITS

1. "As a Child I Was a Tomboy," folder 21, box 1, Barbara Cameron Papers (GLC 63), Gay and Lesbian Center, San Francisco Public Library.

2. "Native American Cultures: Homosexuality & the Family," Oct. 13, 1990, National Convention, Anaheim, CA, Mss. 42, Ser. 006, Subser. 03, Manitoba Gay and Lesbian Archives, University of Manitoba Archives and Special Collections.

3. "Freedom of Women Speech," folder 20, box 1, Cameron Papers.

4. See *Montrose Voice*, Jan. 3, 1986, 4, for a representative example of political opinion among gay and lesbian Indians.

5. Samuel R. Cook, "Ronald Reagan's Indian Policy in Retrospect: Economic Crisis and Political Irony," *Policy Studies Journal* 24, no. 1 (1996): 11–26; Dean J. Kotlowski, "From Backlash to Bingo: Ronald Reagan and Federal Indian Policy," *Pacific Historical Review* 77, no. 4 (Nov. 2008): 617–52.

6. Patricia Fisher, "A Brief Article on Gender Dysphoria," *Pan Transsexual Awareness* (Jan. 1991), folder 15, Burns Papers; Jason Cromwell, "Traditions of Gender Diversity and Sexualities: A Female-to-Male Transgendered Perspective," in *Two-Spirit People: Native American Gender Identity, Sexuality, and Spirituality*, ed. Sue-Ellen Jacobs, Wesley Thomas, and Sabine Lang (Urbana: University of Illinois Press, 1997), 119–42.

7. William Vesterman and Josh Ozersky, *Readings for the 21st Century: Tomorrow's Issues for Today's Students* (Boston: Allyn and Bacon, 2000), 115.

8. Elizabeth Tucker and Ellen McHale, "Two Spirited People: Understanding Who We Are as Creation," *New York Folklore* 19, nos. 1–2 (1993): 155–64; Gary D. Comstock, *Unrepentant, Self-Affirming, Practicing: Lesbian/Bisexual/Gay People Within Organized Religion* (New York: Continuum, 1996), 89.

9. Will Roscoe to Guillermo Hernandez, July 6, 1991, GAI Correspondence, 1988–1989, Will Roscoe Papers and Gay American Indians Records, GLBT Historical Society, San Francisco; *Two Eagles*, June 1990, box 3, Two-Spirit Papers, Jean-Nickolaus Tretter Collection in GLBT Studies, University of Minnesota, Minneapolis.

10. Anthropologist Sue-Ellen Jacobs played an active role as an academic gatekeeper of knowledge about Indigenous gender and sexuality during the 1980s and 1990s. See her revealing letter to Harry Hay, Apr. 18, 1983, folder 13, box 20, Hay Papers. Jacobs also wrote a scathing review of Will Roscoe's

The Zuni Man-Woman in which she dismissed Roscoe's work and lambasted the quality of his writing. See folder 16, box 20, Hay Papers; "Minnesota Two-Spirits," box 2, Two-Spirit Papers; Andrew J. Jolivette, *Indian Blood: HIV & Colonial Trauma in San Francisco's Two-Spirit Community* (Seattle: University of Washington Press, 2016), 17.

11. Carrie H. House, folder 4, Burns Papers. See also Carrie House, "Blessed by the Holy People," *Journal of Lesbian Studies* 20, nos. 3–4 (2016): 324–41.

12. Ruth Beebe Hill, *Hanta Yo: An American Saga* (New York: Doubleday, 1979); Patricia C. Albers and William R. James, "Historical Fiction as Ideology: The Case of *Hanta Yo*," *Radical History Review* 25, no. 1 (Jan. 1981): 149–61.

13. "Ep. 19, Part 1: Randy Burns's Work."

14. Chrystos, *Not Vanishing* (Vancouver: Press Gang Publishers, 1988), 7.

15. Centers for Disease Control, "Kaposi's Sarcoma and Pneumocystis Pneumonia and Homosexual Men—New York City and California," *Morbidity and Mortality Weekly Report* 30, no. 24 (1981): 1431–38.

16. John Portmann, *Women and Gay Men in the Postwar Period* (London: Bloomsbury, 2016), 149.

17. *Outlines: The Voice of the Gay and Lesbian Community* 1, no. 22 (1987): 4.

18. Hugh Stevens, "Normality and Queerness in Gay Fiction," in *The Cambridge Companion to Gay and Lesbian Writing*, ed. Hugh Stevens (Cambridge: Cambridge University Press, 2011), 91.

19. "HIV and AIDS—United States, 1981–2000," *Morbidity and Mortality Weekly Report,* Centers for Disease Control (CDC), June 1, 2001, https://www.cdc.gov/mmwr/preview/mmwrhtml/mm5021a2.htm.

20. Richard A. McKay, *Patient Zero and the Making of the AIDS Epidemic* (Chicago: University of Chicago Press, 2018), 7.

21. In 1959, a man in Kinshasa, Democratic Republic of the Congo, contracted HIV. Genetic analysis of his blood suggested a single source of his infection dating back to the late 1940s. See John Iliffe, *The African AIDS Epidemic: A History* (Athens: University of Ohio Press, 2006), ch. 2; Jacques Pepin, *The Origins of AIDS* (New York: Cambridge University Press, 2011), 7–10.

22. Philip M. Boffey, "Defect in Immune System Found in Victims of AIDS, Scientists Say," *New York Times,* June 11, 1985.

23. World Health Organization, Data and Statistics, https://www.who.int/hiv/data/en.

24. *Daily News of Los Angeles,* Aug. 12, 1990, U3; *Roanoke Times,* Aug. 12, 1990, A8.

25. Melvin Harrison, interview with author, Dec. 12, 2018

26. "HIV/AIDS Among American Indians and Alaskan Natives—United States, 1981–1997," *MMWR Weekly,* Mar. 6, 1998, https://www.cdc.gov/mmwr/preview/mmwrhtml/00051473.htm; "The American Indian and Alaska Native Population: 2000, Census 2000" Brief, February 2002, https://www.census.gov/prod/2002pubs/c2kbr01-15.pdf; Kristi L. Allgood, Bijou Hunt, and Monique G. Rucker, "Black-White Disparities in HIV Mortality in the United States: 1990–2009," *Journal of Racial and Ethnic Health Disparities* 3 (2016): 168–75.

27. *Philadelphia Inquirer,* Sept. 1, 1990. Melvin Harrison, a member of the Navajo Nation and Two-Spirit ally, made the same point when I interviewed him, Dec. 12, 2018.

28. *Seminole Tribune,* February 28, 1990; on LaFavor, see Lisa Tatonetti, *Written by the Body: Gender Expansiveness and Indigenous Non-Cis Masculinities* (Minneapolis: University of Minnesota Press, 2021), ch. 5.

29. Lesbian and Gay Freedom Day, June 1983, folder 21, Cameron Papers.

30. *Seattle Post-Intelligencer,* Nov. 10, 1987, B4; Melvin Harrison interview with author, Dec. 12, 2018; Curtis Harris-Davia, interview with author, Dec. 5, 2018.

31. James P. Rife and Capt. Alan J. Dellapenna Jr., *Caring and Curing: A History of the Indian Health Service* (Terra Alta, WV: Pioneer Press of West Virginia, 2009), 65; David H. DeJong, *Plagues, Politics, and Policy: A Chronicle of the Indian Health Service, 1955–2008* (Lanham, MD: Lexington Books, 2011).

32. IHS Special General Memorandum (SGM) #87-6, Indian Health Service AIDS Policy, July 17, 1987; T. Kue Young, *The Health of Native Americans: Towards a Biocultural Epidemiology* (New York: Oxford University Press, 1994), 87–88.

33. Melvin Harrison interview; Irene S. Vernon, *Killing Us Quietly: Native Americans and HIV/AIDS* (Lincoln: University of Nebraska Press, 2001), 8.

34. Melvin Harrison interview; Dec. 12, 2018; Vernon, *Killing Us Quietly,* 24.

35. John O'Connor, "AIDS in Indian Country: Caution, Health Education and Prevention Seen as Key to Controlling Spread of Virus," folder 4, Burns Papers.

36. *Akwesasne Notes,* Apr. 1, 1989, 25.

37. *Seattle Times,* Nov. 10, 1987, G5.

38. *Tulsa World,* Aug. 11, 1989, A1.

39. *San Francisco Chronicle,* Jan. 25, 1990, A12.

40. *Wind River News,* Sept. 1, 1992, 8.

41. Ken Pinkham, interview with author, Feb. 2, 2019.

42. Paula A. Triechler, *How to Have Theory in an Epidemic* (Durham, NC: Duke University Press, 1999), 11.

43. Roger Hallas, *Reframing Bodies: AIDS, Bearing Witness, and the Queer Moving Image* (Durham, NC: Duke University Press, 2009), 159–61; McKay, *Patient Zero and the Making of the AIDS Epidemic,* 3–6.

44. Ken Pinkham interview.

45. Harriet A. Washington, *Medical Apartheid: The Dark History of Medical Experimentation on Black Americans from Colonial Times to the Present* (New York: Doubleday, 2006); Andrew Woolford, *This Benevolent Experiment: Indigenous Boarding Schools, Genocide, and Redress in Canada and the United States* (Lincoln: University of Nebraska Press, 2015), 235–36.

46. Tom Curtis, "The Origin of AIDS: A Startling New Theory Attempts to Answer the Question, 'Was It an Act of God or an Act of Man?,'" *Rolling Stone,* Mar. 19, 1992, 54–59, 61, 106, 108; Edward Hooper, *The River: A Journey to the Source of HIV and AIDS* (Boston: Little, Brown, 1999); Stanley Plotkin and Hilary Koprowski issued a rebuttal of Hooper's allegations in the *New York Times,* Dec. 7, 1999; Stanley A. Plotkin, "Untruths and Consequences: The False

Hypothesis Linking CHAT Type 1 Polio Vaccination to the Origin of Human Immunodeficiency Virus," *Philosophical Transactions of the Royal Society of London* 356 (2001): 815–23; Philippe Blancou et al., "Polio Vaccine Samples Not Linked to AIDS," 410 *Nature* (2001): 1045–46; R. A. Weiss, "Polio Vaccines Exonerated," *Nature* 410 (2001): 1035–36; B. Martin, "Investigating the Origins of AIDS: Some Ethical Dimensions," *Journal of Medical Ethics* 29 (2003): 253–56. In the winter of 2000, a new scientific theory emerged that suggested AIDS originated in the 1930s. Lawrence K. Altman, "AIDS Virus Originated Around 1930, Study Says," *New York Times*, Feb. 2, 2000.

47. Marlon "Marty" Fixico, interview with author, Mar. 13, 2019; Curtis Harris-Davia interview; Michael W. Ross, E. James Essien, and Isabel Torres, "Conspiracy Beliefs About the Origin of HIV/AIDS in Four Racial/Ethnic Groups," *Journal of Acquired Immune Deficiency Syndrome* 41, no. 3 (Mar. 2006): 342–44.

48. Ron Rowell, "Native Americans: Historic Problems Hamper Aids Prevention and Care," *Newsletter* (American Indians for Development), folder 17, Burns Papers.

49. Gregory Scofield, *The Gathering: Stones for the Medicine Wheel* (Vancouver: Polestar, 1993); Perry McLeod-Shabogesic, *The Medicine Wheel: A Healing Journey* (Union of Ontario Indians, 1995); "Addressing Two-Spirits in the American Indian, Alaskan Native and Native Hawaiian Communities," folder 6, box 9, Two-Spirit Papers; *Idaho State Journal*, Aug. 18, 2005.

50. Dennis W. Zotigh, "History of the Modern Hoop Dance," *Indian Country Today*, May 30, 2007; Trudy Griffin-Pierce, *Sky Is My Father: Space, Time, and Astronomy in Navajo Sandpainting* (Albuquerque: University of New Mexico Press, 1992), 177–79.

51. Friends of the Medicine Wheel Circle, South Bay, folder 4, Burns Papers; "Clyde Hall: About Medicine Bundles," https://www.youtube.com/watch?v=NH8YgwkUbOY; "Ep. 19, Part 1: Randy Burns's Work."

52. "Two Spirits & HIV: A Conference for the Health of Gay & Lesbian Native Americans," folder 4, Burns Papers; George Rutherford to Randy Burns, Apr. 12, 1988, Business, Reports to the Board, 1987–89, GAI Papers.

53. E. F. Duran, B. Guillory, and P. Tingley, "Domestic Violence in Native American Communities: The Effects of Intergenerational Post Traumatic Stress," unpublished manuscript, Indian Health Clinic, San Francisco.

54. *Indian Child Welfare: A State-of-the-Field Study* (Washington, DC: US Department of Health, Education, and Welfare, 1976); "Proposed: The Omnibus Indian Claims Act of 1978," *American Indian Journal* 4, no. 4 (Apr. 1978): 38–39; *New York Times*, Dec. 25, 1978.

55. Margaret Jacobs, *A Generation Removed: The Fostering and Adoption of Indigenous Children in the Postwar World* (Lincoln: University of Nebraska Press, 2014).

56. Indian Child Welfare Act, Hearing Before the Select Committee on Indian Affairs, US Senate, 100th Congress, 1st Session, Nov. 10, 1987 (Washington, DC: US Government Printing Office, 1988), 434–78.

57. Duran, Guillory, and Tingley, "Domestic Violence in Native American Communities," 16; Phil Tingley, "Native American Cultures: Homosexuality

& the Family," Oct. 13, 1990, University of Manitoba Archives and Special Collections.

58. Tingley, "Native American Cultures." Tingley's use of "genocide" refers to the physical destruction of Native people in the context of European and Euro-American colonialism. He uses "ethnocide" to refer to the cultural and linguistic losses in Indian Country from exposure to forces such as Christianity and Western education.

59. Tingley, "Native American Cultures."

60. Barbara Cameron, "Speech at the Memorial of Phil Tingley, 1991," folder 17, box 1, Cameron Papers.

61. Dennis, *The Circle*, Oct. 1989, box 3, Two-Spirit Papers.

62. Clyde Hall interview.

63. *Seminole Tribune*, July 24, 1992, 2.

64. Barbara Cameron, "Bates College Speech," 1992, folder 18, box 1; "Racism," folder 52, box 1; "Family," folder 19, box 1; "Uniting Ourselves: Bridging Our Differences," folder 25, box 1; all in Cameron Papers.

65. Will Roscoe, "Project Agreement," Business, Reports to the Board, 1987–89, GAI Papers; *Gay News-Telegraph*, June 1985, 4; *New York Native*, no. 18 (Sept.–Oct. 1985): 8; *Montrose Voice*, June 14, 1985, 7; *International Gay Association Bulletin* 1 (1986): 27; *Harrisburg Area Women's News* (July 1985): 7.

66. *San Francisco Sentinel*, June 24, 1988, 15; "GAI Anthology Status Report," Dec. 7, 1986, Business, Reports to the Board, 1987–89, GAI Papers.

67. *Ten Percent* 6, no. 4 (1985), n.p.

68. "Telling the Story in Their Own Words: Gay American Indians to Publish Anthology," *The Body Politic*, no. 117 (Aug. 1985): 24; form letter signed by Randy Burns, June 14, 1985, Business, Reports to the Board, 1987–89, GAI Papers.

69. Will Roscoe and Gay American Indians, eds., *Living the Spirit: A Gay American Indian Anthology* (New York: St. Martin's Press, 1988).

70. Contributors included Paula Gunn Allen, Maurice Kenny, Midnight Sun, M. Owlfeather, Erna Pahe, Debra S. O'Gara, Kieran Prather-Jerry, Lawrence William O'Connor, Beth Brant, Chrystos, Anne Waters, Daniel Little Hawk, Tala Sanning, Mary TallMountain, Nola Hadley, Ben the Dancer, Carole LaFavor, Joe Dale Tate Nevaquaya, Janice Gould, and Richard La Fortune.

71. Roscoe and Gay American Indians, *Living the Spirit*, 2–3, 28–9, 50, 61, 74. For additional insights into discussions about changing terminology, see "Notes" on Jason Cromwell, "Not Female Berdache, Not Amazons, Not Cross Gender Females, Not Manlike Women," folder 2, Randy Burns Papers; Jason Cromwell, *Transmen and FTMs: Identities, Bodies, Genders, and Sexualities* (Urbana: University of Illinois Press, 1999), 92.

72. Alfred Robinson's review of *Living the Spirit* is in "Reviews," *American Indian Culture and Research Journal* 12, no. 1 (1989): 111–15. For a typical example of a positive review in the gay press, see Susan Jordan, "Native Americans Re-Examine Traditional Gay Ways," *Empty Closet* (Mar. 2, 1989): 12.

73. Reports to GAI Board of Directors, Aug. 5, 1985, and Sept. 9, 1985, and Business Reports to the Board, 1987–89, all in GAI Papers.

74. Ramón A. Gutiérrez, "Must We Deracinate Indians to Find Gay Roots?" *Out/Look* 1, no. 4 (Winter 1989): 61–67; Ramón A. Gutiérrez, *When Jesus Came, the Corn Mothers Went Away: Marriage, Sexuality, and Power in New Mexico, 1500–1846* (Stanford, CA: Stanford University Press, 1991); Richard Trexler, *Sex and Conquest: Gendered Violence, Political Order, and the European Conquest of the Americas* (Ithaca, NY: Cornell University Press, 1995), 98–101.

75. The focus on gay sex acts in the work of Williams and Roscoe also minimized the complexity of gender fluidity and sexual diversity, according to Native scholars. See, for example, Carolyn Epple, "Coming to Terms with Navajo *Nádleehi*: A Critique of Berdache, 'Gay,' 'Alternate Gender,' and 'Two-Spirit,'" *American Ethnologist* 25, no. 2 (1998): 269–70.

76. Trexler, *Sex and Conquest*, 84–85.

77. Gutiérrez, "Must We Deracinate Indians to Find Gay Roots?," 67.

78. Richard C. Trexler, "Making the American Berdache: Choice or Constraint?" *Journal of Social History* 35, no. 3 (Spring 2002): 625. Trexler adopts a skeptical tone in relation to Plains Indian traditions of visions, insisting that the scientific literature reveals the use of "constraint and force" in visions involving adolescents.

79. Gutiérrez, *When Jesus Came, the Corn Mothers Went Away*, 35.

80. *Out/Look* 2, no. 1 (Summer 1989): 5–6.

81. *Out/Look* 2, no. 2 (Fall 1989): 5. Criticism of Roscoe referred specifically to his *The Zuni Man-Woman, Out/Look* 1, no. 2 (Summer 1988): 56–62.

82. Jason Cromwell, "Not Female Berdache, Not Amazons, Not Cross-Gender Females, Not Manlike Women: Locating Female-to-Male Transgendered People Within Discourses of the Berdache Tradition," Annual Meeting of the American Anthropological Association, Washington, DC, Nov. 17–21, 1993, folder 2, Gay American Indians Collection, 97–34, LGBT Historical Society, San Francisco.

83. Barbara Cameron, "Point of View," folder 52, box 1, Cameron Papers; *The Body Politic*, May 1985, 3.

84. *Twin Cities Gaze*, Feb. 21, 1991, box 1, Two-Spirit Papers; Megan L. MacDonald, "Two-Spirits Organizing: Indigenous Two-Spirit Identity in the Twin Cities Region," in *Queer Twin Cities*, ed. Michael D. Franklin, Larry Knopp, Kevin P. Murphy, Ryan P. Murphy, Jennifer L. Pierce, Jason Ruiz, and Alex T. Urquhart (Minneapolis: University of Minnesota Press, 2010), 150–70.

85. *Two Eagles*, Fall 1990, box 3, Two-Spirit Papers.

86. *The Circle*, Oct.–Nov. 1987, 4, box 14, Two-Spirit Papers.

87. Richard LaFortune to Ron Rowell, email correspondence, Oct. 4, 1994, box 1, Two-Spirit Papers.

88. *Two Eagles*, Fall 1990, box 3, Two-Spirit Papers.

89. Chrystos, "Gay American Indians March on Washington, DC," *Not Vanishing*, 95.

90. *Gaze*, Sept. 1990, 18.

91. Sharon Day interview, *Outwards*, Mar. 5, 2018, https://www.theoutwords archive.org/subjectdetail/sharon-day.

92. "Ep. 19, Part 2: Randy Burns's Trips Out East and Back."

93. Janice Gould, *Beneath My Heart* (Ithaca, NY: Firebrand Books, 1990), 33–34.

94. Shelly McIntire, "The Healing Journey: A Return to the Circle," *The Circle*, Oct. 1989, 1, folder 19, box 3, Two-Spirit Papers; Brian K. Anderson and Ruth Denny, "Acknowledging Homophobia," *The Circle*, July 1990, 23, folder 5, box 3, Two-Spirit Papers; Marcie Rendon, "Sexual Abuse in the Native Community," *The Circle*, August 1992, 11, folder 5, box 1, Two-Spirit Papers.

95. Newspaper clipping, May 17, 1990, box 3, Two-Spirit Papers.

96. "Minnesota Two-Spirits," box 2, Two-Spirit Papers.

97. Ron Pinkham interview; Clyde Hall interview; Marty Fixico interview.

98. International Two Spirit Contact List, box 3, Two-Spirit Papers.

99. Ruth Deny, "National Organization Likely as a Result of 2nd Annual Gay Conference," unnamed and undated news clipping, box 3, Two-Spirit Papers.

100. *Sojourner* 14, no. 2 (Oct. 1988): 7.

101. North American Native Gays and Lesbians, Gathering Together for "Spirituality in the '90's," Aug. 1–5, 1990, box 3, Two-Spirit Papers.

102. *Two Eagles*, June 1990, box 15, Two-Spirit Papers.

103. *Bay Area Reporter*, June 23, 1983; *San Jose Mercury News*, Mar. 25, 1988; *San Francisco Chronicle*, Jan. 12, 1993; *Capital Xtra*, Oct. 18, 1996, 16; *San Francisco Chronicle*, Aug. 16, 1997.

104. Angukcuaq to Gerry Kroll, Apr. 16, 1995, box 3, Two-Spirit Papers.

105. "In the Spirit of Our Ancestors" (2000), box 3, Two-Spirit Papers.

106. *Lavender*, June 19, 1998, 12.

107. *Star Tribune*, Sept. 9, 1991, box 1, Two-Spirit Papers.

108. Will Roscoe to Anuksuk, Dec. 18, 1996, box 1, Two-Spirit Papers.

109. Phillip Brian Harper, "Eloquence and Epitaph: Black Nationalism and the Homophobic Impulse in Response to the Death of Max Robinson," in *Fear of a Queer Planet: Queer Politics and Social Theory*, ed. Michael Warner (Minneapolis: University of Minnesota Press, 1993), 263; Erin J. Rand, *Reclaiming Queer: Activist and Academic Rhetorics of Resistance* (Tuscaloosa: University of Alabama Press, 2014), 19.

110. Curtis Harris-Davia interview.

111. Sarah Deer, *The Beginning and End of Rape: Confronting Sexual Violence in Native America* (Minneapolis: University of Minnesota Press, 2015).

112. *Gay Community News*, July 4–17, 1992; Letter from Randy Miller and William Bland to Anonymous Colleague, June 5, 1996, National Task Force on AIDS Prevention, Tracy Baim Editorial Files (1996), Windy City box J (Alexander Street Press, 1996).

113. *In the Wind*, July 1994, box 15, Two-Spirit Papers.

114. Ron Rowell, "Developing AIDS Services for Native Americans," *Journal of Gay and Lesbian Social Services* 6, no. 2 (1997): 85–95, esp. 89–91.

115. Melvin Harrison interview.

116. Curtis Harris-Davia interview.

117. *San Francisco Chronicle*, Aug. 4, 1987, 8; Ron Rowell, *HIV Prevention for Gay/Bisexual/Two-Spirit Native American Men: A Report of the National Leadership Development Workgroup for Gay/Bisexual/Two-Spirit Native*

American Men (Oakland, CA: National Native American AIDS Prevention Center, 1996); Vernon, *Killing Us Quietly*, 92.

118. *Akwesasne Notes* (Spring 1989): 25; *Char: Koosta News*, Oct. 30, 1992; *Navajo Times*, Nov. 21, 1996.

119. *Seminole Tribune*, Jan. 17, 1990.

120. Gilbert Deschamps, "A Remembrance of Things Past," *The Sacred Fire: 2-Spirited People of the 1st Nations*, 1992, folder 13, Burns Papers.

121. *The Circle*, July 1990, box 3, Two-Spirit Papers.

122. Condoms, "lesbian.com" pen, and "RNW Key Chain," box 17, Two-Spirit Papers.

123. *In the Wind: HIV/AIDS in Native America* (June–July 1997); *The Circle*, July 1990, both in box 3; Joshua Volle, "Native American Lesbian, Gay and Two-Spirit Individual/Community—HIV Prevention Needs Assessment Responses," Draft Report, Dec. 4, 1995, box 1, Two-Spirit Papers; *Tundra Times*, Nov. 6, 1996, 1; *New York Times*, Sept. 7, 1999.

124. Command and Staples quoted in *The Circle*, July 1990, box 3, Two-Spirit Papers. On the role of ACT UP, see Sarah Schulman, *Let the Record Show: A Political History of ACT UP New York, 1987–1993* (New York: Farrar, Straus and Giroux, 2021), 67–93, 173–74, 535–43.

125. Chrystos, *Not Vanishing*, from frontmatter.

CHAPTER 11: LOVE

1. "Gay Marriage in Native America," *Democracy Now*, May 31, 2005, transcript, https://www.democracynow.org/2005/5/31/gay_marriage_in_native _america.

2. Lydia Nibley, director, *Two Spirits*, documentary film, Riding the Tiger Productions, 2010.

3. Judy Gibbs Robinson, "Tribal Officials Refuse to Accept Same-Sex Marriage Application," *Oklahoman*, May 19, 2004, https://oklahoman.com/article /1903369/tribal-officials-refuse-to-accept-same-sex-marriage-application; Joanne Barker, *Native Acts: Law, Recognition, and Cultural Authenticity* (Durham, NC: Duke University Press, 2011), 190–216.

4. The court issued subsequent clarification stating that heterosexual marriages could continue, but the moratorium on same-sex marriages remained in place. Travis Snell, "Judge Ends Moratorium on Marriage Licenses," *Cherokee Phoenix*, Sept. 3, 2004, https://www.cherokeephoenix.org/Article/index/625.

5. "Cherokee High Court Rules in Favor of NCLR and Same-Sex Couple," National Center for Lesbian Rights, Jan. 4, 2006, http://www.nclrights.org/ about-us/press-release/cherokee-high-court-rules-in-favor-of-nclr-and-same-se x-couple; Snell, "Judge Ends Moratorium on Marriage Licenses."

6. James D. Hunter, *Culture Wars: The Struggle to Define America: Making Sense of the Battles over the Family, Art, Education, Law, and Politics* (New York: Basic Books, 1991), 19, 190–91; Valerie Lambert, "Negotiating American Indian Inclusion: Sovereignty, Same-Sex Marriage, and Sexual Minorities in Indian Country," *American Indian Culture and Research Journal* 41, no. 2 (2017): 1–21.

7. Nancy D. Polikoff, *Beyond (Straight and Gay) Marriage: Valuing All Families Under the Law* (Boston: Beacon Press, 2008), 95–97; Barker, *Native Acts*,

145; Cynthia Burack, *Tough Love: Sexuality, Compassion, and the Christian Right* (Albany: SUNY Press, 2014), 175.

8. Angela Nagle, *Kill All Normies: Online Culture Wars from 4Chan and Tumblr to Trump and the Alt-Right* (Alresford, UK: Zero Books, 2017).

9. "Uniting Ourselves: Bridging Our Differences," folder 25, box 1, Barbara Cameron Papers (GLC 63), Gay and Lesbian Center, San Francisco Public Library; Amy Brandzel, "Queering Citizenship? Same-Sex Marriage and the State," *GLQ: A Journal of Lesbian and Gay Studies* 11, no. 2 (2005): 174–204; Scott Lauria Morgensen, *Spaces Between Us: Queer Settler Colonialism and Indigenous Decolonization* (Minneapolis: University of Minnesota Press, 2010), 211; Mark Rifkin, *When Did Indians Become Straight? Kinship, the History of Sexuality, and Native Sovereignty* (New York: Oxford University Press, 2011), 4, 275–76.

10. Sheila Stogsdill and Judy Gibbs Robinson, "Cherokees Working to Ban Gay Vows Lesbian Couple Obtain Tribal Marriage Application," *Oklahoman*, May 16, 2004, https://oklahoman.com/article/1902941/cherokees-working-to-ban-gay-vows-br-lesbian-couple-obtain-tribal-marriage-application.

11. *Asheville Citizen-Times*, Aug. 9, 2005.

12. Melanie Heath, *One Marriage Under God: The Campaign to Promote Marriage in America* (New York: New York University Press, 2012), 168; Joyce Rock, "Baptists Taught Cherokee Bigotry," *Southern Voice*, Oct. 1, 2004, available online at https://www.indianz.com/News/2004/10/01/opinion_cheroke_1.asp.

13. "Gay Marriage in Native America."

14. Barker, *Native Acts*, 196–97.

15. Lambert, "Negotiating American Indian Inclusion," 5.

16. Chelsi Moy, "Opponents Misunderstand Gay-Bias Bill, Supporters Say," *Billings Gazette*, Mar. 16, 2005, https://billingsgazette.com/news/state-and-regional/montana/opponents-misunderstand-gay-bias-bill-supporters-say/article_0810e507-21cf-5381-a102-3a39d82f5951.html. See also Lambert, "Negotiating American Indian Inclusion," 15.

17. Tim Giago (Nanwica Kciji), "Indian Country Copes with Issues of Organ Donations, Homosexuality," *Yankton Daily Press & Dakotan*, Sept. 18, 2003, https://www.yankton.net/opinion/article_43e1ef4f-1bde-5ef1-b33c-3e8f98ca8c67.html.

18. Polikoff, *Beyond (Straight and Gay) Marriage*, 97.

19. Jon Roth, "A Tribe Called Queer," *Out Magazine*, Jan. 11, 2012, https://www.out.com/news-commentary/2012/01/11/tribe-called-queer.

20. Pamela Haag, *Consent: Sexual Rights and the Transformation of American Liberalism* (Ithaca, NY: Cornell University Press, 1999), 132; Nancy F. Cott, *Public Vows: A History of Marriage and the Nation* (Cambridge, MA: Harvard University Press, 2000), 1–3, 16.

21. Annita Lucchesi and Abigail Echo-Hawk, *Missing and Murdered Indigenous Women & Girls* (Seattle: Urban Indian Health Institute, 2018), https://www.uihi.org/wp-content/uploads/2018/11/Missing-and-Murdered-Indigenous-Women-and-Girls-Report.pdf; "Missing and Murdered Indigenous Women and Girls, Trans and 2 Spirited People (MMIWGT2S): Voice of a Family Member," June 19, 2018, http://makeitourbusiness.ca/blog/missing-and-murdered-indigenous-women-and-girls-trans-and-2-spirited-people-mmiwgt2s-voice;

Noelle Phillips, "MMIW Resource Guide," Lakota People's Law Project, May 1, 2020, https://www.lakotalaw.org/news/2020-05-01/mmiw-resource-guide.

22. "Teen Arrested in N.M. Slaying," Associated Press, June 6, 2001.

23. In Indian Country, narratives that connect present-day traumas with the past are "blood memories," what the Kiowa writer N. Scott Momaday referred to as memory that's "renewed in the blood." See N. Scott Momaday, *The Names: A Memoir* (Tucson: Sun Tracks/University of Arizona Press, 1976), 55; Chadwick Allen, "Blood (and) Memory," *American Literature* 71, no. 1 (Mar. 1999): 93–116; K. F. Balsam, B. Huang, K. C. Fieland, J. M. Simoni, and K. L. Walters, "Culture, Trauma, and Wellness: A Comparison of Heterosexual and Lesbian, Gay, Bisexual, and Two-Spirit Native Americans," *Cultural Diversity and Ethnic Minority Psychology* 10, no. 3 (2004): 287–301.

24. Jennifer Petersen, *Murder, the Media, and the Politics of Public Feelings: Remembering Matthew Shepard and James Byrd, Jr.* (Bloomington: Indiana University Press, 2011), 152.

25. Cathy Renna, quoted in Paul Duggan, "Gay Youth's Death Shakes Colo. City," *Washington Post*, Sept. 1, 2001.

26. Brooke Shelby Biggs, "Cathy Renna on the Legacy of Fred Martinez," *Independent Lens*, PBS, June 16, 2011, https://www.pbs.org/independentlens/blog/cathy-renna-on-the-legacy-of-fred-martinez.

27. "Mother Calls Son's Death a Hate Crime," Indianz.com, July 19, 2001, Indianz.com, https://www.indianz.com/News/show.asp?ID=tc/7192001-2; Aspen C. Emmett, "Reflections on the 10th Anniversary of a Hate-Crime Killing in Cortez," *Four Corners Free Press*, June 1, 2011, https://fourcornersfreepress.com/reflections-on-the-10th-anniversary-of-a-hate-crime-killing-in-cortez.

28. James Pickles, "LGBT Hate Crimes: Promoting a Queer Agenda for Hate Crime Scholarship," *Journal of Hate Studies* 15, no. 1 (2019): 50–51.

29. Allison Winter, "Native American Women Are Missing and Murdered. Will the Federal Government Act?," *Colorado Independent*, Feb. 18, 2020, https://www.coloradoindependent.com/2020/02/18/missing-murdered-native-american-women-congress; Carly Wipf, "Indigenous 'Two Spirit' People Find Healing and Refuge from Colonialism," *El Tecolote*, Feb. 27, 2020, http://eltecolote.org/content/en/features/indigenous-two-spirit-people-find-healing-and-refuge-from-colonialism; Alex Bucik, *Canada: Discrimination and Violence Against Lesbian, Bisexual, and Transgender Women and Gender Diverse and Two Spirit People on the Basis of Sexual Orientation, Gender Identity and Gender Expression*, report prepared for Egale Canada Human Rights Trust (2016), https://tbinternet.ohchr.org/Treaties/CEDAW/Shared%20Documents/CAN/INT_CEDAW_NGO_CAN_25380_E.pdf.

30. Nibley, *Two Spirits*.

31. Nibley, *Two Spirits*.

32. Sarah Lamble, "Retelling Racialized Violence, Remaking White Innocence: The Politics of Interlocking Oppressions in Transgender Day of Remembrance," *Sexuality Research and Social Policy* 5, no. 24 (2008), https://doi.org/10.1525/srsp.2008.5.1.24; Cris Mayo, "Intersectionality and Queer Youth," *Journal of Curriculum and Pedagogy* 4, no. 2 (2007): 67–71.

33. Will Roscoe, "Sexual and Gender Diversity in Native America and the Pacific Islands," in *Identities and Place: Changing Labels and Intersectional Communities of LGBTQ and Two-Spirit People in the United States*, ed. Katherine Crawford-Lackey and Megan E. Springate (New York: Berghahn Books, 2020), 76.

34. Nibley, *Two Spirits*.

35. Hillary D. McNeel, "Hate Crimes Against American Indians and Alaskan Natives," *Journal of Gang Research* 21, no. 4 (Summer 2013): 14.

36. Aspen C. Emmett, "Killer Raises Specter of Hate Crime," *Cortez Journal*, July 12, 2001, http://archive.cortezjournal.com/archives/1news1494.htm.

37. Emmett, "Reflections."

38. Emmett, "Reflections."

39. Aspen C. Emmett, "Murphy Enters Plea of Not Guilty," *Cortez Journal*, Oct. 20, 2001, http://archive.cortezjournal.com/archives/1news1806.htm.

40. Emmett, "Reflections"; Gail Binkly, "Fred Martinez's Killer Is Paroled: The Brutal Murder in 2001 Drew National Attention to Cortez," *Four Corners Free Press*, Sept. 1, 2019, https://fourcornersfreepress.com/fred-martinezs-killer-is-paroled-the-brutal-murder-in-2001-drew-national-attention-to-cortez; Bret Hauff, "Man Who Murdered LGBTQ Teen in Cortez Is Released from Prison," *The Journal*, Sept. 5, 2019, https://the-journal.com/articles/151173.

41. Diane Anderson-Minshall, "12 Crimes That Changed the LGBT World," *Advocate*, May 7, 2012.

42. Emery Cowan, "A Boy Remembered," *Durango Herald*, June 11, 2011, https://durangoherald.com/articles/24984.

43. Arnold Dahl, interview with author, Nov. 14, 2017.

44. Arnold Dahl interview.

45. Roger Kuhn, interview with author, Feb. 22, 2019.

46. "Two-Spirit Voices: Returning to the Circle," LGBT Historical Society, San Francisco, https://www.glbthistory.org/two-spirit-voices.

47. Cameron Perrier, "What the National Inquiry into Missing and Murdered Indigenous Women and Girls Means for Two-Spirit People," *Xtra*, July 4, 2019; Madeleine Carlisle, "Two Black Trans Women Were Killed in the U.S. in the Past Week as Trump Revokes Discrimination Protections for Trans People," *Time*, June 13, 2020.

48. Barker, *Native Acts*, 190.

49. Polikoff, *Beyond (Straight and Gay) Marriage*, 93, 97; Barker, *Native Acts*, 192–93.

50. David Stout, "Bush Looking for Means to Prevent Gay Marriage in U.S.," *New York Times*, July 30, 2003.

51. Heather Purser interview with author, Jan. 17, 2018.

52. John Leland, "A Spirit of Belonging, Inside and Out," *New York Times*, Oct. 8, 2006.

53. Heather Purser interview.

54. Madeline Ostrander, "Making It Home: Same-Sex Marriage Brings Healing to Me—and My Tribe," *Yes Magazine*, May 11, 2012; Lambert, "Negotiating American Indian Inclusion," 12.

55. Heather Purser interview.

56. Ostrander, "Making It Home"; Chynna Lockett, "Native American Tribes Are Wrestling with Decision to Legalize Same-Sex Marriage," *All Things Considered*, NPR, Aug. 16, 2019, https://www.npr.org/2019/08/16/751861386 /native-american-tribes-are-wrestling-with-decision-to-legalize-same-sex -marriage.

57. Ostrander, "Making It Home"; Heather Purser interview.

58. Heather Purser interview.

59. Lambert, "Negotiating American Indian Inclusion," 2.

60. "Gay Marriage in Native America."

61. Jeffrey S. Jacobi, "Two Spirits, Two Eras, Same Sex: For a Traditionalist Perspective on Native American Tribal Same-Sex Marriage Policy," *University of Michigan Journal of Law Reform* 39 (2006): 846.

62. Barker, *Native Acts*, 192–93; Ann E. Tweedy, "Tribal Laws and Same-Sex Marriage: Theory, Process, and Content," *Columbia Human Rights Law Review* 46, no. 3 (Spring 2015): 135.

63. Barker, *Native Acts*, 205.

64. "Same-Sex Marriage Ban Becomes Law," NBC News, June 13, 2005, http://www.nbcnews.com/id/8206025/ns/us_news-life/t/same-sex-marriage-ban -becomes-law/#.XvoBBKeZOL8; Barker, *Native Acts*, 205-6.

65. Julian Brave NoiseCat, "Fight for Marriage Equality Not Over on Na-vajo Nation," *Huffington Post*, July 2, 2015, https://www.huffpost.com/entry /navajo-marriage-equality_n_7709016; Felicia Fonseca, "Gay Marriage Is Legal but Not on Tribal Lands," Associated Press, Nov. 27, 2015, https://apnews.com /cd8de7dfe71c41e69723e0bebd0887d8.

66. Trudie Jackson, interview with author, Jan. 26, 2018. For a critical anal-ysis of the third gender concept, see Evan B. Towle and Lynn Marie Morgan, "Romancing the Transgender Native: Rethinking the Use of the 'Third Gender' Concept," *GLQ: A Journal of Lesbian and Gay Studies* 8, no. 4 (2002): 469–97.

67. Marca Cassity interview.

68. Christo Apache, interview with author, Nov. 6, 2017; Curtis Harris-Davia, interview with author, Dec. 5, 2018; Clyde Hall interview; Marlon "Marty" Fixico, interview with author, Mar. 13, 2019.

69. Marca Cassity interview; Trudie Jackson interview.

70. Rebecca Nagle, interview with author, June 4, 2018.

71. Rafaella Gunz, "This Two-Spirited Cherokee Is Bringing Awareness to Indigenous Women's #MeToos," *GSN*, Nov. 24, 2018, https://www.gaystarnews .com/article/this-bisexual-cherokee-woman-is-bringing-awareness-to-indigenous -metoo.

72. H.R. 2965—Don't Ask, Don't Tell Repeal Act of 2010, Congress.gov, https://www.congress.gov/bill/111th-congress/house-bill/2965.

73. Justin McCarthy, "U.S. Support for Same-Sex Marriage Matches Record High," Gallup, June 1, 2020, https://news.gallup.com/poll/311672/support-sex -marriage-matches-record-high.aspx.

74. Debra A. Harley and Pamela B. Teaster, "Implications of DOMA and the Supreme Court Ruling on Same-Sex Marriage for Spousal Benefits," in *Hand-book of LGBT Elders*, ed. Harley and Teaster (Cham: Springer International,

2016), 671–83; Eugene K. Ofosu, Michelle K. Chambers, Jacqueline M. Chen, and Eric Hehman, "Same-Sex Marriage Legalization Associated with Reduced Implicit and Explicit Antigay Bias," *PNAS* 116, no. 18 (Apr. 2019): 8846–51.

75. Bill Graves, "Gay Marriage in Oregon? Tribe Says Yes," *Oregonian*, Aug. 20, 2008, https://www.oregonlive.com/news/2008/08/coquille_tribe_will _sanction_s.html; Lambert, "Negotiating American Indian Inclusion," 6–7.

76. Fay A. Yarbrough, *Race and the Cherokee Nation: Sovereignty in the Nineteenth Century* (Philadelphia: University of Pennsylvania Press, 2008).

77. Trista Wilson, "Changed Embraces, Changes Embraced? Renouncing the Heterosexist Majority in Favor of a Return to Traditional Two-Spirit Culture," *American Indian Law Review* 36, no. 1 (2011–12): 161–88, esp. 164–65.

78. Mikaëla M. Adams, *Who Belongs? Race, Resources, and Tribal Citizenship in the Native South* (New York: Oxford University Press, 2016).

79. Barker, *Native Acts*, 190.

80. Wilson, "Changed Embraces, Changes Embraced?," 178; Lambert, "Negotiating American Indian Inclusion," 6–7.

81. Graham Lee Brewer, "Why Marriage Equality Is a Matter of Tribal Sovereignty," *High Country News*, Mar. 30, 2018, https://www.hcn.org/articles /indian-country-news-why-marriage-equality-is-a-matter-of-tribal-sovereignty.

82. Mark Anthony Rolo, "Same-Sex Marriage in Indian Country," *Progressive Magazine*, Jan. 12, 2006, https://progressive.org/dispatches/same-sex -marriage-indian-country.

83. Wilson, "Changes Embraces, Changes Embraced," 178–79; Tweedy, "Tribal Laws and Same-Sex Marriage," 136–37; Jacobi, "Two Spirits, Two Eras, Same Sex," 827; Barker, *Native Acts*, 195–97.

84. "Council Sues to Prevent Same-Sex Marriage," *Cherokee Phoenix*, Sept. 9, 2005, https://www.cherokeephoenix.org/Article/index/1102; Barker, *Native Acts*, 201–2.

85. "Council Sues to Prevent Same-Sex Marriage"; Barker, *Native Acts*, 204–5.

86. Barker, *Native Acts*, 196.

87. Lois Romano, "Battle over Gay Marriage Plays Out in Indian Country," *Washington Post*, Aug. 1, 2005; Jacobi, "Two Spirits, Two Eras, Same Sex," 827–28; Christopher L. Kannady, "The State, Cherokee Nation, and Same-Sex Unions: In Re: Marriage License of Mckinley & Reynolds," *American Indian Law Review* 29, no. 2 (2005): 266–68.

88. Romano, "Battle over Gay Marriage Plays Out in Indian Country."

89. Barker, *Native Acts*, 202; David Zizzo, "Marriage Could Force High Court Decision," *Daily Oklahoman*, June 27, 2004; Elizabeth C. Lyons, "Normal for Whom? Gender Acculturation in Native American Communities," *DePaul Journal of Women, Gender, and Law* 87 (2011): 93.

90. Jacobi, "Two Spirits, Two Eras, Same Sex," 830–31.

91. LaFortune to Joe Wilson, May 24, 2006, folder 19, box 18, Two-Spirit Papers, Jean-Nickolaus Tretter Collection in GLBT Studies, University of Minnesota.

92. Obergefell v. Hodges, 575 U.S. 644 (2015) https://supreme.justia.com /cases/federal/us/576/14-556.

93. Steve Russell, "The Headlines Are Wrong! Same-Sex Marriage Not Banned Across Indian Country," *Indian Country Today*, Apr. 23, 2015, https://indiancountrytoday.com/archive/the-headlines-are-wrong-same-sex-marriage-not-banned-across-indian-country-5OSYm8SPYU6M8r9JsaUj6A; see also Gyasi Ross, "Smear the Queer, the Supreme Court, and Same Sex Marriage: Love for the Win," *Indian Country Today Media Network*, June 26, 2015https://indiancountrytoday.com/archive/smear-the-queer-the-supreme-court-and-same-sex-marriage-love-for-the-win-t6xAeIBbcUSR8pAI19004Q.

94. Lambert, "Negotiating American Indian Inclusion," 5–6.

95. Marcia Zug, "Why Same-Sex Marriage Bans Risk Native American Sovereignty," *Atlantic*, Oct. 15, 2016, https://www.theatlantic.com/politics/archive/2016/10/tribal-same-sex-marriage-bans/503345.

96. Melvin Harrison interview; Cayla Nimmo, "Navajo Nation's LGBTQ Pride Event Celebrates a Return to the Culture's History," NPR, July 11, 2019, https://www.npr.org/sections/pictureshow/2019/07/11/738099923/navajo-nations-lgbtq-pride-event-celebrates-a-return-to-the-culture-s-history.

97. Diné Equality, "Who We Are," https://www.equalitynavajo.org, accessed May 7, 2021.

98. Navajo Nation Human Rights Commission, *The Status of Navajo Women and Gender Violence: Conversations with Diné Traditional Medicine People and a Dialogue with the People*, report no. NNHRCJUL-26-16 (Window Rock, Navajo Nation [AZ]: Navajo Nation Human Rights Commission, 2016), 47–48; Kyle Ranieri, "New Year's Resolution: Repeal the Diné Marriage Act," guest essay, *Navajo Times*, Jan. 18, 2018.

99. Navajo Nation Human Rights Commission, *The Status of Navajo Women and Gender Violence*, 11.

100. Jacob Anderson-Minshall, "Meet the LGBTQ2S Woman Who Ran for President of the Navajo Nation," *Advocate*, July 10, 2018, http://www.advocate.com/exclusives/2019/7/10/meet-lgbtq2s-woman-who-ran-president-navajo-nation.

101. Following the Supreme Court's 2015 decision declaring bans on same-sex marriages unconstitutional, Reynolds and McKinley successfully filed for a marriage license in Oklahoma.

102. Steve Almasy, "Cherokee Nation Attorney General OKs Same-Sex Marriage," CNN, Dec. 9, 2016, https://www.cnn.com/2016/12/09/us/cherokee-nation-same-sex-marriage/index.html.

103. Jami Murphy, "Same-Sex Marriage License Filed After 12-Year Legal Battle," *Cherokee Phoenix*, Jan. 20, 2017, https://www.cherokeephoenix.org/Article/index/10949; Grant D. Crawford, "Tribal Officials Butt Heads Over Gay Marriage Issue," *Tahlequah Daily Press*, Mar. 22, 2017, https://www.tahlequahdailypress.com/news/local_news/tribal-officials-butt-heads-over-gay-marriage-issue/article_fa27f073-31f1-5114-8b1f-3f8a8e69a2e0.html; Michael Overall, "Cherokee Nation Attorney General Says Tribe Must Recognize Same-Sex Marriages," *Tulsa World*, Dec. 10, 2019, https://tulsaworld.com/homepagelatest/cherokee-nation-to-recognize-same-sex-marriages/article_b4935cb4-c167-5139-a7b7-3329c4ca126a.html.

104. Jonathan Drew, "Handful of Holdout Tribes Dig In Against Gay Marriage," *Tulsa World*, Apr. 7, 2015, https://tulsaworld.com/news/handful-of -holdout-tribes-dig-in-against-gay-marriage/article_f9690b87-8d30-5e71-915b -6cdf736bb4c2.html.

CHAPTER 12: FUTURES

1. Lydia Nibley, director, *Two Spirits*, documentary film, Riding the Tiger Productions, 2010.

2. *Tribal Equity Toolkit, 3.0: Tribal Resolutions and Codes to Support Two Spirit & LGBTQ Justice in Indian Country*, ed. Se-ah-dom Edmo and Aaron Ridings (Mar. 16, 2017), 1.

3. Suzanne N. Fricke, "Introduction: Indigenous Futurism in the Hyperpresent Now," *World Art* 9, no. 2 (2019): 107–21; Alexandra Alter, "'We've Already Survived an Apocalypse': Indigenous Writers Are Changing Sci-Fi," *New York Times*, Aug. 14, 2020.

4. Clyde Hall, interview with author, Feb. 18, 2019.

5. Sunni R. Clahchischilgi, "'I Want to Show Pride': Photo Essay of the Two Spirit Indigenous People," *Guardian*, April 12, 2021.

6. Jeff Friedman, "Spiraling Desire: Recovering the Lesbian Self in Oral History Narrative," in *Bodies of Evidence: The Practice of Queer Oral History*, ed. Nan Alamilla and Horacio N. Roque Ramírez (New York: Oxford University Press, 2012), 73–91.

7. J. Miko Thomas, interview with author, July 13, 2018.

8. *The Paradox of a Gay Native American Veteran*, KQED, Dec. 14, 2016, https://www.youtube.com/watch?v=ho4Tgx4LD2E.

9. Thomas's experience is not unusual. Marca Cassity (Osage Nation) shared a similar story with me. Marca Cassity, interview with author, Dec. 21, 2018.

10. The growing numbers of Two-Spirit people living in major metropolitan areas has recently been referred to as the Two-Spirit diaspora. Nelwat Ishkamewe, "The 2 Is Separate: Decolonizing Justice Through Two-Spirit Sovereignty," *Color Bloq*, https://www.colorbloq.org/the-2-is-separate-decolonizing -justice-through-two-spirit-sovereignty, accessed May 7, 2021.

11. J. Miko Thomas interview. Spirituality is critically important to contemporary Two-Spirit communities. See, for example, Ma-Nee Chacaby, with Mary Louisa Plummer, *A Two-Spirit Journey: The Autobiography of a Lesbian Ojibwa Cree Elder* (Minneapolis: University of Minnesota Press, 2016).

12. Chelsea Vowel, "Indigenous Women and Two-Spirited People: Our Work Is Decolonization," *GUTS*, Apr. 21, 2014, http://gutsmagazine.ca /indigenous-women-two-spirited-people-work-decolonization.

13. Daniel Heath Justice, "Fear of a Changeling Moon," in *The Broadway Anthology of Expository Prose: Third Canadian Edition*, ed. Laura Buzzard, Don LePan, Nora Ruddock, and Alexandria Stuart (Peterborough, ON: Broadview Press, 2017), 442.

14. "Decolonizing Sexuality at the Largest Two-Spirit Powwow in the Nation," *562 Blog*, http://www.project562.com/blog/decolonizing-sexuality-at-the -largest-two-spirit-pow-wow-in-the-nation.

15. John Paul Barmmer, "'Betrayal': Queer Native Americans on the Fourth of July," *Them*, July 4, 2018.

16. "Cecelia Rose LaPointe," *Race Forward, Facing Race*, https://facingrace.raceforward.org/speaker/cecelia-rose-lapointe.

17. Cecelia LaPointe, "Decolonization of Two-Spirit Identity and Anishinaabe Leadership," Weisman Art Museum, Nov. 11, 2019. See also the Two-Spirit program at the Native Justice Coalition, https://www.nativejustice.org/twospirit.

18. Charlie Ballard, "Two Spirit Couple Dazzles Powwow Audiences!," Powwows.com, Oct. 19, 2017, https://www.powwows.com/two-spirit-couple-dazzles-powwow-audiences; Christian Allaire, "This Indigenous Two-Spirit Couple Matches Their Regalia," *Vogue*, Aug. 17, 2020; Ben Alix Dupris, director, *Sweetheart Dancers*, PBS Short Film Festival 2020.

19. Sam Damshenas, "Devery Jacobs on Her Groundbreaking Two-Spirit Indigenous Character on American Gods," *Gay Times*, n.d.; Wren Sanders, "*Lovecraft Country* Creator Apologizes for 'Failed' Attempt at Two-Spirit Representation," *Them*, October 13, 2020.

20. Veronica Holyfield, "Building Bridges with Indigenous, Two-Spirit Identities," *Out Front*, July 20, 2020.

21. Two Spirit and LGBTQ Health, NPAIHB: Indian Leadership for Indian Health, http://www.npaihb.org/2slgbtq; Biju Belinky, "'I Want to Show What It Means to Be Two-Spirit and Trans': The Queer Magic of Mich Cota," *Huck*, Nov. 5, 2018, https://www.huckmag.com/art-and-culture/music-2/i-want-show-what-it-means-to-be-two-spirit-and-trans.

22. Marlon "Marty" Fixico, interview with author, Mar. 13, 2019.

23. Christo Apache, interview with author, Nov. 6, 2017.

24. Christo Apache interview.

25. Harlan Pruden and Se-ah-dom Edmo, *Two-Spirit People: Sex, Gender & Sexuality in Historic and Contemporary Native America*, National Council of American Indians, http://www.ncai.org/policy-research-center/initiatives/Pruden-Edmo_TwoSpiritPeople.pdf.

26. DeLesslin "Roo" George-Warren, interview with author, Dec. 19, 2017.

27. "Buck George: Conquered Barriers to Equality," Freedom Walkway, http://www.freedomwalkway.com/buckgeorge; Andrew Dys, "Clemson Football Legend, Catawba Leader Buck George Dies," *State*, Dec. 23, 2013.

28. "Legendary Clemson Football Player, Catawba Leader Buck George Dies," *Catawba in the News*, Dec. 23, 2013, https://www.catawbaindian.net/newsroom/news/buck-george.php; "Buck George."

29. Vine Deloria Jr., *Custer Died for Your Sins: An Indian Manifesto* (New York: Avon, 1969); DeLesslin "Roo" George-Warren interview.

30. DeLesslin "Roo" George-Warren, interview; Clyde Hall interview.

31. DeLesslin "Roo" George-Warren interview; Marty Fixico interview.

32. DeLesslin "Roo" George-Warren interview.

33. Rebecca Nagle, interview with author, June 4, 2018.

34. Candi Brings Plenty, interview with author, May 25, 2018.

35. Candi Brings Plenty interview.

36. Ken Harper, interview with author, May 20, 2018.

37. Wesley Thomas, "Navajo Cultural Construction of Gender and Sexuality," in *Two-Spirit People: Native American Gender Identity, Sexuality, and Spirituality*, ed. Sue-Ellen Jacobs, Wesley Thomas, and Sabine Lang (Urbana: University of Illinois Press, 1997), 162; Dayna Danger, "Aesthetic Arousal," *Canadian Art*, Dec. 13, 2018, https://canadianart.ca/features/aesthetic-arousal.

38. Muriel Miguel, "Hot 'n' Soft," in *Two-Spirit Acts: Queer Indigenous Performances*, ed. Jean E. O'Hara (Toronto: Playwrights Canada Press, 2013), 34.

39. Kent Monkman, *Honour Dance VR*, video, Sept. 20, 2019, https://www.youtube.com/watch?v=l4qrl-NGa48.

40. *On Art and Resilience: Artist Talk with Kent Monkman—Hirshhorn Museum*, video, May 15, 2020, https://www.youtube.com/watch?v=3FsB_9EI6hQ.

41. Roger Catlin, "These Video Diaries Document Quarantine Stories from Artists All Around the World," *Smithsonian Magazine*, May 11, 2020.

42. Kent Monkman, "Taxonomy of the European Male, Séance," in O'Hara, *Two-Spirit Acts*, 43, 66.

43. Waawaate Fobister, "Agokwe," in O'Hara, *Two-Spirit Acts*, 82, 83.

44. Lisa Tatonetti, "Review Essay: Weaving the Present, Writing the Future: Benaway, Belcourt, and Whitehead's Queer Indigenous Imaginaries," *Transmotion* 4, no. 2 (2018): 153.

45. "Indigiqueer," *All My Relations*, episode 6, Apr. 3, 2019.

46. Joshua Whitehead, *Full-Metal Indigiqueer* (Vancouver: Talonbooks, 2017), 112–13.

47. Joshua Whitehead, *Jonny Appleseed* (Vancouver: Arsenal Pulp Press, 2018), 2.

48. Whitehead, *Full-Metal Indigiqueer*, 48.

49. Anonymous, interview with author, Mar. 12, 2017.

50. Curtis Harris-Davia. interview with author, Dec. 5, 2018; Marty Fixico interview.

51. Curtis Harris-Davia interview.

52. Tony Enos, "8 Things You Should Know About Two-Spirit People," *Indian Country Today*, Sept. 13, 2018.

53. Tomson Highway, "Forward: Where Is God's Wife? Or Is He Gay," in O'Hara, *Two-Spirit Acts*, 7.

54. Richard J. Perry, *Western Apache Heritage: People of the Mountain Corridor* (Austin: University of Texas Press, 1991), 63, 231, 235; Suzanne J. Crawford and Dennis F. Kelley, *American Indian Religious Traditions: An Encyclopedia*, 2 vols. (Santa Barbara: ABC-CLIO, 2005), 1:589; Gregory D. Smithers, "The 'Soul' of Unity: The Quarterly Journal of the Society of American Indians, 1913–1915," *American Indian Quarterly* 37, no. 2 (Summer 2013), special issue: "The Sesquicentennial of the Society of American Indians": 263–89.

55. Marcy Angeles, interview with author, Dec. 11, 2018.

56. Gerald Vizenor, *Fugitive Poses: Native American Indian Scenes of Absence and Presence* (Lincoln: University of Nebraska Press, 1998), 15.

57. J. Miko Thomas interview.

58. Jen Deerinwater, "Our Pride: Honoring and Recognizing Our Two Spirit Past and Present, *Rewire News*, June 5, 2018; Karen Nitkin, "Judy Tallwing, Artist," *Baltimore Fishbowl*, Dec. 2, 2019.

59. Leather Archives and Museum, *Judy Tallwing McCarthy 1987*, video, 1987, http://www.youtube.com/watch?v=_Lizzm7AgbU.

60. *Shake the Feathers*, video, June 26, 2007, https://www.youtube.com /watch?v=DTYqBV76Obc; *Landa Lakes*, video, 2013, https://www.youtube .com/watch?v=vCkoabL5Cng.

61. J. Miko Thomas interview.

62. Marca Cassity interview.

63. Laura Macaluso, "Strange Bedfellows: Indigenous People's History and American Presidential Portraits," *Preservation Journey*, Jan. 20, 2017.

64. Andrea Peterson, "Podcast—UMFA Exhibits a Disturbing View of Western American History," *Saltlake Magazine*, Jan. 11, 2018.

65. DeLesslin "Roo" George-Warren interview.

66. Hayden White, *Metahistory: The Historical Imagination in Nineteenth-Century Europe* (Baltimore: Johns Hopkins University Press, 1973), 267–78.

67. Marty Fixico interview.

68. Marisa Elena Duarte, *Network Sovereignty: Building the Internet Across Indian Country* (Seattle: University of Washington Press, 2017), 29, 57, 85. On Indigenous data sovereignty, see Tahu Kukutai and John Taylor, *Indigenous Data Sovereignty: Toward an Agenda* (Canberra: ANU Press, 2016).

69. Norma Renville to Richard LaFortune, Nov. 25, 2007, folder 15, box 18, and LaFortune to Joe Wilson, May 24, 2006, folder 19, box 18, both in Two-Spirit Papers, Jean-Nickolaus Tretter, Gay, Lesbian, Bisexual and Transgender Studies, Collection 308, University of Minnesota, Minneapolis.

70. "Well Wishers Arrive to Mark 20th Anniversary of International Two Spirit Gathering," Sept. 2, 2008, folder 16, box 18, Two-Spirit Papers.

71. Harlan Pruden, *Two-Spirit Resource Directory*, prepared for the National Confederacy of Two-Spirit Organizations and NorthEast Two-Spirit Society. Understanding the possibilities and perils of these new forms of technology and storytelling is likely to be a growing area of analysis in the coming decades.

72. Harlan Pruden, "Two-Spirit (Women) More Negatively Impacted by COVID-19," *Two-Spirit Journal*, Aug. 1, 2020; Margaret Robinson, "Two-Spirit and Bisexual People: Different Umbrella, Same Rain," *Journal of Bisexuality* 17, no. 1 (2017): 7–29; Rachel Savage, "Walking in Two Worlds: Canada's 'Two-Spirit' Doctor Guiding Trans Teenagers," Reuters, Jan. 8, 2020.

73. Harlan Pruden, "August 4, 2020, 'Two-Spirit' Turns 30!!," *Two-Spirit Journal*, Aug. 3, 2020.

74. Simon L. Lewis and Mark A. Maslin, "Defining the Anthropocene," *Nature* 519 (2015): 171–80.

75. Zoe Sayler, "How Sci-Fi Could Help Solve Climate Change," *National Observer* (Canada), February 20, 2019.

76. "Indigenous Science Statement for the March for Science," https://www .esf.edu/indigenous-science-letter.

77. Aja Couchois Duncan, *Restless Continent* (Brooklyn, NY: Litmus Press, 2016).

78. Hope Nicholson, ed., *Love Beyond Body, Space, and Time: An Indigenous LGBT Sci-Fi Anthology* (Winnipeg: Bedside Press, 2016); Daniel Heath Justice, *The Way of Thorn and Thunder: The Kynship Chronicles* (Albuquerque: University of New Mexico Press, 2011).

79. Sandra Faiman-Silva, "Anthropologists and Two Spirit People: Building Bridges and Sharing Knowledge," Stocking Symposium in the History of Anthropology, Montreal, Nov. 19, 2011.

80. Justice, *The Way of Thorn and Thunder*, loc. 1327.

81. Se-ah-dom Edmo and Ridings, *Tribal Equity Toolkit 3.0*, 1. The *Toolkit* is available online at https://www.thetaskforce.org/wp-content/uploads/2014/09/TET3.0.pdf.

82. Se-ah-dom Edmo and Ridings, *Tribal Equity Toolkit 3.0*, 57, 63, 6, 11, 64, 74, 6–7, 11, 21–22, and 40.

83. UN, Department of Economic and Social Affairs, "Climate Change," https://www.un.org/development/desa/indigenouspeoples/climate-change.html, accessed March 29, 2021.

84. Kirsten Vinyeta, Kyle Powys Whyte, and Kathy Lynn, "Indigenous Masculinities in a Changing Climate: Vulnerability and Resilience in the United States," in *Men, Masculinities and Disaster*, ed. Elaine Enarson and Bob Pease (New York: Routledge, 2016), ch. 12; Kyle Whyte, "Indigenous Climate Change Studies: Indigenizing Futures, Decolonizing the Anthropocene," *English Language Notes* 55, nos. 1–2 (Spring–Fall 2017): 153–62.

85. Luke W. Cole and Sheila R. Foster, *From the Ground Up: Environmental Racism and the Rise of the Environmental Justice Movement* (New York: New York University Press, 2001), 20–28; UN Commission on Human Rights, *Report on the Forty-Sixth Session, 29 January–9 March 1990, Supplement 2* (New York: UN Economic and Social Council, 1990), 134–36, 286, https://undocs.org/pdf?symbol=en/E/1990/22 (supp).

86. Danika Medak-Saltzman, "Coming to You from the Indigenous Future: Native Women, Speculative Film Shorts, and the Art of the Possible," *Studies in American Indian Literatures* 29, no. 1 (2017): 143.

87. Sarah Hunt and Cindy Holmes, "Everyday Decolonization: Living a Decolonizing Queer Politics," *Journal of Lesbian Studies* 19, no. 2 (2015): 154–72.

88. Nick Estes, *Our History Is the Future* (London: Verso, 2019), 14–15.

89. "Ojibwe Elder Sharon Day and the Mother Earth Water Walkers," audio story, PRX, https://beta.prx.org/stories/92997; Maria Manuela, "Check into These Native Lodge Artist Rooms," *New Mexico Magazine*.

90. Whyte, "Indigenous Science (Fiction) for the Anthropocene," 238.

91. Jennifer Weston, "Water Is Life: The Rise of the Mní Wičóni Movement," *Cultural Survival Quarterly Magazine*, Mar. 2017; Shelley Streeby, *Imagining the Future of Climate Change: World-Making Through Science Fiction and Activism* (Berkeley: University of California Press, 2018), 34–36.

92. Nick Estes, "'The Supreme Law of the Land': Standing Rock and the Dakota Access Pipeline," *Indian Country Today*, Jan. 16, 2017.

93. Estes, *Our History Is the Future*, 12; Dina Gilio-Whitaker, *As Long as Grass Grows: The Indigenous Fight for Environmental Justice, from Colonization to Standing Rock* (Boston: Beacon Press, 2019), 1–4.

94. Estes, *Our History Is the Future*, 9–12; Gilio-Whitaker, *As Long as Grass Grows*, 5.

95. Debra White Plume, "Santee Sioux Tribe Rescinds Support for TransCanada's Keystone XL," *Last Real Indians*, May 10, 2013.

96. Natalie Hand and Kent Lebsock, "Lakota Allies Gather to Stand Their Sacred Ground," *Indigenous Environmental Network*, Mar. 15, 2014, https://www.ienearth.org/lakota-allies-gather-to-stand-their-sacred-ground/.

97. Two Spirit Nation, thetwospiritnation.org, accessed May 7, 2021.

98. Rebecca Nagle, "The Healing History of Two-Spirit, a Term That Gives LGBTQ Natives a Voice," *Huffington Post*, June 30, 2018, https://www.huffpost.com/entry/two-spirit-identity_n_5b37cfbce4b007aa2f809af1.

99. Candi Brings Plenty interview.

100. Julia Carrie Wong, "Standing Rock Thanksgiving: A Day of Mourning, Resistance and Jane Fonda," *Guardian*, Nov. 24, 2016; Valerie Taliman, "Thousands of Veterans Descend on Standing Rock to Protect and Serve," *Indian Country Today*, Dec. 4, 2016.

101. Tyson Yunkaporta, *Sand Talk: How Indigenous Thinking Can Save the World* (New York: HarperOne, 2020), 4.

102. Rebecca Nagle interview; Jolene Yazzie, "Why Are Diné LGBTQ+ and Two Spirit People Being Denied Access to Ceremony?," *High Country News*, Jan. 7, 2020.

103. DeLesslin George-Warren, quoted in Alicia Crosby, "Stories from Two Spirit Nation," *Windy City Times*, Dec. 21, 2016.

104. Quoted in Crosby, "Stories from Two Spirit Nation."

105. Tarra Martin, "Portland's Diego Hernandez Has Stood with Standing Rock, and Says the 'Water Protectors' Aren't Going Anywhere," *Willamette Week*, Nov. 30, 2016.

106. As this book went to press, Two-Spirit people were vocal opponents of a slew of anti-trans legislation being proposed in states across the United States. See Surya Milner, "Montana Trans, Two Spirit and Non-Binary Activists Fight Anti-Trans Legislation," *High Country News*, March 10, 2021.

107. Estes, *Our History Is the Future*.

108. Raven Heavy Runner, interview with author, Oct. 17, 2019.

109. Marty Fixico interview; Ava Truthwaite, "Cutting Off All My Hair: A Non-Binary Indigenous Person Isn't Necessarily Two-Spirit," *The Varsity*, March 28, 2021.

IMAGE CREDITS

Theodor de Bry, *Balboa Throws Some Indians, Who Had Committed the Terrible Sin of Sodomy, to the Dogs to Be Torn Apart*, 1594. University of Houston Digital Library.

Stirrup Spout Vessel Depicting Fellatio, Moche ceramic, ca. 100–700 CE. Larco Herrera Archaeological Museum, Lima, Peru. Courtesy Alamy.

Two Women with a Baby, Bahía ceramic, ca. 500 BCE–500 CE. No. GA-46-482-77, Museo Antropológico y de Arte Contemporáneo, Guayaquil, Ecuador.

Theodor de Bry, *Employments of the Hermaphrodites*, 1591, engraving. Reputed to depict a scene portrayed by Jacques Le Moyne but lost in the violence at Fort Caroline. Image no. DG00977, State Archives of Florida.

Nicholas Point, *Marie Quilax a la bataille contre Les Corbeaux (Août 1846)* (Marie Quilax at War with the Crow, [August 1846]), drawing. Manuscripts, Archives, and Special Collections, Washington State University Libraries, Pullman.

George Catlin, *Dance to the Berdash*, 1835–1837, oil on canvas. Smithsonian American Art Museum, Washington, DC.

Kent Monkman, *Honour Dance*, 2020, acrylic on canvas. Collection of the Hirshhorn Museum, Washington, DC.

Woman Chief, or "Pine Leaf." Ethnologists have speculated that Pine Leaf was Bíawacheeitchish. Image from *The Life and Adventures of James P. Beckwourth*, edited by Thomas D. Bonner (New York: Harper & Brothers Publishers, 1856), 203 (public domain).

Lozen and Dahteste, 1886, photograph. PC53, #19796, Gatewood Collection, Arizona Historical Society.

John K. Hillers, *We Wha Weaving*, ca. 1886, photograph. National Anthropological Archives, Smithsonian Institution, Washington, DC.

Mary Wheelwright, *Hosteen Klah*, photograph. Mary Wheelwright Collection, box 26, Wheelwright Museum of the American Indian, Santa Fe.

Alexander W. Chase, *Tolowa Man from Taa-'at-dvn Village (Crescent City, Called the "Old Doctor")*, photograph. National Anthropological Archives, Smithsonian Institution, Washington, DC.

C. H. Asbury, *Ohchiish (Finds-Them-and-Kills-Them)*, 1928, photograph. National Anthropological Archives, Smithsonian Institution, Washington, DC.

Robert Giard, photograph of Barbara Cameron, undated. Yale Collection of American Literature, Beinecke Rare Book and Manuscript Library, Yale University, New Haven, CT.

Stephen Steward, photograph of Randy Burns, 1984. ONE Archives at the USC Libraries, Los Angeles.

Bettina Hansen, photograph of Raven Heavy Runner at the Seattle Pride Parade in 2018. *Seattle Times*, June 24, 2018.

INDEX